Being Better Beings

For Personal, Social, and Global Peace

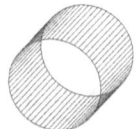

Author's Books
(As at 2021)[*]

__Non-fiction__

The Nature of Love and Relationships 2011, **2016** 2nd Edition
Doubts and Decisions for Living:
   Volume I: The Foundation of Human Thoughts **2014**
   Volume II: The Sanctity of Human Spirit **2014**
   Volume III: The Structure of Human Life **2014**
Relationship Facts, Trends, and Choices **2016**
The Mysteries of Life, Love, and Happiness **2016**
Marriage and Divorce Hardships **2016**
Gender Qualities, Quirks, and Quarrels **2016**
Relationship Needs, Framework, and Models **2016**
Being Better Beings **2020**

__Fiction__

Persian Moons 2007, **2016** 2nd Edition
Midnight Gate-opener 2011, **2016** 2nd Edition
My Lousy Life Stories **2014**
Persian Suns **2021**

---

[*] 12 older books are Enhanced Editions and printed in 2020. They were resubmitted to the Library and Archives Canada Cataloguing as well. If a book's 'print date' on the copyright page is older, the newest version is available at Amazon and bookstores.

Being Better Beings

For Personal, Social, and Global Peace
And for God's Sake Too!

Tom Omidi, Ph.D.

Copyright © 2020 by Tom Omidi

All rights reserved. No part of this book may be reproduced, translated, or transmitted in any form or by any means—graphic, electronic or mechanical, including photocopying, recording, taping or information storage or retrieval systems—without the prior written permission of the publisher or author.

Omidi, Tom, 1945-, author
Being Better Beings:
For Personal, Social, and Global Peace
/ Tom Omidi, Ph.D.

ISBN 978-1-988351-02-5 (Paperback).

1. Art of Being (Psychology, Spirituality).
2. Goodness Structure and Path (Psychology).
3. Human Spirit (Biology, Spirituality).
4. Humanity (Sociology, Philosophy).
5. Interpersonal Relations (Sociology).
6. Corruption Epidemic (Sociology, Psychology).
7. Culture and Character (Psychology, Philosophy, Sociology).
I. Title.

Cover page design by Tom Omidi

Published by Eros Books,
Vancouver, Canada

erosbooks2020.@gmail.com

Printed in 2020

This book is dedicated to all spirited minds and decent beings resisting the world's evil elements, including the arrogant superpowers, incompetent leaders, and greedy elites ravaging humans' basic needs, dignity, and pride so casually everywhere, especially in the Middle East.

I feel sad anytime one of my evil genes
jumps to serve the devil at my expense
and I fail to stop it!

> A tortured, exploring spirit

Table of Contents

	Page
Whining at the Time of Corona (A Last Minute Revelation)	vii
Author's Note: Questioning Our Being	1
Prologue: The Prospect for Humanity	5
Book's Structure	9

Part I: The State of Being

Chapter One: The Broken Beings	15
Spoiled Modern Beings	18
A Natural Personal Initiative	25
The Socio-personal Paradox	27
The Goodness Barometer	32
The Magic of Human Intuition and Spirit	37
Chapter Two: Symptoms of Human Evil and Demise	41
A. Social (General) Malfunctions	44
• Rampant disorder, diseases, and threats	44
• Crimes' senselessness	48
• Corruption epidemic	50
• Widening of economic gap	50
• Global animosity and genocides	51
• Environmental pollution and destruction	52
• Food and nutrition hazards	52
• Population and density pressures	53
• Communication hurdles	54
• Marriage and companionship problems	54
• Job and career related burdens	56
B. Personal (Psychological) Disturbances	56
• Inner conflicts	57
• Loneliness	58
• Insecurity	59
• Psychological defects	60
• Scanty Self-fulfilment	61
• Lower needs deprivation	62
• Struggle for happiness	64
• Loss of identity and confusion	65
The Big Picture	65

Table of Contents (Cont.)

	Page
Chapter Three: The Incentive for Being Better Beings	71
Goodness Challenges	72
1. Building Our Incentive	72
2. Fighting Our Tormented Nature	78
3. Managing Our Demented Logic	82
Assessing Our Being	85
A. The meaning of life	86
B. Our purposes for living	90
C. Our routines' values	91
D. Our mentalities' status	92
The Chain of Existential Thoughts	95
Chapter Four: Humans' Mental Operation	97
Forces Ruling our Brains	98
A. Natural (Positive) Forces:	101
1. Instincts and Urges	101
2. Intelligence and Ego (Personality)	105
3. Identity and Self-awareness	109
B. Imposed (Negative) Forces:	110
4. Rearing Conditioning	110
5. Social Teachings	112
6. Barriers and Limitations	114
The Mixed Effects of Six Forces	116
Making the Best of Our Brains	119
Chapter Five: Our Curious Spirits	123
Mastering Spirituality	125
A. Inward Reflection	126
1. Overcoming our superficial needs	126
2. Gaining inner strength	126
3. Finding inner peace	127
4. Remembering the role of our spirit	128
5. Seeking our being	129
B. Outward Connection	131
6. Focusing on life's larger picture	131
7. Attaining our humility and decency	132
8. Appreciating the world's values and beauties	133

Table of Contents (Cont.)

Page

Chapter Five: Our Curious Spirits (Cont.)
    9. Connecting with the universe 134
    10. Becoming a useful member of society.......... 134
Life's Main Components 135

Part II: The Art of Being

Chapter Six: Goodness Endeavour 139
  Cautionary Points about Goodness 139
  Goodness Pyramid (Structure) 143
  A. Foundation 144
    • Authenticity 144
    • Autonomy 147
    • Vision 148
    • Vitality 151
  B. Form 152
    • Harmony 153
    • Humility 154
  C. Finale 156
    • Divinity 156
Chapter Seven: Badness Epidemic 157
  Badness Pyramid (Structure)....................... 158
  A. Foundation 159
    • Superficiality 159
    • Self-pity 160
    • Naivety 160
    • Negativity 161
  B. Form 161
    • Neurosis 161
    • Narcissism 161
  C. Finale 162
    • Devilry 162
  The Symptoms of Our Badness 162
  The Menace of Social Living 165
  Badness Factory................................ 168
  Badness Factory's Products 174

Table of Contents (Cont.)

	Page
Chapter Eight: Social Mechanisms' Perils	181
1. Education	184
2. Learning	186
3. Occupation	191
4. Marriage	195
5. Parenthood	198
6. Health	200
7. Security	202
8. Justice and Fairness	203
9. Courtesy and Trust	205
10. Morality	207
11. Environment	208
12. Culture	209
13. Democracy	211
14. Economy	213
15. Authority	214
Chapter Nine: Goodness Regimen (Path)	217
Goodness Goals and Practices	219
Goodness Elements	222
Goodness Stages	225
Goodness Scope (Symptoms)	228
Goodness Essence	232
Chapter Ten: Spirituality Haven	235
Outer Power	239
Inner Strengths	242
The Self Synergy	246

Part III: Social Conscience and Consciousness

Chapter Eleven: American Dream	251
The Rise of a Global Perspective	255
The Clues and Lessons	258
The World's Big Dilemma	259
Debate with Our Confused Conscience	259
Hillary Clinton's Debate with Her Spirit	260
Donald Trump's Debate with His Spirit	261

Table of Contents (Cont.)

                                                  Page

Chapter Twelve: Culture Collapse 263
   A Cultureless Social Structure! 265
   The Neo-culture Curse 268
   The Neo-culture Forces........................... 271
   Living for Today 277
   Goodness Culture 281

Chapter Thirteen: Lonely Social Humans 283
   Endless Frustration 286
   Socializing Obsession 289
   General Oppression 292
   Socioeconomic Sources of Stress, Confusion, and Frustration 294

Chapter Fourteen: Mental Restoration and Revolution 303
   Hopes for a Miracle! 314

Chapter Fifteen: A Solemn Conclusion 317
   Main Facts: Dire Goodness Shortage 317
   Not Good Enough Beings 318
   Not Being Good Enough 318
   Not Enough Good Beings 321
   Our Tricky Role as a Human 321

Part IV: World's Political Impasse

Chapter Sixteen: Leadership Mishmash 327
   Pathetic, Lame Leaders 331
   Socio-Political Illiteracy 338
   Scholars' Complicity 346

Chapter Seventeen: Democracy Mess................... 353
   The Marvel of Democracy! 359

Chapter Eighteen: Need for a New Role Model 367
   About Americans 368
   About America 379
   About the World 390

Epilogue: A Divine Being 403
   The Beauty of Betterness 408

Table of Contents (Cont.)

Page

Appendices
- Appendix A : Humans Cognition 412
- Appendix B : Humans' Egological Conditions 413
- Appendix C : Humans' Logic Aversion Drive 416
  - Factors of Human Logical Defects 416
  - Human Logic in Perceived and Real Worlds......... 418
- Appendix D : Human Instincts' Vulnerability 421
- Appendix E : The Summary; Reality Check about Humanity .. 425
  - Dark Realities..................................... 425
  - Our Dilemmas 434
  - The Bottomline 438
  - Our Choices 440

List of Diagrams and Tables

- Diagram 3.1: The Chain of Existential Thoughts 95
- Diagram 4.1: The Forces Shaping People 99
- Diagram 6.1: Goodness Pyramid (Structure) 144
- Diagram 7.1: Badness Pyramid (Structure) 159
- Diagram B: Humans' Egological Conditions 414

- Table 8.1: Fifteen Main Social Elements 184
- Table 9.1: Goodness Goals and Practices................. 219
- Table 9.2: Goodness Elements 222
- Table 9.3: Goodness Regimen 225
- Table C: Decision Inaccuracy Ratings 417

The quotes from esteemed scholars in this book are merely for reflecting worthy viewpoints on related topics without prejudice. They are plausible opinions stated liberally in public domains regarding such philosophical topics, thus have become relevant for general review purposes. Although the author does not agree or disagree with them necessarily, they are precious points that interested readers are encouraged to check in those books for more detail and reflection.

Whining at the Time of Corona
A Last Minute Revelation

COVID-19 pandemic has been a tragic waking call for the world. Thus, its severity and effects had to be acknowledged along with my deep sympathy for those afflicted by it the most. This awful disease has pained us all with a variety of fears and psychological burdens swiftly. The world changed overnight, societies came to a halt, and our lives were put on hold. Most of all, its impact on our personal, social, and global way of thinking would be lasting and deep in terms of our prospects and options for existence.

Besides delaying this book's release a few months, the Covid chaos raised the need to stress on two opposing points. On the one hand, the cynical thoughts in this book about personal, social, and global shortfalls, and the need for a big mental reform, might sound impertinent, like whining at the time people are scrambling to address their urgent worries and are already alarmed by the inevitability of many similar, or direr, disasters in the future.

On the other hand, the emotional and economic upshots of this pandemic, plus the global uprisings against racism and police brutality, have forced the need to ponder the socio-political points noted in this book with a higher priority. Studying humans' vital needs objectively appear crucial for finding long-term solutions in response to looming socioeconomic calamities worldwide. In particular, the following basic facts about humanity and society need scrutiny even more urgently than it is stressed in this book:

1. We humans are vastly vulnerable nowadays more than ever.
2. Our social mechanisms and relationships have low capacities to help us in the long term, especially after a big catastrophe.
3. The world's political systems are unprepared and incapable of handling national and universal demands.
4. The world is much smaller, more integrated, and vastly more vulnerable than we fathom, with half of the globe's population 10-50 times more at risk and desperate.

Whining at the Time of Corona

5. We are unprepared personally and socially, both mentally and logistically, for inevitable future pressures and problems.
6. We have wrong personal views about life, society, and family.
7. Our lifestyles are incompatible with our inner needs and rising social demands.
8. The vast degrees of badness, goodness, and mental differences among people are now more apparent and will keep growing.
9. Family relationships' declining stability and ethics are alarming more nowadays, but also emphasize the need for developing practical principles for relating in society and family, instead of pampering our crude perceptions and ideals about life.
10. Despite governments' past experiences with other pandemics, such as Sars and Ebola, their unpreparedness and confusion during COVID-19 showed the global disunity and difficulty to face even direr inevitable catastrophes in the near future.
11. We should try to imagine the effects of permanent, irreversible disasters, such as climate change that will be so many folds harsher than COVID-19's relatively short-term mayhem.
12. Then, try to imagine the idiocy of many incompetent leaders like Donald Trump running the world with their eternal lies, hypocrisies, and denials, even about the climate change.
13. Imagine how quickly the financial capacities of governments and people would collapse during a bigger catastrophe.
14. Try to imagine a total halt on most social services, including hospitals, food distribution systems and production centres.
15. Try to imagine how inaccurate our views of life essentialities have been in general along with our demented lifestyles, social mechanisms, and political systems that we must depend on.
16. Accordingly, only more evil will grow in people and society.

Can a large world populace learn from COVID-19's aftermath, as an awakening maybe, and ponder their personal and global needs proactively? Can the public and governments grasp the scope of looming catastrophes, think and plan seriously, and be prepared? We need a very different world now with lots more better beings!

Author's Note
Questioning Our Being

Peace is the greatest virtue for personal, social, and global health and welfare. Yet, we haughty humans appear reluctant or incapable to make this ideal possible, as though we were born to cause our own sufferings with bitter determination. In fact, we do everything in our power to prevent civilization and peace by our crude personalities, fanciful ideologies, ineffective social and political mechanisms, and endless arguments over too many juvenile objectives out of ignorance, arrogance, and greed. This suffocating civilization is apparently the best we humans can build! We brag about it, too, along with our endless struggles to prove our ingenuity and success.

All historical evidences demonstrate that our social efforts and philosophical essays to improve human life have been a waste of time and paper judging the looming prospect of humanity. Sadly, the chance of changing people's minds about the vanity of their habits, values, and needs is also small. Therefore, the readers can rightly question my sanity for writing a book about 'being better beings' when I have reached a rather definite conclusion about both the impurity of human nature and the difficulty of cleansing our minds and souls. The truth is that I had mixed feelings from the start myself about wasting time on a book that has so little chance of influencing people and changing anything in this hypnotized world. My friend's rude comment, when he learned about my plan to write this book, still haunts me, too.

"Are you a mad philosopher or preacher now?" he asked me mockingly.

"Why? What have I done now?" I asked innocently, although I sensed his meaning with humiliation already.

"Don't you have anything better to do with your life, wasting so much time and energy to write about society, especially when you have no good relationship with anybody yourself."

His observation sounded reasonable, yet hurtful from a rather simpleton whose own life has been a catastrophe in both financial and emotional terms. Of course, my difficulty to fit in and keep a normal relationship with people has been a sad fact, despite my efforts to humour everybody and hoping not to be an extrovert. Still, my friend's criticism made me think harder and reaffirm my reserved optimism about people's occasional curiosity about the chance, and benefits, of refurbishing their crude, twisted minds in order to find peace and the wisdom of enduring a dying society easier. It felt sensible to believe that some of us have a sketchy drive for self-development. After all, it is easier to keep a bit of hope about humans' knack for ethics and maybe even finding some selfless leaders to guide us out of the mess we have created for ourselves. Some of us still prefer, occasionally, to ponder the possibility of saving humanity somehow, despite our vanishing prospect. Meanwhile, I admit, writing about irresolvable social issues is clearly another clue about my naiveté regarding a few people's interest to promote a universal goal for goodness—at least for curbing our sufferings a bit.

I wrote this book also as a last resort—with minute hope—to communicate with my difficult kids at some point in their lives. They have looked rather insensitive and lost, while I have sensed their innocence and pains, trapped in a heartless society. Still, I believe they can help themselves by adopting the goodness path to become a bit better beings for their own sakes.

Surely, humans' salvation, or even mere survival, remains very doubtful, due to their tenacity to dismiss the vanity of their present mindsets and lifestyles. Yet, we should *at least* realize that we are mostly hurting ourselves with our naïve mentalities and arrogance, instead of helping one another, especially our families, with a finer grasp of human essence and keener efforts to curb the effects of crooked social teachings.

Life is a huge mystery, yet ironically, we all believe to grasp the reality perfectly, know all the facts sincerely, and own the best personalities unequivocally. We all feel like world's experts about existence and social mannerism. However, we are not even smart enough to realize and admit that the rising personal stress and social conundrums are merely due to humans' dogmatism, arrogance, and naivety. The wild history of humanity offers the best clues about our low commonsense and dire disregard for our spirits, which are suffocating under our crude mentalities and lifestyles. Thus, it is not outrageous to say that humans are the weirdest species in the universe or imagine their looming demise, simply due to their resistance to find a more peaceful means of coexistence by using their allegedly educated brains!

Our inability to fathom practical social systems has brought us to such socio-political impasse and causing concerns around the globe, especially in the US—the world's model of civilization. But now what? *Let us hope we do not have to put up a wall at US-Canada boarder soon to stop the flood of American refugees!*

Nevertheless, pondering the ideas raised in this book might at least sharpen our self-awareness, which often stirs an incentive for reassessing our essence more honestly and building a productive lifestyle. As we question our being, we may learn about our urges and authentic needs and boost our identity as a soulful person. Our better grasp of human nature's flaws during this process might in itself increase our compassion and patience for people and easier communication with them, along with an opportunity to build a steadier inner peace even in this crooked social setting.

Author's Note

Unable to overcome my naiveté apparently, I still cannot stop wondering if any solution exists for humans to survive the rising mess. Against all sad evidences and our cynicism, a small chance might still exist for humans to smarten up in the last minute, in a few decades perhaps, when they face annihilation closely. Some of my idealistic thoughts and reasons to stay reservedly positive are explained in the book, although they are probably good only for keeping my hopes and spirit high. Nevertheless, remaining a wishful philosopher serves my psyche better at least and it is surely preferable to dismissing the chance of humans' salvation altogether, despite the gloomy prospects. At the same time, our efforts and conscious learnings for becoming better beings can raise our spirits. Discovering our neglected true 'self' would most likely improve our life prospects all by itself.

Naturally, pursuing this personal ideal is an unconventional, tough challenge—to 'Reassess our essence and basic needs, resist social influences and temptations, curb our egotism and duplicity, find means of building our identities and relationships, and build a stringent routine for becoming better beings.'

The first step is to try to detect and fight our idiosyncrasies, while we learn about humans' rising limitations and helplessness in the new era beyond so much evil already piled in their nature. Then, we can try to work out a basic philosophy and routine for self-development and cleansing our minds and souls gradually.

In all, this book merely intends to suggest a simple perspective about the underlying causes of humans' sufferings nowadays as well as their faltering spirits and sense of being (identity) within such rooted socioeconomic mayhem. If it can help a few people develop the incentive for learning and exercising humility per se, it has achieved a lot. The goal has not been to write an academic or statistical book.

Tom Omidi, Ph.D.
Vancouver, June 2020

Prologue
The Prospect for Humanity

Being a better person sounds ridiculous and insulting to most people, because they believe they are perfect already. Even if a person learns enough humility to consider the option of becoming a better person, s/he would find the task too difficult both psychologically and practically. It is too hard to fight our twisted nature in order to become more civilized human beings. More risky, however, is the chance of being rejected and losing our edge in society if we decide to be less arrogant and wicked unlike the majority. It is tough to disregard social pressures and rewards of becoming as crooked as most seemingly successful people are in line with greed-ridden social norms.

Obviously, religions, cults, and books on soul-searching and self-cleansing have not yet helped people get along effectively or save their marriages at least. They have not even thought us how to explore our essence and spirits to lead a rather independent, peaceful life with a genuine identity and life philosophy. Thus, even pondering the idea of 'being better beings,' or reading a book about it, might seem absurd. Surely, justifying the goodness efforts suggested in this book has been hard, but felt essential for keeping some hope. Still, only a person's faith about the *potential* values of self-development might convince him/her to ponder the idealistic objectives of this book, which are the chances for:

1. **Rejuvenating our identities and spirits:** The mere chance of boosting our spirits and gaining personal salvation, despite the daunting impiety of the environment we must endure, is precious and a viable incentive for becoming a better person. This sacred objective is crucial mainly by realizing our innate identities and potentialities.

2. **Reinventing better options for social coexistence:** Humans can certainly get along better in their relationships, especially marriages, if many people find an incentive to become better beings. Human nature and attitude have been tainted largely over centuries and millenniums due to their genes and urges, as well as social teachings and lifestyles, making them evils. In return, goodness efforts might improve social health and maybe even humans' nature gradually.

3. **Recreating humanity:** We might then even save humanity. Developing a more harmonious and compassionate world, contrary to what our crude civilization has been capable of delivering so far is a precious ideal. Logically, the potential for developing a finer humanity might still exist if we cleanse humans' lifestyles—and maybe even their nature over a long time—by establishing better means of coexistence, including political and socioeconomic systems to refine our minds and needs. Realistically, however, the big question is whether we have enough courage and brains to mitigate our capitalistic mentality and self-gratifying drives for sex and extravagance.

Depending upon our personalities and worldviews, we can choose our life paths, faiths, and duties for materializing any of the above three goodness potentials before it is too late. Sadly, the chances of fulfilling the last two ideals are slim in this author's opinion. However, the rewards for achieving the first goal all by itself could be a huge incentive for anyone with some degree of courage and wisdom to accept the challenge of becoming a better person wholeheartedly. Thus, our efforts to write or read about the ways of becoming better beings, for our own sakes at least, seem rather justified. Indeed, we all have a strong natural urge (an advanced survival instinct) to maximize our health, happiness and success, which we usually try to fulfil with lots of efforts and pains, yet we fail since we look at the wrong places for them.

Besides the above logic for self-development, humans have incredibly curious minds about their identities and destinies. Most people wonder about global affairs and abhor the way humanity has shaped. We like to measure the purity of human nature and establish the traits of a normal person. We also like to speculate about the qualities of an ideal human who surpasses a normal person's nature either as an exception or thru self-development. Indeed, this inquisition feels like an urge for spiritual exploration. Yet, it might also help us set our personal level of trust in society realistically, grow our defence mechanisms properly, adjust our expectations about people and society wisely, and follow a simpler lifestyle that is also practical and compassionate.

Many other existential questions raise our curiosity, too, such as, 'Can living be joyful or at least less painful? Why should we supposedly intelligent humans hurt one another so much and how can we stop it? What should we do to face fewer problems and maybe even capture the secrets of the elusive happiness that we expect both intuitively and traditionally? Can anybody really achieve these ideals even remotely?' However, the most crucial global dilemma is whether societies can *ever* uphold a reliable set of ethics or guidelines to keep people happy together within some manageable and intellectual boundaries at least.

These human conundrums and curiosities need exploration to find viable options for living more peacefully in practical ways. Meanwhile, self-awareness and self-development for becoming better beings are the likeliest sources of happiness. While finding happiness has turned into an obsession for people nowadays, the ways they choose to find this illusive ideal, i.e., thru materialistic and showy venues, are in fact counterproductive and cause more depression. Only by becoming better beings, we get the chance to learn about some essential realities that change our mentalities and outlooks as well, thus permeate deep senses of contentment and fulfilment.

Of course, building a general, absolute path of salvation is impossible, considering the complexity of human nature, needs, insecurities, and interactions. No universal solutions exist, either, as only we can, and must, discover our being (self) privately and build our unique life paths individually. We must make personal choices and take calculated risks. We must boost our spirits, in particular, with a *realistic* attitude towards life—rather positively—thru personal faith and courage, until our inner strengths and potentialities are bolstered to drive our minds and actions.

It is easy, common, and useful to pretend being an intelligent and considerate person, mostly by hiding the evil in humans, all in hopes of being popular and look reliable. On the other hand, it is hard and divine to study our psyches sincerely in order to fight off humans' innate vile nature and genes as well as the effects of horrific social teachings, including greed, conceit, and hypocrisy. Accordingly, one's toughest, but most rewarding, challenge is to build the incentive for going through the laborious self-cleansing and self-awareness process, merely in hopes of becoming a good being for one's own benefits and maybe even becoming a useful social element. *Would not that be a noble gesture?*

Merely opening our minds to various viewpoints and simpler lifestyles can help us learn a lot about varied human relationships and life, boost our spirits, and stir peace at all levels. Instead, we do the opposite nowadays, as we strive to push our crooked ideas during our long, pointless arguments. We like to insist on vanity and naivety. We prefer to waste our lives on too many absurd goals and raw ambitions. We enjoy playing our idiotic games and parading our phony personalities. All along, we take others as idiots, unable to see through our lies and pretences. Overall, our deliberate meanness and spite to serve our crude ambitions and false pride are not just deplorable, but big sources of humans' inability to build a reliable culture and a peaceful civilization.

Personal solutions and salvation emerge from strong minds and spirits, which we can build through self-awareness and faith in both our inner strengths and that mysterious outer power.

Book's Structure

This book has four parts and a Summary in Appendix E, which offers the gist of the book about social realities, our dilemmas, the bottomline, and our choices. A quick review of this summary, and the Table of Contents, can help the readers who like to get an overall feel about the book first. Yet, the details and critical points offered throughout the book are useful for building and mastering goodness through proper reflection and specific regimens.

Part I—The State of Being—reviews the causes of human distress and confusion in the new era. It explains the hurdles for building a peaceful life mostly due to our personality flaws and rising social depravities that have evolved into a global disease and infecting humans' mentality and nature.

Part II—The Art of Being—suggests the path and process of becoming better beings to build our inner strengths at least, if not our mindsets for enlightenment. Our pointless struggles and pains in life are due to our superficial needs muddling our personalities and sense of reality. Therefore, exploring and overcoming our idiosyncrasies on a goodness path would be a big challenge. A transformation to selflessness from the prevalent selfishness—if possible for many individuals—is a hard and long process, but reveals the art of being. Learning about our perpetual, inherent nothingness after a lifelong training to pump our egos would be tough, but a divine experience. Grasping the severe repercussions of humans' vast mental differences can also help us improve our relationships, especially our marriages, somewhat.

Part III studies Social Conscience and Consciousness, while Part IV focuses on the World's Political Impasse and our leaders' inability to build functional societies. A long review of political systems is offered in these two parts, since social conscience and leadership are main goodness attributes. Sadly, the gloomy global state of affairs, especially in the United States, has made humans quite unreliable and controversial, but also deformed their nature and commonsense. Accordingly, the dire absence of leadership is threatening the survival of all beings as well as our planet.

By the way, the four parts and even topics in the book can be read in any order based on the readers' interest. Technical topics in Appendices A through D may be skipped if a person is not too curious. However, Appendix E offers a good summary or long synopsis, while it can also be useful for regular reflections.

This book's ideas appeal mostly to intelligent, naïve people who seek redemption and peace. Naïve in the sense of innocence (due to parental/societal influences and conditioning, and for their submissive beliefs in values that society promotes). Yet intelligent enough to grasp their options and reasons for thinking and acting differently, challenging corrupt social norms, and discovering a personal path of existence and goodness.

The task of becoming a better being is long and tough, thus one must get prepared to devote time and patience during routine practices and meditation to get there smoothly, including the task of reading the book's pages slowly and reflectively. Even though all efforts were made to write the chapters and ideas as simple as possible for general benefit, the readers' big efforts are required all along to succeed. If you feel bored with one topic, move on to another topic that grabs your attention in the Table of Contents. You can switch between topics and sections to give yourself more variety before returning to the older topics later. Surely, do not attempt to read and finish the book fast. Be ready for a few years of challenge and fun on your way of becoming a better being.

After all, finding ways of relieving ourselves from pervasive social influences and identifying more peaceful opportunities for living outside the debilitating rules of our neo-culture is hard. Sadly, we are now broken beings trying to make sense of our existence in a dwindling social setting, while destroying life on this planet as well. Chapter One will discuss this fact in detail, but a big clue about how deeply humans are broken is evident in their vast, growing arrogance, mostly as the result of their efforts to compete in society, compensate for their varied insecurities, and soothe their broken souls. It is hard to imagine that humans have ever been so arrogant by nature. Even our ancestors only a few centuries ago were not so full of themselves the way we modern humans have become, while doing most things wrong, anyway. With no true identities and self-image to communicate amongst ourselves effectively, we only ruin each other's spirits.

Many factors had to be studied in this book about the chances of personal growth and saving humanity by collective efforts of many awakened humans. These general analyses might help us reflect on our authentic needs and the high likelihood of human demise if a large majority of people do not admit to, and fight, the roots of the rising socioeconomic chaos.

The reality we are facing is not bright, yet those who grasp their beings through self-analysis would at least enrich their own souls in a finer realm. Then, we might get a chance to live rather peacefully, though we must still share this planet with too many reckless humans. This personal goal would feel more viable to some people than struggling mindlessly and restlessly merely for keeping a flimsy, questionable social identity.

To be realistic, whether we are an optimist or pessimist about the future of humanity, in the end our options are very limited in terms of what we can do personally with certain years of life in a physical form. We can continue to do more of the same stuff we have been doing in our careers and relationships, or try to find a more meaningful lifestyle that might suit our personalities along with a finer perspective of our being. We can continue to abide by the agonizing principles of social living dominating us nowadays or try to find some basic principles for coping with (living thru) such diabolic rules and relationships without killing our spirits. If we are keen to grasp our options at least, this and similar books will be of value. This book attempts to show why investing time and energy to discover our 'being' would be vastly justified and a rewarding experience. We do these self-cleansing routines for our benefit mostly, but our transformation would also help others. We can also examine the clues around us about our personal, social, and global dilemmas sincerely to get a better sense of humanity.

Grasping the superficialities of modern societies can in itself help us elude the traps and agonies of a hollow existence within such a humiliating setting only in fears of losing some vain social privileges we have taken as our urgent needs. We may realize the inevitability of human extinction if societies cannot find radical solutions soon and revamp people's mindsets by recognizing the essence of human beings and the features of a moral civilization they need. Then, we may also agree that the collapse of prevalent social values would not threaten humans' real needs.

Overall, only through self-cleansing and reflections we might, i) make our lives rather easier and joyous, and ii) find our true 'being' through practical detachment from social vanities.

Sadly, the author might sound cynical regarding the inevitable dire destiny of the planet Earth and its inhabitants accelerating in a loop at the neck of an ominous manmade black hole. Still, the main goal of the book is to goad more people seek the wisdom of goodness and fight socioeconomic systems and values destroying the Earth. It seems impossible to elude social temptations and entrapments, considering our socioeconomic structure's grip over our minds and lifestyles. However, we can try to examine some realities about our being within and outside the context of social living. This book's goal is to goad plenty of personal reflections and soul-searching, as we reassess social life barriers to mitigate its burdens. In spite of our innate scepticism about the meaning or truthfulness of a 'being' that we have not still found in ourselves, some of us can develop the strength to do just that gradually. Many readers might be convinced in the end and set out to do something about their 'being' within this dire social travesty.

PART I

The State of Being

Let them all brag about their generosity,
goodness, wisdom, and all the rest of it;
the fact is that evil engulfs human nature
before the society and people mess them
up even more starting in childhood!

> The same forlorn, old spirit

Chapter One
Broken Beings

Humans evolved from primates over 3 to 7 million years by adapting to new settings and life conditions. The process has been successful in terms of what we can do compared with our distant cousins, apes and monkeys. We became bipedal and learned languages, as nature goaded our ancestors to go find or cultivate food more actively, instead of just fooling around on trees. In all, anthropology and related sciences indicate that intricate biological adjustments, including the superb growth of our brains, have been necessary during a long process in line with humans' environmental and instinctual changes.

The point is that a steady biological adaptation had assured our survival as long as we had stayed in harmony with nature. We also know that if a species has not been prepared biologically for a natural change, it would have faced the risk of extinction, like dinosaurs. Overall, it appears that humans have made most radical changes during their history of evolution based on two main principles: i) Nature has dictated the evolution process, and ii) changes have occurred in a steady, slow, and natural order.

Now, however, suddenly humans have become active agents of an unprecedented artificial evolution. The urgent question at this stage of human history is whether we can adapt to radical changes that we—not nature—are imposing upon ourselves with such exceptional haste and ignorance. In particular, the need for mental and psychological adjustments is too fast and huge.

We are very proud of humans' physical and mental evolution to such level of sophistication and might. However, how proud can we be when we study the recent history of social changes and project them into future human life? It took us millions of years before we became Homo sapiens with high mental and physical capabilities. Then, it took us 50,000 years to progress and prepare our minds to grow into modern human beings who made social systems and began living in communities. Only in the last 10,000 years, organized social structures and rules have emerged, thoughtful humans expressed complex ideas and feelings, and we built our nations. Then, we need to look back only 400-500 years to observe major changes in our thoughts and lifestyles and the effects of post-industrialization era on social values. Finally, we may go back only 50-60 years to witness the fastest growth in the history of humanity in terms of vast technological advancement and their impacts on human life as well as the global assimilation of cultures. The acceleration of technological growth, knowledge, and our ability to travel and mix with various cultures, gave us a new perspective of life and a great deal of expectations. We are now suddenly in charge of our destiny and survival as a species, but have no clues or wisdom to appreciate this responsibility, let alone succeed. We humans now appear like mad or sick creatures with no sense about our actions and their looming consequences.

During humans' natural evolution, we had related to nature instinctually, learned how to live in some form of harmony with our surroundings, and stayed aware of our basic identity within a pure and straightforward context. Then, suddenly, the changes in the last century have revolutionized the nature and structure of our lives in a convoluted manner as we entered an era of futile struggles and constant conflicts. In fact, the changes have been so dramatic we humans have lost our identity, our touch with reality, and our power of adaptation at both social and individual levels. It is easy to envision the effects of these rapid radical changes on our psyches and brains by studying humanity's recent history, including our new habits and social affairs. The amounts of drugs, alcohols, crimes, suicides, and sleeping pills crippling societies are proofs of humans' unnatural efforts for adaptation and their looming future. Many books have already been devoted to this crucial subject, with no tangible effects on our hypnotized minds, mostly because nobody is in charge of our wild societies other than self-serving greedy conglomerates.

Overall, the growth of superficial human urges and needs in fast-changing societies have been too much for human biology to absorb and respond to properly thru a natural process. Especially, our brains cannot adapt to such fierce conditions that are vastly incongruent with our natural urges and tendencies. Now, instead of adapting naturally to new social demands and situations, our brains should constantly seek solutions to face, defeat, or avoid harsh social and environmental threats.

Social living emerged when Homo sapiens decided to create work synergy, minimize animosity and fighting, and maximize harmony and teamwork. Now, it seems that the idea of teamwork that began in the primitive tribes has reverted into a sense of harsh competition and controversy within our demented lifestyles at all personal, social, and global levels. Meanwhile, our lifestyles are too dynamic and problematic to respond to in the same natural way our ancestors could. Therefore, we do the second best thing that our brains tell us to do: Try to find ways of bearing our rising internal conflicts and fighting with expanding external threats.

Most horrifically, we are coping with all these changes not biologically, but only through our vile thoughts and perceptions. Instead of adapting naturally in conjunction with pure thinking and expectations, we are coping under duress. Our ways of facing social demands and the effects of such forced adjustments on our brains and psyches will be discussed in Part II. However, we may simply say that we are inflicting too many psychological burdens upon ourselves merely for adjusting our behaviour to a large load of superficial social demands and for keeping basic relationships within instable, confusing settings. The rising social chaos and personal distress are symptoms of new life structures and values that have evolved recently merely as a result of crude ideological propagandas for some form of coexistence without any coherent plan, but mainly for the benefit of elite groups in our societies. Thus, our constant struggles to cope with these conundrums have turned us into active agents of our own distress and hardships by changing our social conditions and mentalities much faster than we are naturally equipped to adjust to and bear.

Spoiled Modern Beings

Technological progress, crude ideologies, modern lifestyles, vast egotism, and a vile socioeconomic structure have caused a chaos in our heads and societies with lasting effects on biosphere and humanity. The customary natural evolution and adjustments to our brains and psyches would be too slow to handle the speed, force, and impact of humans' aggressive intrusion, fast changes, and mass destructions. Even the wild effects of nature's reactions, like floods and hurricanes, cannot offset the hazards of humans' irresponsibility. These seemingly natural balancing acts have so far been relatively insignificant and superficial in comparison to man-induced damages, although they are actually becoming both more catastrophic and related to our interventions. In this sense, all changes, including nature's reactions, would be a reflection of humans' narrow minds at work making our living conditions scarier every year. Now, the natural order and nature of things on the Earth have altered severely and it seems things will get more out of hand until humans or their evils are eliminated.

Our innovations are *supposedly* for maximizing humans' life expectancy and happiness. However, our attitude and power to manipulate things at large scales so ignorantly and irresponsibly have been ruining both humanity and nature. Mainly hedonism and egotism are driving humans' progress and their life structure, with minimal support of nature. We have disregarded humans' identity and spirit, while other creatures and nature are suffering from our recklessness, too. Now, the world is merely at the mercy of our greed-ridden mentality, industrial ambitions, and egotism towards a catastrophic end.

Maybe that's exactly why God has not populated many other planets with creatures like us? To save the universe at least!

The main causes for alarm and the symptoms of personal and social speedy decline are reviewed in Chapter Two. Yet, the decay process can be felt and defined by weighing humans' lifestyles, mentalities, and depressions; by assessing the enormity of social corruption and disharmony; by gauging main values and systems that are manipulating us; by weighing the sheer size of erratic forces fighting one another at all social levels; by grasping and judging the irrationality of our leaders and their reasons for letting things get so out of control; by calculating the speed that most elements of social structure are moving towards annihilation; and by gathering all the evidences out there about the effects of our existing dogmatism and neglect on our brains.

Altogether, it seems that future environmental changes on this planet will be cancerous, speedy, and devolutionary, instead of evolutionary, unless we find magical solutions soon. Ironically, though, any kind of solutions for stopping the repercussions of the present devolution should come from the same human minds that are causing the mayhem in the first place with no ability and interest to reform their mentalities very quickly. Unfortunately, the formidable new set of unmanageable forces created through humans' selfish intrusion and reckless intentions is promising a gloomy destiny for humanity and biosphere.

We have gotten to this point inadvertently with both positive and negative results, e.g., in terms of higher life expectancy versus higher depressions. However, we now seem adamant to continue on the same path with no long-term plans for humanity. Worse, without a biological evolution to align our brains with new social demands, they must now work too hard constantly to deal with our intellectual and emotional burdens resulting from unforeseen environmental and societal growth. Now, we are expecting our brains to adjust superficially (not instinctually) to events and situations and to fight in many fronts (mentally and externally). We should now struggle and suffer due to our growing conflicts with both our inner self and outer sources, in particular Mother Nature. She is getting terribly mad at us, too!

Furthermore, we are also changing our priority with respect to social philosophy and ethics for the first time in human history! Instead of seeking unity and harmony in family and society, as we had been promoting until recently as part of our instinctive evolution, we are now reverting to our vile, egoistic needs to prove our individualism and fight for vaster territorial dominance and superiority. This type of mentality is prevalent now even in the smallest, and closest social unit, i.e., family. We are resorting to our primitive personal urges and motives to dominate each other, at social and family levels, with hostility and controversy. Our new social setting and attitude are worse than the motives and needs of early cavemen and primates who were unfamiliar with the urgency for social structure and means of cooperation and unity. A major problem is that we do not realize how spoiled we have become as a bizarre upshot of our zeal for civilization. Then, we keep spoiling our kids even more.

Obviously, personal and social problems grow when most of us cannot fulfil our physical and spiritual needs. However, our obsessions with too many idealistic visions and expectations have disconnected our minds from not only one another, but also the harsh reality of existence within a divine universe. We are already so out of touch with the essence of our being we seldom can, or even attempt to, grasp our innate potentialities, prepare ourselves for life's inevitable hardships, find relief, and pursue the sources of self-actualization and spiritualism. Instead, we set materialistic goals and build unrealistic expectations from society, people, and ourselves under the influence of social media that only propagate vanity, individualism, and the lifestyle of rich and famous.

An analogy to stress the effects of unnatural, rapid changes on our brains and behaviour is to imagine forcing people around the world to get only 4-5 hours of sleep a day regularly rather than 7-8 hours required. Clearly, the level of relationship frictions and personal tension would multiply many folds and create vaster social imbalance, hostilities, and sickness due to human contacts and decisions. This is exactly how the radical changes in the last few decades have induced such high levels of social and personal diseases and stress due to long working hours, sleep deprivations, alcohol and drug abuse, rising personal insecurities, etc. In fact, it seems plausible that soon we may not be able to get even 4-5 hours of daily sleep without the aid of sleeping pills due to the rising level of personal and social burdens.

We read and hear so many sad predictions about humans' looming fate, but still have no vision or interest to fight the causes of this manmade abyss suffocating all of us. We still do not find an incentive to seek a better option to live less stressfully in this world. We do not seem to truly sense, or care about, our kids' and future generations' predictable pains, while indulging and ruining them more every day idiotically. We keep thinking there is no cause for alarm and giving up our hopes against the rising odds. With our juvenile mentalities, we strive to remain positive about everything just to prove our resilience and assume everything is under control in the large scale of things, no matter how foolishly we are all damaging our minds, environment, and nature. We still trust our leaders' capacity and goodwill, as well as the existing socioeconomic structure, to prevail and save humanity at the end. We extend great efforts and financial resources to prevent some animals' extinctions, but have no sense or plan to stop humans' looming annihilation after huge sufferings! Simply, our naïveté and gift for self-deception are amazing! *Then again, we also seem badly stuck!*

Anyway, we spoiled, confused, and frustrated beings now face many dilemmas, passively ponder our personal options for living within the boundaries that society imposes upon us, and we strive to ignore all the negative notions about humans' doomed destiny. All along, we wrestle with many plausible questions tickling our subconscious minds at least randomly, such as, "Has the process of social and human final demise really begun? What are the true signs of a natural devolution crippling humans?"

Surely, we want to be rational and objective in our evaluation of humans' state of affairs and prospect. We need concrete clues with respect to the depth of problems and the deterioration speed before drawing any major conclusions and maybe envision some viable plans. We like to identify the main principles and systems that are collapsing and know how badly our future is in jeopardy. More crucially, we like to know if enough willpower, conscience, and opportunity exist in the world to reverse the course of history and secure the fate of future generations.

Assuming we admit the high chance of human annihilation, the next challenge is to establish if any opportunity for changing humans' risky mentality and lifestyle exists considering their vile nature. Many talks and doubts about human nature have spread for many centuries. We have strived to attribute the source of our aggressive, evil behaviour to instinctual or environmental factors. It seems that those arguments are now totally irrelevant and futile since our problems nowadays are simply the results of humans hindering, or even reversing, the slow process of natural evolution. NOW, the question is whether we can change ourselves fast enough to avert our distinction considering the speed of humans' damaging habits and crude nature.

This book's analysis suggest that mainly humans' arrogance and aggressive attitude is behind the underlying personal, social, and ecological decline. We have reached this low quality due to our innate wicked nature instigated by vastly flawed nurture too fast. Everybody is becoming haughtier and meaner just to fit in the society, thus the unstoppable escalation of conceit and spite. Surely, we have instinctual urges and needs that goad our minds positively, though not effectively enough for running a balanced life. Instead, our fast interventions with humans' mental growth have led to their behavioural flaws and low capacity for goodness, while evoking their wilder instincts that might have been partly suppressed during the long process of evolution. All along, the ongoing expansion of technology and societies, as well as new juvenile social ideologies, has also faltered our social adaptation capacity largely. This gloomy conclusion is actually for instilling some incentive and optimism about the possibility of revamping humans' mindset and lifestyle soon in hopes of saving future generations *if we really wanted to and knew how!!!*

Anyhow, the ultimate reality is that our misguided minds are pushing us into bizarre, catastrophic directions, due to daunting effects of social progress on our instinctual urges, e.g., in terms of lust and greed. This reality is not restricted to a specific group of people's vain, modern mentality, the behaviour of convicted criminals, or cases of human degradation. The truth is that all of us regardless of intelligence and social position are now infected by the same deficiencies at noticeable levels. Of course, the social systems we have developed and administer are all suffering from the same diseases and dysfunctions driving human minds and we cannot abolish them until we find a global remedy for what we humans have become—to cure our spoiled minds first. Until then, under present dire circumstances, the process of deterioration will accelerate. Meanwhile, our efforts (solutions) to exert either more despotism or liberalism in our political systems—in order to curb humans' natural or nurtured defects—are also futile for helping humanity. Fighting for capitalism or communism merely shows how our demented minds are keeping us amused hypnotically.

At the same time, it is hard, for some of us at least, not to take the symptoms of deterioration too seriously. Whether we have already, or soon, reach a point of no-return for humanity is hard to fathom, though it feels too daring and fatalistic to contemplate such an utterly absurd scenario. However, too many clues show that we are running fast towards this end so hypnotically and recklessly that reaching the no-return point would be inevitable. We must learn to believe this incredible prospect.

The sad reality is that social and personal problems have grown vastly because we cannot adjust or adapt to the erratic, soulless environments we have built for ourselves. We have also become too spoiled to connect or fit in naturally. We suffer since we do not know how to cope with these changes—even if it were wise and possible to do so. Thus, the quality of our personal lives is also deteriorating fast, while the effects of these speedy social and personal changes are too radical for the survival of families, humanity, and our planet in general.

Nevertheless, instead of merely blaming humans' nature for the growing chaos, we should look for answers about the manner human mind works in general, at a universal level, now in the 21st century. Then, we should find out how it contributes to the growth of hard conditions and situations. Surely, the rising demands on our confused brains induce unpredictable mental reactions and defects in people, while causing changes in human nature much faster than any natural evolution could have accomplished by itself without humans' immense interventions.

Accordingly, we can now also stop viewing human nature as a set of constant attributes resembling the habits of primates and cavemen. Rather, humans' nature should be defined only in terms of its uniformity in majority of people and across cultures at any particular time. In that sense, we are merely affirming the fact that human nature has never been a stable condition, but rather a dynamic state directed by both instinctual and social factors over a long period. Accordingly, we can project the rapid deterioration of human nature thru humans' future history even if they survive their seemingly irreversible looming fate by a huge miracle. Once we build proper scientific tools, we might be able to research and associate changes in humans' nature with common social values and systems that bombard them endlessly so radically. In a sense, the word 'nature' has been misused in the idiom 'human nature'.

More evidences about the deteriorating state of human mind and nature, including humans' demented logic and the effects of socio-political systems, are offered in the future chapters.

A Natural Personal Initiative

Humans' systemic inability to build a functional social structure and promote a moralistic culture is now more evident than ever. We have never had the insight to find the right mix of principles and mechanisms, or a long-term vision, for social harmony and personal solace. However, we have now proven, beyond a doubt, our idiocy and ineptitude to coordinate our needs or cooperate for useful, common goals. The more civilized we have supposedly become, the more controversial and selfish we have turned into. Therefore, we can now safely predict that the chance of building a harmonious life on earth is slim! Instead, even humanity's basic needs are corroding fast now, judging by the escalating levels of corruptions, conflicts, and crimes in all facets of socioeconomic systems and international relationships, not to mention the awful impact of humans' wasteful lifestyles on nature.

It is hard to imagine that even Stone-age humans had endured as much confusions, personal insecurities, pains, and conflicts—despite their perceivable immense life limitations—as we alleged civilized people bear nowadays.

Thus, the question is what makes us so much more inferior than our ancient ancestors despite (or because) of our immense intelligence and innovations?

The direst outcome of the growing world chaos and societal confusion is our loss of personal identities and a lesser sense of our true being. We see and suffer the global mayhem as well as humans' incapacity for coexistence. Yet, we feel helpless to live differently, as we are mesmerized by the illusive symbols of our lifestyles and mentalities, despite our doubts about their validity. Scholars' quarrels over human nature's relation to our dwindling identities in the new era also baffle us further, as we still cannot find approaches and solutions for human salvation.

However, all these symptoms also pinpoint a certain reality to most rational people: That we are now responsible more than ever in history to establish a meaningful identity for humans in line with wiser mindsets and cleaner lifestyles. We must establish 'who we are **and can** be as humans' in order to see and act on a formidable truth: The high likelihood of 'human demise' in a few centuries at most if we cannot fathom solutions soon, mainly by becoming better beings to a large degree somehow.

'Human demise' in this book implies either humans' extinction or at best the survival of small groups around the world living in lifestyles similar to cavemen's, if not in much harsher conditions.

Ironically, many of us realize the ominous direction humans are pursuing and suffer for it daily, but do not grasp the severity of the matter, or do not care about it enough. Instead, we strive to cope with the burdens of social living. We just suffer a sense of helplessness to do anything about humans' growing follies or our personal entrapments.

Still, a 'natural personal initiative' might soothe our souls a bit, and maybe help society, too, if we rebuild our muddled identities and mentalities. We could reassess the forces driving our brains, as outlined in Chapter Four. We could at least see how the rising pains of our daily encounters, experiences, and dilemmas, as well as the growing prospect of human demise, are all simply the symptoms of humans' modern crude lifestyles and mentalities—and deadlier for our gloomy fate than the effects of climate crisis and epidemics. Therefore, building our incentives for goodness in a large scale seems urgent, as discussed in Chapter Three.

Ironically and luckily, we have the greatest chance now to show who we humans are and what our nature is in the way we respond to the accelerating socioeconomic problems and human sufferings. We can show our essence and character in the way we adopt one or more of the following stands about socioeconomic issues and our roles, especially about our mentalities, lifestyles, and the climate change:

1. Simply do not care one way or another for whatever reasons, but mostly for protecting our self-interests or concentrating on personal problems or pleasures.

2. Deny the facts and scientific claims outright due to arrogance, naivety, dogmatism, positive thinking, etc.
3. Realize and accept the problems at hand, but feel helpless to do anything about them personally.
4. Make an effort to at least revamp our personal mentality and lifestyle somewhat in line with the problems at hand.
5. Get fully active about these issues to find solutions even at the cost of personal sacrifice and more suffering on many grounds.
6. Become a revolutionary or find other options for fighting the status quo and gaining our relative independence and peace.

Amazingly, however, we, especially our lousy leaders, believe and act so casually at this point, as if nothing is so fundamentally wrong with humanity, social mechanisms, and our personalities, and that we are not heading for humans' total demise!

The Socio-personal Paradox

Many social and personal pressures always push our nerves and cause us immense psychological disorders. We strive to detect the roots of these problems and seek solutions innocently during some precious moments of reflection. We wonder why our lives have become so shallow and frustrating for no justifiable reasons, and all for nothing. Many of us realize the absurdity of our blind social adaptation, as life's erratic impositions besiege our psyches and we question our strenuous plans and existence.

In all, we face a painful and peculiar *socio-personal* paradox a lifetime. We feel trapped in busy societies built around people's frivolous perceptions and fallacious ambitions. Even our honest, hard efforts satisfy neither people's expectations enough, nor our spirits. Our endless search for tranquility, despite our positivism, good intentions, and diligence, feels futile often, too, as though the whole world had conspired to break our pride and resolve. Instead, our lives feel emptier and tenser every day, while we strive to play many idiotic roles and games for a decent existence, or at least an easier subsistence. Accordingly, as a first step for personal peace, we must recognize the nature and effects of this socio-personal paradox and admit that something is seriously wrong with both society and our personal mentalities, then decide what kind of a person we are or would rather be.

Often, we seem to become victims of our crude perceptions of the world and shoddy decisions, e.g., in terms of our arduous or boring careers and relationships. Yet, our struggles to make sense of this universal madness plunge us deeper into the abyss, mostly due to our egoism, dogmatism, and naiveté about social vanities and values. We seem stuck, though, as we simply cannot ignore our obligations to family and general attachments to society to fit and prosper. We must stay practical, after all!

Instead, we build lots of self-pity and blame mostly ourselves for our hardships—mainly our inability to cope with people and society. Thus, we just try harder to be more like others in order to be accepted in their circles, which in turn makes us more showy, superficial, arrogant, greedy, needy, competitive, and other means of weakness and wickedness. We have become apathetic and only a small group has enough goodness as a basic human trait, although we learn to parade our empathy sometimes, mostly for show or cleansing our conscience. Thus, in effect, we have been causing our own deformation and sufferings with our gullibility and desire to be like others—rather selfish and crooked. Overall, something appears fundamentally wrong with humans' mentality and lifestyles, as well as social norms, as most of us are unhappy with our lives, if not deeply disheartened. Our mundane solutions for salvation are also ineffective, as they revolve around the same narrow-minded principles and norms that we develop egoistically to think and behave with little insight or sincerity.

Ultimately, we must admit that humans' pervasive suffering is mostly due to their: i) high degree of impiety and, ii) inability, or reluctance, to be better beings than they have been historically. Ironically, we have always guessed these simple facts—about the high correlation between human wickedness and their sufferings.

Prophets have hinted about this fact sloppily, too. However, we seem to be deaf and adamant to hurt ourselves and suffer.

Scientists and philosophers have also strived to study human nature and envision an ideal picture of humanity within a moral society where some principles of human relationships can goad a peaceful, productive coexistence. They have hoped to create rules for building healthier and fairer societies that can encourage, and benefit from, human goodness. Yet, clearly, they have failed on both grounds. Even God and His prophets have failed when their efforts to guide humans have caused only more naiveté, distress, and fighting among them. Actually, social chaos has risen fast in line with our deeper attachments to religions or pitiful symbols of civilization. Then, we ponder two amusing ideas (clichés) and feel more confused: Had God meant to create humans pure at all. If yes, why did He fail? And if not, why has He been so eager to change them later thru religions or whatever? These thoughts also challenge the idea of God giving humans willpower and freewill, or His possible eagerness to test our capacity for goodness! These notions do not quite make sense to some of us, so we feel more cynical and hopeless.

Still, our historical failure to recognize and focus on humans' basic, collective needs and a practical society is both depressing and educational. It reveals humans' irreconcilable mentalities and personalities, and their inability to agree on a set of principles for coexistence thru teamwork. It also says a lot about human nature.

Amazingly, all of us play a big role in this horrendous display of human lunacy, as we are driven by our crude desires, naiveté, and insecurities. We all simply feel obliged to fit within a useless, vile socioeconomic setting without pondering our options as a society or individuals. We feel trapped and helpless in this world of our own making around arrogance and greed, while our socio-personal paradox grows and our thoughts about our being and a possible way out feel endless and irresolvable.

While questioning human nature often, rather intuitively, we build a vague vision about it at two odd extremes: A large group *still* insists on the piety of human essence, while another group feels and believes strongly in humans' wickedness. The majority remains confused about this matter. Sadly, this author's studies and experiences have placed him closer to the cynical group's position, despite the gloom this mentality causes him. Besides our wicked genes and urges, many factors prevent us nowadays from being a good person *under normal conditions,* while we live in our addictive, vile societies. Sadly, we like to stay naive, boast about our bullish wisdom, undermine our insecurities, overestimate our abilities, become more arrogant every day, and set higher expectations from life. This pattern of thinking and behaving highly hinders our abilities for becoming better beings and developing a society for peaceful coexistence.

Nevertheless, humans' vile genes and rearing conditions lead to the development of too many wicked personalities and natures across the population. Handling these weird characters has been a big challenge for humans, yet, ironically, we still wonder about the purity of human essence, as though such an ideal were within human capacity. Thus, we quarrel about human nature amongst ourselves as well.

The big irony, of course, is humans' tenacity to keep causing so much chaos for themselves and making one another miserable solely out of naiveté regarding their real needs and spirits, while getting deeply confused by too many artificial needs they have imposed upon themselves. Thus, personal, social, and global problems have kept accelerating with no smart leaders or feasible plans at hand to understand and fight the rooted causes of social distress, and to elude humans' looming demise.

Sometimes, we make great contributions as well, of course, as rulers, reformers, or common citizens, while we examine and redefine our roles in different stages of our lives, too, mostly for coping with erratic social and interpersonal demands. However, the general picture shows that ostentatious rulers and frustrated reformers would keep fighting for their ideologies or the power and privilege of controlling helpless citizens, who must keep struggling with their immediate financial and emotional needs forever. Most of us feel obliged, by habit or necessity, to focus on survival per se in such a hectic environment at the cost of losing our identities and spirits. Accordingly, we have left politics and socioeconomic affairs to some narcissists who enjoy power and business as means of exploiting the world and keeping people in their shells. It is amazing to witness how only a bad example in society, like Donald Trump, can single-handedly contaminate the mentalities of so many common people, leaders, and scholars so fast, while ruining humans' basic integrity and pride recklessly at national and international levels!

Surely, many enlightened leaders and scholars have always lived peacefully within the largely naïve population throughout the history. Some people are in fact obsessed to help others and empathize with their pains. Conversely, many people are not just wicked and cruel, but also driven by a burning urge to hurt others and bask in their sufferings. Many other groups fall between these two extremes, which reflect the amazing, wide range of qualities among individuals in line with the complexity of human nature. Accordingly, humans' unique mixes of qualities and quirks make them look so odd and unbearable to others with little opportunity for teamwork.

Cleansing our malignant urges and giving up our superficial lifestyles are surely quite onerous, because of the way society has moulded us into rigid, self-gratifying, and conceited individuals. We are born into eccentric families, grow up in corrupt societies, and face a hectic, overwhelming world. At the same time, we are trained to expect a perfect environment and destiny that fits our naïve perceptions of life, where people are happy and treat one another fairly and respectfully. Overall, we are living in a fantasy world. Thus, we suffer the consequences of both our ignorance and innocence, since we have difficulty coping with the realities of stressful, harsh social conditions. In fact, this rooted confusion portray the sad state of a normal being nowadays.

At the same time, humans' idealism for a perfect environment and destiny could become a motivator for becoming better beings as the last resort to satiate their dreams! Thus, the good news is that we can help ourselves and maybe even enrich humanity by becoming a bit smarter and humbler. We can do this if we learn to elude social vanities—mainly our superficiality and false pride—that grow through our interactions with people and society so easily during our daily routines.

Nonetheless, grasping the effects of humans' wild nature and wide mental differences on our daily lives is a topic of this book for a possible improvement in our mentalities and interactions.

Meanwhile, the best we can hope to learn from this or any book is to develop enough incentive for initiating the process of questioning our lifestyles seriously in order to save our spirits. Then, our fundamental thoughts about our 'being' would give us a new vision about our authentic needs and means of attaining a healthier mental state. All along, our two main objectives are to: 1) strengthen our beliefs and spirits by testing and boosting the essence of our being personally thru self-awareness, and 2) try to figure out what has gone wrong with our relationships, cultures, and mentalities, for an allegedly intelligent species.

The Goodness Barometer

We have come to believe that three or four groups of people exist—good, bad, marginally wicked or sick ones. Therefore, we (the allegedly good ones) put evildoers in prisons to protect the society and try to show some level of leniency and compassion towards the sick ones. However, the bottomline is that we all are bad and sick at various degrees. In fact, we are most likely quite crooked, despite our big egos making us feel so superior and invincible. At best, we are not good *enough*, judging by the big social mayhem, pollution, hypocrisy, and hundreds of other atrocities we commit regularly around the world. Most people are compassionate and generous occasionally as well, but it does not mean they are good enough regularly, not even for their own sakes. How we hurt one another habitually with our arrogance, obsessions, greed, and many other personal idiosyncrasies is merely shameful.

Goodness is a measure of both a person's moral virtues and mental strengths to make the right choices and grasp the essence of existence. Goodness in the context used in this book refers to our capacity (cognition) to handle life effectively and peacefully. It reflects one's degree of intelligence and insight to develop a rounded personality based on the following three components:

1. **Qualities**, such as passion, compassion, honesty, sincerity, authenticity, generosity, humility, ingenuity, patience, etc.
2. **Quirks**, such as pomposity, insecurities, meanness, jealousy, spite, greed, etc.
3. **Gullibility**, which includes innocence, ignorance, all types of mental incapacities, low cognition, etc.

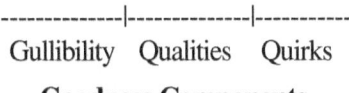

Gullibility   Qualities   Quirks

Goodness Components

We all have some degrees of these three components. Thus, at the end, the proportions of these factors in a person depict his/her character and goodness. Our types of qualities and quirks affect the outcome, too, as some qualities and quirks are more useful or damaging for becoming a better person. Furthermore, personal and social capacities for goodness decline very fast nowadays, since even people's simplest quirks clash constantly and stir more conflicts and badness. In fact, our qualities are often ineffective or crushed under the pressures of our quirks, insecurities, and, most of all, our gullibility. While our quirks, even simple ones, stir tremendous personal and social badness, ironically, gullibility is the most destructive factor hindering a person's efforts to become a better being and it actually induces more badness.

Sadly, as people's encounters stir their quirks and gullibility very fast, social badness and distress have grown to such high levels now in line with larger means and demands for socializing. Again, as a timely, fine example, the author likes to introduce the idiom, 'Trump Effect,' to refer to the depth and speed of badness dissemination in societies and around the world due to humans' high vulnerability for badness, especially when exposed to words and actions of so many ill-natured, lousy leaders.

Nowadays, almost everybody needs lots of self-analysis and self-therapy to defeat his/her drive for badness and build his/her character on a goodness path. Luckily, we can still do so many things intentionally (actively) to become better beings by fighting humans' bad nature and apathy for self-cleansing. Sadly, though, the reverse is truer and more prevalent. Thus, learning how much of our goodness is natural (subconscious or unconscious urges) or intentional (conscious plans and efforts) is helpful in itself.

Becoming better beings requires planning and efforts to defeat our gullibility due to social teachings and propagandas. Instead of letting our haughty self-image and sporadic goodness mislead us, we must learn teamwork and boost our conscience for our own benefit as well as society's. We need exceptional inner strengths to fight the evils of the 'Trump Effect' at least.

The objectives and means of achieving goodness through self-awareness are explained in the following chapters. Nevertheless, the modest goal for goodness is to help the three defective groups (95% ordinary people) learn merely about the merits of being better beings (BBB) somewhat, instead of seeking enlightenment or setting targets unrealistic for most of us.

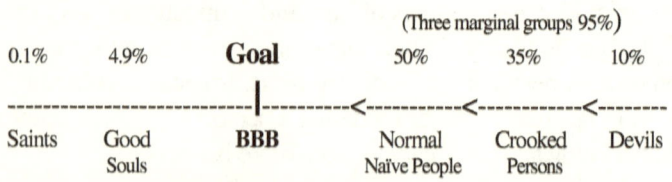

Goodness Barometer: A Modest Goal for Goodness

We might know, or hear about, people who manifest as saints (at best 0.1% of population) in terms of compassion and patience. Some devils occupy the other end of the 'goodness barometer.' Although this diagram shows only five major groups, a wide array of human natures can be detected along the above range. This reiterates the amazing vast variety of human natures nowadays. These differences are too deep to attribute merely to genetics or upbringing conditioning. Contrary to conventional urge to assume a particular nature for humans, this author believes that at least a few dozen clusters of human natures can be formed if we study humans' major characteristics and ambitions around the world. This big variety of human natures mixes with family genetics and rearing conditions, and together they make it too hard for humans to communicate, build relationships, and set their trust levels. The incongruity of human natures is a fact and a substantial factor for humans' extreme degrees of controversy and incapacity to work together and build healthy families, especially nowadays with the added effects of people's rising insecurities and idiosyncrasies due to the lack of proper identities.

At the same time, we certainly cannot (and must not) expect people, or ourselves, to become saints or even good enough. The best we can hope for, and strive to achieve personally, as intended in this book too, is to find means of making the three defective groups a bit better than they have been conditioned to be, though they might never reach even the target at point BBB on the Goodness Barometer shown above. Becoming just a little more conscious and conscientious goes a long way in growing one's goodness all by itself. Especially, learning a basic level of humility is a great start, since people's escalating urge for arrogance to outdo others' is now killing all social fibres and humans' essence. In fact, this growing modern fad among us in itself confirms the looming demise of humanity.

It would be a big triumph for humanity if a majority of people approach the goal of being better than ordinary beings, eventually, mainly by curbing their naiveté and arrogance. Becoming even just a bit better than normal people is not an easy task, yet this modest adjustment would help a lot in reducing our personal stress of living, while helping humanity as well. Amazingly, lots of goodness grows in a person fast only by learning humility, as it curbs the repercussions of his/her gullibility and dogmatism. In fact, the biggest source of the author's reserved optimism for human salvation is his belief that if only a majority of us learn to replace our idiotic arrogance with humility, the chance of human demise would decline by 80%. If a large group of people learn to curb their arrogance, the global effect would be vast, contagious, and hopefully inspiring. Even this basic improvement in personal and social mentalities would be a big achievement for humans, with a great likelihood to also improve humans' nature gradually over centuries. We merely need a culture that advocates BBB philosophy and teaches humility as its core principle to redefine political and socioeconomic structures and values, *at all initial costs*. In fact, it is not farfetched to think that humans might soon realize the need, and invent a method, to grasp their nothingness and learn humility as naturally as they learn arrogance nowadays during childhood. Can societies do at least this one thing right, as a basic means of *being a human*, and gauge the result?

Nevertheless, goodness (the regimen for being better beings) is for exploring our inner self and soul mostly for managing our lives effectively and peacefully. At the same time, boosting our spirits and beings is not meant to be strenuous or an awakening exercise. Rather, the goal is to become somewhat more conscious of, and conscientious about, our actions. The goal is to further our inner strengths, efforts, convictions, and self-reliance. Of course, the ultimate objective is to reduce personal and social gullibility gradually, if possible—if the effects of domineering social forces, mostly our greedy corporate elites and corrupt political leaders, can be somehow mitigated.

Naturally, our personal incentive and efforts are essential for becoming a better being. Yet, social values and environment, as well as national and international politics play important roles in providing the right incentives and atmosphere for individuals to take on the challenge of being better beings and succeed. Then again, social pressures or desperation might also goad a person to find a novel way of living, instead of merely trying to cope with society and hoping to adapt. Anyway, social issues and politics at national and international levels play an integral role in Parts III and IV of this book. After all, the global state of affairs affects people's outlooks and lives around the globe quite deeply—in bad, painful ways nowadays, unfortunately.

For grasping goodness, however, we should first understand the magical roles of human intuition and spirit in line with our authentic needs and basic principles for living.

The Magic of Human Intuition and Spirit

Regardless of God's intention, human nature, and the effects of natural and social evolutions, goodness is a virtue that most of us perceive as an ideal at least. We all wish to live in a healthy world, where people are compassionate and sincere, environment is not polluted and threatening, and social life is not so frustrating and hectic. That is what human spirit so magically demands from us like an instinct or divine urge. So why cannot we respond to this sacred vision within us? Why cannot we build a kinder world for ourselves despite our alleged high intelligence and efficiency? Why are our spirits ignored and dampened deliberately? Why are we burdened with so much nonsensical chaos?

The answer is that we hardly get the chance to study and build our spirits and find our true being even if we are religious. Living in materialistic societies provides no self-discipline or incentive to learn about being better beings (BBB)—as a likely refuge—nor do we have a reliable source of spiritual or social guidance to build our identities and boost our spirits. Even when we believe in the benefits of discovering our inner self, social conditioning and our daily struggles to survive besiege our thought processes and perceptions of life. In fact, it seems that only through certain levels of desolation and isolation we may find the time and urge to grasp our spirits and search for other options of living.

Religions have tried to provide some gruelling guidance and shoddy incentives to look outside the box beyond social norms. Yet, neither their rigid approaches, nor our raw spiritual efforts, have connected us to our spirits naturally and effectively. Instead, we have entrapped ourselves within a world full of fantasies and expectations from life and afterlife. We have never explored our options for healthier means of living, nor realized the benefits of pursuing a personally customized path of life to enrich our spirits. Instead, we have merely tried to indulge ourselves with many juvenile social habits and obsessions. Then, on top of all these sources of mental disorientations, we build lots more fantasies and religious rituals to get ready for afterlife!

Naturally, most people do not see anything wrong with their mentalities, religions, or lifestyles. They are fully faithful to the symbols of social living they are accustomed to, maybe because they have somehow mitigated the sufferings inflicting humanity. This group does not even care to pause and doubt the way social norms and lifestyles have evolved. Another group sees and cares about the problems, yet does not find it necessary or possible to do anything about them. It is too distracted to explore the roots of problems or discuss the possibilities for global solutions. Maybe it encounters and discusses instant barriers randomly, like most of us, mostly as a social habit to whine or just make conversation. Finally, a smaller group feels the problems regularly and suffers, yet believes not much anybody can do to revamp such immense infrastructure that has dominated our minds and lifestyles. In all, we all seem hypnotized and helpless. Still, learning at least which group we belong to is useful for self-awareness, though the idea of changing ourselves into a new being, against how we have felt and behaved a lifetime, feels silly and insulting to us!

Nevertheless, BBB should be mainly viewed as a vigorous regimen for self-development and self-defined divinity with the goal of gaining our soulful identity and individualism outside corruptive social values, while maintaining a civil connection to people, too. This requires wisdom and commitment to replace our vile habits with vivacious principles, while realizing both the difficulty and necessity of making big concessions and sacrifices a lifetime. The big challenge would be to give up certain social privileges and absorb people's apathy towards anybody choosing to live outside the mainstream's norms. Then again, a wakened person seeking salvation and peace would be willing to make these big sacrifices in order to embrace an independent (and rather stoic) existence, while promoting social coexistence, too.

Thank God, (perhaps!), some radical and ethical ideas are still around for reflection and dreaming about a better state of being. Although such crude optimism feels naïve, it still helps us keep some hope about a chance for future generations to live among people with similar perspectives about society and existence.

Fortunately, God has given some individuals the strengths and stamina to resist the temptation of popular slogans, philosophies, and lifestyles. They still derive their energies from some deep inner sources, despite their routine disappointments, rejections, and people's resistance to even hear their unconventional views. They still build and spread their fundamental beliefs about means of redirecting the course of our fated civilization. Luckily, many of us have still not given up our faiths in humanity completely! Despite our bizarre approach all along throughout the human history, let us hope we can eventually emerge as an intelligent species capable of contemplating and rediscovering our beings in line with our revived spirits in charge.

Surely, changing our perceptions of our needs, social values, and personal attachments quickly is hard, and that is not what this book advocates, either. Rather, the idea is to rediscover our being gradually, maybe over three to five years for a normal person. The long process consists of simple self-awareness steps that help us develop deep convictions and faiths to detach ourselves from our habitual, crude perceptions of too many superficial needs, which would then help us develop new thoughts and values.

Being good beings is difficult for most of us for many reasons discussed in this book. However, it is important to remember that becoming a bit better gets easy and feasible if we recognize and seek the benefits of such transformation personally and globally.

The ultimate goal is to fathom humans' essential needs, learn teamwork, and discover our selfless, lonely 'being.' We explore the basics of humanity for peace and connecting to Nature with humility. We admit that humans are not God's privileged creature with the right to abuse Nature, humanity, and society just because they can or are allegedly more intelligent than other beings.

Naturally, these objectives and admissions sound absurd to many readers, at least initially, because most people do not have the motivation or insight to explore their inner self. Without some primary wisdom and faith to think beyond the seemingly clear 'facts' of life, we cannot proceed to delve into our deeper 'self' and discover our humble 'being.' For one thing, we must learn to see human spirit as the third dimension alongside their minds and bodies. Without a divine insight, we cannot perceive the realm and reality beyond social norms. We believe we already know the whole scope of our being and the idea of discovering our spirits is mythical, unnecessary, or impossible. In fact, any small deviation from our preconceptions of social norms and our being would feel abnormal and threatening to us. We mainly like to insist on fooling ourselves with our superficial identities and exploit others emotionally and financially recklessly in line with our twisted mentalities nurtured within a crooked socioeconomic platform. That is how low we have sunk!

Thus, either a strong incentive or a divine insight is needed to abandon our trite mindset and lifestyle to get on goodness path.

Let us hope many of us will get that opportunity eventually, ***because what we have become is just too embarrassing!***

Chapter Two
Symptoms of Human Evil and Demise

The bleak views in this book about humans' low sense for goodness and their looming demise feel more valid and disheartening every day. However, we can never give up. In fact, humans' sacred mission now, more than ever, is to i) grasp the scope of social problems, ii) agree on *if* and *how* we can do something together or alone to avoid humans' demise, iii) assess the role of goodness for personal and social salvation, and iv) *justify* the challenges of this scared mission to ourselves and others.

The public's general naiveté and passivity about global crises are understandable considering their desperation for survival and need for social dependence to maintain at least a job and their security. However, the mentality of our wealthy leaders and their elite sponsors, when they deny obvious facts, for example about the hazards of climate change, is just treacherous and a major crime against humanity. Especially, it is immensely embarrassing to witness our older leaders in their final years of existence still not grasping even a basic sense of their beings. Instead, they look so pathetic like desperate slaves *still* serving their elite sponsors and fat egos to run such idiotic, dysfunctional systems at any cost to humanity and nature. Their deliberate acts to misguide the public or disregard of the clear signs of socioeconomic mayhem all over the world is the biggest calamity and cause for concern—

just another irrefutable clue about human folly. Actually, our greedy leaders' ignorance or systematic denials of facts are often more aggravating than humans' sad destiny per se.

Social living certainly has many advantages that supposedly compensate for its shortfalls and pains that we endure regularly for this privilege. Yet, most of us feel the situation has gotten out of hand and we are paying a very high price for it. Despite all the rewards the present social structure offers, enormous amounts of emerging conflicts are ruining our beings. It does not matter how much we pretend to be enjoying our lives if we are not content deep down and do not know why, either. It is simply ridiculous to call ourselves civilized beings if we do not have the right mind and interest to at least grasp the roots of our social problems and people's anxiety, and then try to envision humans' prospect. It is direly outlandish to just keep on ploughing helplessly and hoping that things would work out in the end and humans would survive one way or another—by some miracles perhaps! This is just such a juvenile mentality to pursue forever! It is foolish to brag about our democracy and open society if these concepts are merely for helping special groups, while destroying the world. In fact, a massive, radical mental revolution is urgent at both personal and social levels to at least figure out if any other option exists for a civil coexistence and avoiding the doomsday.

In the end, we must keep a smidgen of hope about the chance of preventing our personal degradation and universal annihilation. Luckily, we can achieve these goals and elude human demise if a majority of us admit being on the wrong path and stop denying the daunting reality that any sane person can envision by gauging the signs of the catastrophe creeping up fast. A social revolution, mostly in our mindsets, is urgent, despite human nature and brain hindering it! Nonetheless, this sounds like the toughest challenge for modern humans, especially in terms of learning humility.

The catastrophic outcome of human mentality and lifestyles are discussed in detail in the future chapters to demonstrate how our crooked perceptions of life and social pressures in the new era have moulded people into such controversial personalities with low patience and high expectations. Yet, the causes (and effects) of humans' evil and looming demise can be divided into two categories: i) Socioeconomic and political causes that taint humans' spirits and psyches, and ii) Personal (psychological) effects that reflect our inner turmoil and sense of helplessness. We are rather familiar with these pervasive social and personal problems, but a brief discussion of these symptoms of human folly might give us a fuller perspective about the roots of social mayhem and people's inner turmoil. The most prevalent signs of social and personal (psychological) deteriorations are:

A. Social (General) Malfunctions
- Rampant disorder, diseases, and threats
- Crimes' senselessness
- Corruption epidemic
- Widening of economic gap
- Global animosity and genocides
- Environmental pollution and destruction
- Food and nutrition hazards
- Population and density pressures
- Communication hurdles
- Marriage and companionship problems
- Job and career related burdens

B. Personal (Psychological) Disturbances
- Inner conflicts
- Loneliness
- Insecurity
- Psychological pressures
- Scanty self-fulfilment
- Lower needs Deprivation
- Struggle for happiness
- Loss of identity and confusion

The above symptoms are elaborated in the remainder of this chapter, while their consequences are reviewed in Chapter Eight.

A. Social (General) Malfunctions

The main symptoms of failure of our present socioeconomic and political systems, as listed above, and their repercussions on both personal and social health, are evident all around us in all aspects of our lives. A short review of these symptoms follows.

Rampant Disorder, Diseases, and Threats

The main objective of social living is to maximize 'order,' but as we have become more civilized (supposedly), a higher tendency towards disorder and irresponsibility has emerged. In particular, it is infuriating when the main causes of disorder are the very same people and officials who are supposed to establish fairness and order in society. We witness the prevalence of vast corruption at national and international levels among our leaders who are only serving themselves and their corporate sponsors, while deceiving the public by all kinds of unethical behaviour.

The judicial systems and police are often also prejudiced and dysfunctional. With the advent of social media and technological advances in criminology in recent years, now we learn much more about the atrocities behind the scene. DNA tests or random video-recordings reveal how helpless citizens are being killed or convicted out of pure prejudice and arrogance of those in charge of law and order in society. We witness many types of senseless shootings by both the public and police. We hear about innocent people being wrongfully convicted by tampering with, or hiding, the evidence, while police officers' offences disregarded casually. These pervasive practices by governing officers show the depth of disorders that have infected all aspects of society and personal lives, which we must now grapple with forever.

However, the rising social chaos, especially the malice of sworn officers and leaders, also says a lot about the wickedness of human nature becoming more apparent and rampant every decade. Now, almost everybody is showing a good deal of evil in his/her thoughts and behaviour and making life miserable for others. Our intentional recklessness in family and society, while damaging social mechanisms, are deplorable. Practising such dire atrocities out of greed, narcissism, egoism, for securing our jobs, or to flaunt our leadership or authority, reveal the depth of human meanness as a *natural* phenomenon. Even our religious leaders have shown their real, crude *humanistic nature* by abusing their powers. These alleged role models have shown their own share of sexual perversions and hypocrisies. All kinds of atrocities are in fact rising under the name of religion and God even in the 21st century. The ones we hear about almost daily are merely the tip of the iceberg. An account of religions' hurtful role for humanity and towards social disorders requires many volumes by itself.

The problem is that, being only a human, we submit to our inner weaknesses quite often, especially when our leaders and society tolerate, and often, goad crooked behaviour and malice. Thus, instead of seeing more evidences of order, we only witness social mayhem and pervasive disorder. This is not only raising our mistrust about the meanings of social justice and morality, but also forcing us to impose our own share of disorder, even though we may think ours is not as much of a disorder compared to the fundamental injustice in the society. We do it for retaliation or merely out of greed, which has become the root of so much social disorder in the end.

In fact, many of us feel justified to use malice for self-defence at least. We cannot fight evil with reason and goodness, after all. Therefore, we introduce our share of disorder when self-interest or some strong personal incentives goad us to be callous and careless about others. The problem is not merely the fact that our leaders and authorities ignore or undermine their responsibilities. Rather, a much deeper problem is that under these circumstances everybody is gradually losing his/her faith and trust in the whole principle of orderliness and 'order making.' It is also hard to teach our children anything about social order and morality when everybody perceives the society and symbols of piety in such a negative way with little hope for orderliness. Instead, we raise our kids within a fantasy world and then expect them to understand and cope with life's tough realities magically, too!

Many other examples in the future chapters will demonstrate the roots of social disorder spreading personal badness. However, our greed and pomposity stir so many types of minor disorders all by themselves. Donald Trump, sitting at the highest authority in a presumed civilized nation these days, is a great example about the roots of rampant social disorders. Yet, even our general evils weaken many aspects of social structure and raise social costs and burdens on others. For instance, we exaggerate our car accident injuries to maximize the financial compensation. It simply feels weird that, despite all our efforts and costs to develop functional social systems, we witness so much malice by allegedly normal people, too, even among our idols and self-promoting radical leaders elected to restore order and guide the desperate public. Worst of all, these big and small causes of disorder are creating a crooked kind of social mentality and atmosphere. It depresses and confuses everybody, while the capacity for social functioning declines. Our rising sense of entitlement to focus on self-interest, even at the cost of faster and deeper social mayhem, is ruining the human character and any chance for justice and order.

Physical and mental diseases have grown in line with rising social stress, laxity, and irresponsibility. The way our new social values goad us to have free sex has by itself resulted in creation and spread of too much social distress. We have come to rely on more pleasures from sex, alcohol, and drugs to relieve our tension and forget our problems. Yet, we have not only worsened our old wounds, but also introduced new social diseases (both physically and psychologically) for all. We have become mentally weaker and sicker, since our efforts, including more pleasures, to ignore our problems only lead to more agony and depression. We are always on the go and do not know when to relax.

All along, our cynicism and anguish about the rising social disorder is an added source of stress for us, because we feel that something is terribly wrong with the way we humans are living. We grow up with a naive perception and expectation that some basic principles and order govern life in a tidy society. We expect each member of the society play certain roles, especially those holding main official posts. Automatically we presume people realize the responsibility inherent in those official roles and fulfil them diligently to serve the public. The higher and more sensitive the role, the more alert and accountable we believe people must be in discharging their duties. Two main principles behind these assumptions and efforts are that we need social order to: 1) Make the public's life as civilized and safe as possible, and 2) Teach people morality and means of supporting one another against oppressions and threats that still dominate the laws of jungle, in particular among humans in large cities. Accordingly, these rising social disorders make us anxious to find a meaning for life more urgently to save our souls at least before we are totally mad.

Rampant threats, including the fear of terrorism and general unrest among various groups, are also hindering our basic rights and the chance to put our guards down and feel free in our living environments. So much psychological pressures and disorders have turned us into cunning, ferocious adversaries. We get into major confrontations and retributions for slightest disagreements. We do this to each other in work environments, in public places, in families, and in our business transactions. Accordingly, the mayhem of social living affects our life outlooks directly, while it also triggers our cynicism about people and processes burdening our existence. Our innate urge for social order is in constant clash with an endless nightmare of disorders surrounding us and a deep subliminal fear of pursuing even a simple life. The lasting threat of violence prevents us from walking (or even driving) in some streets or parks. The question is how vast and out of control these daily dilemmas and nightmares are going to get and how soon would they cripple the foundation of societies. How can anybody imagine that the outcome of such rampant social disorder would be anything other than more human evil towards total demise?

Crimes' Senselessness

The *senselessness* of crimes in the new era is just overwhelming. Senseless crimes happen in cities, streets, schools, parks, but also include all types of atrocities that nations, especially superpowers, inflict all over the world under all kinds hypocritical disguises. They have been spreading very fast, too, due to the complexities of global coexistence. Distinguishing some crimes as senseless sounds silly as if any kind of crime is rather comprehendible. However, the growing insensibility of some crimes is educational and needs a special emphasis. Sometimes, a crime's nature feels rather comprehensible, for example, when it relates to theft out of hunger or mental disorder. Yet, the natures of crimes are getting weirder and scarier now. Families killing own members out of greed, desperation, or frustration is senseless. Corporations and leaders defrauding the public so readily with such cruelty feel too senseless and out of proportion even for wicked humans. They reflect the high degree of social sickness.

We usually expect a group of citizens' deep mental disorders or deprivations disturb the order of society. Accordingly, we have developed means of helping and curing these disturbed people in societies, mostly for alleviating the effects of their malice on us. However, the matter feels out of control and bizarre when we all cause such insensible and unimaginable crimes at some level. Criminality at various scales is turning into an official business and profession of humans. Many of us invent all types of schemes to extort others, mostly under the guise of marketing and social services, including insurance, banking, healthcare, etc.

Even more depressing, our laws and enforcement authorities do not care or cannot handle the scope of these crooked schemes effectively. How can the fast growth of greed and evil in humans be avoided when our officials, as symbols of decency and justice, are guilty of the same or more offensive crimes and promoting hypocrisy and malice around the world so casually? Accordingly, crimes are becoming more senseless and common every day, too.

People are being killed for a few dollars, over a small argument, in mass shootings, or merely randomly. Major wars all over the world are mostly out of greed and arrogance, while many nations strive to exploit the ill-fated citizens around the globe.

All kinds of criminal gangs are popping out in towns, marking their territories, and terrorizing the citizens. The rise in family crimes is staggering. Especially, when people kill their spouses, children, or parents, by torture and in cold blood, it is hard to grasp what is happening in societies or how we can overcome the roots of all these nonsensical atrocities. Naturally, most of these crimes result from people's mental and personality dysfunctions as well as their awkward perceptions of the world. Thus, we just wonder how and why so much suffering and anxiety exist in the society to make us attempt such senseless acts.

Our mistrust with social order and justice system has goaded many of us to adopt a more proactive attitude to defend ourselves and make our own justice, especially if we can get away with our malice. Often, mere desperation and spite force us take the matter in our hands to survive the social chaos. Some feel justified to terrorize or kill, maybe even a large group in a bomb attack, for self-expression, e.g., about their religious or political ideologies. Besides these common atrocities, many other social malice and crimes erupt indirectly due to our incompetence, honest mistakes, and carelessness. Still, they are senseless too.

The large variety of senseless crimes noted in this chapter stir deep mental pressures and psychological defects in all of us no matter how rational we are and how we try to justify, or handle, the obvious abnormality of human nature and nurture. As much as we try to learn and practice tolerance and compassion, soon we lose our patience and sanity and try to get even somehow. Therefore, the effects of our mental diseases, meditated crimes, incompetence, and carelessness have been hurting not merely certain victims, but also all individuals and humanity at many forms and levels. All these dire symptoms of social living feel terribly nonsensical for supposedly civilized humans!

Corruption Epidemic

Corruption must be stressed here separately as a distinct source of social downfall and distress with deep effects on all businesses, personal relationships, and human mentality overall. It has now turned into a global epidemic and invaded societies and citizens. Besides major corruptions and abuses stemmed from power and money, many petty corruptions have spread fast even among the public and the less powerful and affluent groups. For example, lying, cheating, racial discriminations, false accusations, sexual perversions, abusive exaggerations, malicious propagandas, and fraud have infected the values and ethics within families, political systems, and organizations. The effects of these widespread petty corruptions not only weaken individuals' characters and attitudes, but also destroy people's sense of teamwork due to the lack of trust in one another and systems.

Widening of Economic Gap

All statistics reveal the ineffectiveness of present socioeconomic systems for restoring a sense of equality and equity in society. The common juvenile goal and outcome of profit maximization is making rich richer faster than ever, while poor is getting poorer around the world. This mentality and mechanism is appalling, but also untenable. Thus, at least some level of scrutiny is necessary to gauge the goals and potentials of the prevalent socioeconomic systems for helping humans and societies.

The fact that economic gap is widening is a risky and unfair situation already, but a more dangerous aftermath of this harsh symptom of capitalism is that everybody sets his/her expectations of life at an unrealistic level, too. We presume that any personal aspiration or lifestyle less than what the higher class has achieved would be a sign of failure and our inability to fit within the norms and demands of our socioeconomic system. Thus, the widening gap in economic and social status has caused deep psychological issues for people, too, in addition to all direct problems caused by economic pressures. The effects of varied human inequalities are hurting people at all levels within each society and across nations faster then ever, though now in a more subdued and seemingly tolerant environments. It is bizarre how people appear hypnotized and addicted to social norms, yet suffer a large variety of inner conflicts due to the rising economic gap. Meanwhile, a person's value is set and viewed with even more prejudice than ever based on his/her wealth, power, colour of skin, country, etc. Then, even if one succeeds in acquiring these privileges, one's value would still not be recognized fully if one lacks the ability to show them off in most degrading and pretentious manners. One should in fact become a narcissist to be noticed and receive full recognition.

Global Animosity and Genocides

Our new culture and teachings have pushed us to develop a high sense of animosity and competition amongst humans all over the world. Endless power struggles continue at all levels, globally, nationally, and amongst family members. In this day and age, we still witness vast cruelties and genocide around the world, and nobody seems able to decipher or resolve these conflicts. The United Nation and the international goodwill aim at preventing these atrocities, yet we, as humanity, seem helpless, unwilling, or incapable to achieve concrete results in timely manners (before millions of innocent people suffer or are killed). Usually, a few influential and powerful nations are causing these animosities, as they propagate specific political and socioeconomic ideologies to control the world. Often, power per se seems to justify cruelty and exploitation that one nation exerts upon others. Conflicts and animosities prevail amongst political parties, regions, and groups with varied socio-political ideologies and means of forcing them. Worst of all, weird animosities and competitions amongst the members of families have ruined our basic cultural values and people's compassion. Overall, we are living in a world with a lasting, bizarre appetite for competition, corruption, and war, and a strong aptitude for hatred, spite, and controversy. We nurture and spread a deep sense of racism and contempt for one another, *like a potent essence of human nature!*

Environmental Pollution and Destruction

The perils of industrialization and job creation have been huge in terms of environmental pollution and destruction during the last few decades. Sadly, land and ocean contaminations are piling up fast by all sorts of waste materials. The trends show more abuse of natural beauties and resources, waters, forests, and air due to the need for incessant economic expansion and greed. It seems we cannot stop our reckless views regarding social responsibility and life, while our solutions have been shallow, ineffective, and tentative, too. Our immediate concerns relate to not only the dire effects of pollutions, but also the public's disregard for the evil of our social mechanisms abolishing humans' chance for survival with the support of nature.

Food and Nutrition Hazards

In line with our environmental pollution and population increase, we have been forced to grow vegetables and fruits with the aid of fertilizers and pesticides, and raised our cattle and poultry with hormones and all sorts of animal feed and antibiotics in order to expedite their growth. The low nutritional value of our food sources has been proven and we know how harmful they may in fact be because of all the things we are doing to them, including genetic engineering. These are problems of affluent nations that have food to eat and, in fact, let a good portion of their edible foods go to waste. In less fortunate countries, millions of people are dying every year from malnutrition and food shortage per se. Of course, the number of hungry, homeless and deprived children in modern countries is also increasing fast. Our harmful eating habits are yet another major shortfall. With so much on the go all the time, we have less time to eat at home or prepare wholesome foods. Instead, we eat lots of fat-saturated and unbalanced food at fast-food outlets and restaurants. These habits have ruined our physical and mental health and they cause all sorts of social and personal problems in the long run.

We are not efficient and effective in what we produce either. According to the statistics released in 2020, around 40% of food worth around $80-230 billion that is produced in the U.S. alone goes to waste annually, considering the cost of labour, water, etc. Are we crazy or what?

This staggering waste feels even more stupid considering the points made earlier about our scrupulous efforts to make more food with resort to artificial means and hormones, as well as the pervasive famine and related deaths in many parts of the world.

Population and Density Pressures

Urbanization and population growth are also damaging our living conditions and quality in a hasty pace. We are packing into large cities, struggling in heavy traffic, and facing an immense density of stressed people. Besides the hazards of polluted air we breathe and the increasing crime rate in such environments, we are losing our contact with nature and quieter settings akin to our biological needs. Adding all other effects of this population explosion and polluted environments, the public's rising anxiety and confusion about their roles in society are ruining their mental and physical health. The repercussions of environmental pressures on people are proven in many studies, especially as a main factor of heart attacks. Studies of highly dense animal herds have found clear evidence of special stress syndromes and massive death in a short period. Thus, we may not be far away from big catastrophes just due to social density, stress, lesser feasible options for survival as humans, plus all kinds of real and perceived burdens on people. Yet, nobody cares or can envision a solution. Instead, we keenly embrace capitalism that demands constant growth (in production, work force, population, and consumption) as its basic principle.

On top of all these problems, global conflicts, food shortage, and climate change would force more migrations to liveable countries and add extreme pressures on already dysfunctional large cities around the world. To resist or prevent this inevitable growing force of migrations, national unrests and international atrocities, wars, and miseries would continue to grow.

Communication Hurdles

Despite the communication explosion through internet and social media, we have become less capable of grasping each other's needs at all levels. We have difficulty expressing our true feelings since we seldom communicate with each other honestly. Rather, we are either concealing our true feelings or expressing them in formats that often mislead people or damage our intentions. We have become too needy, pretentious, and pompous, which stir big obstacles for understanding one another. Our communications are not honest due to relationship complexities, our efforts to avoid conflicts, or our desire to remain tactful in personal and social settings for coping or showing our civility. The force to cope with social norms has crippled our minds and communications with no personal or social integrity to keep us in line. The reasons for communication hurdles are discussed in the future chapters.

Marriage and Companionship Problems

As the most important social element, our companionships and marriages are facing a major crisis. With some 50% of marriages breaking up and a large population staying single due to a lack a suitable partner, people have little access to emotional support in society nowadays. Adding the strenuous conflicts and sufferings of couples, marital conundrums remain quite hurtful and a main cause of social chaos. Married couples become alienated towards their partners and, often, not even professional counselling can bring couples together mentally. Communication hurdles due to partners' misunderstandings of each other's needs and humanistic capacity overall are, of course, quite prevalent in families and remain a major cause of separation. As communication problems expand in all directions, couples have less solutions and patience to handle them. In fact, all the personal and social problems noted in Part I of this book make every individual too frustrated and sick to understand, and contribute towards, the real objectives of an effective marital relationship.

Most marriages are also infected by the side effects of social adaptation and modernism, such as people's growing obsessions for individualism, happiness, and success, which often lead to marriages' gradual decay. These common hurdles appear to have expanded in direct correlation with the so-called civilization and the advent of progressive social values. This indicates that family problems are growing in complex manners in line with the rise of general social chaos and people's varied burdens. In all, our crude, idealistic social values and ideologies seem to have made us less patient and understanding of each other, which in turn stir deeper communication hurdles. The question then is why, with progress, we only find new ways and ideologies to alienate one another further, instead of learning teamwork for mutual benefits and goals. Instead of stirring synergy as a main objective of society and family, we stir only more pains and barriers for one another. Another important point people miss about marriage is that for sharing a life with a partner, we should first create a purposeful life of our own, which is in itself highly related to the level of a person's goodness (wholeness). Instead, we expect our spouse to create a fantastic life for us and make us happy. Thus, marital conflicts have turned into a debilitating epidemic and a big social calamity these days, which in turn cause further communication hurdles and social havoc, as discussed later in this book.

Job and Career Related Burdens

Another group of social burdens relates to our jobs and careers. We work hard in our jobs, or struggle to find one. Most often, we are not fulfilled by the type of job we do, and we normally face many work related problems and deficiencies of organizations, where most jobs are. The matter of job insecurity, along with the incongruity of organization and personal objectives, places many psychological pressures on us and affects the quality of our lives. Job and career problems coincide closely with global deficiencies in the socioeconomic superstructures prevalent in the world. Yet, our lives are highly dependent upon financial resources that jobs and business activities provide. Due to this shortfall, we also find very limited choice and opportunity to realize and utilize our true potentialities as a main objective of work as well as a source of self-realization and spiritual growth. Accordingly, we are turning into senseless robots instead of boosting our identities and spirits. All this vanity ruins our sanity.

B. Personal (Psychological) Disturbances

Life pressures and calamities overwhelm our minds and make us think, worry, question, fight, suffer, and cope. The repercussions of these pressures and our corresponding thoughts erupt in many forms in our daily lives and affect our mental health and psyches. At least occasionally, we face some erratic feelings of anxiety and depression that we cannot handle or even fathom their sources. Certainly, people react to these personal dilemmas and inner conflicts according to their characters, outlooks, and mental strengths. However, the ultimate effect on people appears to be consistent, measurable, and damaging. Some of these symptoms are discussed below, while their roots and effects are reviewed further in the future chapters.

Inner Conflicts

The main symptoms of inner conflicts are stress and anxiety, as we feel a big discrepancy between how we intuitively expect things to be and how our lives drag on a painful or boring course vainly. We question the value of our thoughts and efforts. We do not know what we expect to achieve or become in a meaningful manner and scope, yet follow the crowd in a haze, although we do not feel in peace with ourselves about our social attachments, our jobs and activities, and the reasons we are doing them. All our lives, we just try to remain practical and adapt to social norms, while we also notice our foolishness in the way we sound and feel when we pause to judge ourselves with basic intelligence and foresight that normally erupt to guide sensitive people. Trying to elude these questions raise our inner conflicts even further.

Surely, our exhausted and misguided minds cannot help us think straight or gauge the reliability of our convictions and faiths when we are trapped in life's confusing routines. Instead, painful thoughts add to our sense of helplessness, while we struggle with a large variety of social obstacles outlined in the previous section. Occasionally, we object to, or resist, the socioeconomic rules and conditions souring our spirits, as we try to understand our roles as humans and independent individuals. Yet, at the end, all these sources of tension cause only more confusion, stress, desolation, and inner conflicts. We do what we do, because we cannot think of anything better to do! We live aimlessly, since we never learn about a better option for living! This is a hurtful state of being.

Our inability to detect the roots of our inner conflicts, let alone find a remedy, keeps heightening our depression, insecurity, and bewilderment. Then, we begin doubting our identities, life path, and options. We question our sanity, the validity of social norms we follow like robots, and the point of existence altogether. All along, these existential dilemmas and resultant mental vacuum become too stressful and frustrating by themselves. Nonetheless, our inner conflicts are mainly related to our social encounters and family relationships that make us ponder our being and a chance to elude our boring routines towards a more sensible lifestyle.

Although external sources cause most of our inner conflicts during our interactions with people and society, people's personal backgrounds and insecurities also create hurdles, frictions, and inner conflicts, which need even more scrutiny and self-analysis. In particular, the seven common sources of inner turmoil (and personal dilemmas), e.g., loneliness, are studied in the following pages, as they cause deep psychological damages and dampen our spirits and life outlooks. Inner conflicts are perfect signs of a person's low spirit, which is humans' third dimension besides their brains and bodies, as discussed in Chapter Five.

Loneliness

Even when we are married, spend a lot of time with our family and friends, and engage in all sorts of partying and activities, we still feel mentally lonely. Some people do not even have these basic social relationships and distractions, thus suffer much more. They not only miss the limited merits of family cohesion and fun, but also feel inadequate, lonely, and incapable of finding a mate. Meanwhile, most marriages suffer from deep communication problems that turn even the healthiest love affair into a sad state, since partners cannot fulfil their needs, do not feel understood, and are unable to relate. For those who go through separation and divorce episodes, the symptoms of loneliness find still a sadder and deeper perspective. They feel the agony of defeat regardless of whose fault the cause for separation and divorce might have been. Then, they should also tolerate the hassles of readapting themselves to the strenuous routines of independent living after feeling dependent upon someone else emotionally and socially—in the way they had shared all sorts of activities and chores with a partner for many years. This period of readjustment is usually an agonizing, stressful, and difficult long process all by itself, if not turning into a permanent burden or psychosis.

The effects of loneliness are quite drastic on the quality of our lives and raising our badness as discussed in Chapter Eight. Then again, our fear of loneliness has caused many additional problems for us, for example by getting into substandard relationships with selfish, nagging partners who do not share our values and life outlook. In fact, we have lost our natural knack in recent decades for living alone and enjoying the benefits of self-development and self-expression. Instead, we have become too dependent on others to bring us happiness and complete our sense of being. Otherwise, we feel lost and maybe even a failure. In line with our obsession for many superficial things in pursuit of raw fantasies, we have also become too needy for a soul mate, which is getting harder to find nowadays. In particular, when sexual urges mix with the sense of loneliness, the amount of psychological pains, pressures, and insecurity grows immensely. Lust and loneliness are deep pains, but together can kill even an elephant. Sadly, this personal deprivation stirs many other social problems. Now, even radical groups, like ISIS, draw on this international epidemic to recruit the confused youths from all over the world.

As a whole, for most of us, whether single, stuck in a soulless marriage, or dealing with the excruciating pains of separation and divorce, loneliness is a harsh reality that appears to follow us throughout our lives. Therefore, we should somehow learn the art of self-reliance. Sometimes, we may be lucky and feel the joy of communication and attachment with someone we love. Sadly, however, we should be prepared to accept the inevitability of loneliness along with the dire disappointments and desolation that companionships in the new era bring to our lives.

Insecurity

A major impact of loneliness is the loss of self-esteem and the eventual feeling of insecurity. Besides loneliness, many other causes of insecurity will be reviewed in the upcoming chapters. Our insecurities and the lack of self-reliance impair our psyches and lives. Insecurity leads to failures, especially in relationships, which then reinforces the feelings of loneliness and heighten our sense of insecurity. This vicious cycle continues until one loses one's sanity or the cycle is broken by some miracle. Usually if we do not attend to this problem fast and face our insecurities' sources, it becomes difficult to break the cycle, or reverse either the feeling or the effects of our insecurities. When our self-image is ruined, our insecurities root and manifest in various forms of personal flaws, including arrogance, that dominate many aspects of our activities and relationships for the rest of our lives.

Psychological Defects

We all suffer from some forms of psychological shortfalls and the effects of our unique idiosyncrasies. Insecurity was discussed separately due to its widespread effect on general population and becoming a cause of many other psychological and personality issues for most of us. Other psychological defects, which could be minor or complex, like anger, paranoia, or schizophrenia, are grouped here under this general heading without going into too much detail about each one of them. They are either genetic or the results of lifelong pressures and deprivations. The scope of psychological pressures is vast, though we may each be inflicted by only some seemingly minimal and manageable shortfalls. The range and severity of these defects are also wide among various individuals. However, they are usually at least irritating or even excruciating depending on their sources and natures. They affect the quality of our lives as well as people around us. They emerge in many forms, including constant anxieties related to jealousy, anger and aggression, various kinds of perversions, etc. Anyway, judging by the sheer number of tranquilizers people consume, addictive habits spreading in societies, and crimes' senselessness nowadays, we can surmise that prevalent psychological pressures among the citizens all over the world are quite substantial and on the rise.

Scanty Self-Fulfillment

In spite of our hard work and intention to accomplish tangible results, we seldom get a sense of self-fulfilment. Thus, we feel sad about 'who we are' in line with people's negative reactions and feedbacks in society. Meanwhile, the upshot of spending most fruitful years of our lives on activities with little potential for inner satisfaction makes our interpretation of life dull and limited, too. Overall, social limitations and personal misperceptions about life hinder our self-fulfilment. The biggest reason is that we must work hard to make a living, so we do not get a chance to follow our ambitions and enrich our souls, even if we knew how. Still, many people miss their chances to gain self-fulfillment even when they have time and wealth to explore their beings.

Self-fulfilment is a rather high personal need and achieving it demands a lot of spiritual growth, sacrifice, and convictions. We must endure seclusion to build a rather independent lifestyle and mentality, which makes us look odd like an alien, inadaptable to general values and views. Thus, people's attitude now saddens us differently, too. Accordingly, it is reasonable to expect very few people find the wisdom and nerve to focus on self-fulfilment at the expense of alienating their friends and families and depriving themselves from social rewards. Rather, most people place all their faiths and energies into daily routines to satisfy at least some of their lower needs, mainly socializing and sexuality. Still, even fulfilling those lower needs has now turned into disheartening challenges, as discussed in the next section.

The main obstacle for self-fulfilment is that we mostly adopt crooked criteria to plan and gauge our lives. We embrace ideals, beliefs, and life philosophies irrelevant for enriching our souls with a sense of fulfilment. Our lasting search for wealth, love, happiness, and success are illusions that misguide and distract us. They prove meaningless and tentative even when we happen to attain them sporadically. Meanwhile, most of us bypass the path of self-fulfilment, which materializes only by exploring our inner potentialities and a life philosophy towards higher mental growth along with a genuine sense of spirituality.

Diagram 4.1, page 99, shows that Self, which is a purer (and natural) dimension of a person, is trapped inside his/her superficial personality and obsession for expressing (and proving) his/her individualism, while s/he is pressed by people and environment to conform to frivolous norms and values. All the grey areas in Diagram 4.1 reflect the forces that reduce the opportunity of Self finding its roots and place within the universe, which humans are supposedly connected to in a natural way within a mystical realm. At the end, we feel empty and encounter many setbacks, despite our huge hopes and efforts. Then, a lack of genuine sense of self-fulfilment induces pessimism and insecurity. Thus, another goal of 'being better beings' is to find ways of connecting our Self with the universe for reaching the sense of self-fulfilment and peace.

Lower Needs Deprivation

Besides insufficient sense of self-fulfilment, many of our basic and medium level needs are often left unsatisfied, because of the way society contaminates our perceptions of reality and we lose sense of our inner self. Our needs for social recognition, status, relationships, success, and power have just become too strong and distracting amidst social complexities, limitations, rivalries, raw religions, and phony interactions. We spend too much time and energy in hopes of satiating so many superficial needs that even our random fulfilments do not provide any lasting sense of achievement, happiness, or compassion. Yet, we simply seem unable to curb our obsession for our tainted medium range needs built around some idealistic views of life. We cannot control our addictions to many senseless socioeconomic ideologies, despite our rampant disappointments and failures to achieve any tangible satisfaction from our illusive views and heightened expectations.

Our novel and idiotic exaggerations about the meaning of life and our medium level needs, such as success, happiness, and love have reduced our abilities to grasp and handle our daily lives in an effective, simple manner, including our companionships needs and marriages. For instance, our view of individualism has turned us into controversial, selfish, and demanding persons with low patience, compassion, and sense of Self. With our aggressive, haughty personalities and exaggerated self-image, we have lost even our minimal capacity for exploring our finer qualities and utilizing our inner strengths, including our primary instincts and wisdom. While trying too hard to grow a phony personality and a conceited self-image, we have lost track of our authentic identity, thus become incapable of pursuing a simple life path enriched with self-reliance aimed for peaceful co-existence.

Ironically, humans' medium needs are now mostly superficial urges that we have invented idealistically in line with our crooked new social values and high expectations from life. Even our need for socializing is contaminated, nowadays, though still left mostly unfulfilled, due to our superficial means of relating to each other with false pride, pomposity, and emphasis on a foul impression of individualism. Our ability to socialize in a sincere and natural manner has been eroding fast, which in turn makes relationships and friendships too shallow and unreliable.

In this unnatural convoluted environment, our efforts to fulfil even our lower needs, such as sex, security, and teamwork, lead to conflicts, stress, frustration, and hostility. Then, these physical and mental pressures cripple most of us to think straight and deal at least with our basic needs, which then jeopardizes our abilities to handle our marriages and careers in a practical manner, let alone find a chance to explore our spiritual dimension through self-analysis and self-fulfilment.

In all, while we are wasting a lot of time and energy on our superficial medium level needs, we neglect both our basic needs (e.g., true individualism and self-reliance) and higher needs (e.g., self-fulfilment and spirituality). The irony is that both our basic and high level needs can help us revive our essence of being and lead a happier life, while our obsession to fulfil our medium level needs are only making us sicker and needier. Accordingly, social mayhem has kept growing in line with a wide range of demented social and personal philosophies in search of pleasure and success (medium level needs). So much stress on medium level needs, such as obsessions for socializing, wealth, and status, is the result of our crude mentalities grown in our alleged modern societies.

Struggle for Happiness

Many prevalent deficiencies noted in this chapter have besieged our lives and disabled us from achieving even a sense of peace and contentment, yet our demand for happiness is at its highest. We have pleasures and good times occasionally, too, when our depression and problems subside a little tentatively. However, we eventually learn that these pleasures are transient and soon we must face the same old problems and questions. In fact, we often have difficulty even defining the sources of happiness. How can we even imagine its nature with no grasp of its major factors and components? So, we keep seeking pleasure erratically and hitting brick barriers, hoping to eventually break through and embrace happiness behind one of those walls. Our struggle for happiness is a fundamental and funny topic in modern societies due to the three essential forces driving it: 1) we carry a sense of entitlement for happiness as a new social fad and part of our positive thinking efforts, 2) we conceive happiness as an antidote for sadness and depression that are soaring in new societies, 3) humans carry a subliminal, mysterious urge for happiness, like a genuine, forceful energy that must be released during regular experiences of life. Accordingly, we forget that happiness is an innate state of mind that erupts naturally from within a person in line with his or her wisdom and contentment, not from external stimuli, such as love, wealth, or success. We simply expect deep, enduring happiness without a sensible clue about its meaning or source.

Loss of Identity and Confusion

Social disorders and psychological pressures would gradually confuse us about the purpose and meaning of life. We lose track of our personal life objectives even if we ever get a chance to develop them. Thus, we eventually lose our identities and do not know who we are. We usually do not realize these repercussions of social living besides feeling disheartened and upset regularly. We behave like a robot and pursue the same goals and paths day after day, amuse ourselves with shoddy aspirations and needs, and remain content with occasional pleasures we are addicted to. However, we still feel an overwhelming sense of confusion and helplessness most of our lives and we get anxious usually when we fail to detect even the causes of our tension or the meaning of the niggling unrest often burdening us.

Accordingly, humans' inherent need to gain selflessness and explore their spirituality dimension is not recognized or nurtured properly. Most of us never get an opportunity to even reflect on the authentic means of existence or realize the aesthetic beauties that nature and our own creations offer. These divine dimensions of life and self are necessary for developing our identities and personalities, yet they get the least attention. This topic is reviewed more later along with self-recognition and self-reliance. Anyhow, the lack of personal identity appears readily in our selfishness, instead of selflessness, as we get buried under our raw ambitions and fantasies and feel more confused every day, yet remain so full of ourselves!

All the personal (psychological) symptoms noted above infect our brains early in our lives and induce plenty of inner conflicts, quirks, and insecurities. *Then, all this vanity also ruins our sanity!*

The Big Picture

Humans have never faced such a wide mixture of dilemmas and idiocy in history. At the start of the third millennium, we witness a significant mark of human fatigue and failure despite the fastest and most amazing technological progress in recent decades. The way all these seemingly social and technological developments have created so many problems—instead of enriching our lives and making us wiser—is the oddest and saddest dilemma we are facing at this crucial time. In fact, this point in history (2020) should be recorded as a turning point for losing our last chance and hope for saving humanity and learning to be better beings. From now on, it will most likely be merely a fast decline towards absolute devilry with the last grains of human goodness dissolving gradually. It is interesting how most of us feel and associate with social decay and agree passively that urgent actions are required. Yet, we have tried only superficially, individually and globally, to recognize the roots of problems and find solutions. Meanwhile, we are suffering more arguments and aggravation for not making any headway. We are simply wasting time fighting relentlessly amongst ourselves on 'how not to fight.' We are blaming only others for making us feel miserable.

Sadly, the big picture about humanity looks dismal if we grasp the symptoms of human evil and demise listed in this chapter. Thousands of evidences exist all around us, for example in terms of the amount of alcohol we consume daily to forget our pains and existence. Yet, the majority of us cannot see the big picture, although we keep nagging about, and suffering from, injustice and malice all our lives. In fact, as a more amazing symptom of human demise, all these addictions to alcohol, drugs, sex, money, greed, hypocrisy, and thousands of other idiotic social habits feel quite natural to us, like expected norms for modern existence. We are simply lost within our socio-political traps towards extinction. The raw positive thinking fad all by itself prevents people from pondering the scope of demoniac forces in society seriously, let alone seeing the big picture and grasping the gravity of humans' doomed destiny. Thus, even criticizing these symbols of human folly sounds old-fashioned and foolish. We sound like preachers trying to edify the naive population and salvage people's souls.

A big obstacle for human salvation and global peace is that no feasible solutions seem to exist, or could possibly emerge, as long as we lack a socio-political system with immense power, vision, and interest to enforce drastic and effective changes. On the one hand, any solution short of an overhaul of political, economic, social, and value systems would at best offer only a tentative remedy before we return to our vile habits, short-term vision of society and the same routes of destruction. On the other hand, this wide overhaul seems to require a totalitarian political mechanism to hold all the needed authority and determination.

Accordingly, the matter of human nature must also be raised again, as some of us believe that all these personal and social problems mostly relate to the essence of humans, especially their dire egoism and greed. As noted before, scientists have attempted to prove humans' wild nature and aggressiveness through many ethnological studies of primates and generalizing their behaviours. In this sense, they suggest that our true nature resembles other primates and the backward tribes of South America or Australia. Many forms of proof have been cited for humans' instinctual urges to kill and be territorial. If this is true, then the solution for world problems might come only from authoritative governance of the common people, genetic engineering, and perhaps race purification. But, of course, these are all nonsensical solutions that we can hopefully avoid if only we learn to become a little wiser and try to be just a bit better human beings.

A more basic paradox is that any such radical socio-political reform, or the possibility of any solution, in fact, requires a drastic revamping of people's narrow mentalities. As long as people are trained to be so xenophobic, self-centered, and greedy, we can never put a global rescue plan together. The way it appears now, we rather annihilate humanity and our planet than put our heads together and devise a long-term global solution and plan.

The reality we face is that without a fundamental revolution in our thinking and deeds, human deterioration and demise would accelerate out of control, yet this radical expectation feels like a fantasy by all accounts. People merely lack the capacity even for simple mental reorientations, let alone a big revolution requiring such a drastic deviation from their regular logic and urges. We prefer to put our self-interests and patriotism ahead of humanity and high risks of our present lifestyles. Thus, even the idea of a socio-political overhaul and revamping of the public's mentality sounds like an absurd dream. Pondering and building a process to force these ideas, including the need for powerful conscientious global governance, would be even more idealistic.

Our leaders' and scholars' various solutions for restoring the world order have proven naïve and superficial, while they have lost their credibility in the process. Their solutions and arguments merely raise our agonies, while they try to prove their viewpoints hastily and arrogantly by resorting to shortsighted solutions and even overstating scientific information and findings for publicity. They also fail due to other major dilemmas noted in the above paragraphs. Then again, their ideas, efforts, and failures at least demonstrate the scope of social issues and the global frustration with the existing systems and environment.

Thus, we feel trapped deeper in a dying society; and the more we struggle to free ourselves, the faster we sink and the tighter the devil's grip becomes. Many of us feel the scope of social evil, the inefficiencies of socioeconomic and political systems, and our personal contributions towards the demise of our surroundings and ourselves. However, even if a good majority of people knew what is wrong, and why, we cannot find a viable solution until we prepare ourselves to make major sacrifices and revamp our extravagant mentality and demanding attitude.

The bottomline is that while human nature and society drive our mentalities and personalities, our values and actions ruin the social order and contaminate the environment in return. Thus, it appears that only an unlikely mystical vision and intervention might help us avert the path of social and human demise.

Accordingly, a few vital questions cross our minds: Would humans ever build the mental capacity to grasp, and the character to do something about, humanity's tough situation? How do our brains operate and how bad human nature is? These important topics are explored in future chapters.

Meanwhile, we may at least admit personally that the existing mayhem, including governments' incompetence and corruption, is mostly the result of citizens' naïve mindsets, short-term vision of social structure and needs, high expectations from life, greed, and crude criteria for electing our leaders. This acknowledgment by most of us would be a big step to address human dilemmas noted above.

As another part of the big picture, we cannot stop wondering about the chance of many of us becoming better humans if we could mitigate the influence of crooked social norms and allowed humans' natural virtues to flourish. What if we could make better judgments about our needs and means of salvation? What if we could build a more constructive path of life for ourselves by using all the facts about social realities, for example, about the difficulty of relating to people due to their insincerity and phoniness? Maybe we could even learn to become more compassionate and tolerant of other people's naiveté and malice, while learning self-reliance to elude too much social disappointments. Sadly people, including our families and friends disappoint us and deter our enthusiasm for socializing in a setting revolving around such dire mentalities and attitude. Luckily, though, people cannot kill our 'spirit for living' and they cannot stop our chance for personal growth if we adopt the right identity and attitude for our own benefits. Thus, learning about the real (largely devious) nature of humans could be useful if we stay realistic and positive in setting the course of our own lives more effectively.

Naturally, so many wrong things in society agitate people and lead to a conventional (and crooked) view of life. Ultimately, however, mostly our erroneous perceptions and hasty reactions to those outside events and situations stir our inner conflicts and anxiety. The important point is that if our outlook and perceptions were managed more consciously and wisely, we might be less influenced by many outside events so drastically too often. We should get ready to face social barriers and through resilience, resolve, patience, and passion.

We usually view our problems as barriers or threats originated by some external sources, individuals, or situations. They subdue our senses and ability to think objectively, so we feel frustrated and paralyzed. Eventually, we may seem to resolve the problems or forget them gradually until a new condition or event triggers our primitive (undeveloped) defence mechanism again. We feel inner turmoil, anger, burden, and react harshly to defuse those outside sources of threat to our being. Yet, people, events, and situations are often stimuli that provoke our pumped egos, false pride, and raw mentalities. Our hasty reactions are usually the products of our own insecurities and frailties, which are inherent in many aspects of our psyches and personalities. Thus, we get agitated and lose control over our lives often only because we are unprepared to face them patiently or ignore them divinely.

Often, the answer to, 'What is wrong with our lives,' can be traced in our hasty reactions to outside events and the way we let them distort our thinking and agility. In the end, while we must beware of outside problems and nuisances, and why and how they often cause such big headaches, they must be viewed merely as stimuli that stir our own deep insecurities and idiosyncrasies. The source of our chronic inner turmoil relates to our egotistical life outlook and reactions towards social and personal challenges. Social pressures and threats are deep and real, yet mostly our grasp of reality matters. We could remember that mostly our egos ignite our radical reaction to real or perceived problems.

At the same time, the main point is that social hurdles, our perceptions of them, and our reactions to outside pressures all require an overhaul in order to give enough people a chance to become better beings.

Chapter Three
The Incentive for
Being Better Beings

Humans'[1] needs and insecurities, along with social hurdles and pressures, have made them too defensive and offensive at the same time. Thus, with their urges for aggression and arrogance intensified, they never get a chance to explore the limited goodness in them and they never build an incentive to ponder or pursue the goal of being better beings as a worthwhile routine, if not a natural drive. Even when a person finally realizes that only self-analysis and self-development might help him/her gain at least a minimal sense of solace and salvation, the intensity of psychological and social pressures nowadays diminishes his/her chance or incentive to grow goodness. The fact that gurus and clerics have tried to inject a sense of goodness in the public, and the way religions have played such a controversial and influential role in humans' life, prove the erosion of our natural tendency, intuition, or interest to be better beings on our own for personal benefits at least. At best, we demand some kind of prize, such as a promise for a fantastic afterlife in heaven, in order to accept the big challenges of being a better person and make all the personal sacrifices and efforts necessary to get there. Then, we do some rituals superficially with no personal conviction about the means and meaning of goodness!

Goodness Challenges

The mere existence is a tough enough task for humans already, but being better beings is an immense struggle for everybody due to the constant pressures on us to adapt ourselves to social norms at least for defending ourselves better among illogical humans.

Accordingly, the main challenge for becoming a better person is to keep this sacred objective in a proper perspective, instead of making it feel too abnormal. Rather, we remember that pursuing such a tough endeavour is only for achieving two modest goals: 1) to become a better person than we have been so far, and 2) to be better than common people, especially those around us. Of course, accomplishing even these two rather realistic objectives usually proves difficult considering the variety of forces defying our efforts. In particular, the main challenge would be to tame our egos in order to reassess our mentality and logic. **Surely, the idea is not to become a saint or stoic.**

The goals and process of building goodness are explained in Part II. They will be useful for proceeding on the goodness path smoothly. First, however, it is helpful to build a mindset to pursue this task and grasp the obstacles for success. In particular, it is crucial to: 1) build our incentive, 2) fight our demented nature, and 3) manage our crooked logic. Our naiveté and idiosyncrasies are other negative forces and goodness obstacles, as explained in previous chapters. After all, keeping our faiths and high spirits to become a better being within our convoluted social setting is tough, despite our strong curiosity to explore goodness.

1. Building Our Incentive

Finding our personal reasons and incentives for becoming better beings is a novel, sacred choice for making our lives and social relationships tolerable at least. However, accomplishing this ideal is challenging for most of us. In particular, two dilemmas must be resolved: **First,** we must convince ourselves that being a better person is rational! **Second,** we cannot change ourselves *easily* due to our forceful crooked genes as well as social pressures to adopt pervasive values, relate to others, express ourselves, and make a living—all in phony, pompous manners.

Ironically, people do not seem to care much about a person's goodness, and in fact, often resent his/her guts for trying to be someone that majority does not find appealing or practical, for example, if they feel our apathy about religions. So, 'Why would anybody want to be an open-minded, better being when most people misinterpret his/her goodness or resent him/her for being different from the rest? Why should we take on the challenges of becoming a better individual and then suffer more, even if we succeed?' Naturally, we would suffer until we learn to disregard people's apathy towards oddballs.

Then again, a tangible incentive for becoming a better being is to unravel the mystery of happiness, which has now turned into an obsession for people. We have come to believe that happiness is not only a reality, but also our right. We believe we deserve it and not finding it is a sign of our incompetence and dire failure. Naively, we all try to solve the mystery of happiness, but only some lucky individuals discover eventually that only by fulfilling the lengthy regimen of becoming a better being a person might embrace some degree of happiness. Only thru goodness, one finds the *wisdom* of happiness, too, essentially by learning the art of contentment and self-development. Even then, enough times we still get sad and mad at ourselves when we recall our 'old being' and our dire deeds—before we had begun our goodness journey. How could have we been so naive and selfish, while behaving very much like the devil?

So, we can say 'goodness' is the secret for happiness. Wow...! The mystery finally solved!! In fact, we could all be happy just by being better beings, but, apparently, that is not what we want, *or not exactly the kind of happiness we have cultivated in our naïve minds.* So foolishly, we have come to see happiness merely in terms of sexuality and extravagance! Therefore, in the end, we are not interested in finding happiness. Instead, we seem eager or obliged to do everything in our power to be bad and sad.

Actually, humans' *natural* incentives for goodness have also declined in the new era due to our obsessions for sexual freedom, success, and happiness. We are now victims of our fantasies, yet we can escape if we build our inner-strength on the goodness path and satisfy our need for spirituality. At least our lives would feel rather easier without relying on sex and success to fulfil us.

At one extreme, most people are less naïve regarding religious promises, thus choose self-gratification and freedom without the fear of God's eventual retribution, *or they hope to repent and receive absolution in the last minute.* Conversely, some fanatics still resort to religions in hopes of pushing some decency and sanity in our vastly corrupt minds and lives. The war between these two groups to stipulate humans' needs within a meaningful social structure is definitely causing more suffering for people than helping them find peace or explore spirituality personally. Meanwhile, social destruction, personal stress, and hatred are spreading fast globally and ruining our spirits, mental energies, humanity, structural assets, and cultures. We are now forced to live in a cruel, depressing world and try to amuse ourselves with illusions of happiness, sex, freedom, and a crooked democracy that people can neither grasp nor cope with. We are naively driven by fantasies that are either unachievable, e.g., happiness, or beyond our normal capacity to face sensibly, e.g., equality, liberty, democracy, afterlife, etc. We have proven to merely get carried away and lose our commonsense and identity even more as we strive to assert our desires for happiness and freewill.

Accordingly, we whine and wonder what is wrong with life, society, and our fates. The answer usually depends on a person's personality and his/her mood and state of mind in any particular moment, in line with his/her most recent experiences. Although life experiences play a major role in our perceptions of the world, current events stir our mood swings dramatically at any point. At the same time, our experiences and mood swings are internal reactions to some external stimuli, e.g., when people provoke or attack us. They create many vague perceptions of life that we rely on to judge the path and quality of our lives.

For this book's purpose, we are mainly interested in knowing the effects of 'external stimuli' and our 'inner response' in terms of perceiving problems. This information is important for shaping our outlook and making life decisions wisely. We need a proper perspective of society, our existence, and our personal problems (or perceptions of problems) in order to gauge and manage our thoughts and decisions easier. Our ways of facing life (internal reactions) are as much, or maybe more, destructive for perceiving life problems than any external stimuli that we often view as the causes of our problems and struggle to abolish. In fact, the major sources of our problems are within us and relate to either personal flaws or our methods of facing external stimuli.

Sadly, we never learn how to live effectively and peacefully, because our raw ambitions and devilish drives, such as sexuality, hinder our perceptions and judgments about our real needs. As we focus on many superficial needs, we forego our capacity to detect our *genuine needs* that can support an effective and peaceful life for us. Thus, we need a 'goodness regimen' and mentality to do self-analysis, improve our outlook, and find better principles for handling both external forces and personal erratic sentiments. This regimen would help us manage our lives effectively and live more peacefully. The final goal is to develop our inner strength and identity to handle various social problems with confidence, while curbing our conceit and need for extravagance. Ironically, this natural goal of helping ourselves live healthier and easier also turns us into better beings. Yet, this irony makes total sense as well, because: Goodness stirs inner peace and vice versa.

Overall, the most natural and logical way to make our lives meaningful and easier is to explore our needs and personalities. Actually, fulfilling this existential drive (for self-awareness) also provides the best incentive for becoming better beings.

The 'goodness regimen' helps us assess our options for living, especially in terms of the value or vanity of our present lifestyles and all the needless stress they cause. Thus, we find an incentive to do things differently and lead a more stoic life path, mainly by trying to be better human beings for our own sakes. As a start, we should realize what a *spoiled modern beings* we have become. We must have realized by now that our contemporary solutions for a peaceful existence have not worked due to so many hurdles noted in this book. Especially, our religions have mislead people and raised their naiveté instead of making them wiser and better people. The extremism and corruptions in religions, in this day and age, have made us lose our trust in this old method for either making us better beings or saving humanity. Religions have failed us miserably at both levels. Thus, perhaps we should view and apply 'being better beings' as a novel philosophy or strategy, maybe as our last refuge, to attain what our leaders and religions have failed to do for us all along. Meanwhile, finding a chance to build a peaceful personal life, through some degree of goodness, might help humanity and stir social order for coexistence, too.

Sadly, social structure, including religions and culture, have only kept people in a primitive mental state mostly for exploiting them. At the same time, people have become too emotional and naïve by nature to think objectively and ask themselves the right questions about their existence. Thanks to humans' naiveté and exploitive nature evolved in dwindling, corrupt societies, only more incentives for badness and malice have spread amongst them. People seem to prefer and enjoy their wickedness naturally, too, while increasingly lose their chances to grasp the merits and means of becoming better beings. Thus, to propagate the need and incentive for people's pursuit of morality—as a worthy social ideal—the sources of their naivety, including materialism and religions should be somehow mitigated, *by a miracle perhaps!*

Some fundamental questions cross our minds: How and why would a person adopt an unconventional lifestyle and mentality in hopes of achieving the elusive benefits of goodness, and what kinds of personal qualities and convictions should s/he have to succeed? The answer is that *a person is usually drawn to this position rather intuitively* after pondering the ideas and questions similar to the ones raised in this book. S/he realizes intuitively or through learning and meditation that a more productive path of existence is at hand, which also turns him/her into a better being gradually, even if s/he does not have many high qualities and convictions at the outset. His/her drive for emotional stability, self-awareness, and natural happiness raises his/her curiosity to explore the option of being a better being. This happens to people in many ways, maybe even by reading a soulful book. However, it occurs mostly when a person seeks peace and independence truly, often through a divine inspiration or after bad experiences with people and life. Then, s/he does some self-analysis and grows an incentive to gauge his/her being. S/he might gain a deeper sense about his/her Self, build self-reliance, fortify his/her character, develop a divine resignation, and find a better path of life, all for becoming a better being.

Sadly, modern humans have no strong incentive for being good, despite their curiosities about their spirits and spiritualism. No natural urge or cultural norm drives goodness nowadays in present corrupt societies where people feel obliged or encouraged to be crooked. Thus, building our incentive for goodness is now a personal task. This book opposes the idea of depending on myths, e.g., religions and heaven as a reward, to develop our goodness incentive, either. Instead, we may rely merely on certain personal wisdom and convictions to keep ourselves motivated on the goodness path by thinking and behaving morally. This is surely a hard mission to envision and pursue. Not everybody has the talent and temperament to accept such a colossal challenge and risk losing his/her status amongst the mainstream as well.

Still, we might someday feel the need to detect the hidden sources of our turmoil and unrest, defeat our crippling confusion, and curb our inner tensions. Thus, we find an incentive to revamp our identities through meditation and self-awareness regimens.

We reassess our life path and reset our values and convictions, but also realize and cope with the difficulties of pursuing the path of goodness and self-development steps patiently.

2. *Fighting Our Tormented Nature*

The second goodness challenge is to discover the sources of our idiosyncrasies, which mostly relate to human nature, and see how they affect our mentality and attitude during our interactions with family and society. We like to know how much of our defects are due to, i) our instincts and primary needs, or ii) societal influences over millennia leading to our petty characteristics now (humans' evolving nature). This knowledge can help us during the process of building our incentive for goodness and mitigating our defects. After all, the gravity of personal and social distress nowadays reflects the malice in human nature evolved in vile societies now and hindering our efforts for BBB and living in peace. Can we learn to tame our tormented nature a bit?

Two main facts can help us establish a realistic view about the practical role of human nature nowadays: **First,** gauging our own and other people's malicious behaviour—especially our political and spiritual leaders'—reveals that many of our primitive drives, including lust, narcissism, and hypocrisy, are too rooted in our nature to allow purity ever being an inherent feature of humans. Then, our personal experiences show that humans' ambitions and high expectations from life nowadays force them to be impure intentionally, as if goaded by some devilish, innate deep urges in human nature. In another word, human conscience is quite low in general in new societies. **Second,** even if human nature had been pure originally by a slight chance, restoring it to its initial state is inconceivable due to the lack of personal incentives and social mechanisms to propagate goodness and control the chaos around the world towards a moralistic lifestyle.

Overall, scientists' current debates about the piety of humans' primitive nature are not helpful even for forming a reliable stance, let alone applying this knowledge to speculate about their present nature. Yet, it is more plausible that humans have been inherently impure all along. In fact, as a fundamental argument, we can say that humans' vast appetite and drive for lust alone curtail their chances for goodness, not to mention their seemingly instinctual drives for greed, jealousy, etc. God would not have dispatched so many prophets in hopes of making humans more reliable, either, if He had ever trusted their nature. Thus, it is rational to assume that even God knows how humans' basic urges would always debilitate their capacity for goodness, let alone purity. *Ironically, all religions have failed to tame human nature a bit, too!* Still, studying the psychological implications of human nature are quite intriguing, and thus noted throughout the book, including the extra notes in Appendix D.

In the final analysis, the purity of humans' original nature does not even matter as long as we are now moulded into such rigid and frigid characters and cannot elude the influence of our dominant, crooked societies. Instead, we must remember one vital fact and two possibilities: The vital fact is that regardless of the purity of human nature, we are now trapped within our defective societies, mentalities, and lifestyles and cannot reverse the dire effects of social living. Instead, the present social mechanisms stir almost all the social and personal problems, while deteriorating human nature along the way, too. Thus, the two possibilities are:

1. If we have a pure nature, we should still find a way to escape social conditions or change them drastically in order to grow our chances of revamping our nature and redeeming our true spirits and peace gradually.
2. If we do not have a pure nature, it might still seem wise, to a special group of people at least, to find ways of overcoming or controlling their innate weaknesses and urges to the extent possible for the precious objectives of goodness. If we agree that our peace and happiness depend on our knack to manage our needs and urges, then hope exist for all of us to develop

some good qualities that can enrich our being. We just need more incentive and stamina to stay on the goodness path.

On the one hand, we can never prove the level of humans' original purity or regain it, which most likely cannot still handle present social setting, anyway.

On the other hand, we have lots of evidence and knowledge about some positive attributes of humans that, if nurtured, would not only compensate for our evil, but might overwhelm the scope and content of social life gradually, maybe to the point everything else, including our vile urges, can be suppressed and abolished eventually. We have discovered that a special 'being' resides in most humans that, once developed, can bring out not only their good qualities, but also protect them against the hazards of social interactions and the evil within us. Once we attain our authentic 'being' state, we can benefit the life of a pure human regardless of our nature.

Naturally, our 'being' is somewhat related to our basic nature even now, in this new era, despite the pervasive repercussions of social living. Otherwise, even the divine senses of passion and compassion, which at least some humans can produce rather naturally, would not have existed. However, the goodness of our 'being' and the piety of human nature are not necessarily the same things. A pure nature, even if likely, would be just an innate state of existence. Yet, discovering our 'being' entails thoughtful processes, logical contemplations, and spiritual growth. Reaching our true 'being' requires *special* hard work and conscious efforts.

These spiritual efforts are needed for self-awareness, anyway, to break through the deep layers of social conditioning covering us tightly like a thick cocoon and suffocating our divine essence. Thus, can discovering our 'being' bring us closer to our origin, our self, and possible purity? This is also debateable. Anyway, the task of discovering our 'being' is crucial merely for the ultimate goals of growing our inner strengths as humans and alleviating our social problems towards a more peaceful coexistence. In all, as a conclusion regarding humans' original nature and its likely relevance today, we can make the following arguments:

1. Blaming mainly nature or nurture for humans' evils seems futile, since people show fluctuating degrees of purity at any period of history across and within cultures, and even among the members of a family due to their unique genes as well as the psychological formation of a person.
2. Studying our distant cousins, i.e., gorillas or baboons, would not provide a definite answer about humans' essence, e.g., regarding our urges for aggression or being so territorial.
3. Even if we could relate humans to gentler primates in terms of nature at the time they were in the same level of biological development, the vast effects of our independent evolution during the last few million years cannot be ignored or even studied easily. Humans are too complex now to be compared with such an ancient biological origin.
4. All the studies about our primate cousins have turned out to be inconclusive and unreliable, anyway.
5. Even if these findings could be generalized, they cannot be properly interpreted, since we are using humans' crude logic to analyze animal behaviour million years ago. At best, these interpretations would be vastly speculative and theoretical rather than a pure science.
6. While the debate about human nature's piety continues, it is hard to accept the arguments of its proponents or opponents, due to the lack of enough proof. Still, the impurity of human nature seems to stand on firmer ground. Most likely humans have never had a pure nature, even if social conditioning and psychological influences during the last 30-40 millennia, in particular in recent centuries, could be abolished. Applying the traits of baboons or gorillas to study primitive humans has also been unrealistic and inconclusive. Our findings in this regard cannot offer a uniform knowledge about animals' nature, let alone humans that have built complex characters through millenniums of their independent evolution.

7. Overall, it would be both useless and impossible to think of humans' behaviour and thoughts in their primitive form in order to arrive at a generalized theory about human nature as a determinant factor for practical purposes NOW.

Thus, while some scientists' efforts to prove human nature's piety in hopes of stirring goodness seem futile, we can personally find ways of circumventing this limitation—our natural flaws—to reduce our sufferings as well as the burdens of social living.

3. Managing Our Demented Logic

Most of us perceive our logic superior to everybody else's. With this kind of mentality besieging our objectivity and judgments, we have become quite opinionated, pompous, and controversial. Thus, we never give ourselves a chance to undertake a proper self-assessment, and explore our qualities and quirks realistically. We do not learn about our vulnerabilities, sense of being, and need for humility. We make wrong decisions, interpret the world erroneously, and never realize the meaning and purposes of life. We never grasp our nothingness and the privileges of being better beings. Thus, we lose our opportunities for enlightenment, simply because we are all so sure about our logic and wisdom. At the same time, ironically, we consider others fools or mad. Surely, this equation cannot hold water when we all feel this way. The odd meaning of this general mentality is that we are all both very wise (in our own minds) and very mad (by other people's logic). Since we cannot all be so wise, the latter option, i.e., universal naivety and madness, appears more accurate for defining the state of human mind and logic.

Discussing the reasons for our highly erroneous self-image and pomposity is not the purpose of this book. Rather, the whole purpose of discussing the extreme limits of our commonsense, logic, and even science, here is to overcome our dogmatism, which would be a big step for self-analysis and even selflessness.

Mainly our egos make us feel so highly about our logic and wisdom. A more crucial point is that we humans have not yet appreciated this condition (our naïve egotism) as a generic human flaw that prevents us from learning who we really are and finding natural incentives for becoming a better being. Instead, we have become too dogmatic to grasp the finer aspects of our being and life's essential values, as our egos make us trust our logic and conclusions totally. We also fail to observe the world with open mind, thus lose the opportunity of recognizing the meaning and purposes of life. Our fat egos and demented logic have prevented the establishment of fairer societies and human morality, because a big majority of people prefer to stay ignorant and self-absorbed all their lives.

Human logic is flawed also because we rely so much on our raw perceptions of things, people, concepts, and a general reality we have nurtured in our heads hastily. Our perceptions are not only too flimsy and unreliable, but also vary drastically among people based on their intelligence, experiences, and personalities. That is why finding a uniform rule of logic has been difficult in spite of our logic-ridden scientific successes. Our commonsense is even more unreliable and flimsy.

Another great proof about the fallibility of human logic is that we have not still figured out our logic's fallibility in general, but mostly for finding a way to get along better in peace with less greed. The ways we elect our leaders and define democracy also show the infancy of our logic. In all, we must admit that human logic is highly inconsistent and unreliable despite all the scientific knowledge we have mustered and in spite of humans' egotistical dogmatism about the accuracy of their personal views of reality.

Ironically, our logic and science also suggest some plausible notions about the existence of an unparalleled *real world* beyond our convoluted perceptions of reality. For now, however, our logic and science are applied mostly in the *perceived world* to answer only basic questions, though we still cannot even do that effectively—to agree on vital social issues that affect humanity!

Many of the scientific laws and human logic might be wrong, because we do not understand much about the real world, while our rooted perceptions definitely obstruct our learning process. Still, we believe that the universe is a major phenomenon that constitutes the real world beyond our perceptions. If we deny this principle, everything becomes a figment of human perceptions, including the concept of creation and the creator, all the science, and anything that any philosopher or a prophet may say about spiritual souls and divinity. However, for now, even from within our perceived world, we can imagine the existence of a real world, based on a unique mix of personal experiences, logic, and inferences. We can attribute these testable physical phenomena, and the logic that explains them properly, to a fundamental world of real realities. That is, we are hanging in bewilderment within a realm shared by both real and perceived realities.

Ironically, we are hoping and struggling to cross over from our perceived world to the real world with the use of our logic, in particular about the chance of going to heaven! We often believe that both levels of creations—the universe and a cell or embryo—are parallel fundamentals of the real world. Thus, we conclude that our logic and science are viable tools for explaining all the other questions in time, if our brains ever build enough capacity to ask the right questions that are testable within a natural setting.

Meanwhile, we keep relying on our *presumably perfect* logic, thus remain incapable of agreeing even on basic principles for running our socio-personal affairs effectively. For example, we are incapable to agree on a specific logic to address the looming climate crisis versus our capitalistic ambitions. Then again, we cannot second-guess the validity of things (not even perceived facts), which have been proven through logic and science, on the grounds that they may be merely our perceptions and not real. Ironically, we do not even accept human *intuition* as a logical tool or process, *just because we want to stay logical!*

Our huge trust in, and love of, our logic is very interesting to study for learning about humans' personalities and minds.

To avoid complex discussions, other big flaws of human logic are explained in Appendices B: Humans' Egological Conditions, and C: Humans' Logic Aversion Drive at the end of the book

For becoming better beings, we should doubt and reassess the validity of our logic personally and use this exercise mainly for accessing our purer Self that has been burdened by our phony personalities and raw perceptions. This sacred exercise is mostly for improving our sense of humility. It is for helping our Self find its connection to the universe despite all the pressures preventing us from reaching this goal, as shown in Diagram 4.1, page 99. In all, besides the chance for a divine feeling and enlightenment, the sacred incentive (and logic) for becoming a better person would always stay valid and a final refuge for suffering less in our lives.

Assessing Our Being

We usually follow a common life path that has evolved randomly within societies without people giving enough thoughts about its structure and purpose. Philosophers and prophets have tried to put some sense into people's heads and offer some other options for living harmoniously by building a valid social superstructure. However, they have failed miserably to draw our attention or make substantive contribution to the development of our cultures. So now, we have inherited a broken and hurtful society that is heading fast towards its final demise. Most disheartening, within such an inefficient, rigid system, almost nobody finds the time and incentive to think independently *even* about the viability of his/her personal life. Nor do enough people have the incentive or guts to question the value and validity of the social superstructure imposed on us, including religions. Ironically, humans are rather intelligent and artful by all accounts, in particular considering our scientific and artistic achievements throughout human existence. Yet, most of us are also very naïve, malicious, and bad-tempered. Thus, it has become hard to grasp humans' essence considering the immense contrast that exists between their high qualities and extreme quirks. Saddest of all, of course, is the fact that we do not find, or give ourselves, a chance to grasp our beings in a personal manner, elude some avoidable hassles of living, and maybe even enjoy a peaceful existence. Only some lucky individuals acquire the intellectual capacity and incentive to pursue the sacred goal of finding their salvation and Self rather successfully. The rest of us wonder what is going on and what we are doing in the midst of this mess! Still, we grapple with some existential questions and personal dilemmas a lifetime, at least subconsciously, to figure out our being. We wonder about:

- The meaning of life
- Our purposes for living
- Our routines' values
- Our mentalities' status

These fundamental thoughts often cause confusion and stress, because we are making many assumptions and decisions based on our best judgments about these issues, e.g., the meaning of life. We have tentative, often fantastical, impressions about these vital aspects of our lives. Yet, our doubts about the accuracy of our perceptions never subside and our failures to enrich our lives prevent us from reaching concrete conclusions about our spiritual being. Actually, our philosophical doubts about the purpose and value of our daily routines, along with our strenuous efforts to maximize our life opportunities and pleasures, cause deep inner conflicts, but also reduce our chance for self-analysis. Therefore, a brief discussion of these four main human dilemmas is crucial for self-awareness and building our goodness incentives.

A. The Meaning of Life

We fuss over the meaning of life mainly when we get flustered about our fate or the difficulty of handling people. Otherwise, we accept social processes and purposes as a valid path and meaning for life. We usually do not have time or incentive to question the common perceptions of life, so embrace two wrong impressions that: 1) finding happiness is our main mission in life, and 2) by adopting social norms and values, we elude life's demands and obstacles better, while maximizing our chances to find happiness. In reality, however, the only way to find some relative peace of mind and perhaps even a chance for salvation is to reassess all these assumptions and the validity of social teachings. Then, we might perceive and develop our own unique philosophy of life around our simpler needs and expectations for living and relating to other humans. In fact, life is just a long process of mental and physical hardships that we should master very artfully. This is a vital truth to accept!

Especially, the way we see 'socializing' as life's main feature is causing us lots of confusion, frustration, and mental distress. While we are too keen about socializing, keeping even simple relationships are becoming difficult, especially in our marriages. Instead, our obsession to feel accepted and popular is minimizing our abilities to gain independence and self-reliance or define our lives more realistically outside the socializing aspect of it.

Naturally, socializing and other sources of relief bring us joy, but capturing happiness is not life's inherent purpose or merit, especially the way we humans are eager to hurt one another and destroy nature. In fact, life would always remain a big mystery for humans and other species, although we may get a basic sense for it during our spiritual endeavours. Especially, two inevitable life requirements cause many hardships for us:

1. Marriages and companionships have become too unreliable and torturous. Therefore, we often wonder about the purpose of the life we pursue so hypnotically. We wonder about the point of struggling to build and maintain an unappreciative family and still feel so lonely at the end.
2. The work we do for living is mostly boring, frustrating, and painful. The amount of time and energy we spend to perform some unpleasant jobs all our lives, our worries about finding and keeping one, all the politics and quarrels at work, and the

fear of losing it ruin our sense of life largely. More ironical and torturous, humans are programmed inherently to work or go nuts out of boredom and a sense of uselessness. Actually, joblessness tortures most people more than working so many hours every day for running a lousy life in all other respects, too. Meanwhile, nowadays job contents, work relationships, and working hours are getting less favourable, which cause more agony and depression for all. Things will get even more complex and frustrating in near future when robots replace many jobs, population and work force grow, and societies become incapable of providing at least the basic needs of so many unemployed, insecure, and angry souls.

At the same time, nowadays we have become obsessed about grasping the meaning of life to enrich our existence—although ironically again, we want to do it through self-gratification. Since nobody can find a satisfactory answer for this puzzle, we pain ourselves and others so much due to our disappointments. We keep undermining the value of our existence and lose the chance of enjoying the simple privileges of life, since we always search for a true meaning for life that can bring us eternal happiness, perhaps along with a reliable, loving companion. Yet, all these fantasies merely frustrate and prevent us from understanding and accepting the sad reality of existence gracefully with lesser pain.

Ultimately, we should admit that life has no special meaning whatsoever. We can philosophize and dream about it, but those thoughts and expectations would only misguide our brains and pain our psyches in vain. Even if humans happen to live many more millenniums, they can never unravel the mystery of the universe or find any special place for humans in it. Maybe some of us just go insane when we reach this point and accept this sad reality about life's lack of meaning; Then, we may even become a philosopher to handle the situation!!!

Ironically, we easily find other animals' life fully meaningless and discard any chance for their relevance within the universe or in God's kingdom. This is a fine analogy for inferring exactly the same thing about the meaning of human life. We are just another animal with no particular purpose or meaning for our existence within the context of a mysterious universe.

Even if the universe or humans' existence has any purpose or reason, grasping it would always remain beyond our logic no matter how smart we become and how much science we muster. *God would have shared it with us by now if He had meant it to be public!* Our arrogance and religious propagandas are useless for sharing a particular meaning for life as well.

Life is merely a monotonous span of time within a mix of manmade and natural settings filled with conflicts and constraints. Therefore, looking for a particular meaning for life, especially within the context of society, is a waste of time and a source of suffering. Only when we are old, wise, and blessed, we may get just a tiny private sense about the meaning of life, which is often too late to use this raw wisdom for finding either happiness or salvation, other than possibly learning to live the rest of our lives with some degrees of resignation and divine contentment. Life offers some solace occasionally only if we get wise enough to appreciate some special features of our being per se.

At the same time, it is conceivable that our instinctual urges for self-fulfilment and spirituality are somewhat responsible for our craving to find a meaning for life and the chance of finding some form of happiness. These basic urges actually offer sacred clues about the real world behind our perceptions. Then again, we should not let these ideas confuse us with a crude meaning for life, a hasty hope for spiritualism and enlightenment, or a fanciful anticipation for happiness only with the aim of self-indulgence.

B. Our Purposes for Living

While life has no particular meaning, we can set many meaningful personal purposes for our existence per se. This strategy is, in fact, the best way to minimize the hardships of living and possibly create our own personal meanings for our being, too, to make up for the lack of a general purpose for life. Most of us try to do this subconsciously, anyway. In that sense, life can offer a special meaning for a person based on his/her needs and personality. All s/he must do is to focus on defining and pursuing a sensible path of life leading to some profound, specific targets. S/he might still fail to achieve all his/her goals and feel a definite sense of purpose for life, but even the mere mission of defining his/her meaningful purposes and following a goodness path to get there would make his/her life rather fulfilling and peaceful. Ironically, this strategy also stirs a high incentive for becoming a better person. In return, becoming a better person can be a great means of finding our specific purposes for living.

The meaning of life and our purposes for living are two crucial and related philosophical questions that our brains struggle with forever, mostly subconsciously. While we should dismiss the first dilemma rather readily as an irresolvable mystery of the universe, we could devote a good portion of our thoughts and energy to choose our purposes of living and then spend a good chunk of, our lives to fulfil them as prudently as possible. Surely, it is not possible and wise to give up our social needs and duties if our main purposes of living might jeopardize our chances of keeping a practical life in society. This is another tricky dilemma, because appealing personal purposes that might validate our being often contradict the general social means of survival and connectivity. Thus, grasping the risks and setting a delicate balance is crucial to elude the possibility of getting carried away by some juvenile purposes for living that might seem appealing to us merely due to our life inexperience or naivety at certain age.

Finding both practical and wise purposes for living is not easy and fast. It requires lots of thinking and self-analysis to grasp our unique personal needs and means of self-fulfilment, which are often outside our careers. It needs building our life philosophy after years of experience, studying social structure, meditation, and facing odd people and mainstream values. Then, we might become wise enough to envision our personal life philosophy and specific purposes for living. Still, it takes months and years to test our convictions before devoting our energy and mind to some life purposes with little risks of regretting our actions and efforts later. Only then, we are ready to proceed with some degree of certainty that our purposes would be rational and not too risky to devote the rest of our lives to.

C. Our Routines' Values

We envision certain outcomes for pursuing a special path of life. We build our life philosophies, plans, and hopes that drive us to engage in some activities and establish certain relationships. This outlook would provide enough motivation to keep on struggling and working after a person takes the time to set his/her personal purposes for living and accepts the required challenges and tough sacrifices. However, even carefree people who have no defined life philosophy, purposes, and path have a life outlook and expect certain outcomes from their pursuits within society. This general expectation provides a rather good incentive to keep living and maintaining hope about finding some kind of value (meaning) for our activities and relationships ultimately.

We try hard to enhance our being by finding better reasons for our actions and living, but often end up creating more headaches and instability due to our naïve assessments and decisions. For one thing, a majority of people go through divorce and separation nowadays or resent their marital conditions and yet refuse to seek better means of relating and living, or questioning the essence of their being as an independent, self-fulfilling person. Thus, they suffer more every day and consume antidepressant pills regularly to maintain their routine activities and lousy relationships or to endure loneliness.

To grasp the essence of our being, we can gauge the process and outcome of our routines and relationships either actively or sloppily in our subconscious. Often we ponder our sanity, too, for bearing all the hardships related to those relationships or routines merely out of a sense of obligation or neediness. We wonder if our views of life and our Self are correct and if we have other options to make our lives more fruitful and joyful. While causing pain and stress, these thoughts are also quite fundamental and risky depending upon our grasp of reality and decisions. Finding the right balance for our confusing needs and routines, while keeping a practical life in our chaotic societies, is hard. Grasping and facing this intricate human dilemma is rather impossible for most of us, unless we have spent enough time on the difficult mission of building a personal life philosophy and purposes, as noted in the last section.

D. Our Mentalities' Status

As we struggle with the three above noted means of assessing our being, we seek stability and peace, while ponder the possibility of humans ever growing a suitable mentality for coexistence and attaining a relatively peaceful state of mind. The answer seems to be a resounding 'no' in general. We humans have always been too controversial and arrogant to learn how to get along civilly and live in peace harmoniously. It has never happened and it will most likely remain only a dream. Yet, some of us can reach a peaceful state of mind personally under certain circumstances by following a more independent (rather stoic) path of life. Again, ironically, pursuing this path of life makes us a better being as well. Being a better being and pursuing a pure, productive path of life (away from social rules) seem to be highly related adventures and prerequisites of each other.

Of course, being a better being can also help us get along with the right people (and often with the general public as well) easier and nicer, which is an added incentive for those who still crave love and belongingness or cannot bear loneliness.

Overall, it is astonishing how we can reach a relative sense of peace individually if we really put our minds and faiths into achieving such a divine state of existence. On the other hand, it is just amazing how we insist on pursuing lifestyles that have no chance of offering us any sense of psychological harmony and mental control over our destiny. We do not even like to stop and gauge the possibility of living and relating to one another in a different manner than society dictates upon us. We simply obey those norms and values with complete trust, as if some intelligent rulers or philosophers had designed our existing way of life with adequate diligence and understanding about humans' true needs and temperament. Yet, the fact is that our civilization has been shaped too randomly, mostly around the urges of certain groups who have known how to make propagandas for brainwashing and exploiting people financially and emotionally thru politics or religions. At the same time, amazingly, we now do not wish to abide by our Gods' presumed guidelines. We are defying our religious beliefs fast in recent decades or expect the clerics make drastic changes to those guidelines to accommodate our new crooked needs, e.g., more sexual freedom. We are too eager to recreate even our religious guidelines based on demented values we invent for our pleasure-seeking minds and sex-driven views of our being.

By the way, using 'Gods' in plural is for reflecting our present confusion about this matter, too. That is, the inconsistencies and hostilities among religions show that they must have come from either several gods or a confused one. We must choose! A more plausible option, of course, is that prophets have listed many of any God's instructions based on their misperceptions or needs! Thus, we can ask who those so-called prophets were, making such bold claims and offering us some wishy-washy guidelines. Or, in the worst-case scenario, all these religions and their varied rules are the figments of some humans' imaginations and desires to dupe the public. Now we can choose and decide who we are!

While religions have never been a reliable means for defining our identity and being, their basic notions of ethics and guidance, had been of some minimal value for humans to keep at least a sense of decency and self within a simple culture. They imposed some level of social harmony as well. Now, we do not have even those primary controls over our psyches and superficial needs that society wants us to fulfil at any cost, even by crushing each other's pride, mind, and spirit. Meanwhile, we are also destroying nature, which has served us in many ways, including as a divine venue to connect with the universe and our essence.

The way we have developed such an amazingly irresponsible mentality and reached such a futile state of being demonstrates humans' low capacity for goodness and good sense at so many levels, at least for grasping the gravity of our demented lifestyles, logic, and looming demise. We have created this havoc ourselves by living in a fantasy world. Instead of preparing ourselves to face life's hardships with patience and compassion, we just keep paining ourselves with our juvenile illusions of love, happiness, success, and afterlife that society expects us to believe are real, attainable, and personal entitlements.

Humans' enormous misperceptions and illusions regarding the role of religions and spirituality have hindered their ability to grasp and grow their life philosophies and plans, besides stirring gullibility and infecting their mentalities substantially. Chapter Ten discusses the shortfalls of religions and current spirituality means and suggests a simple method to refurbish our minds as an urgent personal mission. We can build our spirituality guidelines and feelings in line with humans' innate needs and urges through an enriched state of mind, which can be developed independently gradually. In fact, some readers may prefer to read Chapters Five and Ten regarding human spirit and its connection to spiritualism before starting the next chapter.

The Chain of Existential Thoughts

The above four existential thoughts (dilemmas) are interrelated and common amongst humans as shown in Diagram 3.1. They function together like a chain of innate curiosities and stir mental burdens for humans all their lives.

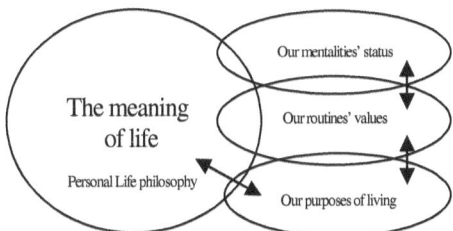

Diagram 3.1: Chain of Existential Questions

We intuitively realize our state of mind importance (degree of mental health and peace). Mental health and tranquility become possible if the outcome of our relationships and activities are meaningful and offer high values. Furthermore, we realize that our activities and relationships find values if our life purposes are meaningful and we can pursue them successfully. This mental process is natural and proper for leading a useful life. Yet, we also believe our purposes of living should coincide with a general meaning for life. This is the only link in this chain of 'existential thoughts' that we all have difficulty reconciling, thus we hurt one another and ourselves in hopes of establishing a viable definition for life. Ironically, we cause all these pains for mitigating life's hardships and possibly finding salvation!

The idea of a basic uniformity among human thoughts and aspirations, and possibly a general meaning for life, is probably a myth and another symptom of our flawed social mentality grown over millennia. Such an ideal about the uniformity of existential thoughts and beliefs (maybe in hopes of creating harmony among humans) would be a fantasy and not a feasible human condition. Thus, while ultimately the above four related existential thoughts are crucial to meditate on, we must be prepared to fail in finding a universal meaning for life or a viable social structure to support such a huge dream. Instead, we must stress on our own meanings of life based on, i) a well-thought, diligently defined purposes of living, ii) a master plan for getting sensible outcomes out of our routines and relationships, and iii) a path for building a strong and stable mindset. Our refined personal life philosophy can delineate our private meaning of life as well.

Developing this personal life path feels like a natural mission as soon as we gain the incentive for becoming a better being.

And vice versa: BBB helps in answering those four existential questions perfectly.

*****

Some keen readers might object to a plausible contradiction in the existential arguments in sections A-D above. They may question the value and meaning of establishing and pursuing personal life purposes (B above) if we believe life itself has no special purpose or meaning (A above). This valid conclusion can be accepted or rejected with equally strong justifications depending on one's personal choice and philosophy regarding existence per se. The intriguing pro and con viewpoints for living at all in a purposeless life can be developed in a major book by itself. Yet, ultimately, we cannot deny or alter the fundamental fact A, about life being a meaningless compulsory journey imposed upon us accidentally. Yet, once we grow up, build a strong mind, and choose to keep living, we should define and make this journey very purposefully, instead of only exist in vain. We must defy the purposelessness of life itself in order to become a worthy human rather than a bum. *Maybe that's also God's hidden agenda for humans, you'd never know!*

Chapter Four
Humans' Mental Operation

We all have a basic idea about a good person's attributes, which mainly relate to his/her level of compassion, sincerity, generosity, etc. We also view these qualities with both awe and envy rather stealthily, yet admire our own cunning and cocky personalities even more. Sometimes, we even wonder why we lack those virtues, yet we do not pursue the matter seriously to find the real causes of our crookedness and disinterest to become better beings. Therefore, this chapter reviews the forces stopping us from being as good as our subconscious sometimes ponders as an option for living—maybe like a bizarre mystery.

Well, while most of us prefer to remain as we are—so naughty and dogmatic—it is useful to be more specific why we cannot, or refuse to, be better beings. Does this mean that humans have no capacity for being good in general, or just social evil is killing our spirits and basic intuition for goodness? The answer probably is that a mix of human nature and culture has limited our capacity to grow a peaceful character and vision of life. More importantly, however, we must ultimately blame our lack of time or interest to delve into these types of thoughts and analyses, i.e., about the roots of rising social corruptions and personal problems. That is why even pursuing humans' basic goal to make a living and keep a family has become so laborious. Thus, our rising depression and stress are mostly our own creations due to the lack of a spiritual urge, while we pain one another regularly in our relationships. In all, humans' low capacity for goodness has two basic sources:

1. **Our low consciousness** about our real needs, surroundings, and people. This also means we are unaware of, or careless about, our idiosyncrasies and the forces that have made us think, act, and feel foolishly and superficially.

2. **Our high inner conflicts and mental damages** due to our crude encounters with people, society, family, etc., as they hurt our spirits, psyches, and thinking ability drastically.

The above two sources are also the causes and effects of each other. In particular, our low consciousness about the six forces controlling our brains and attitudes (listed below) raises our inner conflicts and makes us evil, divisive beings. After all, humans' inability or disinterest to learn about the path and purposes of goodness is the reason we usually end up paying such a big price for social living. Then, our crude mental operation has damaged our delicate spirits drastically, too. As noted in the next chapter, we need our spirits as much as, if not more than, our brains to maintain our sanity and a peaceful life. But then, only our brains can helps us understand the importance and needs of our spirits!

Forces Ruling Our Brains

Our deep urges and needs trigger opposing, interrelated forces (stimuli) that direct our brains and affect our knack for goodness. They are either natural or the result of our reactions to a stimulus, perception, question, or event at some level of consciousness. In all, the forces running our brains can be grouped as follows:

A. Natural (Positive) Forces	**B. Imposed (Negative) Forces**
1. Instincts and urges	4. Rearing conditioning
2. Intelligence and Ego	5. Social teachings
3. Identity and self-awareness	6. Barriers and limitations

Naturally, it is difficult for normal, busy people to feel and distinguish the inner workings or effects of the above six mental forces during their daily activities and encounters. These forces are usually interacting and reinforcing one another so deeply that attributing our reactions or attitude at any point to any particular one of them is hard. Nevertheless, these distinctions are useful for learning about some aspects of human mind. The natural forces are mostly positive, as they reflect our pure, independent views and conclusions about things. The imposed (negative) forces, on the other hand, demonstrate our dependencies and subordination to externally instigated stimuli or training. The more crooked our perceptions of reality, and the more we are attached to teachings of society and our parents, the more we are inclined to trust the rules and values of society and follow them blindly. In all, a mix of the above six forces drives our minds constantly and shapes people's personalities. The interrelationships among these forces can be depicted in a diagram such as the following:

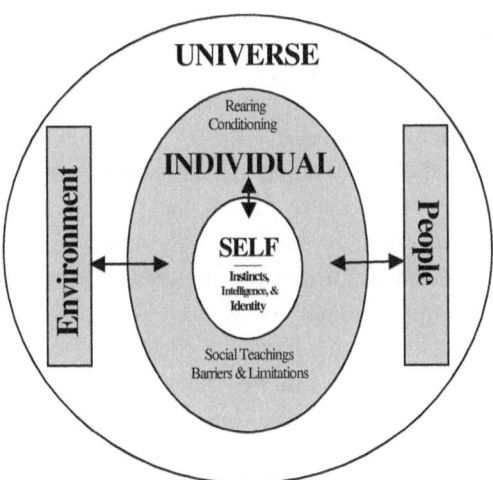

Diagram 4.1: The Forces Shaping People (Their Personalities)

In Diagram 4.1, the innate qualities of a person are amassed in Self, the inner white circle. Then, his/her total personality evolves within the outer grey circle according to his/her rearing and social conditioning, as s/he grows means of circumventing both natural and social barriers for connecting to the environment and people. The eternal, intricate relationship between an individual (grey) and his/her Self (white) is quite intriguing and critical for his/her health and happiness. White and grey fight often for a variety of reasons, including our hidden drive and curiosity about goodness.

As illustrated, our instincts, identity, and intelligence define our Self, which is rather pure and authentic. They are positive forces in one's brain, but this instinctual human capacity is beset by negative forces nowadays. Consequently, we develop many superficial needs and wicked personalities. Although each group of forces make up a segment of one's mental ability in a special situation and time, together they reflect one's overall capacity for independent thinking. These forces are interrelated, as our brains not only mix their effects during any particular mental exercise, but also have been shaped around their collective interactions a lifetime. For example, when a person's intelligence or instincts are subdued, other forces, such as social conditioning, affect his/her character easier and deeper.

These forces also affect a person's cognition, which includes his intuition and grasp of reality. The higher the effect of positive forces, the higher would be one's cognition, which reflects the clarity and awareness of mind regarding one's surroundings and ability to make sound judgments. At the same time, a person's purity of mind declines as the effects of external conditioning and limitations grow. A person's mental capacity and independence reflect his/her cognition level (the overall influence of all forces) that s/he draws upon. Accordingly, human purity, autonomy, and cognition decline as a person's capacity for independent thinking or use of his/her instincts is jeopardized. By the way, 'Inner Self' is the term explained in Chapter Ten and contains all the 'Self' attributes noted above plus our 'spirit.'

The six positive and negative forces shaping one's personality are reviewed in the remainder of this chapter, while Self is stressed as a sacred entity. At the same time, it is crucial to face up to a sad, profound question: If our rampant minds are causing all the drastic changes in our biosphere, what catastrophic ending is awaiting humanity and how much more sufferings we would inflict upon ourselves due to our mental distress, arrogance, low cognition, and universal stupidity, which are all growing too fast? Obviously, the growing social chaos and looming human demise directly relate to our rising naiveté and the way our brains work, including our logic and emotions. Therefore, we must review the forces stirring our minds and get a good sense about the way our crooked urges and environmental conditioning have ruined our brains and humans' fate. We might then build the incentive and guts to make fundamental changes in our habits, recondition our minds, and redeem our spirits.

This chapter's discussions about the 'forces ruling our brains' also confirm that humans' destructives motives and acts are not due to human nature or nurture per se. Rather, they reinforce each other immensely quite regularly during this accelerating process of human decay. More crucially, and of great concern, however, is our utter disregard for these mixed mental forces damaging our characters and lives so deeply.

A. Natural (Positive) Forces:

1. Instincts and Urges

Surely, instincts constitute the most positive force for all creatures to manage their lives. Our prominent urges for food, safety, and sex are a few examples of these primitive instincts, which emerge automatically in the form of a need or feeling; so are most of our natural habits like eating, speaking, fearing, thinking, reacting, etc. These fine properties and genetic information are built within us, which we normally cannot override easily by conditioning. In extreme cases, intensive conditioning might suppress or deform one's instincts, yet they are parts of people's genetic formation, unconscious mind, and inner Self forever. On the other hand, the rising influence of other mental forces has been undermining our ability to draw on our instincts quite readily and effectively.

Human urges are mostly uniform, yet fine differences can be detected among people and across cultures due to their genetic heritage. For example, some people have a higher potency and urge for sex or develop a seemingly abnormal orientation, e.g., as bisexuals. Moreover, social values and personal priorities boost certain urges in some groups more easily and forcefully than they affect average humans with common inclinations. Naturally, this is one factor raising these groups' vulnerability and gullibility and making them susceptible to external influence and manipulation.

In all, while basic human urges are rather universal, they are not felt or pursued equally depending upon their prominence in a person and the effects of social values on him/her. For example, while everybody likes to express him/herself and his/her talents, many people have a substantially higher need for self-expression, belongingness, creativity, or achievement.

Our instincts and natural urges often seem distinct in the sense that some types, or strengths, of innate urges vary in individuals, although humans share the general instincts driving those urges. Moreover, the matter has gotten too complex because we have also developed a large array of artificial urges and needs, such as happiness, love, luxury, acceptance, etc. These new urges are unrelated to instincts or natural urges, but they complicate the operation of our innate urges. The rivalry between our real and artificial urges confuses and jeopardizes our mental operation. We have also intensified our needs related to some of the most likely natural urges, such as greed, belongingness, and narcissism at various degrees, though mostly towards extreme, due to rapid changes in relationships and social values.

Thus, the three following possibilities about humans' instincts and urges are plausible:

First, the complexity of needs and urges that humans have gradually grown for social living has become the source of their sufferings and setbacks. These complex artificial needs, such as belongingness, acceptance, achievement, self-esteem, status, and love have become so prominent in our lives that we sense and consider them as our natural needs consciously or inadvertently. Although they may have some instinctual roots, they cannot be considered completely instinctual at such prevalent extremes that appear like obsessions among most people now.

Second, some of our behaviours and reactions, such as anger and spite, have become so natural and prominent we believe they may in fact be part of our primitive instincts. This idea makes us wonder again about the causes and origins of humans' wild and aggressive behaviour and learn about our nature's badness level.

Third, a good portion of our instincts and natural urges has been suppressed during civilization and many of us have been deprived from recognizing and utilizing them. For example, our needs for self-actualization and spirituality are gradually subdued, yet they are extremely crucial positive forces (if not natural urges) that goad the development of our brains. In fact, self-actualization and spirituality appear quite instinctual and akin to our spirits, as if related to our innate being and spirit itself.

Grasping the effects of these three likely evolutions, especially the first and third ones are crucial for building the right mindset and incentive for becoming a better being. Thus, they are studied throughout this book, especially in Chapters Five and Ten.

In terms of the second possibility, it is quite likely that both nature and nurture have bolstered the foundation of our minds and jointly contributed to human aggressiveness and the related problems we create for ourselves and everybody else. For one thing, humans have possibly evolved from a mix of soft-natured and wild mammals. We may be the outcome of crossing between baboons, which are wild and aggressive, and gentler apes that show traces of compassion. All along, humans' nature and nurture have merged and reinforced each other, too, to develop such a muddled species that we have become.

Surely, discovering humans' original nature might have been interesting and useful at least for revealing the severity of social conditioning on our mentalities and aggressiveness. Yet, finding a methodology to gauge the effects of nurture on our nature over millenniums appears quite unlikely. More importantly, however, such discovery would not help humans enough to relate more effectively, anyway. Our skirmishes would not end even if we could establish the type or purity of humans' original nature. We cannot stop the rampant personal and social conflicts until we learn to control our egos and prejudices and stop our means and mentality of manipulating and controlling others for personal or political interests. We have now created societies that thrive on keeping people naïve in their shells. Now humans are merely brainwashed to pursue some immature ideals that serve only some elite groups running the world.

Our instincts provide both insightful thoughts and means of self-preservation when explored and rejuvenated properly, or at least not repressed so dramatically. They can help us make sound judgements and stay conscious of our surroundings more vividly in relation to our natural needs. They help us grow a productive personal image and a truthful personality. As a positive force guiding our minds, instincts also restrict the influence of negative forces working on our brains. However, the power of negative forces is subduing plenty of our instincts. Even when glimpses of primal instincts hit us and we are blessed with some insights, we ignore them quickly. We are usually quite doubtful about the meaning and wisdom of those clues within the context of social rules. Instead, we embrace social norms rather blindly and turn them into personal prejudices we cherish with no sign of personal initiative and integrity, while also suffocating our natural urges for contemplating healthier living options.

Personal and social extreme interferences have overwhelmed human nature gradually and it will be practically subdued very soon in terms of helping both humans' mental strengths and their environmental functionality. Because of our new lifestyles and raw philosophies, which undermine the role of nature, we are also losing our natural ways of living and thinking. As a result, when there is no nature to relate to and when our life is anything but natural, we would eventually lose our instincts as well. This destructive process has evolved and built such an immense speed and momentum that reversing the direction of social and personal deteriorations seems almost impossible.

More discussions about human instincts and nature are offered in Appendix D at the end of the book.

2) Intelligence and Ego (Personality)

Unlike instincts that reflect humans' general attributes, ego and intelligence reveal a person's unique cognition and temperament. They goad our *efforts* to manage our urges, especially for building our inner strengths and resisting our raw instincts, erratic whims, and crude norms that seem irrational and meaningless. They also influence our choices and drives for independence, freethinking, and minimizing the effects of family and social conditioning. The more developed a person's ego and intelligence, the more s/he questions social norms and resists the pressures for conformity. Overall, while a person's ego and basic intelligence are shaped by genetics, his/her ultimate mental growth depends on his/her interest in, and exposure to, inspiring experiences and thoughts. These facts reveal humans' inherent power and option to choose a fruitful path of life and become better beings for their own sakes if they really find the wisdom and incentive to do so.

In fact, as we lose a wider range of our instincts every few generations, intelligence and personality would be the only line of defence to build against the negative forces infecting the content and operation of our minds. Furthermore, if we can develop our intelligence and ego somewhat vaster, we might even awaken our suppressed instincts and rediscover our natural needs that are lost in the midst of a wide scope of artificial ones. Of course, the question is how to pursue all these self-development regimens, i.e., boost our mentality, personality, and primary instincts. The main challenge is to overcome our naivety, which sounds like an impossible mission when social teachings and formal education are hindering our urge for self-awareness and personal growth. The mindset, personality, and awareness required for accessing our true being—our 'self'—and finding the purposes of our lives cannot be found in the academic world or religious disciplines. They are acquired through exposure to particular thoughts and intuition. Usually, we need a sacred insight to reach the deeper and sounder aspects of our being—like the intuition and freedom we acquire mysteriously sometimes at a high note of despair. These moods and states of mind occur to many of us when our emotions are evoked luckily or our minds are stimulated by some unexpected situation or event. When we are desperate and cannot find solutions in mainstream's values and lifestyles, we begin to seek alternatives. We look outside the box seriously. During such times, we may read soulful literature or do some self-analysis to access the depth of our 'being.' Reflecting on wise philosophers' thoughts and exploring our higher personal needs and urges also give us the temperament and wisdom for building a platform to uplift the positive forces within our minds and find our true 'self.' The hurdle is that we do not draw on such circumstances and insights seriously and return to our mundane habits and thoughts quickly. We hardly find time and patience to contemplate and cherish our insights. Even worse, people live self-destructively nowadays due to their poor intelligence and personalities. They react to their setbacks by either committing suicide or killing the public, since these prevalent options feel easier and faster sources of relief than doing self-analysis and self-cleansing.

A basic level of intelligence and personality is needed to resist the global gullibility forced upon us through endless propagandas and eerie social values. Then, a person's keen urge and courage for freethinking reflect his/her unique characteristics, including a capacity to explore his/her real needs and personality, while s/he strives to understand him/herself and life through self-awareness. In return, his/her grown consciousness and wisdom support his/her drive for independence and reassessing common values and lifestyles as well as his/her living options and relationships.

Intelligence and ego are positive forces for controlling one's mind, yet high personal incentives and qualities are required to build them systematically and apply them well consciously. We also need objective means of defining positive intelligence and personality. In effect, our intelligence and ego must be driven by a proper life philosophy and personal identity, which we should develop around our valid life purposes for guiding our values and path of existence. Instead, in real life, we boost our egos merely for power and competition, instead of seeking selflessness, thus turn into pompous individuals with little brain, compassion, and inner security. Sadly, most people's intelligence and personality are inadequate for fighting off the vast level of social challenges, and thus turn into negative forces upon their minds instead of positive. Everybody believes to be smart and have one of the best personalities in the world. Therefore, our criteria for gauging our intelligence and personality are also arbitrary and subjective. Hence, humans are stuck in a frightening abyss.

While our mind operates mainly according to our intelligence and ego, our wisdom, personality, and consciousness are in return developed under the influence of all positive and negative forces. It is impossible to know exactly which forces play a prominent role in the way our minds learn to operate. Some scientists think that our instincts and genetics play a bigger role in making our characters and all the problems we create for ourselves due to our low capacity for goodness. Yet, all the six forces discussed in this chapter have major impacts on our psyches and who we become, depending upon various circumstances and conditions that are unique in each individual's case.

The effects of negative forces, i.e., social conditioning, family rearing, and environmental limitations for ego and intelligence developments are two folds: **First,** they influence the formation of personality and intelligence during the early stages of our lives and fix our personality, consciousness, and wisdom. **Second,** it becomes difficult to overcome our predispositions in the later stages of our lives, as they are engraved in our unconscious and direct our personalities forever. Actually, these negative forces expand their influence upon us incessantly after our personality, consciousness, and intuition are developed as an adult. That is how these negative forces have multiple (at least double) effects in forming (and deforming) our cognition and mentality. That is, with our frail personalities, consciousness, and intelligence, we become too susceptible to endless family pressures and social limitations, but also become too dogged, idealistic, and arrogant. Accordingly, the effects of negative forces are quite severe for any normal individual to resist or overcome easily. Only a magical incentive or insight can give him/her the strength to fight the deep impacts of negative forces, not to mention the influence of his/her bad genes. Thus, the nature and quality of a person's intelligence and personality also become obscure, though usually reflect his/her substandard character and convictions.

Intelligence and instincts are basic human properties that raise our curiosity and an incentive to explore our being thru goodness. Like a car engine, they can be restored and boosted thru valuable thoughts (e.g., our life purposes) even if they stay idle for many years when we neglect to tune them up properly. This is good news about our chance for maturing and redeeming our spirits. Our main challenge is to give our minds a proper tune up and start them up for riding on a mind-awakening path. Newer thoughts and intelligence erupt, while our personality grows, too. Actually, one measure of high intelligence and strong personality is our ability to develop foresight and conviction to tune up our mentalities through self-awareness and by exploring the purposes of our lives.

Surely, intelligence and personality (ego) constitute different dimensions of humans and they are studied separately. However, they are also interrelated qualities and prerequisite of each other, thus discussed in parallel in this chapter. For example, as one's intelligence increases, his personality becomes more flexible, humble, and 'self' oriented. In turn, the strength of personality brings a person the opportunities to explore new ideas and to question the validity of values and systems s/he is attached to. S/he starts to doubt his/her intelligence and priorities, which leads to higher exposure to new thoughts, thus higher self-awareness and intelligence. Moreover, a person's ability to influence his/her mind effectively relies on both these positive forces, i.e., his/her high intelligence and personality strengths. Together, personality and intelligence can create a synergistic force to overcome the negative forces bombarding our minds all the time.

3) Identity and Self-awareness

'Identity' signifies a person's essence and inner strengths—the nucleus for building a solid character and convictions as a robust and stable being. We often feel lost or depressed for no tangible reasons. The cause of these mental unrests is the lack of identity, though we might be quite intelligent and have a good personality. Sadly, the effects of social living and values have made us feel empty and purposeless despite our arduous activities, high social status, avid socializing, and ambitious goals we pursue all day. We strive to use our intelligence and personality most effectively and shrewdly to present ourselves in a polished format in society and impress others, get along with them, or manipulate them. This goal and mentality, however, comes at the cost of ignoring and dampening our identity largely. We merely try to hide our flaws and intentions to show off our phony personalities. Thus, while the 'personality' we grow so selfishly is just for pretending 'whom we desire to look like,' our identity reflects 'who we are' in terms of our genetics, thoughts, passion, abilities, etc. A strong personality goads us to find and boost our identity, and vice versa.

Identity is a positive force for being better beings, because we realize that exploring it (the identity or Self) would relieve a good portion of our social burdens, mainly because we abandon our tiring efforts to be like others. Instead, we learn more about our 'Self' for increasing our capacity to follow a self-sustaining path of goodness and to explore our inherent potentialities, including spirituality, through self-awareness and by heightening our level of consciousness. Nevertheless, most of us do not get a chance to recognize or develop our identities because of our low urges for self-awareness and consciousness.

The most crucial step towards self-awareness is to learn about our personality aspects, their interworking, and symptoms. This topic can be studied in this author's book, *The Nature of Love and Relationships (GARP)*. In particular, we can learn to:

1. Monitor our behaviour in terms of each personality aspect, i.e., ego, model, and self, regularly. Learn how each one is driven by many motives or impulses and then find out what they are. Reading Chapter Thirteen, and maybe Twelve, in *GARP* is useful.
2. Assess the integrity of our motives and decide objectively if they are suitable for an enlightened person who does not need to play games or retaliate. We should apply Self and Model aspects of our personality to control our selfish motives and improve our tactics for managing our daily routines.

B. Imposed (Negative) Forces:

4) Rearing Conditioning

Only few individuals are lucky enough in the way their parents or guardians teach them valuable life lessons. The rest of us do not get this opportunity and instead our instincts and personalities are suppressed during the rearing period. In fact, parents often cause so much of our psychological dysfunctions, usually inadvertently. With the increasing life pressures on adults, providing a healthy environment conducive to the sensitive mind of a child is hard. Parents have lost their sense of parenting in recent decades, while nobody is quite certain about parenting requirements and how to train his/her children. It seems, however, that kids in developed countries are being spoiled much more than they are taught about life challenges and hardships and how to prepare themselves for all the agonies of living. Even when parents have patience and time to stir a mind-nurturing life for children, it is hard for them to grasp all the right things about life and teach to their children without spoiling them. We do not have a viable culture anymore to guide and support parents do a proper job in educating their kids, especially about life essentialities. Instead, even parents' instincts to teach basic stuff is hindered in societies satiated with demented norms and so much toys. Moreover, a child's sensitive, naive mind may misinterpret his/her parents' life conditions and intentions, which at the end makes his/her views of him/herself and life blurry and confusing at best. Even if we do not grow up with self-doubt and insecurity, we still may not grasp our real identity and purpose of life. We are left alone in a fantasy world to sort out complex matters on our own in the most confusing years of our lives, i.e., during adolescence.

Together with our distinct genetic characteristics, the rearing conditions cast our personality traits. Naturally, our obsessions, drives, and experiences in search of love in the early stages of our lives also play major roles. Meanwhile, our strong sexual urges have quite an influence on the development of the main features of a person (identity), which we all have to live with in harmony or conflict (mostly the latter) for the rest of our lives. Depending on our levels of sensitivity and intelligence, we may grasp and admit some of our personality dysfunctions and find an incentive or urge to do something about them. Even so, overcoming our idiosyncrasies and personality flaws—if we notice and accept them—would be a difficult and lengthy process. Of course, even pondering a valuable thought, such as the idea of self-awareness to overcome our flaws, is precious for becoming a better person.

Even such minimal convictions provide a good chance to gauge our identity and welcome insights and revelations that can affect some aspects of our minds and lives gradually.

Anyway, the chances are that we never recognize, admit, and overcome our rearing hang-ups. Thus, our psychological flaws turn into major negative forces that dominate and drive our minds persistently and hinder the liberation of our 'Self.' The symptoms of 'Self' negligence manifest in our chronic gloom and agitation for no special reasons, yet cannot free our minds to ponder the situation and make a useful self-evaluation. We never grasp our problems' sources that relate to our genetics and rearing abuses, which we do not (care to) ponder or understand.

5) Social Teachings

We pay a great price for social living in the new era. We are merely helpless members automatically, since we are born into a world of illusions and grow up according to hypocritical rules, values, and conditions imposed upon us without realizing how deeply we are hypnotized. Everything in social living seems so natural and necessary that hardly ever we think of other options, despite our routine setbacks and frustrations. We get absorbed in mainstream's rules, as our social identity and success depends on our ability to comply with prevalent routines. How social values and norms have evolved to such idiotic forms of superficiality filled with egoistic goals requires a book of explanation in itself. However, the outcome is that we remain a helpless entity, with no identity, driven by complex socioeconomic parameters. Even if we had some autonomy and integrity to oppose the process of deterioration in family, society, and environment, there is so little we can do as a person, as a community, and perhaps even as a nation. We are merely at the mercy of powerful forces revolving around rigidly interwoven relationships and conflicts of some elites' interests at national and international levels. In fact, even if all the people and nations came to their senses and agreed that our ways of ever-increasing production, consumption, and waste bring us only more personal distress, pollution, and irreversible damages to humanity, so little options exist as of now to reverse the process quickly. In most respects the damages are already done. Although the dire effects of our selfish pursuit of capitalism and materialism may not be seen totally yet, all the evidences reflect we are bound for major disasters in the near future—in less than 50 years or so.

Yet, even all the scientific data and official reports about the looming catastrophes due to our crooked lifestyles do not move us. We simply remain unconvinced that humans are destructible, too, and the last grains of our civilization and social order are at the verge of collapse. We just do not realize or care about the fact that, without a healthy nature, human existence will soon become too painful before their final demise. Our amazing arrogance and ignorance have made us oblivious of our looming *terribly* painful end! Now, bringing more helpless humans into this world is also a crime!

Another negative aspect of social life is reflected directly in the level of stress and anxiety that everybody must endure due to the low quality of our jobs, social relationships, marriages, etc. We drink alcohol, smoke, and take sleeping pills and addictive drugs in order to forget our problems, but in effect add to our level of depression and helplessness. We are just trying very hard to cope with the process of deterioration in any way possible, because we do not seem to have the wisdom and conviction to reverse the trend of social disorder and to reassess our horrific, outmoded criteria for coexistence. We are simply content with our presumed freedom, pleasures, and mottos like democracy, which is only allowing idiots and hypocrites rule the world!

Social conditioning is a negative force on our minds in terms of reinforcing a crooked life outlook, besmirching the meanings of success and individualism, and paralyzing our senses to grasp the scope of problems we are creating for nature and ourselves. Thus, we are also losing our capacity to find plausible solutions.

It has become a double jeopardy when our tentative solutions reflect our helplessness in taking drastic actions and finding better alternatives for living more harmoniously in a natural setting. All these delays to reassess our social living and its direction reflect our weakness in recognizing our demeaning values and giving up some of the superficial means and methods of living that we have so naively adopted as natural and useful. No doubt, the negative forces of social teachings are responsible for the fast decline of our inner strengths, biosphere, and social order. Meanwhile, our dependence on some misperceptions of personal needs and social values keep deepening, as evident in our falling spirits, misguided ambitions, and insufferable lives. Now, we have no mindset and incentive to make our personal lives a bit easier at least!

6) Barriers and Limitations

The first five forces noted above rule our brains naturally and routinely, and their effects appear in our thoughts, feelings, and attitudes. They reflect either our genetic attributes or parental and societal conditionings that are carved in our minds. These forces also boost our dogmatism, as we always believe we are right in all our thoughts and deeds. Some of us might even realize our unique personality attributes (both positive and negative ones, including eccentricities) due to the five mental forces, especially our genetics, imposed upon us all our lives and making our brains perform in peculiar manners. Nevertheless, these forces have the greatest impact in the manner we feel, think, and act, because we associate with them rather naturally, mostly subconsciously.

The sixth force, however, consists of limitations and barriers we face directly and consciously as outside threats to our plans and beliefs. In addition, we must waste a lot of time and energy to fight them as much as possible. These limitations and barriers emerge in our relationships, during our struggles towards some goals, and in our attempts to find our social identity. They affect our nerves and minds in many ways, mostly negatively, and quite differently from those other five forces. Our sense of despair due to the effects of barriers and limitations damage our minds, as we get frustrated about so many obstacles hindering the pursuit of our goals and living peacefully. Facing people's incompetence, carelessness, and manoeuvres for abusing us is too frustrating, in particular. Therefore, we suffer from these setbacks due to not only arduous mental instigations and inquisitions, but also our severe biological (and physical) reactions. All these barriers and limitations affect our attitudes, minds, outlooks, and personalities due to our disappointments and failures.

Often, however, life barriers and limitations are the products of our naive perceptions. We imagine many shortfalls or setbacks due to our demanding mentality and high expectations from life. These self-made limitations appear like, and become, barriers for fulfilling our social, economic, or relationship needs. Especially, our fantasies about love, happiness, and marriage lead to major disappointments and perceptions of problems and limitations. Instead of curbing our wild ambitions and perceptions of life, we stir more limitations for achieving what we think we deserve. Thus, we keep creating many newer problems for ourselves due to our rising neediness. In all, we have lost our sense of reality, as we have become obsessed with many juvenile fantasies about existence. We have been born into a life of constant struggle for more of everything, although we have been warned about the personal (psychological) cost of these never-ending consumption habits on both environment and humanity besides our sanity.

The constant pressures of fighting social limitations on our minds and spirits burden our psyches to the point we become insane and psychotic. Thus, we react drastically and contribute to the build up of those social barriers and limitations in many ways ourselves, e.g., through our spites and animosities. We are guilty in two ways. First, we do not grasp the right sources of social decline, such as capitalism and materialism, and the need for a viable society within a practical socioeconomic setting. Second, we support the debilitating social mechanisms by increasing our personal needs, consumption, and demands from life, instead of accepting a simpler lifestyle in a healthier society.

Our selfish habits seem quite natural to us, too, as we are not convinced about the necessity of controlling our superficial needs and fat egos. We simply do not admit that destruction of forests and the rise of carbon dioxide and other chemicals in atmosphere are due to our own untamed appetite for more of everything. Now every member of the family believes s/he must have his/her own car. Our lifestyles do not advocate sharing our belongings, using public transportation facilities, or riding bicycles anymore. We need larger houses that consume a lot of lumber to build and a great deal of fuel to maintain. We buy too much clothes and other useless stuff to make ourselves more appealing to each other, yet we are only alienating one another more every day with our egoism and greed. We have become addicted to extravagance in order to follow social trends without realizing the dire effects of so much waste on the purity of our spirits and nature that are the ultimate sources of peace and benevolence. Most amazing, of course, is our tenacity to undermine the severity of global issues, such as greenhouse effects, ruining all aspects of our being very soon.

At the same time, we are allowing our shoddy perceptions and ambitions turn into negative forces that muddle our minds and create horrendous stress and frustration for us all. Thus, we are ultimately creating many of our problems and limitations by: i) our rising neediness and fantasies, and ii) perceiving inherent life realities as barriers and limitations.

The Mixed Effects of Six Forces

Although the above six forces affect our perceptions of people, society, and life, the sixth one stirs our pessimism and depression the most due to the severe effects of our perceived limitations and barriers on our psyches. As the first five forces stir a consistent outlook, the risks of distress and inner conflicts are small. Yet, goal incongruence and inner conflicts grow fast when we swiftly perceive some specific social disorders and pressures as personal limitations and barriers rather than rooted social deficiencies per se. In other word, we feel safer within our illusive worlds than thinking outside the box to fathom life realities more realistically and seek simpler options for living. Certainly, the mere sense of existence and need for adaptation, to withstand social life's rules and tyrannies, torment us vastly already, as we live in a muddled state of ignorance and hypnotism. The only merit of this state of hypnosis (thoughtlessness) for a naive person is the possibility of feeling rather carefreer and safer due to his/her naiveté. However, social barriers damage people's spirits eventually. All along, low self-awareness and naiveté also stop people from discovering their innate potentialities and the essence of their being.

Thoughtlessness curbs living pains at the cost of ignoring the virtues that a mature, pensive person can achieve, though wisdom has its own pains. Thus, we can choose a life path by gauging our desires, views, and values through self-awareness. Like old tribes who lived in harmony and peace for ages, despite a much higher degree of natural threats and deprivations, we can learn to live a rather quiet and tranquil life by disallowing social demands and external forces taint our minds and values so relentlessly.

Social chaos, anxiety attacks, and depression would not be so pervasive if social structure could be developed around people's natural needs and intelligence. The incessant personal conflicts and pains that people face in the new era in family relationships and society are due to erratic forces and changes in social systems and settings. Our sufferings are due to vast inner conflicts when our random intuitions reject or question superficial life values and ways. As we face all types of limitations and barriers during our encounters with life, our frustration and distress turn into intense negative forces and irrelevant concerns that besiege our emotions and minds and taint the quality of our lives. Moreover, we never learn to relax and be authentic with a set identity. Accordingly, our hypocrisy infects other people's brains, too. Thus, we hasten the process of deterioration in social morality, personal values, individualism, compassion, humanness, integrity, patience, piety, true happiness, personal sense of security, innocence, natural beauties, environments, and global welfare and harmony.

Another major source of our frustration is our dire feelings of helplessness when we face many (often self-made) barriers and limitations, and when our vision of life contradicts the symbols of social growth and wealth. We feel our inabilities as individuals, or even as a devoted group, to induce worthwhile causes, such as preventing worldwide water contaminations and destructions of forests. We feel helpless and restrained by economic and political forces that some greedy elites have imposed on our way of life and thinking. We feel too many barriers crippling us to act for the welfare of society or even object to our leaders' inability to grasp or stop social decline. Then, we suffer more wondering if they are just stupid or crippled, too, like us! It is shocking to witness the big disparity in people's, especially our leaders', beliefs and visions about the environment, social priorities, and a valid sense of who we humans are in our corrupted societies nowadays.

Our inability to relate to each other as members of the same species is a horrendous barrier and raises our frustration regularly. We humans feel alienated towards one another, as our differences are much beyond usual conflicts arising from personality clashes and egos. Rather, our quarrels are fundamental and philosophical notions about human life per se. So, we cannot relate effectively as members of the same species. We are angry with ourselves since, after so much show of intelligence and historical evolution, we still seem incapable to understand who we are, or wish to be, as a human being and as a species. We have major differences in our views of 'humans,' because we do not know whether we are supposed to be a conceited domineering species or a benevolent defender of all life in a more natural, harmonized manner. *Can we ever agree on this basic dilemma at least?! And then maybe build a functional society around it for those who choose to live!*

In the final analysis, we are all at fault for the stressful effects of too many barriers and limitations in societies. Every one of us has become a barrier for others, since we do not know how to restrain our unleashed expectations from life and others merely by embracing a less showy lifestyle in a natural environment. If only we develop a simpler, more practical social structure based on a logical restraint on our needs and appetite for consumption, we would not have to suffer relentlessly from the limitations and barriers that are mostly self-imposed and driven by our childish fantasies and humans' general naivety. Ultimately, most of our social burdens, limitations, and barriers reflect the vanity of our mentalities boosting the absurdity of our present social structures. Ironically, our weakness to limit our needs—our neediness—is the reason we suffer so much from the limits that social systems should impose on us to sustain themselves. Meanwhile, our basic needs also remain unfulfilled. These negative forces crush our minds, because we do not train our brains thru self-awareness to elude superficial needs and seek contentment in nature's aesthetic values and nonmaterial means of happiness.

Surely, our crude economic and political systems, especially capitalism, are the main culprits for inducing people's mentality for endless consumption as the only way of living and flourishing in society. This is a horrendous, rooted problem, for which we do not seem to have a solution. Therefore, all our other efforts and personal sacrifices for being better beings would have minimal effect on humans' fate and welfare until we can figure out, by some miracle, a more functional socioeconomic system.

In all, we perceive and carry too many barriers and limitations in our lives, simply because society has made humans too naïve and one-dimensional.

Making the Best of Our Brains

Our minds develop and function based on the forces discussed above plus general information. The noted positive forces induce intuition and dynamic stimuli in our minds and motivate us to take sensible actions. Conversely, the negative forces normally create anxieties, psychological dysfunctions, pessimism, lethargy, and we usually react unproductively, too. This basic rule can be useful for managing our lives somewhat more constructively by detecting and empowering the positive forces, while studying the negative ones more consciously, too. Sometimes, negative forces may push an individual to seek other options of living in order to elude the agonies of his/her present lifestyle. Even depression may lead to remarkable intuitions and energies that might exceed even our high intelligence and cognition. In fact, negative forces might instigate positive thoughts and actions, too, although not as an expected routine or normal process. Appendix A at the end of the book explains the features of 'human cognition' briefly.

In all, it is crucial to remain vigilant about both positive and negative forces stirring our minds, emotions, and actions. We should remember two crucial points in particular: First, our minds are under constant attack by negative forces mostly due to family and social interactions and influences. Second, we amplify the effect of negative forces on our minds by conceding to the values and influences imposed on us, instead of using our brains and intuitions more aggressively to defeat or offset the negative ones. We do not use self-awareness, intelligence, and intuition enough to make independent judgements and assess alternative ways of living. We let the dominance of negative forces upon our minds simply push us follow the same social trends that advocate vanity and winning at any cost to our psychological and physical health as well as the environmental welfare.

Sadly, now we appear to have no control or intuition about the path of life we are following erratically, while socioeconomic and environmental collapse is looming due to humans' narrow minds and aimless actions. Our intelligence and instincts have now been suppressed to such low levels that we perceive only the existing superficial, imposed values as the sole viable course of existence. Surely, even intelligent, intuitive individuals who have objected to our crooked way of life cannot do much about the deteriorating social conditions, as the whole humanity appears helpless under present circumstances. Sadly, no one can change a world where most people and authorities are unwilling or unable to appreciate and do anything about the symptoms and effects of a capitalistic social structure on people's psyches and spirits.

Collective voices, mass protests, and social revolutions are eventually needed for changing societies and bringing civility and ethics into people's lives. However, more urgent and crucial is humans' mental readiness to realize both social problems and personal defects, then build the courage and incentive to become a better being first. We must fight social and personal naiveté first and confront corrupt authorities, so that we might get a chance to come together and build a sustainable, healthier life on this planet. In fact, all revolutions and proposed radical mechanisms will fail if a very large population around the world are not good enough beings with much less gullibility, strong commitments, selfless minds, and high ethics to change things. However, this sounds like an infantile desire!

In particular, reducing humans' gullibility, instead of pushing more phony ideologies and needs on people, is crucial for solving personal and social conundrums. Then again, it is hard to fathom the kind of magical, super power that could envision and achieve this horrendous mission. Overcoming humans' rooted arrogance and naiveté at this scale feels impossible considering the level of personal, social, and global endeavours required to grasp humans' authentic needs, including spirituality, propagate self-awareness, and overcome our petty needs, habits, and emotions. We see many demonstrations for climate change and other big causes, but wonder how many of those demonstrators are really serious and capable of changing their own mentalities about capitalism and reduce their neediness just for the sake of saving humanity! These challenges and principles may make sense only to those who find incentives to become better beings.

This chapter has meant to achieve two objectives: **First,** to show how our **minds**, and each one of us as a naïve member of society, are responsible for contributing towards social and environmental demise at the start of the 21st century. Even more disturbing, we feel too helpless—regardless of our level of consciousness about what is really happening—as there appears to be so little anybody can do to reverse the accelerating deterioration process.

Second, the information about the positive and negative forces influencing our minds will be used in the future chapters to learn about ourselves as individuals and human beings, as well as our plausible options to address the daunting stalemate in society. The limited discussions of social problems and environment in this book are only for the purpose of signifying the impacts of our weakening social infrastructure on our minds and welfare, *and vice versa*. In the final analysis, we can note that our problems and unrest result from the way our minds have been trained to operate under the influence of certain hypnotic forces. We are perhaps unaware, thus not guilty of the problems our minds are inflicting on us and nature. However, by learning about the forces running our minds, we can explore some other life paths open to us for gauging our needs and attitudes better, and thus raise our self-awareness. Then, we might even learn to become a better person, too, as the only solution for personal, social, and global salvation. Heck, we might even wish to do it for God's sake as well! Apparently, He wants us to be better beings than how He has created us! *We would never know why He is so keen about our goodness, though, especially since He made us so defective!*

The discussions in this chapter reiterate another important fact to consider as well about human badness and all the personal and social mayhem we have brought upon ourselves: Often, badness is not by choice, but by chance. We usually do not get a decent opportunity in life to learn about the path of being a better being and we do not see our badness due to our crooked genes and dreadful parental and societal experiences.

Goodness is always by choice, though!

Chapter Five
Our Curious Spirits

The points made in previous chapters about humans' overall incapacity for righteousness must be clarified, since we have a divine curiosity about goodness and we have an arty spirit that seeks purity. The hurdle is that we have lost touch with our curious, sacred spirits due to our lifestyles and religions draining our mental energy. We are surely made of body, mind, and spirit. However, our focus on body and mind, especially the former, has come at the cost of neglecting our spirits' needs the most. The hurdle is that we do not know about, or believe in, the existence of a spirit that is equally, if not more, important than our brain and body for our welfare in the long run.

Humans have a few complex dimensions that are reviewed in Part II of this book when the topic of 'knowing our being (self)' is reviewed. However, a brief discussion of humans' spiritual urge is useful at this point for arguing the existence of our spirits. In return, our spirits drive our urge for spirituality, which is mainly for finding our high qualities, becoming better beings, and living easier through our boosted spirits. Therefore, a natural zeal for goodness is hidden in humans, though we do not notice or know how to access this god-given trait and empower it through a self-developed regimen of spirituality without relying on religions or other people's interpretations of divinity.

We imagine, and sometimes feel, the connection between our spirit and our urge for spirituality, but do not pay attention to their inherent places within, and for, our being. When we feel sad or need solace, we resort to religions or some form of spirituality to soothe our sorrows. Yet, we miss the innate force of the spirit that thrives only through a sincere sense of spiritualism to keep itself intact, while helping us find peace. We are unaware of the role we must play actively to maintain this sacred link. We do not know how to touch our spirits on a regular basis and we do not appreciate our need for spirituality, although our frail spirits strive to stress on this high personal need subliminally, especially when we feel down.

Besides stirring our need for spirituality, our spirit plays many other functions. It drives our curiosity about humans' higher needs, including artistic and intellectual explorations and self-actualization. It stirs our curiosity about humans' goodness and purity. It serves as a barometer for gauging the state of affairs in our lives, including the cause and level of our stress. Therefore, it reveals the health and stability of our being, including our body and mind equilibrium, in the midst of our busy lives as we plough on hypnotically. We regularly use the phrase, 'My spirit is high or low' and we know what it implies, yet we do not use 'spirit' in a proper context every day as a vital entity of our being, similar to our brain and body.

Most of all, our spirit has the sacred task of making us better human beings and raising our zeal for existence. In return, our goodness regimen keeps both our spirit and inner-strength high.

Accordingly, we need an effective medium to make our body and mind operate in line with our spirit, and boost it, too. We have learned to call this medium spirituality, though it has always sounded like a supernatural or mythical endeavour that gurus follow for hobby or divine purposes. Yet, spirituality is just the medium (a goodness regimen) that feeds our spirits, as humans' third vital dimension. So how can we master spirituality?

Mastering Spirituality

People usually view spirituality as a formality for contacting their creators through some bizarre rituals without truly realizing their meanings or purposes. However, spirituality is merely a principle and practice to sharpen our senses through 'inward reflection' and 'outward connection' in ten fronts listed below. Mastering these ten commandments of self-awareness and Self-realization boosts our mental capacity to reach a divine sphere and mentality called spirituality. A few words about each of these ten goals are offered in the following pages, while Part II will explain the guidelines and process for achieving these goals, while building our *personal* sense of spirituality through goodness.

A. Inward Reflection is for:

1. Overcoming our superficial needs and revamping our naive perceptions about life and its capacity to offer a lasting sense of happiness and success.
2. Gaining enough inner strength to withstand life's inevitable hardships gracefully with minimal stress.
3. Finding inner peace and the wisdom of living independently.
4. Remembering the role of our spirit and its needs regularly.
5. Seeking our being and a personal purpose for life.

B. Outward Connection is for:

6. Focusing on life's larger picture, while raising our patience and compassion towards people.
7. Attaining a higher sense of humility and decency.
8. Appreciating the values and beauties of the world instead of ruining all aspects of nature.
9. Feeling our delicate connection to the universe.
10. Becoming a useful member of the society by being a better person rather than living narcissistically and robotically with so much pretension. This mission is mainly complemented by 'Inward Reflection' steps noted above.

A. Inward Reflection

1. Overcoming our superficial needs and naive perceptions

A main hidden cause of social downfall and personal stress is our rising need for superficial things, love, and belongingness. We have become too needy, which is the strongest poison for killing our spirits. In return, our spirits are so depleted we cannot build a resilient character merely based on the merits of our potentialities and compassion, so we have become too needy for belongingness and love. Our weak, wicked personalities make us desperate for superficial means of feeling alive and expressing ourselves, while we remain inherently fearful of loneliness. With less needs and neediness, on the other hand, we can free our spirits and feel the essence of our beings after establishing our beliefs through our growing sense of spirituality. Thus, another function of spirituality is to provide a strong platform for us to gauge our needs and scarp most of unauthentic ones that have been built gradually in our psyches under the influence of capitalism and materialism. We really do not need them!

Through spirituality, we also realize that our perceptions of society and life are too naïve, as they cannot fulfil even a small fraction of what humans hope to achieve—despite all the positive thinking propagandas—, especially about the meanings of love, happiness, and success.

2. Gaining inner strength to withstand life's hardships

It is true that life is full of physical and psychological hardships. However, we should not take this matter too personal and grow self-pity for our bad luck or lack of enough opportunities, which we think we deserve with our inflated views of our potentialities. We need a more realistic view of life's capacity to fulfil our dreams. We must build a far more modest perception about what we, as individuals and humans, deserve. In fact, we deserve very little, contrary to all the social propagandas for individualism and positive thinking. We humans are too naïve, greedy, conceited, and cunning nowadays to deserve the kind of compassion and love we imagine we deserve and should get. Instead, our massive sense of entitlement is ruining our spirits.

At the same time, we must realize that despite humans' huge weaknesses and idiosyncrasies, we could be both happier and better human beings if we grasp the means of achieving goodness by learning about our identity and developing major personal convictions. We should realize that we can gain inner strengths through spirituality, to not only bear life's hardships easier, but also attain some degree of personal grace and divinity. We can boost our spirits to guide us achieve these precious objectives for living, instead of only dreaming about some raw measures of success and happiness.

We must stop being an idealist or perfectionist in a world that is incapable of offering even simple harmony and peace. Even nature is too impersonal and cruel often, despite its incredible harmony, beauty, and intricacy. Then, of course, the societies we have developed with our demented perceptions of reality have no capacity whatsoever to be even remotely adequate, let alone offer the kind of perfection we envision in our naïve minds. It is merely our views of self, life, world, and society that need a big overhaul.

3. Finding inner peace and the wisdom of independent living

Living is becoming more confusing and painful as we humans keep doing all the right things for destroying the world and nature and alienating people everywhere in large societies as well as small family units. Our limited wisdom and crooked solutions, including drugs, wars, suicides, and various types of crimes, to fight social mayhem have no power to save our souls or bring some level of solace into our lives. As a last resort, some of us are now realizing that only some *personal* sense of spirituality could help us cope with this havoc and find a relative inner peace.

In particular, spirituality is a very useful process for learning the wisdom of living independently, which provides a sense of self-reliance and conviction to take life in our strides with some practical levels of realism and optimism. It is getting hard these days to rely on others to help us avoid loneliness. Therefore, we should depend on our own wisdom and spiritual power to feel rather complete alone. This wisdom would not only eradicate our sense of helplessness around the mass of egotistical population, but also bring us a soothing sense of inner peace and goodness.

4. Remembering the role of our spirit and its needs regularly

The inherent link between our spirit and drive for spirituality was noted before. Humans' obsession to invent and practise religions provides another clue about the reality of spirit and the strength of spiritualism boiling within humans and possibly other beings. The reason we often feel lost and depressed is that our spirits deplete when we engage in so much activities related to brain and body without considering their effects on our spirits. While mind and body activities, including pleasures, are useful for our mental and physical health, overindulging them through strenuous thoughts and vain pleasures ruins them. Actually, we ignore the crucial needs of our minds and bodies to stay healthy, too. We have no sense of equilibrium required for body-mind connection to stay alert and peaceful. A role of our spirit is to gauge, restore, and fortify this equilibrium for our ultimate personal health through spirituality exercises. In return, spirituality is for remembering our spirits' special needs, which mainly include the attributes we expect in a strong character, like pride, self-awareness, integrity, conviction, love for other beings, etc. These sacred, unique needs will be discussed in Part II. They are the same characteristics we often ponder and adopt for becoming a better being.

Thus, grasping and strengthening the sense of spirituality is crucial for feeding our spirit constantly, which would in return keep the balance and health of our brain and body. As a first step, we must always view ourselves in three—not two—dimensions as shown in the following triangle.

Besides the importance of remembering the spirit-mind-body connectivity, the priority must always be given to spirit, as shown in line A below, instead of indulging ourselves as noted in line B.

A. Spirit⟶Mind⟶Body   (Correct Priority)
B. Body⟶Mind⟶Spirit   (Demented Priority)

Naturally, these three primary human dimensions are meant to work together and serve one another all the time. At the same time, spirituality can be considered an auxiliary dimension for serving the above three primary human dimensions. It should be developed for keeping a healthy balance in our psyche and life[*].

In the end, our main task is to boost our spirits through self-developed spirituality routines to keep our bodies and minds healthy. Meanwhile, our bodies must be viewed mostly in terms of their ultimate task of severing our spirits and minds. Instead, we focus on indulging our bodies by seeking the best means of physical pleasure, which leads to crooked thoughts and mental burdens, as well as the demise of our spirits.

5. Seeking our being and a personal purpose for life

We struggle a lifetime to cope with our mundane lives and make the best of our opportunities. We educate ourselves, work, build a family and worry about so many tedious details along the way

---

[*] Psyche and spirituality are explained further in this author's book, *Doubts and Decisions for Living, Vol. II, Appendix C*, as two (auxiliary) human dimensions.

just to maintain some kind of identity in society. Still, despite our efforts to stay logical and practical, we often get confused about the purpose of living like a robot. In fact, we often dwell on three major dilemmas: We ask ourselves, 1) who am I supposed to be amidst this big social chaos with so many philosophical or idiotic interpretations of life around?, 2) how have both my identity and personality been (de)formed so fast in society?, and 3) is my 'Self' or spirit somehow linked to a higher realm or the universe?

If we are serious about finding answers for these existential questions, we need a spiritual mind and conviction to examine the depth of our thoughts and deeds. Only through spirituality, we may find 'who we are' as a primary step to also fathom and adopt a personal purpose for life in line with our unique life philosophy and routines, including our careers and relationships. Meanwhile, by sincere, deep reflections on these self-exploratory questions—in a kind of meditation—we reach moments of Self-realization gradually and build a personal sense of spirituality.

Any wise person tries to learn about him/herself for not only coping with social demands, but also building a strong character and boosting his/her spirit. However, to grasp 'who we are,' we need a process to do some self-analysis objectively. Spirituality is it—the routine to view ourselves in a selfless realm after learning to stop our egos and superficial needs from running our minds and emotions relentlessly. The only way to feel our true being in a selfless sphere and find relief from life's agonies is to grasp our inner self thru spiritualism. Yet, this would be a tough challenge, as explained later in this chapter and Chapter Ten.

The above five spirituality functions are for focusing inwardly to grasp our being and boost our spirits for making our routines more bearable. The second half of spirituality focuses outwardly to delineate humans' divine dimension beyond their social status. It seems quite plausible that we are part of a bigger picture, much beyond the tight cocoon within which the society and religions have kept us trapped. Spirituality's big goal is to help us explore our roots and realize our nothingness in the scope of existence.

B. Outward Connection

6. Focusing on life's larger picture, while raising our patience and compassion towards people

Our personal life philosophy begins to delineate our purposes for living nicely when we keep our spirit high and let it lead our daily actions and decisions. In return, our high spirit keeps us focused on the larger picture of life, which means letting go of trivia and those features of existence that we cannot control, in particular people's crookedness and social havoc overwhelming the world nowadays. Meanwhile, our compassion and patience towards people grow not only because we realize humans' helplessness to be better beings, but also for making our own job of relating to everybody much easier and less stressful.

We must also accept that people's varied personalities reduce their abilities and chances to relate effectively. Thus, we need lots of compassion and patience to run our communications and retain some level of harmony thru our high spirits. We cannot expect others to think or behave like us, nor should we force ourselves to imitate others and adopt phony identities merely for getting their approval or making them happy. Meanwhile, for building our being and boosting our spirits, we should strive to revamp our personalities—especially our egos—for becoming better beings. Indulging ourselves with so much greed, arrogance, ignorance, sexuality, and dogmatism forever has killed our spirits and dried our personalities.

'Focusing on life's larger picture' has many objectives, but its crucial role to raise our senses of humility and decency is further stressed in the following section.

7. Attaining a higher sense of humility and decency

Self, Nature, and the universe are the three main elements stirring our senses of survival and spirituality. Yet, a fourth element, i.e., other humans, plays a vital role for completing our sense of being and spiritualism. In fact, we often feel more connected to, and in love with, other humans than we do toward nature or the universe per se. Surely, our connection to, and love for, other humans is too selective and tentative. We do not like or care about most people and we even turn against our friends and lovers if they hurt our egos. Yet, through self-developed spirituality, our views of humans improve vastly, too, and we become more selfless when judging people. We become more compassionate, tolerant, and forgiving, which in return soothe our own spirits.

It is bizarre that all religions have caused lots of human rage and hostility despite their mottos for mercy and goodness. So, we question the legitimacy of their supposedly divine attempts and claims to enlighten the public and bring people together. We doubt religions' spiritual potency when people have become so arrogant and spiteful towards one another due to their religious prejudices and crude ideologies. On the other hand, our basic self-developed meaning and practice of divinity would make us view all humans with higher empathy, despite all the malice and corruption that people keep spreading in society. Most of all, we also grow a sincere sense of humility—another failure of religions—as we grasp both humans' nothingness and helplessness.

We must overcome a great deal of misperceptions and hatred within us to achieve humility. In fact, we are so self-centred and ignorant that almost everybody not only thinks that the earth and human existence are the locus of the universe, but also imagines him/herself to be at the centre of the earth—as a crucial element of existence. Therefore, it is hard for us to realize and accept that these perceptions are not even remotely true. We cannot grasp the reality that we are simply as important within the context of the universe as a mere amoeba! While many religions rely on some slogans, such as "God loves you," to stress humans' special status, we must not rely on such self-indulging imaginations for defining who we are, or for building our personal spiritualism that must be based on grasping our nothingness! Then again, as we master spiritualism, an outer power's magical support of our being feels like love and boosts our inner strengths to live peacefully.

On the one hand, it is hard to fathom why people, even the very ordinary ones, are so full of themselves. Who do we think we really are? On the other hand, as a graver, sadder problem, we believe we can defend ourselves and prove our self-worth only by being as selfish as the mainstream. We feel obliged to behave arrogantly merely for handling people or getting their respect. Sadly, this self-imposed sense of deficiency and self-pity without lots of false pride feels rather natural. Therefore, egotism has now become a primary feature of human nature. It has also turned into an outlandish reason for the acceleration of conceit in society towards humans' total degradation and extinction.

8. Appreciating the world's values and beauties instead of ruining all aspects of nature

We are so 'inwardly focused' that we hardly get a chance to look around attentively and see the magical beauties surrounding us and the real values of existence that have remained hidden from us due to social distractions and our never-ending quarrels with one another over trivia. Surely, our selfish 'inward focus' hinders our chances for contemplating and practising spirituality as well. Instead, humans' common 'inward focus' these days reflect their extreme level of self-centredness, confusion, and hypnosis within a society that has been misguiding and exploiting them. We have learned to set our life priorities based on infantile criteria built around our narrow views of the world and our one-dimensional perspective of life for boosting a fake personality and succeeding in a corrupt socioeconomic setting. Our flimsy minds are not in sync with our spirits to separate society from the natural reality.

Thus, the role of spirituality in this regard is to remind us of our origin, which is not the society or even our parents who have been instrumental for us getting a physical existence. We learn to feel and praise the beauty and intricacy of nature, gain a special capacity to live a bit more harmoniously within ourselves and with our chaotic world, and—most important of all—build the conviction to do something about humans' tenacity to destroy all aspects of nature merely out of ignorance and greed.

9. Connecting with the universe

Through spirituality, we also acquire a sense about the universe that resides beyond the visible and accessible nature. We feel a connection to this rather mythical sphere without religious beliefs or practices that mostly (mis)guide us with imaginary perceptions of God or afterlife. Instead, our feelings of connection are merely useful for building our life philosophy and faith realistically, and for relieving our sense of loneliness in society where compassion is eroding too fast.

Obviously, the idea of connecting to the universe is the most abstract part of spirituality, since this ultimate level of divinity materializes only at the highest degree of practice and patience, after we reach a sacred state of being. Thus, we should not lose faith if this ultimate divine sense of spirituality does not happen to most of us quickly or at all.

10. Becoming a useful member of the society

Ultimately, all our efforts for exploring our Self and building a personal sense and regimen of spirituality is to keep our spirits intact, so that we can survive the endless tyrannies of existence, including the symptoms of social living and encountering all kinds of weird personalities. We need our spirits intact also for exploring and exploiting the essence of our being, while we stay a useful member of the society. We like to live practically as much as we aspire to connect with the universe. We like to stay in peace with the rest of the world and people, which can happen only by becoming a better person ourselves.

In particular, we must learn to be much less naïve, stubborn, and arrogant, by building a solid spirit and strong convictions to withstand all the social hurdles and personal flaws discussed in previous chapters. More details are offered later about social and personal limitations that we should be ready to tackle.

Naturally, gaining a proper mindset and mood to enter the sphere of spirituality is difficult all by itself, let alone fulfilling its ten commandments diligently enough to attain a tangible level of mastery in it. Still, even our smallest efforts to strengthen our spirits through some form of personal spiritualism can produce enough focus and incentive for us to seek the wisdom of living freer and becoming a better person at the same time. Another crucial point about spirituality is that we must grasp its ultimate meaning and outcome for us personally. Spirituality has nothing to do with religions and it is not a process to imitate or learn from some alleged experts or clerics. Instead, we must build spirituality gradually within ourselves based on our grasp of its meaning and objectives, in line with personal emotions and devotion required to fulfil this ultimate mission of our being.

Spirituality is vital for finding a stable and meaningful outlook and pursuing our lives effectively and peacefully. It is essential also for appreciating the sanctity of existence per se, as we adopt a proper mindset and path for handling our shoddy social norms, which are mostly uncivilized, painful, and moronic. More details about spirituality are also available in *Doubts and Decisions Vol. II*.

Life's Main Components

The discussions in Part I of this book reiterate that human life has three main components:

1. Existence—that is complex, daunting, beautiful, mysterious, and amazing all at the same time, therefore connecting with it adequately is too difficult for humans.

2. Social structure—that is chaotic, uncivilized, and moronic, yet we have adopted it hypnotically, and, in fact, cherish many aspects of its self-indulging mechanisms and propagandas.
3. Inner Self—that we must build proactively, effectively, and authentically with the power of spirituality. However, we do not have enough patience and wisdom to explore and employ our spirits, boost our inner strengths, and develop our personal life philosophy and purposes to embrace our inner self.

The way we distinguish and view these three components of life and the way we analyze and synthesize them are crucial for establishing our life philosophy and making the right decisions for living. Life's lack of a particular, common meaning seems to be inherent. But, even if it had a hidden meaning, it is impossible for humans to fathom it, because nobody learns how to view, distinguish, and analyze the three life components in his/her head effectively and handle each one separately in ample depth before creating a total picture about his/her role within, and connection to, these components.

We have no control over the first two components, though we could try to make a bit of contribution to social welfare, despite the remote possibility of reducing people's gullibility or stirring even some basic thoughts for the long-term benefit of society. However, we could establish a vast degree of control over our inner self and personal life within society and the universe thru self-awareness and meditations. Only then we might get a chance to enjoy our existence with awe after we learn to cope with social demands and chaos somewhat, while pursuing our stoic existence with conviction. Accordingly, we also discover an easier way of adapting to the social structure and learn to handle our frustrating and dispiriting encounters with our families on top of our painful relationships with ordinary folks in the society.

PART II

The Art of
Being

The Art of Being lies in one's ability to learn humility and apply one's primary intuition and intelligence against one's dogmatism and arrogance.

                                A budding spirit

Chapter Six
Goodness Endeavour

Perhaps one day we get a mysterious inkling to become a better person, maybe after a divine experience or reading some books like this! We either feel the need to escape the crooked reality crippling our existence or are awakened by a notion of spirituality. So we suddenly have a strong incentive to explore our better side of being, but do not know how to do it and what to expect along the way. We like to understand the basic elements of goodness, adopt the right process and principles to follow, and develop a constructive lifestyle and mentality, while maintain a civil relationship with our families and society as well.

Cautionary Points about Goodness

Most people can become at least slightly better than they are by improving their personalities and outlooks to gain independence and peace. We ponder goodness since, 1) we are desperate for a manageable life, and 2) we are romantic, so like to imagine, i) an ideal human with strong character and sense of ethics, and ii) the chance of developing our own abilities to embrace love and relate rather peacefully and easier. These issues are tackled in Part II, but the following cautionary points are crucial to remember to remain realistic about our sacred mission of goodness:

1. Only a small group of people has the mental capacity, and gets the opportunity, to become good enough. Most of us fail to make this leap, due to our severe genetic defects, daily life pressures, and the effects of family and social conditioning. Still, we all can be just a bit better if we really wanted to.
2. This book's criticisms of greed, materialism, capitalism and similar causes of social distress might convey an impression about rich people not being as good as the poor. That is not true. In fact, poor have shown an equal or higher tendency for badness than rich, especially when they show less vigour and ambitions due to their gullibility and lethargy. Poor is not necessarily pure or plain victims of social malice.
3. This book's loud criticisms of humans and societies relate to their historical inability to think and act at a macro level to help humanity's long-term welfare, although their success and ingenuity at micro levels are amazing—yet not useful for saving them.
4. While we strive to be good and get along with others without compromising our identity and pride, people often ignore our good intentions and keep responding in their own crooked manners. Thus, we must be ready to absorb people's malice, instead of hoping to be appreciated or acknowledged for our goodwill and goodness efforts. We must not get discouraged and lose sight of our sacred goal.
5. Instead, we should always remember our goal of being better beings only for our own inner satisfaction without any other motives or the need to get outsiders' approval of who we are. We must also remember that talking sense to most people or advising them is often futile and harmful for our relationships with them. Not only human logic is too varied and impotent to appreciate our intentions, but also people's dire dogmatism prevents a sensible exchange of ideas among them.
6. Many people never get acceptance or a simple recognition no matter how good and caring they become. Popularity seems mostly akin to charisma regardless of a person's goodness or

his/her efforts for getting recognition, while bad people are often more charismatic as well. Charismatic evils are more accepted and successful in general than normal decent people who just strive to keep simple relationships with others. This condition seems like a mysterious or sacred phenomenon amusing humans all by itself.

7. Naturally, charisma and goodness are not the same thing or even remotely related qualities for humans. At the same time, charisma is hard to gain, if possible at all. Yet, goodness is both possible and more precious (needed) for self-realization.

8. Still, another mysterious phenomenon is that good people seem to get punished unfairly or face more life barriers than evils who in fact find plenty of room for self-indulgence and prosperity. This idea sounds insensible about a just creator, too. Anyway, this unscientific remark is only a hypothesis—not a clue about any supernatural power forcing any type of either fair or crooked reward system that religions assert about a divine entity or God. The common practice to relate goodness and God is futile and untrue.

9. The anomaly related to some evils' continued luck may have some form of mysterious reason behind it—maybe even as part of a divine wisdom, e.g., for testing people—or be only a random occurrence, e.g., as a sign of nature's innate ferocity. On the other hand, the likelihood of our goodness efforts paying off is not far-fetched, e.g., in terms of peace and inner wisdom we gain. This self-induced reward system appears like a big incentive for anybody to pursue without any other earthly or divine expectations, including afterlife or even a means for spreading fairness and justice.

10. Ironically, humans seem destined to suffer regardless of their nature and goodness efforts. Through goodness, however, we learn how to bear life's burdens and pains more effectively and gracefully. Still, it seems we all eventually get what we deserve, i.e., too much pain and setbacks, due to our general flawed characters. We can argue that we are being punished

for no fault of our own, since we are born helpless with such wicked genes, develop naive mentalities, and are trained to adapt ourselves to all kinds of devilry in society. Most of us suffer in life since we are formed improperly and usually do not get the opportunity to be better beings.

11. The notion of all humans deserving lifetime agonies is surely harsh and against all religious beliefs about a divine power rewarding or punishing us for our deeds and characters. It is also against another contentious religious premise in terms of our ability to control our vile urges and behaviour. Yet, it is hard to attain solace in life, instead of suffering, considering the accelerating social immorality in line with humans' rising appetite for greed, controversy, and arrogance.

12. We never get used to inner conflicts and pains that besiege our psyches all our lives, although they become easier to bear with a spiritual mentality, while pursuing the goodness path with faith and compassion.

13. Altogether, although the word 'goodness' implies achieving certain goals (as mainly listed in the next section), we should keep our expectations moderate in terms of how good we can actually become. In fact, as noted before, the main goal is to become just a bit better than what we have been all along. Expecting an absolute state of goodness is unrealistic, as it would be a very difficult task for most of us. As a premise of this book, our efforts to be slightly better than what we have been all our lives is a big step in the right direction towards a possible full salvation. The next step is to be somewhat better than average people in society are, while we hope and plan to improve every day, too. Accordingly, the term **'betterness'** is applied occasionally in this book to imply the notion of 'being better beings', rather than always expecting, and using the word, goodness.

14. **Betterness or Bitterness:** A main property of betterness is its potential to eradicate the pervasive sense of bitterness that most people feel and show nowadays. People's incessant

frustrations and disappointments during social interactions, while enduring other people's bitterness and malice, have led to an endemic social distrust. Accordingly, a deep sense of bitterness has overwhelmed the foundation of social structure and turned us all into permanent adversaries with a great deal of superficial (showy) good intentions. In fact, we can recite and remember the idiom 'Betterness vs. Bitterness' daily as a potent motto to practice and promote our drive for goodness.

15. To pave our path towards goodness, we must beware of the inner and outer forces (noted in Chapter Four) that often stop us from ensuing our goal for goodness, and then defeat our evils and their sources, as explained in the next chapter. Still, understanding the 'goodness structure and goals' first can prepare our mindsets and raise our incentives for goodness.

With these rather peculiar precautionary notes in mind, let us try to pinpoint goodness virtues, goals, and platform in this chapter, and then analyze its elements and process in Chapter Nine.

Goodness Pyramid (Structure)

Goodness is not meant to refer to a person's moral virtues per se, but rather to reflect the wholeness of his/her character to sustain a peaceful, productive, and passionate life with a high degree of consciousness and minimum conflict with people and the world. A person can adopt many qualities for becoming a better being. Yet, ultimate goodness requires a wholesome, strong character built progressively over the following six pillars of goodness and discussed below briefly.

A. Foundation	**B. Form**	**C. Finale**
• Authenticity		
• Autonomy	• Harmony	Divinity
• Vision		
• Vitality	• Humility	

While the six pillars of goodness are developed together as a person proceeds on the goodness path, we must place a higher order and emphasis on creating the *foundation* (i.e., Authenticity, Autonomy, Vision, and Vitality) to establish the right *form* (i.e., Harmony and Humility) towards the *finale* (i.e., Divinity).

Boosting the six pillar of the goodness pyramid is actually the path of spirituality that raises one's spirit, as one moves slowly towards divinity at higher goodness mastery.

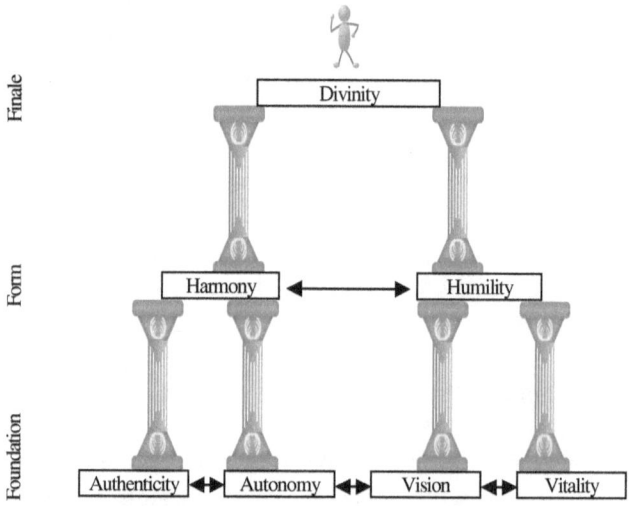

Diagram 6.1: Goodness Pyramid (Structure)

Obviously, reaching selflessness and divinity, as the ultimate goal at the height of the goodness pyramid, is rarely feasible for most of us, yet we can become much better beings by studying these six pillars of goodness. Then, we can learn to contemplate and direct our efforts on areas that seem to lack enough strength. This pyramid also stresses on both the goodness regimen and goals, as explained in more details in Chapter Nine and Table 9.1. A crucial point about these goodness pillars is that they all have been vastly weakened within individuals in the new era, which is exactly the reason for so much chaos and wickedness in society.

A. Foundation

After developing our incentive for becoming a better person and preparing ourselves for the pain and frustration we must endure to succeed on the goodness path, we set out with great hopes and enthusiasm to build a goodness foundation by working on its first fundamental four pillars, as briefly discussed below.

Authenticity

We have lost our identities in a world that promotes pretension and vanity as its core values. Our personalities reflect parental and social teachings that push idealism with an erroneous view of individualism and revolve around conceit, deceit, false pride, big misperceptions about humans' needs, sexual overindulgence, and self-gratification. With no interest in developing and sharing a harmonious world, we all merely embrace lifestyles and values that represent neither our inherent identities nor serve our lonely, disturbed souls (Self). In fact, our phony personalities only goad us follow some raw ambitions and seek power, social acceptance, and popularity with no regard for human dignity and integrity. Therefore, we never grasp who we really are and why we have imposed such a tiresome, stressful existence on ourselves.

All along, people's level of trust in one another has declined vastly, because we realize that almost everybody is too phony and unreliable to put our guards down when dealing with them. Often, people's words are not worth the air carrying them. This mistrust has turned into a pandemic and inflicted us with deep senses of loneliness and helplessness. Ironically, everybody still looks for more love and belongingness, while fewer people can offer true passion and compassion.

At the same time, our rising neediness for love, things, and power is making us so unreasonable and unrealistic regarding people's capacity to offer compassion and about societies' ability to fulfil so much artificial needs that people are now pampering and demanding. Thus, we feel depressed and disappointed due to not only our failure to achieve everything we desire, but also our rising personal oversensitivity when people cannot relate or fulfil each other's high expectations. The bottomline is that we are running around and hurting one another with our odd perceptions and personalities, which are the outcome of our low authenticity and the social fad for superficiality. Thus—the most hurtful fact of all—our spirits feel betrayed and lonely.

Besides causing communication hurdles and deep mistrust in society, our superficial personalities singe our psyches, as we feel confused, rootless, and dispirited, yet we refuse to see our pitiful phoniness. Thus, we lose our spirits and chances to explore our potentialities, including our urges for socializing, psychological growth, self-fulfilment, and spirituality. Surely, we cannot nurture goodness in ourselves while we stifle our spirits deliberately daily —when we are wasting all our energies and time to perfect our fake personalities in hopes of either exploiting people or getting their approval. The lack of authenticity annihilates our sense of reality and weakens the chance of working on other pillars of goodness, too. Our vanity and neediness impede our chances to develop our inner strengths and Self, as we nurture modern social values that promote evil and narcissism at the cost of killing our spirits and humanity.

Building authenticity and a solid identity is vastly hindered by our severe growing-up conditioning. However, we can strive to curb our phoniness and neediness, explore our inner essence, and become a better being. We can explore who we truly are through self-analysis and self-awareness in order to revamp our outlooks, personalities, and lifestyles. The goodness regimen and elements are discussed for self-analysis and self-development in Chapter Nine.[*] We get the benefits of building a self-oriented, conscious, and conscientious identity in a simple lifestyle instead of pursuing

---

[*] Studying the seven elements of self in Chapter Two of this Author's book, *Doubts and Decisions for Living, Volume II,* would be useful as well.

a torturous, meaningless life among the mainstream in search of illusive success and happiness. Although we must give up many facets of our self-gratifying addictions for reaching the ultimate sense of self, we can still try to maintain some level of attachment to society while building our new purer identity. Self-awareness is the main path for, and product of, building our authenticity.

Autonomy (Self-reliance)

As we proceed on the goodness path, lots of autonomy and self-reliance are required to cope with the outcome of breaking our addictive, self-indulging attachments to society. The less phony we become, the more people perceive us as an outsider and lose interest to include us in their games, which feel wasteful, wicked, embarrassing, and unbecoming to us more every day, anyway. They detect our cynicism in our reluctance to participate in so much vanity and pretences or play so many roles and games. They resent us for our calm encounters per se even if we keep all our new beliefs to ourselves. Therefore, the risk of being snubbed or rejected grows, and we should learn to rely on ourselves for satisfying most of our emotional and existential needs personally, *without loving ourselves more as well, of course!!!*

Surely, autonomy is becoming a necessity these days, since we have difficulty trusting people, even family and friends, or relying on them seriously. They often disappoint us at the worst time when we need them. On the other hand, the rising social pressures and demands make us too needy for love and support to mitigate our pains and stay sane. Solving this deep emotional conflict is one of the main life challenges, yet we must favour the stringent option of self-reliance largely to avoid the humiliation and agony of trusting or relying on others naively.

In particular, family relationships are becoming too unreliable. Most of them collapse after we invest a great deal of time and emotions in hopes of creating a refuge against all the tyrannies that life imposes on us at work and other social settings. Thus, we must foresee and prepare ourselves, from the early stages of our lives, to grow a high degree of self-reliance along with a prudent level of trust in people to avoid too much paranoid or alienating them. That would be a very delicate balance to demand from our tired brains. In all, the task of developing a virtuous self-reliance, without appearing (or getting) too pompous, would be hard, but necessary for becoming a better being.

Unfortunately, no longer any mechanism exists in our cultures to teach autonomy (as well as the other pillars of goodness) to people in a practical manner. Instead, people are misguided, e.g., through positive thinking gimmicks, to feel too important and capable of achieving anything. The goal is supposedly to teach them confidence and individualism. However, people's crooked self-image and their convoluted perceptions of individualism and independence make them more vulnerable and needy in society, instead of learning the fine art of self-reliance according to right criteria for becoming humble and reliable themselves.

Self-reliance is developed gradually through contemplation and proactivity, while we strive to also grasp the true meanings of individualism, independence, confidence, and pride. Our vanity and false pride are replaced with altruism and self-esteem, as we learn to forego many of the luring features of living within our poorly structured society without hurting our souls or wasting our precious energy on rivalry, resistance, and rebellion. Instead, we try to grow more patience and tolerance against the cruelties and hostilities that people and society inflict on us in retaliation for our seemingly weird stoic attitude, or merely out of spite.

Vision

We are being exploited in society mostly due to our naivety and poor inner strength to resist people's luring promises and traps. We are not good and strong enough to elude the games they play to manipulate us. We lack a proper vision of the social structure and norms dominating our minds and lives.

Vision also refers to a person's level of insight and foresight to build and pursue a productive life, make the best use of his/her potentialities, and stay pragmatic in terms of compromises s/he should make in society to get along with people. Vision means building genuine short and long term plans according to a solid personal life philosophy that we choose, and then pursuing those plans with fortitude and faith. Our sensible, clear vision is for facing many inevitable setbacks and each time only raising our spirit and resolve to work even harder without letting despair or negativity cripple us.

Furthermore, vision refers to a person's strong 'ingenuity' to explore and express his/her niche and spirituality urges. Ingenuity in the context used here does not mean an extraordinary insight about the universe or art of living. Rather, it refers to our ability to test the validity of our perceptions about our lifestyles and the senselessness of our expectations from people and life in general. This special kind of wisdom reflects our appreciation of personal limitations as a human being, instead of feeling so superior and smart. We must try to grasp, i) the social and personal hurdles for building ethical societies, and ii) people's options for coping with the inevitable demise of our cultures, civilizations, and humans. We must find the wisdom of living in a mess that is impossible to cleanse and with people who are not going to be even remotely objective and fair. We should learn that all the advertisements to sell us all those useless products are merely means of exploiting our naivety. Believing in those propagandas and commercials are only making us stupider and poorer. All those junks we keep buying are not adding any value to our characters or wellbeing, but only making us more needy, vulnerable, and wicked.

Building enough vision is a gruelling task due to humans' dire aversion to learn anything beyond what their crude mentalities insist to be the reality of existence, especially in terms of personal and social needs. Accordingly, it is hard to imagine the chance for a higher social consciousness and political reform. This is simply not going to happen, so we had better get used to this sad reality and map a viable path of life for ourselves. Developing a realistic vision about humanity makes social coping easier with a better chance of boosting our spirits as well.

How many times must we let our leaders and political parties fool us with their empty promises and solutions for improving socioeconomic conditions? How much longer should we trust the promises of peace and prosperity by all these self-serving elites and useless organs of society? Is not it the time to get a bit wiser and look at the larger perspective of social structure and its dire incapacity to reform itself? How much longer we wish to believe that capitalism—or any other mechanism depending on people's greed and vanity to sustain itself and people—is viable or capable of serving the public?

Reflecting upon these and similar questions helps us grow the kind of simple wisdom and vision that can free us from all the nonsensical and impractical ideologies about social living, hope, happiness, prosperity, and all the other sources of our entrapment in a delusional world. Our newly grown sense of reality beyond the perceived reality imposed by our odd neo-culture would give us the power to look within ourselves to discover our true needs and abandon all the artificial ones. We gain the vision for being better beings and getting along with people easier.

This vision reflects our intelligence, logic, and perseverance, mostly for self-analysis, learning about our idiosyncrasies, and boosting our self-awareness. We become thoughtful as a habit for choosing and chasing a life philosophy, and for making our life decisions rationally in line with the needs of humans' emotional and spiritual dimensions. We become flexible and open-minded towards other viewpoints and people's preferences, no matter how illogical they appear to us.

Vitality

Goodness is usually misperceived to require, or result in, a rather passive attitude towards people and society (and their prevalent tyrannies). While a civil type of stoicism is partially helpful for meditation and attaining the wholeness (goodness) of character, we should inject lots of vitality and passion in our lives to fulfil our physical and mental needs, while stabilizing our connections within society, too. Therefore, the type of withdrawal that, for example, monks and sages adopt to meditate is not compatible with the goals of goodness principles used in this book. In fact, we must be quite alert, conscious, proactive, and agile to foresee and defeat the unavoidable routine hardships of living, while also defeating the random tyrannies that sneak upon us from different sources.

So many battles we all must fight regularly—to stay afloat—drain so much of our mental and physical energy. Most of us need antidepressants, sleeping pills, alcohol, and drugs to go through another day. To maintain enough vigour to survive in a rather hostile society like ours, we need a good mix of optimism and passion for some worthwhile form of art or activity. Sadly, our hopes usually turn into helplessness when we fail to achieve our objectives or realize that our dreams had been only a mirage that would offer no solace or a remedy for our sense of loneliness and despair. Our efforts to think positive and stay optimistic feel futile and shaky. At the end, we often lose interest in our passionate views of life or certain activities, too, again due to either social pressures or pains of loneliness. So, expecting people to maintain so much optimism and vigour to satiate their spirits and become a better being, too, sounds rather too strenuous and unreasonable.

On the other hand, we cannot simply give up. In fact, we must somehow find good sources of energy for performing our daily routines, making our bodies healthy, and keeping our spirits high in pursuit of some worthwhile purposes for our lives. We need vitality even for becoming activists and revolutionaries as part of our mission to advocate personal and societal goodness.

Fortunately, this kind of divine vigour can be induced through deep spiritual beliefs and practices, though building and keeping those kinds of sacred beliefs cannot be straightforward.

A reasonable question that readers may ask is, 'How to raise our vitality and build all other pillars of goodness when our spirits are so dampened and we have lost all our hopes and faiths about life and society?' The simple answer is that only through gradual self-awareness—once we get the incentive to gauge and revamp our mentality and lifestyle for a chance to redeem our souls—we can gain the needed energy to pursue the path of goodness and attain our *personal* sense of spirituality. The whole purpose of this book is to stress on the challenges and benefits of 'being a better person' for a variety of goals noted all along, but mainly for gaining the incentive and vitality we need to build a more meaningful life for ourselves. Pursuing a goodness path is a very challenging process as much as it would be worth our while.

B. Form

While building the foundation for becoming a better being, we go through a huge transformation. Our inner and outer perspectives begin to reform, our new character forms around a fundamental life outlook, and we feel a rising level of harmony and humility as discussed below. Our personality flaws and identity crisis will begin to heal and a new form of being emerges from within us as we learn to behave in a more compassionate manner.

Harmony and humility begin to develop as a person masters all four elements of authenticity, autonomy, vision, and vitality to build the foundation of goodness. However, the two elements of authenticity and autonomy are more crucial for stirring harmony, whereas the vision and vitality elements are more instrumental for developing one's humility. Our self-image grows realistically, too, as we cherish only our humility, integrity, sincerity… Our ability to distinguish right from wrong grows, as we practise our being constantly based on proper worldviews and pure identity. The opportunity we get to dispose of our chronic arrogance and spite is by itself quite precious.

Harmony

As our self-image and self-esteem develop, a new sense of being brings us peace and harmony gradually, as if a solid, warm shell grows over the frigid skin that had covered our phony personality with a sense of vulnerability all along. We meet our helpless self and view the imposing outer forces, entities, and people in a new light. This progressive perspective is simple and real, while we accept the inevitability of life's hardships, people's helplessness, humanity's looming demise, religions' irresponsibility, God's ambiguous presence, social injustice, nature's beauty and cruelty, genders' growing disparity, the messiness of global conflicts, the universe's awkward awesomeness, and humans' spiritual knack behind their naivety and failures to find a meaning for existence and a functional family. Now we have grown into a resilient and reliable form with a rather sensible mentality. Thus, instead of expecting people to grasp and empathize with our viewpoints and needs, we strive to cope with their idiosyncrasies and naiveties mostly driven by social teachings. We become open-minded and flexible when dealing with people, especially family and friends.

A main feature of this harmony is a noble urge for sincerity with our soul as well as other people, even in light of their lack of appreciation for our modesty and honesty. We also build a higher degree of fairness, patience, and tolerance. In fact, we must get ready for people's deeper animosity and faster rejection when our new mannerism, especially civil stoicism, defies their values. We are not swayed or irritated by people's persistence to push us with their conventional means of thinking and behaving. Our tactful disregard for their lifestyles still upset people who are addicted to their showy mentalities and mannerism and trapped in a wide network of lies and deceit. In fact, another big feature of our sense of harmony is a rising level of compassion, which we show towards everybody, despite our disappointments with people, family, and society. Again, open-mindedness and flexibility are crucial for building the desired harmony.

For being better beings, we must grasp the responsibility and art of playing a few dozen roles throughout our lives, as men, women, spouses, companions, parents, children, citizens, leaders, neighbours, employees, managers, mentors, teachers, humans, friends, etc. Every one of these complex roles has a unique set of characteristics and demands, so mastering them with a practical, harmonious attitude would be both hard and crucial for building social values, cultures, families, and becoming rounded better beings. We should understand and play all these roles diligently, while thinking and behaving within a harmonious frame of mind and philosophy for serving and boosting our Self, integrity, and self-reliance. These roles have many conflicting elements, in fact, so playing them simultaneously, e.g., as a man, husband, parent, and leader, would become quite hard and risky, since we should satisfy many other people, while remaining as faithful to our principles and convictions as possible. A big book can be written about the principles and objectives of each one of our roles and then even a bigger book about balancing all these roles to fulfil our own personal stoic needs, while humouring or helping people in each special category, too.

We also realize the merits of having a simple life for keeping our inner peace and bearing the burdens of living better. We learn to rely on our grown sense of harmony, honesty, and compassion to withstand loneliness and relative isolation with grace.

Humility

The other prominent feature of our evolving form (our authentic individualism) is humility. During the process of developing the main pillars of goodness, we learn about our nothingness as a person and human. Thus, we grow a genuine sense of humility that is useful for connecting to our essence as a being, but never as another mechanism to humour or humiliate others.

Nowadays, people are extremely eager to prove (and force) their individualism, which they assume is achieved through a show of pomposity and superiority. People are driven to build phony confidences and convictions, while trusting their showy attitudes to acquire lots of love, wealth, and power as symbols of success. Actually, the more naïve, insecure, and incompetent a person is, the haughtier s/he behaves in order to compete in the ongoing social war for portraying a crooked individualism. Thus, people have a very low knack for teamwork as well as a natural sense of personal image, dignity, independence, compassion, and pride—the true parameters of individualism. *Amazingly bizarre, in fact, showing humility feels quite unnatural and embarrassing to most people nowadays!*

Therefore, as a shocking and significant realization, while building the six pillars of goodness, we learn how wrong our definition of individualism has been. We learn that humility, not haughtiness, is the main property and sign of individualism among many other important parameters that must also exist in a person. Yet, the humbler a person becomes, the higher his/her chances would be to acquire and maintain the right characteristics of individualism and spiritualism. Actually, individualism is not a personal property the way we like to show it off publicly to gain approval and power. Rather, individualism is just a *self-cleansing mechanism* for building the right foundation and form as a human and reaching the ultimate sense of goodness, i.e., selflessness. Although individualism and selflessness are different concepts, their mix grows our personal sense of spiritualism. Individualism refers to personal attributes that we develop for our easier daily encounters, but mostly for smoothing the process of gaining our ultimate goal of selflessness and inner completeness. In return, selflessness helps us discover and keep our individualism intact within a phony social realm.

Developing humility need not be a big task indeed, but rather a natural process. In fact, it is amazing we still have not realized our (humans') nothingness. More astonishingly, we actually feel embarrassed to adopt humility as a natural knack for living and relating to other people and nature. Instead, we strive to build conceit by forcing our psyches believe in our superiority, while we abuse others and brag. This huge human misunderstanding of its being has evolved through history and worsened in the new era due to crooked social teachings that have also tainted human nature and ego gradually. Our egotism merely reflects humans' juvenile mentality grown so unnaturally over centuries and now turning into an epidemic. Accordingly, we all behave so foolishly and destructively contrary to a wise individual's unconditional, prompt acceptance of his/her nothingness!

C. Finale

Some privileged individuals gain enough harmony and humility eventually to reach divinity and selflessness as the final stage of goodness, then live the rest of their lives in peace with themselves and others within a personal sense of spirituality.

Divinity (Self-wholeness)

The more conscious we become about our 'self,' during the process of building the six pillars of goodness, the more complete we become. This would induce a sense of divinity merely in terms of self-wholeness but also selflessness. This sounds like a big irony to lose self (become selfless) when we crave and strive to grasp it all our lives and finally achieve it with our feeling of self-wholeness. However, this complex, delicate feeling of both self-wholeness and selflessness is yet another mystery about self and goodness, which will be explained later. Of course, a bigger mystery, which is rather resolved in this chapter, is that goodness and self have an inherent link. We like to believe that goodness is the only venue to penetrate our highly private and neglected self. And we believe that only by grasping our self we gain the power to maintain our goodness on a long-term basis. In fact, goodness is the art of mastering self-wholeness and selflessness together. The art of being!

Chapter Seven
Badness Epidemic

The goodness endeavour outlined in the last chapter—to boost our spirits through spirituality—is a strenuous task. In particular, the self-cleansing part is tough, since badness is more akin and appealing to human nature than goodness. Too many wicked urges bombards us regularly and we enjoy our cockiness so much, whereas we should extend lots of efforts to be even slightly humble or show a noble gesture. Besides the big variety of quirks that almost everybody develops and becomes bad enough already, most of us pamper many devilish feelings and thoughts in order to satiate our sick psyches and vile urges. Our horrific drive for sexuality alone ruins our lives, as we feel too helpless to curb this maddening urge. In all, we are too bad in general to even realize the purpose of goodness, let alone remain loyal to our sense of decency or even ponder a plan for testing the chance of cleansing our souls.

On top of our untameable nature, we are born into a culture that renders (and often even promotes) all sorts of incentives and justifications to maximize our sinful urges. Accordingly, humans now contain too much aggressiveness, arrogance, and spite to get along harmoniously or explore the means of developing a more peaceful character. In fact, we enjoy creating hostility and tension every day at so many fronts as a normal way of relating. Wars are escalating all over the world between nations, religions, ethnic groups, political parties, genders, and within families, while the new generations of parents and children have become estranged. We are in war with nature and environment. We are in war with our spirits when we do not know how to resolve our loneliness, yet cannot stop alienating people with our arrogance, either. We are in war with God too, as we have lost our faiths in general, while we question His wisdom for allegedly sending us all these contradictory religions in hopes of teaching us to become better beings after creating us so faulty to begin with.

Badness Pyramid (Structure)

Unlike goodness that grows gradually as a person gains certain virtues, badness builds fast automatically since people lose their identities and characters quickly in childhood. Thus, they develop vast idiosyncrasies, smother their spirits, and contract too many social and personal diseases noted in this chapter. The badness pyramid (structure) has a 'Self'-damaging Foundation, turns us into a crooked Form, and leads to Devilry as Diagram 7.1 shows. While the six pillars of badness are fully in contrast and parallel to the six pillars of goodness, they have specific effects on human psyche that must be studied and curbed effectively first. One must face up to one's evils and their deep sources, while building one's goodness incentive and plans for a long goodness endeavour.

A. Foundation
- Superficiality
- Self-pity
- Naivety
- Negativity

B. Form
- Neurosis
- Narcissism

C. Finale
- Devilry

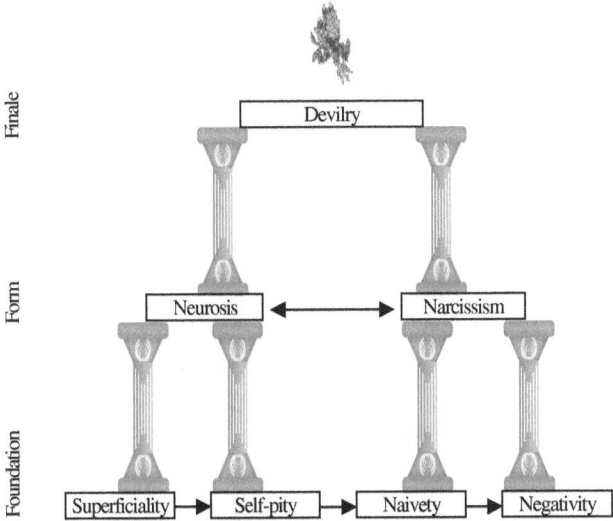

Diagram 7.1: Badness Pyramid (Structure)

A. Foundation

The badness foundation is deep-rooted in humans' substandard nature and solidifies by enormous social and parental influences that contaminate our personalities and spirits. It entails a pervasive self-destructive process, during which we build up self-pity and a sense of entitlement, learn superficiality, become too naïve, and develop lots of negativity about life, people, and ourselves.

Superficiality

Instead of grasping our real needs, authenticity, and self, we learn to develop and portray a phony personality to fit in society, be popular, look happy, appear positive, hide our idiosyncrasies, fool people, show off our power, brag about our success and wealth, etc. Accordingly, without an authentic identity or a solid personality, we remain confused, shallow, and susceptible to all kinds of negative forces in society that goad more badness. Of course, superficiality is not merely an antonym for authenticity, since a person can be neither. That would reflect a kind of passive or undeveloped identity with many causes and effects of its own. The point is that a person's level of badness usually grows along with the rise of his/her superficiality for a variety of reasons.

Self-pity

Instead of growing a proper self-image and true confidence that are necessary for developing self-reliance, we are too needy for attention and affection nowadays. Accordingly, we grow a lot of self-pity, as we feel ignored or lonely in our highly mechanical, materialistic societies. While we believe we deserve a lot, people appear apathetic towards us with no appreciation of who we are. This condition is also the result of our excessive self-indulgence and dwelling on our bad luck or life's hardships. Mostly, we keep raising our sense of failure and self-pity, as we struggle to enjoy life in its fullest, capture happiness and love, and receive so many other alleged merits of social living that we feel entitled to.

Naivety

Instead of striving to envision life's harsh realities, adapt wisely, and search within our inner self to explore our potentialities and ingenuity, most of us remain too idealistic about life, society, happiness, etc., usually around too many raw ambitions. We live in delusion with a load of misperceptions about the purpose of living and the kind of life philosophy that can bring us peace of mind. Most damaging and stressful are our perceptions of life, political systems, socioeconomic environment, and society's role and capacity to work for people. We waste our energy, time, and money on trivia and struggle for so many materialistic goals. We suffer a lifetime simply due our naiveté and our inability to grasp and handle life's hardships that are mostly caused by our own crude means of thinking and building our societies.

Negativity

Instead of preparing ourselves for lifelong confrontations with social and human evils through spiritual vitality, we have become vastly negative, nagging, and lethargic, though still feign positive thinking, too. In fact, as our rising ambitions and expectations from life make us too needy and sensitive, every simple setback agitates us and we feel defeated and offended. Along with our crooked perceptions of reality, we fail to grow a proper vision of life, thus build more illusions and negativity in our psyches.

B. Form

Neurosis

The four elements of badness discussed above contaminate the foundation of our being and prevent any possibility for bringing some sense of contentment and harmony into our lives. Instead, we turn into angry, spiteful, and wicked persons, even though we often try, and succeed, to hide our outrage and bitter personality. Without the goodness foundation (e.g., authenticity, autonomy, vision, and vitality, as shown in Diagram 6.1) people develop a great deal of idiosyncrasies already. However, when the badness foundation overwhelms a person, his or her neurosis increases extensively. Instead of harmony and peace, we grow a great deal of inner conflicts, insecurities, anxiety, and confrontations with people and society. We also become too rigid and spiteful.

Narcissism

Ironically, we have also become the most arrogant humans ever, instead of learning humility. It is truly amazing that we still have not realized our (humans') nothingness and instead hope to build our characters around arrogance and ignorance. We are adamant to live in delusions and dreams and prove our stupidity forever!

C. Finale

Devilry

At the end, with a personality developed over a shaky, wicked foundation, many of us are formed into neurotic, narcissistic, and nervous people who think and behave like the devil. The more we have supposedly become modern and civilized, the more we have lost touch with our true being and soul. We are crooked and deceitful mostly due to our life experiences that construct the foundation and form of our being according to badness elements and factors noted in this chapter. Then, we hurt each other, create big incentives for devilry, and cause social chaos in the process.

The Symptoms of Our Badness

The extent and effect of our badness and stupidity are evident in our daily actions and the way we treat and threaten one another. Throughout this book, especially Chapter Two, many symptoms of human badness have been noted as hurdles for being better beings. Yet, reiterating the main factors of the Badness Epidemic along the six pillars of the badness is crucial. Especially, we are getting snottier and phonier due to our zeal nowadays to establish and express our individualism without knowing its properties and purposes. Our naïve perception of independence has stirred a fast process of disintegration at all social levels rather than finding means of bringing people together. On the one hand, we are keen to create an odd social identity for ourselves in hopes of finding wealth and happiness and possibly even some respect and relief. This endless search and pretensions already reveals the extent of both our desperation and neediness. It reveals how vastly we have become dependent on one another and symbols of social life. On the other hand, we seek separation quickly with the first sign of inconvenience. We feel lonely and lost without other people's attention, but do not have the right mentality and mood to sustain our relationships without causing so much agony for one another. We fail to understand and balance our conflicting needs for both dependence and independence at personal or global level or within our cultural or ideological groups. Different social and political factions are seeking independence and separation, while realizing their deep vulnerability to survive without other nations' help and a balanced harmony and unity around the world. The simple fact is that we humans do not have commonsense, mental capacity, right nature, and pure incentives to set our priorities straight. *At the end, we do not even know what we want or is right for us!*

For a supposedly intelligent species, it feels that our priorities are totally screwed up. For example, we spend so much time, money, and energy on building all kinds of sophisticated armoury to engage in useless wars, which bring us only more destruction, misery, and alienation across the globe. We do not learn how to elect leaders who are not so utterly corrupt and ignorant. We do not learn anything from our failures in Vietnam, Afghanistan, Iraq, Libya, Syria, Yemen, and dozen other places. At the same time, it is not hard to envisage how healthier and happier people could live if these monies and efforts were devoted to humans' welfare fairly. Instead, we allow corporate elites build more war equipments and ideologies to stir citizens' minds for systemic badness, devastating exploitation of nations and people, and promoting hostility at global, social, and personal levels.

Our extensive efforts and costs in space exploration is another example of our misplaced priorities. While scientific discoveries along the way have been impressive and important, it seems odd that we try to explore the possibility of life on any other planet, which we can never even reach, or living on Mars or Moon when most people have no basic life on our own dying planet. We want to tame hostile planets and learn about aliens, while ignoring the fact that we are killing our perfectly habitable and lively planet and refuse to find easier ways of understanding our own kinds—such deprived humans. Space exploration is mostly for expanding nations' control, surveillance, and commercial capacities, which are more akin to humans' appetite for vast controversy and vanity than harmony. It is even weirder that at least half of us still deny the facts about the speed we are destroying our own planet and human life. We cannot feel how people's endless struggles with their miseries are sucking life out of them. Our fantastic and raw scientific curiosities are used to produce TV sitcoms and movies for pushing commercials and selling more useless stuff to people and sinking them deeper in a delusional world, while killing their spirits' innate curiosity for goodness all along. All these wastes and vanities reveal a lot about humans' irrationality, low foresight about their real needs and priorities, and the absence of a global vision and coordinated efforts for everybody's benefit in the long run. These are all great evidences of humans' wicked nature and chronic badness on top of their dire stupidity.

The point is that expanding our territories or even the science we can master cannot help us if we cannot fulfil even our basic needs, including a calm psyche and spirit, or find the means of a basic level of social harmony. It just feels ridiculous to expend so much effort on fantastic and futuristic goals when human demise looks so imminent and when humans' ability for coexistence and peace feels so vastly questionable. Should not we devote at least half of the energy we are wasting on so many auxiliary, complex objectives to find simple solutions for urgent, obvious problems facing humanity? Why is it hard for humans to see these simple points? What is the point of trying so hard to grow national GDPs just for running our crooked socioeconomic structure, produce more junk food and goods, waste 50-60% of our good food, fill our lands and oceans with plastic and garbage, and raise the world's helpless population to work as slaves for sustaining such nonsensical ways of living at the cost of polluting the biosphere and killing nature? Are not we mad, bad, and sad enough yet?

The main symptom of our badness is our inability to learn anything from our mistakes and stop being so stubborn about our flawed ideologies and economic systems. We are sacrificing our souls and health, wasting our energies in vain on piling up useless stuff and technologies, making and watching so much foolish movies, disregarding our basic needs for living with dignity, and sustaining a demented social structure that concentrates only on the immediate interests of a bunch of inept elite capitalists.

This lack of social harmony and direction has badly infected people's mentality on top of all the tension and suffering they must endure. More sadly, we spoil our kids according to so many frivolous social values that raise their expectations from life and people unrealistically, too, rather than teaching them the growing complexities of life in the new era. Our kids grow up thinking about having fun and an exciting life more than they learn and think about having a peaceful existence within a healthy family and keeping it together and happy. Therefore, most people end up living without a family or suffer in dysfunctional ones with lots of stress and depression. We have simply shown no capacity to set our priorities straight to at least avoid adding to our hardships with our naïve, narrow minds. Social living is now confusing and hurting us more than giving us chances for personal development and inner peace. Thus, we can say that humans' mentality and priorities are badly screwed up, while our badness is hurting us personally as much as it damages society, all beings, and nature.

The Menace of Social Living

In our demanding, demeaning, and daunting world, we witness a great majority of people waking up everyday merely worrying about the crooked roles and games they should play all day like senseless, heartless robots. Their minds are set to find gimmicks to sell all kinds of products and services to people with lies, propagandas, and advertising. The saddest part of this mentality is our sense of entitlement, as we have now come to believe that our attitudes and expectations are acceptable and normal, if not admirable. Meanwhile, all these social pressures to sell, buy, or discard stuff turn us into stressed, vengeful people. Accordingly, social living is most responsible for the badness epidemic, while people strive to, i) cope with corruption and malice besieging all social systems, and ii) relate to, or tolerate, the mass of pompous, phony people.

Humans' mentalities are systematically formed around shoddy principles and plans nowadays to serve their egos relentlessly and maximize their wealth and self-gratification at all costs. We think we must play along with this prevailing social game if we want to succeed and get accepted amongst the mainstream. Accordingly, we now judge people's beliefs, personalities, and worthiness based on the same shallow criteria we apply to define happiness and success with the biggest emphasis on materialism. We value only those who are playing the same wicked games and roles to get wealthy and advance in society according to their appetite for corruption and aptitude for exploiting the public. In all, we now ponder and plan how best to manipulate others for satiating our vast emotional or financial hunger regardless of the effects of our actions on other people and nations.

It feels weird when we realize people respond to our knack for snobbery more than they appreciate our humility. Thus, we grow more arrogance and ruin our spirit just to make a living or keep a minimum social contact. Sadly, instead of exploring our individualism with honour and integrity through goodness path, we eventually think and behave foolishly like the mainstream in order to handle these conceited clowns. We are forced to play too many crooked roles and games if we wish to be accepted and stay in the flock. In the end, the lure or necessity of being a crook is too high to resist. That is how social living turns us into bad individuals, and then we feel lousy about it *sometimes*, too! That is why we hardly get a chance to explore our inherent qualities as a human. In such an addictive, tempting environment, we surely need a superhuman power to come down from the clouds with our haughtiness and admit to our nothingness. Therefore, the transition from utter selfishness to pure selflessness would be more like a miracle. Achieving such a huge personal growth and commitment would be a very big challenge and a major leap.

That is why we never get a chance to nurture our self and true individualism or develop moral principles.

The stupider a person is, nowadays, the more snobbish he/she behaves in hopes of building some kind of image and self-worth for him/herself. His/her embedded arrogance as a routine means of communication, while trying to mix it with his/her fake friendly gestures and calculating words, is just embarrassing. In return, this infantile epidemic for snobbery and showiness reveals the sheer size of fools hurting this planet and the depth of insecurities and foolishness in society. Then, it also makes us wonder often, 'Why humans cannot grasp their nothingness.'

Despite our rising pomposity, we have become too emotional and oversensitive as well. We get annoyed quickly when others mistreat or snub us, thus we retaliate harshly because of our oversensitivity and rash emotional distress. Meanwhile, another emerging psychological paradox is people's extreme insensitivity when judging others, despite their own oversensitivity in similar situations. They become offended and sad quickly when they feel mistreated, but ignore how their own carelessness hurts others—again reflecting their insecurity and vanity, of course. Ironically, often their oversensitivity turns them into spiteful, cruel persons. They dismiss quickly any hints they get about their insensitivity, too. Instead, they just get more defensive and hostile, while still strive to justify their attitude with some lame logic or aggression. People's dual tendency for both oversensitivity and insensitivity is in fact a complex paradox—another bizarre phenomenon of the new era. It is somewhat like their obsession nowadays for both dependence and independence erratically.

Sadly, human logic does not work properly, either, for settling our differences or at least communicating a bit more effectively. We often have difficulty expressing our logic or making others see our points. Accordingly, we get frustrated and discouraged when we try to reason with people (e.g., about their loose, vicious dog attacking us whenever we stroll in the neighbourhood). They usually take our logical, calm approach the wrong way and abuse us more (even in defence of their mad dog). Our efforts to state our concerns calmly go to waste, whereas craziness and bullying deter people from hurting us somewhat. It feels even weirder when we go out of our ways to be nice and do favours for people, especially our family and friends, and they mistake our goodwill for our vulnerability and neediness. Instead of appreciating our gracious gestures, they merely become more demanding and careless and enjoy their snobbery like another triumph for today.

Badness Factory

It is sad that people give one another space only through illogical and boorish behaviour, as if only lunacy and intimidation (instead of reason) work in the new era. This purposeful irrationality, i.e., bullying tactics, apparently works best for those with low mental capacity and vindictive characters, including most of our leaders! However, the rather saner half of the population cannot bear, or function within, this malicious, humiliating environment. This demented option (i.e., abuse and bullying) surely cannot be used to solve personal, national, and international problems. Still, this is how people, nations, and leaders have been behaving all along and hoping to succeed. Even when some flickers of hope grow in the horizon occasionally about nations finding a calmer means of relating, the leading nation, the deemed superpower, elects a bully as its president to terrorize the world with his nonsensical views, words, and actions. Thus, we ignorant human species are doomed, *according to my logic!*

The badness epidemic discussed in this book proves humans' innate inability to relate either naturally or civilly! It stresses our preference to communicate mostly by direct or subtle snobbery. The situation has gotten ten folds sadder and tougher since all these painful symptoms of social downfall have also infected our loved ones whom we must face illogically with abusive tactics, e.g., when they try to snub us or misinterpret our soft emotions towards them. It hurts, especially, to feel that the more successful (and busy) our children become, the more snobbish, careless, and uncompassionate they become, which only reflects the perils of social adaptation in this badness factory. In fact, family members' attitudes, even those seemingly normal ones, make us angry and sad about the way people's values have infected their judgments, deeds, and sensitivity just for adapting and proving themselves in society, yet only towards social and human demise.

Obviously, family quarrels raise our cynicism about humans' growing badness much faster and deeper. Then, we destroy our spirits, too, as we keep reminding and forcing ourselves to be equally careless and bad, just to avoid being hurt or disappointed again and again in society, even by our close family. Surely, we strive to be cunning or tactful about our badness, too, hoping to conceal our malice and intentions. We pretend to be honest and compassionate, which only makes us also look like fools. All along, we drain our spirits even further for all the roles and games we play a lifetime, while bearing the pain of all our pretences and insincerity as well as others', especially our loved ones. It is weird how we all believe to be playing our roles perfectly to fool people and imagining they cannot detect our shams!

Amazingly, we all still believe to be wise, wonderful, flawless beings! Of course, sometimes we feel or guess people's cynicism about our sanity and sincerity—which simply sounds too absurd and nonsensical in our minds. In fact, not only we believe to be perfect individuals, but also expect people to think and behave exactly like us, based on our impressions of life and perfection. Yet, ironically, we often resent people with idiosyncrasies similar to our own. We simply do not see, or care about, the same defects in ourselves, which we usually cherish in ourselves, in fact.

Anyhow, our societies have now turned into a huge badness factory for perfecting people's drive for malice and abuse. It is a depressing situation when we witness even good people become careless and cruel out of necessity, merely for coping with other people's arrogance that appears even in their simple gestures, e.g., not answering their phones or returning our calls as another snubbing habit. Then again, we are all tired of answering our phones due to telemarketers' non-stop intrusion to sell us useless stuff or to con us with all kinds of schemes that crooks and social pests are inventing. The volume of daily calls and nuisances, e.g., to offer hearing checkups, financial services, furnace cleaning or other services, waste lots of our energy and patience. Many real estate agents call to convince us sell our residents, as if we were silly to make that kind of decision spontaneously, e.g., when they insist a swift surge of buyers has created a lucrative market and demand *in our neighbourhood*. Of course, too many naïve people fall for these gimmicks and intrusions, which in turn stir many salespeople and agents copy one another to lure people with their schemes and sales pitches. The number of scams thru internet, phone, TV, and mail is driving people mad and our governments cannot, or do not want to, do anything about this daily torture if people answer their phones or read their emails.

The depth and scope of badness epidemic, i.e., people's sense of entitlement and self-interest, feels *fundamentally absurd* when professionals, even professors, politicians, presidents, police, and lawyers lack enough compassion and competence, and instead strive to screw up people out of ignorance and greed. Especially, it is maddening when almost all medical doctors and dentists now focus on money, instead of duty. A big book can be written about this depressing social phenomenon all by itself! It sounds crazy, but more plausible everyday, to believe that doctors deliberately delay curing people or maybe even making them sicker merely for raising the volume of our visits and maximizing their profits. What is the nature of our societies now, then? How much more devilish we humans want to think and behave?

The effects of capitalism on this badness factory and on our mentality are horrendous. Now, people's thirst for materialism, instead of morality, has made them insensitive, irresponsible, and deceitful all around and ruined any residues of piety that might have been in human nature. The saddest result of this capitalistic mentality is that we trust one another very little these days for good reasons. In return, our distrust of people, especially family members and doctors, is ruining many other facets of social structure and families. It is shameful that even our rising levels of cynicism in society and families are the effects of our new value systems built around greed. It is simply disheartening and hard to believe how we have let our socioeconomic systems and values turn us into such tainted and tormented species.

In this chaotic society, people are forced to get rude to deter so many social pests, who are victims of the current socioeconomic setting themselves. We are either turned into fools that indulge these crooks and fall for their gimmicks, or realize that the only way to minimize these daily intrusions and deceits is to be rude and aggressive ourselves. So, how could anybody remain patient and caring in such an agitating, hopeless social environment? How should we behave, then, when it feels risky these days to be fair, trustful, and open? Do we have any choice but getting more wicked ourselves every day?

In the game of death in France, 81% of contestants obeyed the authority and decided to impose the highest level of electric shock and pain on each other. They did it while knowing the high risks of hurting other contestants, just for increasing their own chance of success in the game and for winning the authorities' approval. Only 9 out of 80 people disobeyed the authority and stopped playing the game in order to avoid inflicting more pain on other contestants. This tiny group is most likely perceived as weird or chickens by the cruel obedient group and others as well. These types of statistics demonstrate humans' wicked mentality and nature these days and reflect our way of setting our personal priorities even if it means abandoning our basic sense of decency and compassion for other human beings.

Therefore, those who insist on the purity of human nature seem fully out of touch with reality, given all the clear evidences around us about humans' inferior genetics and crude mentalities. In fact, grasping the causes of human badness and admitting our weaknesses is the first step on the path of goodness. We should accept the ultimate truth, once and for all, that humans are created too weak to curb the large assortment of crooked urges for deceit, rivalry, thievery, jealousy, controversy, revenge, power, and many others—especially our sexual drive. Even the allegedly devoted clerics have major difficulty remaining faithful to their beliefs, despite all their pretences, bothering themselves and us with their lectures about the possibility of inhibiting our sins adequately. We must be under no illusion: Human nature is horrible! Simply, God's original design and implanting all sorts of unmanageable human urges are behind this entire badness epidemic. We are bad by nature and need special awareness and efforts to overcome our god-given flaws, *if we are interested in being better beings!*

If only we could be honest and objective enough to reflect on our various thoughts and deeds in a day, we would realize how deeply bad we are as a person and how wicked human nature is in general. All honest people would reach the same conclusions about the depth of human wickedness, despite humans' urge for self-love and regular misperceptions about our virtues. Thus, the patience and resolve required to pursue our goodness regimens within this badness factory must be huge!

Of course, there are always heroes who take risks or sacrifice themselves to help others. Some even jump in rapid currents in order to save a drowning person or rush to a burning car to rescue a trapped driver even if they realize the futility of their courage. This phenomenon, i.e., our selfless eagerness to help others at the time of crisis, somehow appears to make the job of assessing the nature of humans harder. Yet, people's rather random gestures of goodness do not make up for their inherent, systematic urge to be self-centred and bad. Their random pity does not help humans' inability to find the means of living together in some relative peace and harmony. The main proof of our inability for goodness is the wholesome social mayhem that humans have created and their inability for teamwork and agreeing about a lasting order in society and a kind of lifestyle that could support that. We are not good enough to at least avoid human race's looming destiny.

At the same time, many people suffer in their deep conscious about their rather forced sneaky badness just to survive in society without getting hurt too much. Deep down they still ponder the merits and moods of goodness and fear the outcomes of humans' devilry. The only advantage of people's low capacity to change against their deep genetic nature is that 'finer people do not change' their characters and become evils as fast and easily as most people do, even when exposed to badness. However, their inner conflicts perturb them for not being as cunning as others naturally—due to their passive personalities or perhaps even their naïve, natural goodness.

Ironically, we already seem to know all these sad facts about the menace of social living nowadays. Many of us acknowledge the inevitability of our demise and some religions look forward to it eagerly in fact. This poses yet another cause for concern about human logic and sanity when people accept, or fight fiercely for, such nonsensical religious mottos—e.g., ending humanity to reach afterlife faster. Relying on some sort of juvenile faith for a better world beyond our present realm—in hopes of a more bearable or less terrifying existence—certainly reveals the depth of humans' pains and naiveté. The way those fanatic groups crave the chance of human demise as a fateful beginning toward Armageddon and reaching afterlife and relief, along with eternal pleasure, is quite educational. Their inadvertent admission of humans' inability to ever build a liveable setting on earth—despite all those religious teachings—is also enlightening. However, more amazing, is their naiveté about another form of self-gratifying existence, which is their entitlement and definite merely due to their blind acceptance of a certain religion, which many have admitted its teachings' vanity passively. What a helpless species we have always been! Still, even weirder is how dumber and sadder we are becoming every day! *For humour only, it is interesting to add that we are apparently also certain that at least the lucky group going to heaven would automatically know how to get along very nicely without any more confrontations! Is God going to change our nature on our way to heaven, or we swiftly learn how to behave and communicate properly? Or maybe no human interaction is allowed or needed in heaven!*

Meanwhile, even those raw traditional ethics and forces that deterred human evil somewhat seem to have lost their potency nowadays. Maybe this is due to the growing social burdens and badness, as well as our rising doubts about the value of religions or living at all. On the one hand, questioning our existence and a divine dimension, maybe even afterlife, is a useful natural drive in our DNA. This curiosity stirs our philosophical ideas, spiritual beliefs, and arguments that could goad us to explore goodness. On the other hand, our evil deeds and justifications for badness feel more natural every generation. The reason is that our urges for badness increase when they feel so necessary and natural, and when we are less fearful of retribution by society or God. *Many of us are fed up with existence, anyway!*

Badness Factory's Products

Sadly, the badness factory is getting more efficient and effective every day as socioeconomic mechanisms falter faster worldwide. We have become more reckless and sinful every decade in line with our growing doubts about religious values and promises, as well as our scepticism about society altogether. For one thing, our sexual perversions have skyrocketed and become a way of life in the new era. Thus, even when we mature in one way and doubt the rationality and usefulness of religious teachings, we just abuse our new wisdom to become more reckless and bad in other ways. Now, the badness business is booming with unprecedented speed, since we are simply adamant to ignore all the warnings about humans' looming fate and resist to mature. Instead, our modern wisdom is that, *we should enjoy our lives as much as possible!*

Well, this new radical philosophy—*crooked wisdom*—sounds like a rational principle to all of us. However, the problem is that we get carried away with our imaginations and drive for liberty.

First, we imagine that enjoying life is easy or even prudent for us to put too much thoughts and energy into it. We misinterpret this wisdom, as we have come to believe that 'as much as possible' is an emphasis to overindulge ourselves regardless of its rationality —even at the cost of ignoring many other important aspect of life and reality. We see the goal of enjoying every minute of our lives *as a holy criterion to dilute our social obligations and spiritual needs.* We downplay our moral principles and health just to enjoy ourselves. We ignore our families and friends when they seem to hinder our urge for pleasure. We sacrifice our marriages, pride, and personal integrity to pursue some fantasies about happiness and love in other places and in other people's arms.

And of course, we get opposite results! We fail to enjoy our being, since our crude notion of 'enjoying our lives to the fullest' is simply fooling us. Instead, we cause ourselves more frustration and depression, because all our illusions about love, happiness, and pleasure are merely making us less conscious of our being and less conscientious about other people's needs. We think our welfare and even imaginary whims should take precedence over everybody else's needs and our moral obligation towards them. Our juvenile justification for self-gratification—since we live only once—is ruining our identity and feeding our evil nature further. These infantile social values and ideologies have pushed us into a world of delusions, mostly about the meaning and implications of happiness, family, social life, and love. Family relationships and values had evolved in old cultures after centuries of reflections and trials and errors. Yet, in the 21st century, we have thrown out all that wisdom quickly in hopes of capturing happiness and more pleasure, with such horrific results and so much gender conflicts.

We have now become spoiled mentally due to the effects of materialism, individualism, and commercialization, even on the type of reading materials and ideologies sold to the public only for profit motives rather than their values for building humans' character and families. We are only nurturing people's urges for badness instead of following a reflective path to goodness, which is by the way the only path to enjoy life realistically in the long run, anyway. Our raw, erratic pleasures cannot provide a lasting sense of self-realization and self-worth, which are the only means of gaining the wisdom for love and happiness.

Besides the fundamental flaws of our new crude philosophy regarding self-gratification (enjoying our lives to the fullest), this juvenile objective is only raising stress in society. This is because people think, or push themselves, so much about the means of fulfilling this goal—often as a show of modernism—and to prove their success in pursuing this moronic path of life. Yet, in reality, they strive to hide all their failures and frustrations for not getting anywhere. They must try hard to ensure they are not perceived as failures, incapable of achieving the success that people should find and parade energetically. They should pretend diligently—like everybody else—to know the secrets of happiness and signs of their presumed accomplishments so far. Deep down, however, most of us often feel like the only loser in society and question our ability and luck for finding happiness, love, popularity, and success the same way others seem to be enjoying and flaunting it around us. Therefore, at the end, the more we seek gratification, the more we stress and confuse ourselves. All along, we carry the burdens of all these concealments, games, and pretensions. Thus, we lose our identities, too.

Another product of our obsession for 'enjoying our lives' is our addiction to over-socializing in the new era. In particular, the youths feel obliged to spend 5-6 hours every day on their phones to stay within social circles and norms. This waste of time and brain leads to mental health problems–mostly among girls.[*] This trend is another symptom of our desperate attempt to find that illusive happiness that everybody is seeking as a social fad in his or her popularity contests. Instead of learning about the means of defining our identities and strengthening our friendships and self,

---

[*] This is according to Dr. Corine Carlisle findings–Clinical Head, Youth Addiction and Concurrent Disorders Service at the Centre for Addiction and Mental Health in Canada.

we just follow some pathetic ways of finding more friends, repeat some faddish slogans to one another, and parade our phony ideas and personalities like a bunch of deprived juveniles. Nowadays, everybody must adopt and obey these silly popularity rules to build his/her shallow and showy identity—since s/he just cannot build an authentic identity to begin with.

Our needs (especially youths') for attention and passion have skyrocketed in the new era for absurd reasons, mainly insecurity or drive for self-gratification and fame. However, the rising level of people's mania for this type of mentality, as an expression of individualism, has created so much alienation and loneliness in society. We have major difficulties finding right companions and we have a harder time sustaining our relationships. People opt for separation and divorce too quickly in hopes of finding a more suitable partner soon. Overall, people have become too picky, grumpy, demanding, impatient, and arrogant to be satisfied in any relationship that would have been considered quite normal a few decades ago.

Then, our rising obsessions for raw individualism, happiness, and love fuel our sense of loneliness, too, as those illusions and ideals hardly materialize for most people. In fact, individualism, love, and happiness are often too contradictory ideals to aspire as a package. Thus, we get testy and vengeful because of all these failures, deprivations, and rising insecurities. Our badness urges are triggered severely and faster, too, when we feel lonely and insecure, as we imagine so many people out there having fun and enjoying lots of free love. Ironically, the sense of loneliness and insecurity does not fade for most of us, anyway, even if we are pushing ourselves in random relationships in hopes of feeling happy and getting a taste of love. Even if we have a family, the high level of conflicts and alienation with our spouses and kids makes us feel so terribly lonely psychologically, which is often worse than being alone merely physically.

Accordingly, the mere sense of loneliness, with or without a family, aggravates our badness towards society and our families.

We try to retaliate, as we usually do not know how to be more self-reliant. We cannot fathom civil manners of handling people's apathy or showing our frustration, either. Instead, we often feel obliged to react in either snobbish or sneaky manners, too, mostly for hiding our insecurities or defending ourselves, until we finally lose our sanity and get violent, too. Thus, people raise not mere badness in society, but rather the worst of themselves and one another due to their loneliness, insecurities, games, neediness, and sly reprisals. Naturally, they also hate those people they cannot manipulate easily. The cleverer a person is, the more s/he tries to exploit others financially and emotionally, as if s/he feels obliged or driven to be abusive just to prove being smarter than others!

Besides raising people's overall evil, loneliness and insecurity cause deep depression and suicides these days, as people are not trained and prepared to face life's realities alone. After so much optimism and incessant efforts to enrich their lives through love and reliable friends, their hearts and souls shatter when they face reality by repeated failures and their sense of loneliness grows.

At last, many of us learn to cope with loneliness thru a mixed sense of resignation and despair, or by accepting a mediocre mate to share a lousy life together. Either way, both our badness urges and depression heighten as we just try to cope with our despair and mental fatigue without getting a chance to explore our being. Naturally, under these circumstances, it feels quite silly to ponder or foster goodness and try to solve our social and family issues with patience and compassion. Instead, we now let more badness, aggression, and rebellion dominate our thoughts and deeds.

The big irony is that the reason for many people's loneliness is not the lack of enough people for socializing. Rather, the major hurdle for our inability to find the right companion is our own controversial personalities, arrogance, and high expectations from life and one another. We do not get along or enjoy each other due to our misperceptions and erroneous ideologies about life, but also disappointments with our lousy love affairs and friendships, as people's pretensions make them look so phony and unreliable, while they in effect prove their uselessness regularly. We get tired and bored with so much vanity.

Sadly, the loneliness epidemic is too hard to tackle. The good news is that plenty of desperate, crooked people are available for companionship if one prefers a lousy relationship to solitude. Our choice depends on our desperation for a companion, despite the high price we usually pay for it. In contrast, personal freedom and solitude appear like a more viable option for some, in particular those who decide to at least learn about, and possibly follow, the path of goodness. They give themselves a chance to develop their beliefs and a meaningful life mostly alone.

Nevertheless, until we develop our goodness spirit, especially self-reliance, we get disheartened and anxious every day in many ways during our routines to cope with social and family demands and badness. The menace of social living and wrestling with our phony lifestyles infect and infuriate us regularly, and yet we do not seem to realize the source of our rising tension and confusion. Soon, we lose all our energy and motivation to indulge people or even think rationally. Meanwhile, the products of badness factory are becoming more destructive personally and socially every day.

Ironically, the entire world now appears mesmerized by this freaky neo-culture (the badness factory) that has spread fast due to people's sudden obsessions for a vast amount of superficial needs and fake social identities. Our minds have been trained to envision the world and life purposes based on shaky and shallow pleasures at the cost of losing our souls. Our new, global culture has no capacity to offer us guidance or a chance to build healthier characters and sustain a tranquil existence for ourselves and our families. Instead, it has promoted a huge level of addictive social and personal values that have entrapped people in a suffocating shell and causing severe depression and desperation worldwide. Surely, these psychological pressures also affect our life outlook and philosophy in odd ways, which in turn goad us to become the kind of person we choose to be with some level of propensity towards goodness or badness, usually the latter. Now we must add the impact of physiological burdens that many of us should endure for many years, especially as we age, merely for fighting social evils bombarding our tired psyches and weakening bodies. All these added pressures on some individuals simply make them evils, way past badness. Sometimes, some of us even feel sad and sorry when we fail to stop our wicked genes or quirks that jump to serve the devil at the expense of our tormented spirits!

It feels bizarre and pitiful when we look around and see how weird we humans have become! It also feels bizarre that the more we keep a safe distance from people, the better we become and feel as a person, despite the occasional feelings of loneliness and sadness. Being such sentimental and oversensitive people these days, we both feel lonely often and fear the risks of getting close to others, putting our guards down, and expressing our boiling emotions. Our sense about the high chance of getting hurt haunts us a lifetime and causes many added inner conflicts.

Ironically again, the badness epidemic is growing fast around the globe in line with people's ambitions for a more civilized, happier existence—a rather legitimate notion that modern nations envisioned before spreading it too fast and deep around the globe. That is, human badness seems highly related to people's rising expectations from society and life, while our socioeconomic and political mechanisms seem unable to cope with all these demands. The less affluent people around the globe now imagine lots of luxury and happiness out there, become envious, and raise their expectations from life and society. Thus, a large deprived mass are becoming delusional, aggressive, depressed, and resentful without realizing the truth about the rising general misery in the Western world. Their fantasies about happiness in some corners of the world make them rush to either migrate or fight the rest of the world viciously. They dream a lot, grow hostility, revolt, and become increasingly bad within this global badness factory. In the end, all these growing sources of badness are due to people's ignorance and misperceptions about life, along with deepened social numbness and global confusion.

Chapter Eight
Social Mechanisms' Perils

The badness epidemic explained in the last chapter reflects our lack of willpower and courage to curb our passion for addictive social rewards and greed-ridden ambitions. All social elements have also been contaminated by this general mentality, which means not enough people get incentives for goodness or to attend to their higher needs for self-fulfilment and divinity. In fact, such ideas feel too naive and unnatural. Meanwhile, coping with ineffective social processes imposed by self-serving elites and political leaders is also tough in spite of our devotion to this intimidating social structure. The pressures of living within these crooked social elements and norms sadden and madden us. Yet, in the end, we should only blame ourselves for being so attached to a vile, dysfunctional, soulless society hypnotically, instead of learning self-reliance to sustain an easier life, maybe even alone, without abandoning society. Nonetheless, grasping the nature and perils of main social elements is crucial for gauging our options when facing them personally and collectively as worried humans.

We believe society has built the best structure for human life in line with a valid of vision of our needs. We think everybody has a chance of becoming successful if s/he puts his/her head into it and work hard, while we trust all kinds of propagandas and adopt positive thinking jargons thrown at us. Thus, while people imagine society has a potential to fulfil a variety of our natural and superficial needs, the cost of satisfying even our basic needs, if possible, has proven to be quite high. Then, we lose our souls, integrity, and serenity further in hopes of getting rich, becoming successful, and feeding our restless egos.

Social structure and its elements are for sustaining basic order and supporting people, while in return people should safeguard and boost these social elements and mechanisms. Yet, running and supporting these social mechanisms, such as justice system and the police, have become quite cumbersome, controversial, and ineffective nowadays. In fact, they have turned into sources of social chaos and human agony. Thus, we have become cynical about prevalent social systems quite rightfully, although also feel obliged to abide by them somehow. After all, we are not only addicted to so many superficial features and values of society, but also pressed to cope with all its tyrannies and injustices. *We are simply trapped and must struggle desperately with little prospect! Our sense of guilt for our seeming failure to cope with this chaos is an added pressure of its own, in fact.*

Even the main elements of social structure, such as learning, education, work, and marriage, have become ineffective these days and quite incompatible with our natural needs. These social elements are not driven by a master plan for social coherence and development of a meaningful culture, either. No authority in the world has the vision or a plan for a social infrastructure to help people and humanity in line with their true needs. For example, while we try to teach our kids many subjects, they are learning less about self-reliance, family, and teamwork. While corporations compete ruthlessly for higher profits, they brainwash people to buy all kinds of useless stuff. They push their employees to sell products and services to people who cannot afford them or do not need them. Or while we work so hard to live lavishly, we lose touch with our families and true personal needs. No congruity exists among social elements, while the contents and processes within each of these elements of social structure are too shallow and shaky to offer reliable lasting solutions for human miseries.

In fact, social mentalities and systems are now rooted in such contaminated grounds that rescue seems impossible. Meanwhile, nobody knows how to go about building a functional society or reforming humans' mentality even within a century before we lose our last chance for survival entirely. Too many conflicting social elements and needs make it impossible to even envision a way out of this mess. Instead, the long fight for socialism versus capitalism would drain the last grains of humans' sanity.

Following social rules and demands is rather justifiable for a large portion of population obliged to work hard to survive, as long as they do not get absorbed in self-indulgence and vanity as well. Yet, luckier rich people still pursuing the same routines and games to gather more wealth and power, instead of discovering their being during the final stage of their lives, are just deplorable.

Discussions in this chapter about the fifteen social elements show that they neither serve us adequately, nor provide a natural setting to find our peace personally. Instead, their frailties stir dire social decay and malfunctions like those noted in Chapter Two. Thus, understanding the shortfalls of these fifteen social elements might be useful for thinking proactively regarding humans' social and personal needs, especially for becoming better beings.

Learning is in itself the most critical social element, because if people's mentalities cannot be revamped, other social elements and systems would never get a chance for scrutiny and overhaul. The chance of human salvation without a solid social conscious and wisdom in line with a sound mentality and morality would be zero, anyway. Nevertheless, we could gain big insights and a wiser life perspective by, i) building our objective views about these social elements' potencies, pressures, limits, and demands, and ii) developing our coping mechanisms for gauging, using, and fighting them, as necessary at times. Sadly, societies have so far failed to provide proper guidelines, values, and means of building our mentalities and lifestyles. Instead, they been the main cause of humans' gullibility and sufferings.

Table 8.1: Fifteen Main Social Elements

(**Religion** is purposely excluded here due to its contentious nature, though it is a crucial element)

1. Education	2. Learning	3. Occupation
4. Marriage	5. Parenthood	6. Health
7. Security	8. Justice & Fairness	9. Courtesy & Trust
10. Morality	11. Environment	12. Culture
13. Democracy	14. Economy	15. Authority

1. Education

The main problem with the present education format is that it gives people the impression that they are learning some useful stuff, especially about the validity and ability of social structure to avail a practical life for all. However, in fact, it mostly teaches people to become more pompous, competitive, and self-indulgent with no cognizance of their beings and reality.

Another repercussion of our lengthy, structured education is that it is intended for career purposes rather than preparing people to live practically in a cooperative manner and maybe even help them become better human beings. It does not improve our social behaviour and interactions, either. Spending up to two decades of our precious lives on education indicates our present wasteful method of schooling, especially when it teaches people very little about humanity or even basic means of relating to one another. Definitely, this amount of time and all those educational efforts could be structured better to prepare people for the hardships of life and relationships at least. Instead, our shoddy educational contents and settings mislead children and youths with superficial notions like consumerism and happiness, raise their expectations from life, and spoil and exploit them with positive psychology. Our educational systems and society make us less compassionate by propagating competition, materialism, greed, pomposity, etc. They give people, especially the youths, an erroneous perspective of life, which then only makes them feel worthless, humiliated, wasted, and defeated later when their premature ambitions and exaggerated expectations do not materialize.

Learning and education have found different, often clashing, purposes nowadays, and unfortunately, we seem to have lost our wisdom on both grounds. Neither our educational systems teach us the authentic means of living, nor do our sporadic efforts to learn help us become a better person. Over the last century, in particular, the depth and content of both education and learning have not helped us understand ourselves and our world, thus we have become less capable of relating in families, communities, and across the nations. It is just amazing and sad that the public's intelligence is kept so low deliberately all along, considering the long history of humanity and our interest about learning, relating, and being a better person. Worst of all, the majority of education we get over two decades finds no practical application, as most of us end up doing jobs that do not require our formal education. It often proves a waste of time and energy. This is true, especially, when we presume the main purpose of education is to develop and spread useful, and maybe even moral, values in societies and around the globe. With social values deteriorating so fast beyond repair, the damages that our educational and learning processes have caused, especially in the new era, are horrendous.

Despite the rising amount of education in terms of student/ hours and more university education throughout the world, we have become less honest and productive as individuals even in modern countries, while get stressed regularly. People's naivety and dogmatism appear in their superstitions, religious beliefs, greed, egotism, low financial sense, and high demands from life. Overall, formal education is not useful in crucial areas of human concern. Instead, it has become mainly a means of brainwashing and exploiting humans for running our greed-driven economies with marginal benefits for the majority. Ironically, we all should share the blame for this mayhem, since we stress on education instead of learning. We miss the facts noted here about education and do not make our leaders reassess our educational systems and contents. We are letting evil forces in society keep the public in ignorance simply because we do not question our raw beliefs and shallow values in our failing societies. Education and modernism have also damaged our cultures and their teaching capacities.

For becoming a better person, and as concerned citizens and parents, we must reassess our needs for conscious learning, rather than depending on our old-fashioned perceptions about the value of education. It does not make sense to encourage our kids to do college and higher education if such efforts cannot even help them build a related career or means of fulfilling their financial and emotional needs. We must grow a more sensible, proactive mentality about the role of education and teach it to our children.

2. Learning

Society's stress on education for career and income purposes has been at the cost of losing our chance to learn about life's essential needs and values. We do not get the training or incentive to learn about 'self' and find a soul-satisfying life path. We do not learn how to gain and protect our modest individualism mostly through self-awareness for a lasting peace of mind, which is the ultimate goal of learning. Thus, people are less authentic and able to grasp life's harsh realities, while fooling themselves with their college degrees and a mirage of success and happiness. They never learn that only certain kinds of knowledge supports their psychological growth and helps them keep a positive outlook about humanity and existence in general. Thus, a long review of learning process and its importance is particularly crucial here.

Besides our outmoded educational processes, our learnings are random and not purposeful for grasping who we are and what our life philosophy and efforts bring us. These general learnings through society, family, or educational systems are ongoing and automatic according to our interests, intelligence, and stamina. Thus, we usually learn lots of useless or wicked stuff from one another and thru media. Meanwhile, we hardly learn the purposes and principles of social living; or the possibility and importance of human coexistence. Instead, we stress on 'individualism' as a new fad without learning the meanings and goals of individualism and socialism or their relationships. Ironically, we love social living and are allowed to use the word 'social' in any context, except for 'socialism'! Weird species!

Luckily, everybody can learn insightful stuff thru 'conscious learning,' build a peaceful life, and maybe become a better being, too. In particular, s/he must learn about the sad state of our doomed society, revamp his/her naive mentality, and adjust his/her lifestyle and expectations accordingly. Many topics discussed throughout this book require a much higher focus by most people to weigh their lifestyles and mindsets. Especially, we must grasp the true implications and importance of the main social elements discussed in this chapter. For example, most of us like to ignore the basic fact that democracy—as an ideal human aspiration—does not work within capitalism, despite the propagandas about their close correlation. In fact, we are brainwashed to perceive democracy as a symptom or symbol of capitalism and vice versa. We are trained to perceive socialism as a taboo. Thus, we simply cannot conceive or believe that no democracy is attainable while humans are so naïve, poverty exists, and corporations and elite groups exploit the majority under the name of free enterprise and freedom. Our ignorance, when being fooled by such vile jargons, shows that we have not learned enough about the impracticalities of capitalism and democracy, even if most leaders were not so incompetent and corrupt. Democracy would never work until we can impose proper systems for curbing the evils of free enterprise mixed up with humans' horrific, selfish nature.

As stressed in this book, people's widespread naivety renders a horrendous hurdle for forcing a fairer and more effective social structure, besides rendering democracy useless. Our hypnotized minds about social teachings' validity and social systems' viability are the roots of our chaotic lives. Thus, learning how to overcome our naiveté and reassess many fundamental facts about the vanity of current social values is essential for saving humanity, while becoming a better being as well. Especially, we should learn that our general dogmatic mentality nowadays is a main reason for our inability to build a moral culture for humanity.

Social and personal mayhem indicate that we all must grow new mentalities about life and society by lots of urgent learning about means of coexistence. Then, 'learning' about our essence is a major device for gaining our identity as a human and as a useful citizen. That is also the only way to enhance our lives' qualities, mostly because our formal and social education distracts us from true learning, growth, and finding peace. Sadly, however, most of us have the least amount of interest, ability, or time for learning the right stuff about life. Thus, all these ideas about learning to curb our gullibility most likely sound absurd.

As a worthy challenge to redeem our dignity and soul at least, we should learn to see 'learning,' especially about Self and social elements' intended goals, a mandatory part of personal education and growth. In fact, this personal learning is particularly crucial because formal education is distracting our focus, while pumping our egos to believe we know everything better than everybody else does. We believe we understand the purposes and problems of social elements perfectly, yet choose our leaders based on their shallow promises and our personal whims and greed. We still do not realize that no president or government can repair the state of economy or return employment and prosperity to a city when economic conditions change over time. Our assumptions about socioeconomic factors, as well as our criteria and principles for making our judgments, are naïve and self-serving. We are quite unfamiliar even about the purposes of social elements for a moral society, let alone the required mechanisms for them. Ideally, all these learnings must be mandatory as part of formal education.

More importantly, we must realize that 'learning' is not just an exercise to pursue sporadically only when we find time or an incentive, for example for becoming a better person. Rather, we should see it as a daily routine for self-analysis and sustaining a high level of consciousness about reality and our life choices. Of course, discussing 'learning' without offering the path for taking on such a horrendous task is unfair and unproductive. Thus, the readers interested in the rules and mechanisms for 'learning' are encouraged to refer to this author's book, *Doubts and Decisions for Living, Volume III.*

As a start, we should distinguish conscious learning sources (e.g., reading, meditating, experimenting, etc.) from unconscious training and culture (e.g., television, social trends, friends and family, etc.) Surely, it is hard to resist the influence of everything we have already learnt, or to break our information-gathering habits. Still, we can learn and revamp our mentalities and habits vastly by observing our actions, reactions, and relationships more consciously. We may unlearn harmful aspects of our unconscious learning if we at least acknowledge their debilitating effects. We could stay vigilant about the types of learning that our superficial lifestyles impose. Then, we could stress on the kind of learning that supports self-awareness, instead of filling our brains with so many juvenile ideologies and slogans that give us only an illusion of individualism and happiness.

Conscious learning evokes our innate potentialities, drives our psychological growth, and nurtures our sense of spirituality. The mere significance of these types of learning for one's psyche and spirit reveals the triviality of all other learning, and the futility of all our efforts related to them. For example, we learn how foolish our greed and egoistic power struggles are; we recognize how crudely we are driven by such vast amount of worthless teachings to satiate our egos and social addictions in our modern world.

In all, we must view and adopt 'learning' as a major personal endeavour, rather than general knowledge acquired on a random basis. Learning from media, internet, and social propaganda only raises our naivety and addictions to trivia. Instead, we must focus on the goals, processes, and sources of conscious learning—to help us compare various viewpoints and choose the right career and lifestyle, too, with the chance to explore our real potentialities and study our 'self.' Most of all, only this kind of learning can help us become a better person.

Ultimately, only conscious learning can help us, i) choose our life purposes realistically and find peace amidst the pressures and stress that social living causes, and ii) fulfil our socioeconomic needs and aspirations better by adopting simpler lifestyles. The goal is to explore our innate potentialities and spirituality in line with humans' inherent needs, instead of all the superficial ones promoted as symbols of civilization. Of course, we cannot ignore other types of learning needed for our survival and professions. Yet, we should balance our learning efforts wisely based on their likely effect on personal happiness and psychological health.

Our lifelong mission is to gauge our conscious 'self'-learning and 'self'-fulfilling efforts to ensure we are not merely driven by social teachings and our pleasure-seeking attitude. We must also monitor our mentality regarding the effects of our professional training and education, their purposes, and outcome. Do they cause more stress or serenity? In the process, we learn a crucial lesson about *happiness,* too. We learn that it requires plenty of sacrifice and work, mostly in terms of learning the right stuff of life. Therefore, we can say that a main objective of learning and self-awareness is to find that elusive happiness, mostly in terms of learning the art of contentment.

To capture true happiness, we must in fact become conscious of our learning habits deeply, defeat (unlearn) our idiosyncrasies and egocentricities, and revamp our personalities and outlooks. This is a major challenge for most people, because it is hard to modify our old learning habits and channels that we have pursued subconsciously all our lives. It is almost impossible to develop an almost new mindset and personality. We must try to become and remain conscious of all involuntary learning, which are imposed upon us, including social values and upbringing lessons. The goal would be to detect and reverse the effects of conditional types of learning, conscious or unconscious ones, ongoing or old sources.

Turning conscious learning about the right stuff of existence into a daily routine is a major step for becoming a better being. Then again, making humans believe in these heretical ideas or build some interest in conscious learning sounds too dreamful!

3. Occupation

Several reasons, but mainly financial needs, goad us to work and often we have little choice in the kind of jobs we end up doing in order to remain practical and survive in society. However, it is still important to ask ourselves two essential questions when planning for, or pursuing, any occupation, 'How does this kind of work affect my spirit? Does it make me a better person or I am only another hypocrite doing a sloppy job selfishly with no, or little, regard for its effects on the people I am supposed to serve?' 'Does my job and the way I do it boosts the validity and value of the social element I am supposedly serving?'. Of course, these questions, especially the last one, sound too idealistic for normal people to ponder, as we see our jobs only as a source of income.

Work has always been the most relevant social element for both making a living and establishing our identities as productive members of society. However, its role and nature have become less defensible and too stressful in the new era.

After doing a lot of technical education and learning so much useless stuff from family and society, we strive to keep a job to make a living, help others and society, and maybe fulfil some of our personal aspirations in the process, too. Sadly, we often fail to achieve most of these goals, especially the last one, due to flawed contents and conditions of occupations we end up finding.

Like everything else in modern societies, the nature of our jobs is highly mechanical nowadays and overwhelmed by human egoism and insecurities. Thus, we end up working too much or too little and often wonder why making a living has become so torturous and humiliating. We pursue various professions, mostly in hostile and stressful settings, merely for a measly subsistence, feeding our ego and self-esteem, or getting rich. Yet, fulfilling even our modest expectations takes a lot of labour. Ironically, we consider 'work' an essential part of life structure, which we take on for economic reasons, to mitigate boredom, or merely for not being called a bum. Sometimes, we work out of a sheer sense of responsibility to self and others. For these reasons, 'work' needs scrutiny as a major social element, but also because our rationale for doing all that work and self-sacrifice might be questionable within the larger scheme of one's life philosophy. *Who says we must work so hard or at all, anyway, and for what end?*

Although labour feels like a natural part of life, justifying it personally is getting harder every year if we are not getting any self-satisfaction out of it, or at least some sort of appreciation, not even from our family. We often wonder about the purpose of our labour in such debilitating, stressful environments just for feeding our addiction to extravagance. Is this kind of work habit natural? Especially, the rising social disorder and the decaying state of family relationships make working so hard feel senseless—just to buy more things or accumulate wealth! If it is all for leading a happy life, is the prevalent 'work' format in modern societies a relevant or distorting factor for a sensible means of existence? What is work supposed to be, anyway? A paying job, a career, a means of survival or building wealth, labour, some physical or mental chore to fill our days and fight boredom, a way of serving our Ego, a social conditioning, a habit, an obligation to society or family, all of these, a balanced mix of them? What? We ought to know, yet most of us do not have time to even ponder these ideas. Thus, our doubts (mostly subconsciously) about the purpose of our work, and our reluctance or inability to find more appropriate work routines, ruins our spirits and minds. In fact, our present attitude to see work just as a financial vehicle makes us greedy and wicked, as we pursue work only for self-gratification instead of self-actualization. This one-dimensional view of work also hinders our chances for reflections and becoming better beings.

Our occupations can be viewed in two ways: 1) we must work to fulfil our financial and emotional needs, and 2) we like to work as an inherent urge to build our identity and mental strength. Our 'self' and spirit are characterized highly by the nature of our work. So, defining a personal work philosophy gets complicated, as we must satisfy both our social and spiritual needs through our work. Balancing these two perspectives of work is both difficult and impractical in our societies. In the end, the matters of practicality, personal priorities, philosophy, and balancing our wide range of needs goad us to choose our formal and side occupations.

Then again, our lifelong inner conflicts and nagging attitude (subconscious doubts) about work as a seemingly forced duty distress and confuse us, especially because we cannot readily revamp our mentality and responsibility for making money. We cannot ignore our egoism and ambitions or the pressures on us to sustain a particular lifestyle by working hard. We simply cannot think outside the box past the parameters of the prevalent social structure. We cannot bypass the conventional norms about work objectives and its role for developing our phony personalities and lifestyles. Thus, we never get a chance to touch our spirit and find our identity as a soulful creature living for worthy purposes.

Often we must do some kind of work just to survive and stay practical. That is understandable and honourable. Beyond that, however, we must resist the cultural norms that view work only in terms of its financial benefits. If our occupation does not offer a sense of self-fulfilment, we must at least find good reasons for doing that job within the context of our life philosophy.

The first two concepts that cross our minds when we hear the word 'work' are, i) *money* (greed and crude ambitions) and ii) *labour* (hard work and pain). In spite of our adolescence dreams to pursue a particular appealing profession, we associate work mostly with the 'job we must do,' which is expected to be tough based on what we hear from our parents and society. Yet, this does not have to be true. We may at least gauge our options and criteria about achievement versus individuality regularly, instead of only following the crowd, growing a phony personality, and perishing in society. We may adjust our mindsets to explore our being and identity now and then, while also fulfilling our primary needs for working.

Work stress comes from many sources and affects individuals based on their personalities. We may not feel it directly, or merely get absorbed in an organization in order to mitigate its tyranny, but the overall work hardships are evident in the growing stress level of office workers the most. These sufferings are also evident from the way we contaminate our relationships outside of work with our families. The rising relationship failures in the present culture are highly related to the individuals' work issues. We are getting more wicked and unaware of our true needs and inner self due to the type of work we do mostly for maximizing our income and wealth regardless of its value for our long-term welfare or the amount of deceit and false information we spread to succeed.

The ideal would be to figure out a kind of profession we could carry out from youth to the last stage of our lives for fulfilling our authentic needs, mostly spirituality. Instead, we are usually forced to labour during the most productive years of our lives merely for subsistence and then, when we get older, we are forced to retire and live idly with some kind of lost identity. We do not have any useful work to keep our spirits intact when we need it the most during old age. Therefore, in effect, we kill our spirits by not only our inability to do the right work during our youth, but also not having anything useful to do during the final stage of our lives when we need a set identity. Nowadays, hardly anybody gets a chance or mindset to define a work philosophy for him/herself, since grasping and reconciling it with its practical perspectives all our lives is hard and painful. Meanwhile, it is crucial not to get too philosophical at the cost of losing our sense of practicality.

Nevertheless, we must question our work objectives, although we may never get a chance to have an ideal work. Satisfying this personal curiosity is useful for self-awareness and finding the right path of life eventually. Especially, any work that kills our spirits and integrity could be a direct source of our depression and evil. If we never get a chance to discover our potentialities and explore our 'self,' a deep void in our psyche causes frustration and stress. Discovering our innate potentialities and using them in the 'right work' are two major tasks on the same continuum. They must be planned together practically early on in our lives to avoid lifetime disappointments, endless burdens of boring works, and suffering absolute vanity and idleness during old age.

As part of defining our life objectives and philosophy, we must assess all the above noted dimensions of work, especially its purposes and inherent potentiality to boost our spirits and support our identities. We must at least learn about the principles of coping in organizations[*] and keep our aspirations and Egos in check. Before planning a long-term miserable life in organizations, we must gauge our options and needs. That is one way of preventing our individuality getting smashed during power struggles within organizations. It is especially crucial to understand both human nature and the nature of organization work before doing many years of higher education and planning for a career that we may end up doing and abhorring a lifetime.

4. *Marriage*

Marriage has become the touchiest social element these days due to the chaos that feminism and modern relationships has caused for people and societies worldwide. Marriage and companionship have become the biggest sources of stress in life, as both options of living alone and with someone else bring us pain and distress nowadays. Loving someone often makes us feel even lonelier when we cannot relate to him/her effectively. We feel helpless, unappreciated, and desperate too often. This endless source of

---

[*] The perils of working for organizations and coping methods are explained in this author's book, *Doubts and Decisions for Living, Volume III*.

doubt and disappointment is a reason why marriage has become such a difficult dilemma to sort out or cope with.

At the same time, people are unaware of relationships' needs and hurdles nowadays, while their impressions and expectations are highly incongruent with new realities and couples' growing inability to relate. Accordingly, marital failures cause stressful family conflicts and social chaos, while also turning into direct sources of people's rising naiveté and badness in general. Thus, grasping the roots of marital conflicts, as a pervasive, debilitating social element, is a crucial aspect of self-awareness and a main topic for managing our lives and becoming a better being.

Love and loneliness have also become major life dilemmas for most of us nowadays, since we feel incapable of mastering viable means of living and loving. We do not know how to relate and love effectively, but we are not trained to live independently, either. Instead, we are consumed with all sorts of fantasies about love and filled with the fear of loneliness. All along, the pressures on our psyches and spirits pile up when we should also cope with organization and occupation demands, as noted in the previous section. The pressures caused by our dependency on organization to have a job, and the way it competes with our higher needs for self-realization and independence, already deplete our spirit and energy. Then, love and companionship needs result in an even higher level of dependence and desperation.

Accordingly, our love and loneliness dilemmas reduce our chance to respond to our urge for independence, because we find ourselves needy for love and being loved very soon in life. Then, our efforts to distinguish, consciously or subconsciously, between our love needs and sexual drives turn into an added source of confusion and doubts. All along, our frustration and deprivation raise our bitterness and dormant urges for badness.

In the end, our desire for independence and our inevitable submission to our urges for love and sex cause stress and major inner conflicts throughout our lives. We struggle helplessly and uselessly all along to solve these painful dilemmas by fixing (and balancing) our feelings somehow. While we enjoy some feelings of control and independence during some periods, we soon revert to our need for love and the feelings of dependence that come with it. For either love or sex, or simply eluding loneliness, we should depend on somebody else who is willing to share similar feelings or experiences with us. Our relationships require mutual dependence, understanding, commitment, respect, and integrity in order to stabilize into a reliable form that can satisfy our need for a companion. All these requirements create a major paradox in people's personal lives and raise their level of bitterness, but also increase the chaos across the society.

Our ceaseless failures to satisfy our need for dependence or independence cause many other psychological shocks, too, that lead to depression and malice. For one thing, we start to doubt our identity and 'who we are' without a companion. We doubt our sense of love and companionship and the effectiveness of our approaches to find and manage them in our already hectic life. We doubt our ability to judge and decide about our preferences and options regarding this matter, and about our ability to be an independent person. We get entangled between our emotions and logic fighting forever, while our insecurities pile up, too.

A major problem is that we have created our own subjective perceptions about the purposes and potentials of relationships based on our personal needs and superficial values around us. We have invented a fantasy in our heads about the nature and role of relationships and their success factors. Thus, we set ourselves up for failure, since our naïve expectations cannot be fulfilled. After a short period, couples realize their mistakes and begin to resent their partners and themselves for being dragged into suffocating relationships incapable of satisfying their personal needs, which are superficial most often, anyway. The vast level of suffering caused by our marriages around so many superficial needs ruins our characters and turns many of us into devils.

To cope with the rising companionship chaos, we must show willingness and patience to study relationships' unique needs. In particular, partners must be much more patient and understanding than they are nowadays. They must be a much better being than a normal person is. Sadly, however, finding good-nurtured partners is becoming difficult, and the chance of both partners being good enough to build a healthy relationship is even more remote.

5. Parenthood

Parents' capacity and duty to teach the right stuff of life to their kids has always been an essential social element. Yet, the social confusion and disorder have now eroded family ethics and power drastically, too. Nowadays, parents have no proper guidelines or knowledge about parenting, so kids grow up with no role models and discipline to learn anything useful. Instead, every generation has become more spoiled and lost in terms of life's realities.

Advising our kids is risky and tough nowadays, anyway, as no reliable or cultural principles are available for managing our lives in such overly complex, chaotic, and superficial societies. In particular, explaining the meanings of success and happiness is impossible these days, as we witness the dreadful outcome of our supposedly astute search for life's virtues. How can any sensible person not doubt the validity of his/her interpretations of success and happiness? Thus, only a few wise and selfless parents might know life's secrets. Even then, their ideas would appear absurd and radically contrary to the alluring lifestyles that push youths only for more pleasures and prosperity.

Meanwhile, many parents overindulge their children to boost their self-image and chances of success in our vastly materialistic environment. Accordingly, kids have become too self-absorbed and spoiled to pay attention to their parents' random cautions and teachings or grasp the intricacies of life. Some parents, especially 'mothers,' go to the odd extreme of adopting their kids' juvenile values and lifestyles just to show their modernity and support. Surely, something is wrong with the society where adults imitate their children as part of parenting. In this type of environment, parents and children have difficulty coping with pressures on them to learn and do the right things and be accepted in society, too. Instead, they are getting more confused every day.

Parents' inexperience and mentality nowadays hurt their kids' characters, anyway, whether they attempt to become a mentor or remain rather passive to let their kids figure out life on their own. Most of us are naïve about life and driven by social demands and the upbringing flaws of our own parents. Thus, we damage our children's psyches as well as our relationships with them by the time they reach adolescence.

On the one hand, the youths' tenacity to doubt their parents' wisdom, like a subtle rebellion, is often a blessing, because most of us have nothing useful to teach our kids, anyway, or do not know how to do it. Their resistance could *potentially* help them become freethinkers and listeners with objective mentalities if the society and media did not confuse them so tenaciously.

On the other hand, the absence of guidelines or reliable role models for children, due to cultural collapse in societies, hinders the youths' chance for building even a primary foundation of thoughts and developing their own life values and ways. In this passive and senseless environment, our children are helplessly at the mercy of a society that has no intention or capacity to teach them life's true meaning and issues. Instead, the effects of rising financial insecurity and social deprivations for youths only make them more restless, desperate, and radical.

Nevertheless, both parents and society cause immense anxiety and confusion for youths with their superficial teachings, phony lifestyles, and idealistic ideologies. Peer pressures and influence during adolescence hinders youths' desire to think objectively and independently as well. While our children might inherit some positive attributes from us, many irreversible psychological flaws infect their mentalities. They imagine we hurt them deliberately, too, even despite our overindulgence. Even when they do not show hostility and anxiety, they often suppress an enormous level of traumas and cynicism about their parents—sometimes rightly and sometimes due to their misperceptions. Unfortunately, even as adults, they (like the rest of us) seldom get a chance to reflect and recognize their idiosyncrasies and the means of overcoming them, in particular the ones etched in their unconscious minds during childhood. The outcome is that every generation, in the last century at least, has become less cultured and more doubtful about the authenticity of their lifestyles.

Sadly, not enough intelligent books are available, either, to help the youths understand the sad nature of the world they are inheriting. Books must give them enough facts and ideas to think for themselves, instead of filling their minds with trivia, fantasy, and corny conclusions. Books must offer practical techniques and tools to identify their options for living, instead of raising their soppy sentimentalities and high expectations from life. Youths must know the most likely outcomes of their major life decisions and personal dilemmas before their hasty choices lead to lifelong depression and a dismal way of subsistence. These books should reflect only our sincere lessons from life without pushing popular values to justify our own lifestyles. We need books that address major life issues in a simple language for youths, to discourage consumerism, vanity, and self-gratification. Educating the youths, mostly thru school curriculum, is our last chance to prevent their ultimate mental deterioration and distress due to the influence of misguiding books, TV, video games, and social media.

6. Health

People's health is in great jeopardy since we do not know how to attend to our physical, psychological, and spiritual needs. Instead, people consume a great deal of alcohol and drugs to cope with occupational stress, unemployment, failing relationships, and loneliness. The kind of food people consume is making them obese and sick. Our psychological and mental pressures are also rising due to the superficialities of modern lifestyles, life's vanity, and our failure to find the purpose of our struggles. In this setting, our spirits and morale are sinking too fast, while we have no knowledge or incentive to explore our spirituality needs. We are just getting more entangled with our illusions about pleasure and sexuality daily, which heighten our insecurities and neediness. Our identity and dignity are also shattered, as we get absorbed in our juvenile thoughts and activities all our lives.

Need for physical and mental health is common knowledge, yet many of us do not honour it consciously for living effectively. The general health is, in fact, only the first step, since we have the ability and drive to expand our minds largely to lift our spirits for optimizing our health and happiness. We can explore the higher consciousness and wisdom that most humans can potentially muster for not only living healthier, but also reaching a fulfilling enlightenment. We only need willpower and maturity to curb the effects and demands of our perceived world. We need the divine power of 'self' to elude the lures of superficial needs and values that society advocates. We need radical visions and thoughts to revamp our misperceptions, especially about the purpose of life and our futile search for the elusive happiness in a corrupt social framework. We need a strong spirit to reveal our gullibility and childish whims to us, and then perhaps direct us to those blissful territories of higher wisdom and energy, which only a healthy mind and body can reach.

While people's health is declining fast in all regards, society is becoming less compassionate and capable of addressing their needs. Society is not only making people sicker in so many ways for so many reasons, but also getting less capable to offer proper medical attention. Health insurance is getting too expensive and the cost of drugs is too high. Physicians and pharmaceutical companies are allowed to charge outrageous prices and prescribe useless, addictive drugs, which are only making some companies richer and the public sicker. In fact, physicians may be making the public sicker rather knowingly for getting richer. In all, a sad state of affairs prevails at many levels regarding people's health issues and societies' incapacity to handle this basic human need.

7. Security

Security has become a highly stressful social element these days, because individuals' physical and mental welfare is threatened within our pressed, complex social structure, while national and global conflicts are affecting the whole humanity on a large scale. These rising threats relate to political and economic instabilities around the globe and the fast decline of governments' capacity, as well as the United Nation's, to stir peace around the world and fulfil people's basic needs. The sources of conflicts, nationally and globally, have been historical and deep, so finding workable compromises seem tough for our arrogant leaders and capitalists. For centuries, some nations have exploited others to serve their industries and citizens, while accumulating enormous wealth for some elite groups. Now that those oppressed nations are fed up and oppose this global travesty, we face much wider arrays of international conflicts. Developing countries and radical groups also resent and resist the rise of the Western corruption, bullying, and values, thus the whole world is in war, while finding practical solutions appear more remote every day.

Within such big global turmoil, a large number of displaced populations around the world are on the move to find refuge in more stable countries, while the growing immigration of poor refugees has become another sore point and source of insecurity for citizens of the overwhelmed nations. At the same time, many affluent and educated people are also immigrating to best places on the planet to enjoy themselves and safeguard their assets. The outcomes of these rapid displacements of people, global misery, capital and brain drains, and cultural shocks would stir higher insecurities for people regardless of their origins and final places of residence. Accordingly, global insecurities, cultural clashes, and extremism are rising due to vast immigrations, the widening segregation of rich and poor, and the effects of climate change. At the end, no sense of harmony and security exists, not even in rather stabler places, as long as the rest of the world struggles with poverty and insecurity.

Aside from our fears of rising general violence in the streets, wars, and terrorist attacks, we feel deep psychological insecurities related to our jobs, careers, marriages, and other sources of inner conflicts. The annihilation of family values, low social empathy, and the absence of moral support are adding to people's growing insecurity, stress, mental imbalance, and the loss of motivation to search for better ways of living or a desire to live at all.

Overall, we are all responsible for many types of horrendous social and personal pressures that are making us feel insecure. Yet, ironically, our persistence to live in our delusional worlds, based on our idealistic perceptions and expectations from life, is further rising our level of anxiety and insecurities.

8. Justice and Fairness

Our grasp of daily news alone suggests that justice and fairness are merely fantasies, as people's cruelty and their lack of both conscious and conscience appear too deep. In fact, humans seem to be programmed to conspire, lie, cheat, and harm one another regularly not merely for personal interests, but also out of habit, if not pure malice. Yet, we seem incapable of giving up our fantasy about justice and fairness. We still wonder if any chance exists for decency in this world, as we feel abused and misunderstood by people. We wonder whether humans can ever create a fair and compassionate society. *Does God play any role in this matter at all, like a game or something?*

On the one hand, we seem to be inherently, or maybe even spiritually, driven to expect justice and fairness as humans' basic rights. We cannot stop thinking that unfairness and injustice are merely due to humans' low ingenuity, morality, and willpower to create a more harmonious society for themselves. On the other hand, fairness and justice feel like fantasy in any society where such deeply flawed, selfish humans are in charge of generating social values and systems. Creating a society to restrain humans' crooked nature and finding leaders to sustain that setting appear far-fetched. With pomposity, racism, and inequality so prevalent around the world, expecting any sense of fairness or justice is too naïve nowadays. Especially, with rich and poor around the world being segregated even faster and more visibly, the possibility of keeping a harmonious social structure to induce justice and peace would be impossible even in small communities. Therefore, we believe people and societies would never mature enough to instil any form of justice and harmony.

Nevertheless, our obsession for justice and fairness in either this world or afterlife puts a lasting burden on our psyches, as we seem adamant to capture these ideals. We seek refuge constantly, while we feel obliged to live in broken societies that burden our spirits with so much injustice and unfairness. We are unwilling to give up the alleged privileges of many phony social attachments, even when we feel our lifestyles' vanity and role in causing the added injustice and unfairness in society. With respect to our imaginations about any afterlife compensation for our sufferings, we have even less grounds to trust religions or any spiritual motto for an ultimate—divine—justice and fairness. Instead, our naïve perceptions about, and passion for, fairness and justice cause us an unsettling, irresolvable dilemma all our lives.

Our lingering scepticism about human nature along with their keen struggles for fairness and justice are causes and effects of each other, while we strive to stay optimistic as much as possible. However, ultimately, our fundamental pessimism about human nature and capacity to be just and fair seems quite justifiable. In fact, we must accept and cope with this reality once and for all, so that we can manage our lives just a bit more practically in the light of all the inevitable unfairness and injustice imposed upon us. We might be able to fight our urges for living so callously and vengefully like everybody else, and maybe even adopt the path of goodness as a preferred lifestyle for a conscious person seeking justice and fairness merely as his/her personal life philosophy.

We might even gain the wisdom of seeing, feeling, and practising 'goodness' as a very potent defence mechanism to fight off all the badness and injustice.

Naturally, coping with this fundamental social deficiency and building such a progressive, cynical mentality would be tough. However, a main purpose of pursuing a path of goodness is to strengthen our characters and build strong convictions for curbing our idealistic ideologies, especially about justice and fairness, with the goal of enjoying a stoic, but productive, life.

9. Courtesy and Trust

People have become less courteous and considerate, as the level of arrogance in society has climbed to the roof and everybody feels so important and special. Accordingly, the overall level of trust has almost disappeared, too, because we are learning not to depend on others or trust their words and promises, not even our friends' and family members', especially our spouses'. We feel we should remain vigilant, if not cynical, about not only people's words and values, but also the viability of our social structure. Now, we can hardly trust our government officials and politicians to do the right things for us and humanity as a whole, although many people are still naïve and fall for the nonsensical promises that our elected officials, especially our top leaders, keep offering for fooling us. With the advent of internet and telemarketing, the level of courtesy and trust has declined even faster, as we should now be overly cautious about all sorts of fake news and scams to defraud us. At the same time, no society can function or survive with such widespread cynicism keeping people always on their guards just to protect themselves.

Worst of all, too much mistrust in society leads to people's chronic insecurity, cynicism, frustration, and depression. Then, it grows badness, as people become selfish and cruel just to survive in terms of both avoiding social abuse and making a living. In addition, people's chronic mistrust is causing contagious personal idiosyncrasies, such as higher pomposity, oversensitivity, and rudeness towards others. Overall, it is not hard to imagine the kind of social environment all these aggravated feelings, actions, bitterness, and reactions are causing throughout the world and alienating humans for good. It is disheartening that even our basic contacts in society result in so much evil and cynicism.

Nonetheless, we should predict the rise of both global chaos and human badness in line with people's growing mistrusts in their governments, social systems, spouses, religions, and people. Ironically, most people are still revealing their deep naiveté, too, as they fall victims to all sorts of manipulations by politicians, salespeople, advertisers, etc. Despite our chronic mistrust, we still keep falling in tempting traps that stir our sense of greed or when we look for relief from our rampant miseries. Our inability to use even our deep sense of mistrust to protect ourselves is an odd phenomenon all by itself. It demonstrates our level of confusion as our spirits, ridden by our urges for goodness and justice, clash with so many inner conflicts and insecurities as well as flawed social elements and processes all the time.

In Part IV of this book, the US Presidential election of 2016 is reviewed for its amazing educational values regarding people's wishful thinking and juvenile imaginations when they suddenly put all their faith in a person mostly because they have lost their trusts in their social mechanisms and leaders. It is amazing that people have all these mistrusts about most authorities and their governments and still follow the same means of choosing an even lousier leader based on his childish promises and arrogance. It is simply amazing how we can even imagine that these phony leaders can be of any use or perform any better than the previous ones we have trusted all our lives to make miracles for us. Even worse, we simply do not grasp the depth of our own naïveté that is causing the chaos in the first place—all these social mistrusts and frustrations along with further confusions and gullibility for the public.

10. Morality

It is rather logical to expect a civilized society teach and practise morality as its core value. Yet, societies have always waited for some outsiders—mostly prophets—to force such ideas on the public, and even then, our leaders have fought with those ethical teachings for preserving their own powers or for other reasons, sometimes with good justifications. Nevertheless, while religions played a role for spreading morality, other social systems and norms remained in some harmony within such overall mentality in terms of values people envisioned and shared among them. Now, we no longer have the same vision or opportunity. With the decline of religious influence, we have not been able to find a universal means of pondering and spreading morality or adopting a personal path towards a simple form of spiritualism to maintain at least our integrity and identity. Instead, we have been doing the opposite. Our new social values encourage us to be reckless and adventurous in hopes of capturing happiness and success. We behave selfishly and strive to enjoy our lives at any cost with no regard for morality or psychological effects on our psyches. The widespread alcoholism, addictions, stress, sexual perversions, and our increasing needs for sleeping pills, antidepressants, and other drugs, do not seem to convince us that something fundamental is wrong with social conscience, values, and structure. We merely think superficially and fill our lives with meaningless, fleeting pleasures, mostly through extravagance and sexuality. Yet, at the end, we suffer due to our shallow perceptions of the world and the way we miss the opportunity of building a peaceful lifestyle according to some solid personal principles and a basic level of morality at least.

Society is now too contaminated to guide people in terms of morality. Actually, it acts contrary to those old perceptions about morality. Now, instead of teaching people some ethical rules for common benefits, it hinders their basic intuition to find the sense of decency and ethics personally for their own purposes at least.

Many discussions in this book show why 'being good' is a major challenge within our pushy socioeconomic setting that is merely surviving around all kinds of immoral principles and a knack for manipulating the public.

11. Environment

The horrendous damage our mentalities and actions are causing is not merely social and personal. Our irresponsible attitude and crooked social mechanisms, especially our obsession for more wealth and power, have destroyed our planet, too, and we seem to have reached a point of no return regarding the environmental calamity we have caused. Yet, we still do not seem to care, and often, in fact, appear mentally incapable of envisioning any ways of living without our capitalistic ideologies even one day. It seems that our fascination with our present socioeconomic mechanisms and lifestyles can never be restrained to reverse their dire effects on environment and our own future. How many of our leaders are willing, or dare, to speak up against conglomerates' interests around the globe in order to save the environment or humanity? But, truly, it is ultimately our varied weaknesses and gullibility, including our choices of leaders, that cause social chaos and damage the environment, too. We are all guilty of wasting food, energy, clothing, etc., and for supporting social trends and norms so blindly. We must blame our materialistic minds, low spiritual sense, and deep-rooted gullibility as main sources of damage to environment. We allow industries and elites destroy our planet while fooling us about our potentials to be rich and happy like them by being greedy, ambitious, and ruthless towards nature and other people's basic needs and dignity. Are not these incentives tempting enough for people to nurture their badness? How could anybody even discuss, let alone practise, the goodness path in this intimidating setting without becoming a subject of total ridicule and abandonment?

Then again, without goodness engulfing large segments of the world population soon—a highly unlikely scenario—we will not find the incentive and courage to save our planet, either.

12. Culture

Culture is for creating a uniform mentality for people to gauge social elements and mechanisms properly and design productive processes to get the best results for the public. The objective is to propagate useful values, feel nature, and enjoy the finer aspects of life, including humans' creativity. However, as discussed in some length in Chapter Twelve, culture is not playing an effective role now as a crucial social element. Instead, people's mentality has focussed on whimsical values and lifestyles. Our modern drive for a crooked sense of individualism has by itself undermined our cultures and the need for a harmonious social vision with lots of teamwork. Some of the newer countries, like the United States, did not even get a chance to establish a proper culture, anyway, since they learned quickly to focus only on money, guns, killing, and means of exploiting others for personal and national interests. Capitalism replaced the need for a culture. Then, older countries were exploited initially before being lured with capitalistic goals that eroded their primitive sense of humanness, too. Accordingly, now even the old cultures, including the basic unifying influence of religions, have been flushed down the tube.

Now, we do not have a culture to measure and consider the fifteen social elements discussed in this chapter in a responsible manner. Very few people care about having a proper direction for the world culture. The norms and values that we often mistake for culture nowadays are only ruining our spirits and depleting the last grains of humans' ingenuity and consciousness about the right means of living and the way all social elements must work together effectively for the benefit of all, not a very tiny group. The whole world is now losing its sense and willpower to ponder the meaning and purpose of culture and how to go about instilling a functional process in society. Instead, we are just getting more absorbed in our corrupt, doomed neo-culture—the dire mentality to concentrate only on sexuality and money. We have not even defined the meaning and parameters of civilization—the world we use so much now!

Now, in our neo-culture, any individual or nation that resists capitalistic propagandas and values is labelled undemocratic and uncivilized. Any group against the norms of our showy societies and commercialization is doomed, while the entire world is being demoralized and demolished by allegedly modern lifestyles and ostentatious personal mentalities. Our shallow neo-culture and people's numbness in this setting are ruining the meaning and purpose of society, election, democracy, economy and all other social mechanisms. The world must now face many unsettling conflicts and bear the consequences of actions by narcissistic leaders like Donald Trump misguiding the public further and abusing their gullibility.

If we ever contemplate the means of refurbishing our culture, surely the only solution is for so many of us to start being better beings. We should demand and develop a culture in which the fifteen social elements are designed realistically for a common purpose with a long vision—a culture to goad people and nations help one another rather than spread hatred and hostility. Common people must grasp life's real values and essentialities, instead of wasting their brains and energies on trivia, imitating the lifestyle of celebrities, and envying the rich. Many urgent human needs and duties require people's cooperation instead of spending their lives on shallow socializing fads or bragging about their wealth.

The growing social havoc, including rising depression and addictions, is the outcome of our cultureless lifestyles. The fifteen social elements are now faltering with no congruity and cohesion for building a foundation for an ethical culture. If we ever find the wisdom and urge to at least consider the need for a viable culture, we must decide about the role and nature of each of these fifteen social elements and their congruity to serve humanity properly.

13. Democracy

Democracy is a big social promise and process, but it has proven to be merely another means of fooling people with some luring jargons like voting right, freedom of assembly or speech, free enterprise, capitalism, etc. Most intelligent, objective people know by now how useless these jargons are. In fact, democracy in the sense of free vote and speech is not going to help humanity as long as people are so naïve about politicians' promises and their ability to make common people's lives easier. Democracy would not work also as long as people cannot grasp both the complexity of social structure in the 21st century and the looming threats in the next few decades, for example, the fact that robots might abolish the need for 50-80 percent of work force in most industrial and service sectors. In particular, democracy is unattainable and meaningless in cultureless nations. The effects of humans' flawed nature in general and the absence of practical and moral social mechanisms are two other obstacles for accomplishing even the preliminary intentions of democracy.

Another major flaw with the present application of democracy is its emphasis on immediate needs of people and politicians, rather than pursuing a long-term vision for nations and humanity. In fact, the main reason for the rising, irresolvable social mayhem is the stress on short views and immediate interests of people that drive our present democracy. Now, people choose their leaders according to their promises for quick fixes and actions, instead of a vision for long-term national and international cooperation and peace. This mentality cannot help people and societies. In fact, humanity will collapse without a reliable process to make viable long-term decisions and build a balanced, harmonious, and free world. Then again, this way of thinking requires many personal and social sacrifices that we are not willing to make.

On the one hand, people's votes are vastly tainted by so much lies and propagandas that candidates and their rich sponsors inject into people's desperate heads. We commoners have no interest or expertise to grasp the overall socioeconomic conditions or worry about long-term social needs and complexities around the globe. We make our choices only based on our juvenile ideologies and beliefs or our immediate personal interests, such as promises for more jobs, tax relief, and preposterous incentives, which reveal those candidates' narrow views of the world affairs already.

On the other hand, politicians and leaders are handling their responsibilities too superficially and selfishly, merely for satiating their personal needs for power, influence, and affluence. They are merely concerned about winning, which means they try to be politically correct to exploit people's greed and insecurities. They worry only about their careers, while gauging the public's mood and the means of fooling them again during the next election.

Therefore, instead of bragging about our useless democracy, we should reassess its ultimate purpose and potency for building functional societies and sustaining humanity. Actually, we should blame our superficial democratic mechanisms and propagandas these days for present instability within social structure and the gloomy socioeconomic conditions around the globe. With our mishmash democracy, we are preventing our chance for creating fundamental plans that might serve people eventually within a stable environment. Instead, now the zeal for democracy is only serving wicked or pathetic leaders to fool us repeatedly. Some of these leaders might even believe in their actions and political compromises with various social groups, environmentalists, and industries, as a better option than letting a crooked dictator force tyrannical solutions and ideologies for running the country.

Overall, we have been misleading ourselves with our naïve perceptions of democracy. It is simply impossible for common people, or pathetic leaders like Donald Trump, to understand the complexity of national and international affairs and about the practicality and implications of democracy in the new era. Instead, socioeconomic chaos around the globe is heightening, all thanks to our naive impression of democracy, while conglomerates and elite groups abuse our incited emotions and deprived needs. Now merely the ruinous symptoms of capitalism are spreading faster all over the world under the auspices of democracy and human rights, while people and leaders get greedier and snobbier with no capacity to serve others or their countries.

14. Economy

National and international economies have been under pressure rather regularly throughout human history, but the situation has gotten worse in the new era and will get out of control in a few decades due to the accelerating deteriorations of even the basic principles sustaining capitalism. With so many conflicting forces at play in society, e.g., environmental issues and pollution due to consumerism and industrial expansion, finding the right balances and satisfying people have become impossible. No leader can solve these fundamental problems, although many simpletons or charlatans keep promising to do all that and more so arrogantly during elections. The problem, of course, is again our naiveté to fall for such nonsensical, self-serving propagandas. The obstacle is mostly our reluctance to realize that creating economic fairness and stability is impossible before inventing an entire economic foundation and structure totally outside the current capitalistic ideologies that depend on wasteful consumerism to grow with so much pain for people and nature. The looming catastrophes in relation to nations' growing debts are worrisome, too, of course.

Unfortunately, people have no expertise or mentality to help themselves out of this perplexing economic confusion. They cannot see and accept the sad reality that capitalism, at least in its present form, can never fulfil the needs of a just, peaceful society. People should accept that production centres would continue to move around within nations and around the globe. So expecting our leaders to revive old jobs in our towns and communities is simply futile and ludicrous. Production modes and sites would continue to change quite rapidly and people must be willing to move around in search of new jobs. And this is just the beginning of even harsher realities when robots would take over a majority of jobs and when economic depressions eliminate even the chance for basic social services. Our jargons and boasting about democracy in this climate, based on flimsy economic principles, is meaningless or in fact shameful, especially when some nations insist on selling capitalism and democracy to other nations under the slogan of human rights! How brazen and arrogant humans, especially politicians, can be is just amazing!

Instead of supporting our outmoded systems and mentality and promising unrealistic economic solutions, both our leaders and people should develop a new mindset about the economic catastrophes awaiting us all. We are doomed, unless we start to overhaul our existing economic models and mindsets. We have at best only a few decades to ponder our lifestyles and the world's economic systems to save humanity possibly.

15. Authority

While social problems have accelerated and besieged all people and nations, no leader in any part of the world has the vision and power to do anything about humans' sad future. We rush to help the victims of storms or earthquake, etc. Yet, the roots of all these mayhem, e.g., climate change, are ignored. Nobody can help this dire situation, it seems! However, our arrogant disregard of what is happening, what our goals are, and where we are heading, is the silliest part of this social demise. We simply seem oblivious to humans' faltering fate, instead of rushing and pushing for a way of helping ourselves—the worldwide victims—before it is too late! Instead, our elected officials are only interested in their own political agendas, people's crude votes, and their sponsors' immediate needs more than they worry about the lasting welfare of common people and their nations. They just appear pitifully useless when the welfare of humanity and planet is discussed. Most of our leaders and elite groups only care about exploiting their authorities and our broken political systems. The checks and balances imposed to prevent the authorities' abuse of power are comically ineffective and in fact causing their share of chaos and bottlenecks.

Often a prime minister or president is incapable of doing the right things simply because the opposing party controls the senate or parliament. Even when one leader succeeds to do something more in line with the welfare of majority, such as a decent, fairer access to healthcare, after only a few years the next leader or party in control repeals those laws. Under these circumstances, and within such dysfunctional systems, no authority exists or can run the affairs of a country, let alone the whole globe, effectively on a fair, consistent basis. Thus, the whole world is in shambles, on a fast-declining path, because of all the games that political parties and world authorities play against one another and their people. Only the powerful conglomerates continue to enjoy these muddied waters.

Not only our leaders are too naïve, helpless, or self-serving, but also the immensity of conflicts among various leaders within and among nations disallow even a uniform perception of global problems and plausible remedies. People and nations still think merely in terms of their own interests regardless of what happens to their neighbours, other countries, or humanity overall. Surely, this mindset would never help anybody, while we insist to ignore the need for an international grasp of human misery and social problems, and the need for universal solutions. Could anybody envision a remedy for human salvation in this corrupt setting?

All the social elements numerated in this chapter, plus religions, need a major overhaul if we are interested in humanity's future, yet no leaders and authorities are at hand to grasp the problems and take charge of the required revolution. For example, the large varieties of problems related to health insurance and the costs of drugs, limited social services to help people, the poor quality of food, and low conscience among doctors and pharmaceutical companies all add up and put deep pressures on people's physical and mental health. Every one of these areas of neglect requires major attention and action, but, most of all, a long-term vision is needed for coordinating these social elements and processes somewhat effectively and efficiently. Yet, authorities and leaders simply refuse even acknowledging the depth of the problems and finding sensible plans to address people's sufferings according to a long-term vision for humanity. They have failed to build proper processes for any of the main social elements, let alone an overall plan with some degree of harmony and synergy among all these fifteen social mechanisms.

As noted before, religion, as an essential social element, was deliberately excluded from discussions in this chapter due to its contentious nature, although enough ideas about spirituality and religions are offered throughout the book, especially in Chapter Ten. Nevertheless, religions need major attention and an overhaul due to the damages they are inflicting upon humans' minds and causing deeper global naiveté, as well as all kinds of conflicts and wars around the world. These religious sources of human demise are merely too embarrassing at this day and age.

The main purpose of reviewing social elements and processes in this chapter and drawing a rather full picture of our doomed social structure has been to build a realistic personal perspective for pursuing the goodness path. Understanding the influence and burdens of the noted social elements might also help us realize why it has become so difficult to find real friends or companions, especially when they aggravate the inherent evil in human nature, as explained in the earlier parts of this book. Most importantly, perhaps some people, the youths in particular, realize the need for a real revolution, in line with mature and practical goals, as a last resort for human salvation. Then do something about it too.

Realistically, we need simpler socioeconomic and political structures in less complex settings with no need for constant economic growth, while keeping the size of global population manageable and stressing on people' wiser mentalities thru self-realization in moralistic societies.

Chapter Nine
Goodness Regimen (Path)

Bad news: Human nature is impure, the neo-culture and democracy are harmful, our demented social values bring on the worst in people, and world leaders and authorities have no sense, interest, or power to save the world and humanity.

Good news: Most people realize the rising social evil and try to resist badness *randomly* when facing injustice.

Therefore, many people are potentially equipped to be a bit better beings, in spite of humans' innate wickedness nurtured in highly efficient badness factories around the globe posing as modern societies. The question is whether enough good people can gather to help at least one another within a cohesive group aiming to coexist outside the norms and pressures of a disorderly globe.

Ironically, humans have always dreamed about, and tried to invent, a harmonious society. Despite all the inner and outer forces pushing us towards chaos and evil too often, we envision and prefer a rather stable, ethical society. Our occasional grasp and loathing of badness help our conscience and psyche. Even this raw conscience and sense for morality is promising at least as a tentative restraining force against our inherent evil.

The big hurdle is that we do not have an incentive or guidance to internalize betterness as a valid strategy towards social stability and pursue it consciously every day. We have failed to grow a social mentality to define the means for a harmonious world or at least attain a relative personal peace. In fact, humans' reluctance or inability to work together, in spite of their desire for a practical, moral society, is a mysterious, bizarre paradox. That is, we could have invented a civilized means of cooperating and relating better globally for a moral, calmer coexistence by now if we had learned how to use our alleged high intelligence that we humans like to brag about so much. Instead, our inability to think of a functional social structure has led to the growth of human evil and global chaos way beyond humans' flawed nature has.

Still, humans' innate desire and thoughts about ethics affirm their potential for becoming a better being if a person decides and learns to become somewhat conscious of his/her authentic needs and circumvent the social influence on him/her. In another word, a certain path of goodness exists for some wiser people towards personal salvation even in our chaotic society and in spite of our flawed nature. They can build their convictions and self-reliance to resist the lures of social compliance and rewards in order to find their own individualism, identity, and peace.

The first step towards goodness is to believe in our reasons for becoming a better person sincerely. We must grasp the goodness goals and elements, and then focus on the strenuous, long process of sustaining our incentive for being a better being through steady reflections over those goals and the topics discussed in chapters 2 and 5. Building this divine capacity is neither easy nor feasible for some people with deeply sullied souls and minds, especially the matter of abandoning our destructive habits and perceptions. Still, we would never know until we strive sincerely to help ourselves. At the end, the success would depend on a person's conviction, the same way some addicts kick their habits easier than others would, while most of them keep living in misery and dying in disgrace. Maybe our obsession for malice and corruption is not as fatal as drug addiction, but it is equally as daunting, crushing, and hard to kick. Most of all, it is too embarrassing.

Goodness Goals and Practices

The goodness pyramid (structure) presented in Chapter Six shows the 7 goodness goals that are achieved thru the 7 practices listed in Table 9.1. We strive to develop our *authenticity, autonomy, vision,* and *vitality* as foundation to build our sense of *humility* and bring *harmony* into our lives, and then maybe even approach the realm of *divinity* as the highest level of goodness.

Goodness 'regimen' has 5 stages, 7 practices, 10 elements, and 7 goals, which are explained in this chapter gradually and shown in Table 9.3 on page 225 right after the goals and practices are explained. (You may take a pick at Table 9.3 now and maybe photocopy and use it as a map thru the detail review of 'goodness regimen' in the following pages and as a guide for reflections in the future.)

Table 9.1: Goodness Goals and Practices

Goodness Goals	Goodness Practices
Authenticity	Do Self-cleansing
Autonomy	Build Self-reliance
Vision	Develop a Personal Life Philosophy
Vitality	Help Others with Positive Energy
Harmony	Develop a Knack for Teamwork
Humility	Master Selflessness
Divinity	Show Devotion and Self-sacrifice

Self-cleansing is the first practice of goodness for building our *authenticity*. It requires a sense of purpose and commitment, to strive for a higher stance of 'being' towards selflessness. We should pinpoint and acknowledge our wicked urges, learn how to curb them, and resist the temptation of hasty reactions to people's attitude and words. This means constant cognizance and control of our egotistical urges to be mean like others just for being good *to* ourselves—to serve our interests and ego. Instead, we strive to be good *for* ourselves mainly through 'self' realization, at the cost of regular humiliation in the face of the tyrannies that people, in particular our families, impose upon us.

Again, building this level of maturity and stoic attitude is hard, mostly for the simple reason that our tricky egos are grown too powerful to tame. Moreover, we have a hard time seeing even our most obvious defects, e.g., obsession for lying and deceit. Our brains have a knack for denying reality, especially when it hurts our egos and interests. We just have no capacity to see our flaws, let alone the guts to acknowledge them. It is bizarre and amazing that sometimes we even lie and do nasty things in our dreams, and then in the morning wonder, often for fun, about the interpretation of our open badness in our dreams. We wonder and laugh about the evil that resides deep down in our unconscious and then emerges with such vengeance in our dreams. So maybe we are not as good as we usually think to be, we wonder!

Nevertheless, we should try to penetrate our subconscious and maybe unconscious through meditation and self-assessment. This exercise would help us raise our self-awareness, detect the roots of our idiosyncrasies, and find the means and courage to defeat them gradually. Pushing our brains for self-cleansing and finding the roots of our flaws is a major practice that anybody serious about goodness adopts as a start.

The second goodness practice is to develop **self-reliance**, as it is simply impossible nowadays to depend on people and society to be compassionate and caring when we need help. In particular, our families and friends keep disappointing us, while the crooked social values push them to be self-centred and careless about their obligations. As it is getting harder to trust people's integrity and commitments nowadays, we must learn to build a personal life based on a high degree of self-reliance in line with our beliefs and inner strength. We should define our individualism in a sensible manner mainly on the power of our *autonomy*.

The third goodness practice is to develop a **life philosophy** (vision), and devise a plan to accomplish all the goals that every smart person should aspire for living nowadays in addition to all his/her social responsibilities. For becoming a better being, one must have both a *vision* and a plan for living, which would boost his/her self-reliance as well.

The fourth goodness practice is to **help others** in any way we can by boosting our positive energy about self and life for our own and other people's benefits, and maybe even goading more people ponder the option of following the goodness regimen themselves, thus revitalizing societies in a few centuries perhaps. This practice both requires and grows *vitality*.

The fifth goodness practice is to empower or develop our **knack for teamwork** by sharing our thoughts and interests with others, especially our companion, rather than focusing merely on individualism. This expertise stirs *harmony* in our own lives.

The sixth major goodness practice is to grasp the meaning and means of **selflessness**, mostly by working on our relationships with people, especially family, in the light of rising social barriers making relationships unreliable, humiliating, intimidating, and tough. We must raise our tolerance and patience by curbing our dogmatism and arrogance in hopes of making our relationships as calm and productive as possible. Actually, we must learn to cope with society and people effectively and fairly, while making social contributions, despite all the pressures they impose upon us daily. Raising our interest in humanity and coexistence is another goodness practice—to master selflessness and *humility*.

The goodness practices are interrelated and work together for self-cleansing and raising our self-awareness to achieve the seven goodness goals, and perhaps even *divinity*. At this high level of enlightenment, 'devotion and self-sacrifice' feels like a natural practice for being. Overall, deciding about a right path of life and succeeding to fulfil its goals are important for making our lives less erratic and hectic, and for stirring peace and harmony in our personal lives.

Goodness Elements

As we follow the 7 goodness practices explained above, we focus on, and learn, the following 10 goodness elements.

Table 9.2: Goodness Elements

1. Genetic Capacity	6. Patience
2. Resignation	7. Forgiveness
3. Stoicism	8. Identity
4. Conviction	9. Personality
5. Tolerance	10. High Consciousness

These goodness elements are ranked by their priority, though they must be studied and practised rather collectively through a long *process* of experimenting and learning.

A **'genetic capacity'** for goodness is the first element to check, as many of us either lack or do not get a chance to explore due to varied reasons. Thanks to poor social teachings, usually we do not know if we have a genetic knack for goodness or not, since most of us are simply convinced of being excellent beings already. We are quite certain about not only our goodness, but also our perfection, especially in terms of mental superiority. Thus, a prerequisite for assessing our capacity for goodness is to understand and admit that nobody is ever pure enough, at least due to crooked family and social teachings. In fact, trying to build a basic modesty and acknowledge our definite shortfalls is the best practice for gauging our 'capacity for goodness.' Then, we test ourselves through self-assessment and meditation during the lengthy goodness regimen outlined in the next section. In the end, many of us might realize our lack of temper and capacity for goodness—mostly after feeling and admitting that our obsession for evil and self-gratification is too strong and precious to us to sacrifice even for the chance of growing our peace of mind and gaining salvation. Conversely, some people recognize and exploit their capacities for goodness gradually thru sincere self-cleansing and meditation practices, while pondering the goodness goals and building their incentive for becoming a better being.

Assuming we feel and nurture our capacity for modesty and truth, we sense plausible signs about our aptitude for goodness. Then, we can attend to the task of **'resignation,'** which is merely the notion of admitting to ourselves that we would be on our own —rather alone—in our journey of goodness, while we should abandon so many privileges of belonging to a crooked society built upon a big load of showy, shallow values. We resign from the games and role-playing in society and with people largely. Accordingly, we must develop a civilized sense of **'stoicism,'** as the next element of goodness required for coping with the new environment and living in our delicate, private universe, which we are planning to create around ourselves.

The next element of goodness is **'conviction.'** We must build the courage and faith that should sustain us in our long and lonely journey on the goodness path. Without a strong conviction, we would soon abandon our goodness goals after encountering life's harsh realities continuously, including people's antipathy towards those with low enthusiasm about the mainstream's obsessions for vanity. We should build a profound conviction and resilience to withstand people who take our resignation and stoicism as a sign of weakness and lack of ambitions. Some may even see it as a demented or radical type of arrogance.

Naturally, to deal with these negative side effects of pursuing a goodness path, including people's malice and low view of humbler people, we must develop a great deal of **'tolerance,' 'patience,'** and **'forgiveness.'**

While gauging and practising the main elements of goodness noted above, including our efforts for modesty and resignation, we begin to develop our authentic values and sense our **'identity'** emerging out of a heap of superficial forms and needs that we had been cherishing as our main purposes for living. We refurbish our inherent integrity and sense of 'being' merely for our own benefit without fussing about compliance and imitation of mainstream's norms. Meanwhile, our comprehensive new identity connects us to society and people easier and sincerer, despite the difficulty of humouring too many conceited and shallow individuals.

All along, we align our **'personality'** with our 'identity' to fulfil our authentic needs, while learn the art of living peacefully with people easier. Personality is different from identity and has three distinguished aspects that are discussed in other books.[*]

Finally, we might reach the state of **'high-consciousness,'** which is the tool for grasping our true self, connecting with the universe in a genuine manner, and gaining a divine wisdom.

As we master the above ten elements of goodness gradually in line with our genetic capacity, we become a better being every day. A small group with no genetic capacity for goodness might find a huge incentive by a miracle and then work much harder than others to build their beliefs, follow the goodness regimen, and possibly even reach an incredible divinity.

To stay on track and remember the purpose of our efforts, we must adhere to a rigid routine that we must build personally and follow seriously. We call this routine the goodness regimen.

Goodness Stages

Goodness regimen is a routine for mastering the ten elements of goodness and achieving the goodness goals. We take certain steps gradually in line with our rising personal awareness and growth. Table 9.3 shows the goodness elements, practices, and goals in five stages. During each stage, we try to understand and perfect some elements of goodness towards specific goals listed in Table 9.3 and explained on pages 219-221, which would then prepare us to move on to the next stage and build up goodness virtues— maybe even enlightenment and divinity. Our routines keep us on track, as we reflect on goals and practices of goodness.

---

[*] See this author's book, *The Nature of Love and Relationships* or *Doubts and Decisions for Living, Volume I.*

Table 9.3: Goodness Regimen

Five Goodness Stages	Ten Goodness Elements	Seven Goodness Practices	Seven Goodness Goals
Experimenting	Genetic Capacity Resignation Stoicism	Self-cleansing Self-reliance	Authenticity Autonomy
Awakening	Convictions	Life Philosophy Helping Others	Vision Vitality
Internalizing	Tolerance Patience Forgiveness	Teamwork	Harmony
Salvation	Identity Personality	Selflessness	Humility
Maturation	Full Consciousness	Devotion	Divinity

The goodness regimen begins when we feel an urge to grasp the noted goals and elements. This basic musing helps us affirm our incentive for being a better being, then get ready to practice the ten goodness elements noted above for their specific purposes, e.g. self-cleansing. We study the means of mastering the elements, meditate, gauge the effects on our way of thinking and acting during our dealings with people, create our routines for testing and practising these goodness elements, and feel humbler. All along, we analyse the changes in our thoughts and behaviour in relation to goodness goals and strive to determine our progress in terms of each element and goal.

Table 9.3 suggests the five stages of goodness in line with a person's level of engagement and development. They are:

1. Experimenting

The experimenting routine is for working on goodness elements slowly and gauging our goodness capacity. During months and years, we try to boost our incentive for being a better person than we have been. Deciding sensibly about our genetic capacity for goodness is tough, so we should initially stay positive and work on elements related to self-cleansing and self-reliance. Our mood and consciousness about our being grow slowly, while we sense our genetic capacity for becoming a better being. Otherwise, we may wish to accept our incapacity for goodness and give up.

After affirming our incentive and genetic capacity, we would continue with the task of resigning from our social addictions and growing a fresh perspective about life and people. We would also try to attain a sense of stoicism, which would help us go through this preliminary stage of self-cleansing and building self-reliance smoothly towards the two primary goals (virtues) of goodness, *authenticity* and *autonomy*.

2. Awakening

At this stage, we establish strong convictions for ourselves and build a solid personal life philosophy to guide us for the rest of our lives. As a result, we can achieve the next two goals (virtues) of goodness: i) building our personal *vision* and life philosophy, and ii) Growing *vitality* to fight life pressures and sources of stress, and to maximize our power of insight and ingenuity.

3. Internalizing

At this stage, we master the arts of tolerance, forgiveness, and patience. The outcome is a serene sense of peace and *harmony* in our lives for the first time, despite the fact that we still have to live within the same corrupt environments. We learn about teamwork and connecting to others and society in a civilized manner, and we try to help people with our positive energy.

4. Salvation

At this stage, we finally find our inner self and true identity. Our shoddy personality is transformed into a truthful and confident character that knows how to deal with people civilly, despite their wickedness and spite. Accordingly, we achieve the sixth ultimate goal (virtue) of goodness, *humility,* through selflessness. We just acknowledge our nothingness in contrast to the immense level of the haughtiness we have felt and shown around all our lives. (Another 23 *Goodness Symptoms* are also listed below.)

5. Maturation

Finally, some extremely lucky and diligent people might gain full consciousness about their being and sense their innate connection to the universe. These enlightened people reach the highest level of goodness, *divinity,* through self-sacrifice and devotion.

Of course, a basic sense of serenity, or even divinity, is felt slowly during the 'Experimenting' stage already, as one begins the goodness regimen. It is an enriching sense and worthy of our endeavours in itself, even if a person loses the chance or desire to pursue the other stages of goodness. Our efforts and sacrifices for being even a bit better beings, instead of persisting to remain too egotistical and dogmatic, could go a long way in improving our personal lives as well as our relationships with others.

The goodness regimen entails long reflections and self-analysis consistently to grasp our insecurities, acknowledge our flaws, do self-cleansing, and determine our purposes for living. Through meditation and self-evaluation, we test our new convictions and boost our goodness elements, such as compassion and tolerance when we face people. We remember goodness goals and practise humility the most, especially when people's attitudes humiliate or hurt us, or when their words threaten our egos.

A primary principle of the goodness regimen is to do almost everything contrary to what our ego often goads us to do. Both our natural defects and social demands force us to be bad. So fighting our dire egos and social habits is the best tool for self-awareness and cleansing our flaws. Learning humility is particularly useful for gauging our genetic capacity for goodness.

As we meditate and draw on our growing inner wisdom, we begin to perceive the world and people in a new light, while our level of consciousness about life and the universe increases, too. Slowly, we attain a sacred sense of enlightenment, as we build and climb up the goodness pyramid that consists of *foundation* (i.e., Authenticity, Autonomy, Vision, and Vitality) to establish the right *form* (i.e., Harmony and Humility) towards the *finale* (i.e., Divinity), as explained in detail in Chapter Six.

Therefore, the goodness regimen entails a spirituality outlook, as explained in the next chapter. Eventually, we might even attain the kind of enviable enlightenment that usually spiritual gurus claim as a presumed divine connection with the universe.

Goodness Scope (Symptoms)

Offering a broad account of goodness attributes would be both impossible and impertinent. Yet, pointing out a few symptoms and benefits of goodness could be useful. Certainly, any kind of deception, perversion, and malice would feel awkward to an awakened person wishing to stay on the goodness path. More importantly, however, the ingenuity and self-reliance resulting from goodness goad us to:

1. Discard our idealistic perceptions of life, society, religions, people, and the universe.
2. Embrace goodness merely for the sake of personal salvation, which has nothing to do with promises of rewards or reprisal, now or afterlife, for who we are and what we do. We might then learn how to stop our gullibility, emotions, and fantasies goading us to trust the nonsense that society and people, even some dubious spiritualists, advocate.
3. Abandon our juvenile habits, needs, and addictions to social norms, propagandas, and false news.
4. Admit that our logic is vastly tainted by our predispositions, dogmatism, ego, and crooked social norms. Thus, its value is quite low for studying human essence, recognizing social needs, or judging people's attitudes, needs, and intentions.
5. Take the gigantic leap to come down from the clouds and fight off our haughtiness to find our nothingness.
6. Admit that, despite their holy intentions, all religions have caused human gullibility and horrendous animosities. So, we

become more realistic about many unnatural or contentious ideas, including afterlife and God. We study and decide alone about the possible role that any religion may play for making anybody a better being or only raising his/her gullibility.

7. Build a strong mindset without becoming dogmatic, stick to our convictions without condemning others, and get fearless to resist social evils, including capitalism and consumerism, without getting reckless or fighting people.
8. Grasp the true meaning and implications of individuality, which evolves through humility, contrary to our misguided impression as an excuse for pumping our egos.
9. Learn about the goals and effects of our contentious gender aspirations in our families, society, politics, etc., in line with various roles that we are so eager to play nowadays.
10. Recognize that gender conflicts and quarrels have become a major cause of badness, while also minimizing our chances to explore our goodness. Thus, addressing this dire epidemic more effectively is urgent and essential.
11. Live naturally with an authentic personality, instead of trying so much to impress others. We can learn to live based on our personal principles (that we should develop gradually), often against mainstream's values. With all the high qualities that a person could build for enlightenment and divinity, and with all the things s/he could do and learn for self-actualization and contentment, why would s/he even wish or consider any shallow lifestyle for impressing others, even his/her lover?
12. Learn how to be a better man, woman, father, spouse, child, employee, citizen, etc, in addition to being a better human. We learn to play each one of these roles in line with its own needs and goodness criteria for helping everybody.
13. Realize that we all have our moments of doubts (relapse) about either indulging a mere existence or seeking goodness, which requires lots of efforts and sacrifice even for a primary enlightenment. Yet, we can curb such moments of weakness,

while we learn that existence and goodness are mysteriously related in a way beyond our primitive impression of being.
14. Realize that building a realistic, divine personal philosophy is essential for delineating a peaceful life path and making our lives less erratic and hectic.
15. Recognize how naively we strive to live in a fantasy world, especially in terms of our crude perceptions about happiness, love, success, and relationships. We have become this way in recent decades due to the world's dire commercialization even with respect to art and literature.
16. Build a wise balance between solitude—for peace of mind—and social inclusion to cope with society's harsh realities. Eluding the contentious reality of life, despite all its burdens, is imprudent. Living requires lots of vision and involvement, even though tranquility demands isolation and deprivation.
17. Realize that while mind development routines, such as yoga and meditation, help our self-awareness and peace, building goodness requires stable consciousness, commitment, and a rather stoic mind on a long virtuous journey. At the same time, living a normal life—working, building a good family, socializing, etc.—is both necessary and precious.
18. Boost our faith and ingenuity for creating a practical balance for mastering goodness and handling social living hardships patiently. Instead of hoping to bask in our being in seclusion, we should know how to face troubling situations and cope with random, unfair impositions of existence that often drag us into long, agonizing games and make us play idiotic roles. Accordingly, we should remain conscious of our convictions, social coping mechanisms, and our rude reactions. We attain this goal by strengthening our goodness attributes (inner self).
19. Decide whether resistance (or even violence) has any role within the goodness path. We often realize that it does, but scarcely, merely for fighting rampant social naivety, people's incompetence, and capitalism.

20. Realize that nobody can ever be good enough, never mind perfect, even despite all his/her efforts and sacrifices to build the goodness elements and goals noted in Table 9.3. Yet, most of us can imagine those human attributes that sound honourable as symptoms of goodness. Keeping Table 9.3 handy and consulting it every day would also be useful.
21. Realize that our spirits embrace the sanctity of goodness and fill our hearts with joy and wisdom once we mature. Yet, we have simply not acquired the incentive and chance to explore goodness as a pertinent social exercise and to experience its attributes and feelings as a sensible option for being. We are either too mesmerized by pervasive social perversions or too weak to fight with common norms and values, as well as our egos and obsessions. Thus, our spirits' sufferings are of our own making largely.
22. View Goodness Regimen as a personal spirituality ritual that can boost our spirits and help us build our inner strength for the long confusing life journey. This is an important topic that is addressed exclusively in the next chapter.
23. Embrace our **Nothingness** and build humility as the ultimate virtue of goodness and being.

Grasping our Nothingness is a personal mission, discovery, and triumph. It signifies our progress towards enlightenment past self-awareness. This process also entails three distinct stages for revamping our three personality aspects (Model, Ego, and Self)[*]: First, **understanding our nothingness**, which entails our ability to curb our Model personality that goads our urges for showiness and pretension. Thus, we grasp our authentic needs and purposes of living. Second, **accepting our nothingness** by eradicating our Ego. Third, **feeling our nothingness** that happens when we get close to our inner Self and embrace the sense and meaning of our being and nothingness together.

---

[*] For personality aspects' descriptions, see this author's book, *The Nature of Love and Relationships* or *Doubts and Decisions for Living, Volume I*.

Goodness Essence

Following the goodness regimen is for examining our Self and its seven elements in a brighter perspective and building a fulfilling, realistic, self-image (see footnote on page 146 regarding the seven elements of Self). Along the way, we realize that being good is merely *for* our own sake (salvation) compared with our pervasive obsession to focus solely on being good *to* (indulging) ourselves at any cost. This would be a delicate, gratifying discovery per se.

Being good *for* or *to* ourselves means different things. In fact, they reflect two opposite mentalities, incentives, and attitudes. The goal of being good *for* *ourselves (for our own sake)* is to find means of self-sufficiency and self-control. In contrast, the goal of being good *to* ourselves reflects merely the common urge to think only about serving our egos, often at the expense of hurting or humiliating other individuals. The crucial point is that we can be good either *to* or *for* ourselves until we gain goodness. This mainly implies that we cannot be good *for* ourselves if we are still obsessed with the mentality and objective of being good *to* ourselves the way the public usually think and behave. Being good *for* ourselves reflects the art of self-cleansing and our ability to muster high levels of resilience, humiliation, and self-reliance required for reaching a good degree of selflessness. Conversely, being good *to* ourselves (in our present culture) reflects our urge for selfishness. Being good *for* or *to* ourselves also represents the sources of humans' inner conflicts, as we wrestle with the two extreme forces of goodness and evil in our psyches regularly. Ironically, as we gain goodness gradually, being good *to* or *for* ourselves begin to mix and reflect the same notion of selflessness in a sacred sphere eventually. This is the goodness essence.

Some other features of the two alternatives of being good for or to ourselves are as follows:

1. **Being good to ourselves,** as a pervasive social practice, only makes people both naïve and dogmatic, while they submit to

their selfish urge to serve themselves at any cost. This means that we are often forced to be bad towards others, including our family, merely for indulging (being good to) ourselves—mainly to protect our egos, interests, or sanity. However, these external pressures to be bad like other people sadden us subconsciously, while they impair our spirit's chance to play its crucial role in our lives as noted in detail in Chapter Five. For example, if we have an abusive family, we eventually get fed up and show our displeasure by some actions and words that often sound insensitive or like some kind of retaliation to them. Most people, particularly our children, dismiss their own poor attitude and insensitivity and still expect us to be good to them. So even our simple act of treating them somewhat strictly, in line with their boorish behaviour, not only makes them angry and hostile, but also makes us feel down for behaving at their level. We usually try to react in line with what people deserve, yet, this rather logical habit (just for serving our egos) always stirs both senses of badness and sadness in us quickly, especially if we have a rather fair and fine conscience and an intention for being a better being. In all, the common urge for being good to ourselves is the prevalent, selfish method of reacting harshly towards any perceived threat to our egos at the cost of singeing our spirits. Sadly, arrogance is killing humans and humanity.

2. In contrast, **being good for ourselves** is a radical option that helps us to ignore other people's malice largely. We can train ourselves to become more conscious of our retaliatory habits and behaviour. This would be a hard task, especially when we are burning with rage and feeling a severe temptation to show at least our displeasure about, if not a harsh reaction to, people's insensitivity. Nevertheless, learning a high degree of self-control is an important objective of following the path of goodness. Naturally, reaching this level of enlightenment happens only gradually over the years and decades. Yet, this ultimate goal must always remain in our heads as a yardstick

for pursuing the goodness regimen. We must build our inner strengths to absorb social and psychological burdens on the path to attaining a soulful identity eventually—*after growing a divine capacity through self-control and self-cleansing.*

On the one hand, being better beings *for* ourselves (for our own good) is the most rational way to keep our sanity and peace, while keeping a civil, stoic contact with people, too. These are valued goals of goodness. On the other hand, the idea of focusing on our Self for personal welfare and self-realization, mostly by giving up on socializing opportunities, due to people's naiveté or evil nature, might sounds a bit selfish in itself. Still, the objective of being good *for* ourselves, as a tool for self-improvement, is better justified than the selfishness of being good *to* ourselves just for the sake of socializing. Our resistance to learn anything about goodness or to curb our urges for badness—while mixing with the mainstream and striving to serve ourselves—would damage our psyches and relationships even further. In contrast, as we learn to be good for ourselves, we can be good for others, too, or at least gain a higher conscience to avoid hurting others, which is a nasty social habit nowadays.

Chapter Ten
Spirituality Haven

Spirituality is merely the serenity and wisdom that grows on the goodness path gradually. It reaches its height when a person approaches selflessness and divinity during the final stage of enlightenment, as shown on the goodness pyramid. Therefore, besides its urgent goals, goodness is a long journey for a possible grasp of spirituality as a personal haven, though not for reaching heaven. Neither goodness nor spirituality is for seeking outwardly rewards or performing some showy rituals mindlessly. Instead, their common objective is to access our Self, explore our innate potentialities, and build a solid personality with truthful beliefs, mostly for bearing people and life's tyrannies patiently and gracefully. Grasping this inherent link between goodness and spirituality, as well as their basic worldly goals, is vital. Goodness and spiritualism are just two complementary notions for building an active, self-reliant character. Both are for gauging and growing our self with the intention of curbing our egos, attachments, and addictions to mainstream's pleasure-seeking mentality.

As explained in Chapter Five, our spirit drives our inner urge for spirituality as an exercise for manifesting and boosting itself —the spirit. At the same time, both our spirits and spirituality reflect our search for goodness roots in humans. Overall, both our spirit and curiosity about goodness goad us to seek the meaning and means of spirituality to enrich our lives. The journey begins when we feel an urge and incentive for being a better person, and then pursue the rigid process of becoming a better being. If we succeed, we attain a certain level of spiritualism automatically. Without our initial, sincere interest to follow a goodness regimen, hoping to attain spiritualism is a futile, superficial attempt. We should be mentally ready and convinced about our honest need for goodness, instead of hoping to find spiritualism and its alleged virtues by adopting some raw rituals or faiths. This mentality is contrary to the customary practice by organized religions or cults. In fact, the goodness goals and regimen explained in the previous chapter provide a practical, simple platform for developing our personal spirituality thoughts and routines without the need to invent some peculiar rituals or rewards for spiritualism.

The problem with religions and most spirituality practices is its inherent futuristic perspective rather than its potential for some limited personal benefits only now. They make people adopt a bunch of juvenile beliefs and rituals in hopes of reaping some rewards mostly afterlife. Faith might even push some people to tame their devilish urges and thoughts or observe some goodness measures based on their religious or spirituality guidelines. Yet, faith per se does not make people grasp spiritualism or goodness as a being. They fail, as they start with raw assumptions at the wrong end of the goodness/spirituality spectrum. That is, people seek spirituality before they are mentally convinced and socially prepared to be a better being per se regardless of reaching the end privilege of spiritualism or not. Like most things we humans have done throughout our history, our goodness and spirituality efforts are pursued in the reverse order as well, by force, for the wrong reasons, and superficially. Our religious rituals or spiritual beliefs without an initial personal incentive for goodness are useless. These practices are in fact against goodness principles due to the high level of gullibility that blind faith and devotions to religions and raw spiritualism induces, whereas goodness is mostly for abolishing gullibility.

Spirituality is an authentic, high-level need of humans, which satisfying it would empower our psyches and mental health.[*] As such, it must be practised naturally, instead of getting hung up on some crude ideologies and beliefs, such as God or afterlife. Blind faith and rituals based on naive desires or assumptions regarding afterlife are ridiculous and solid proofs of gullibility. Instead, any kind of faith, or our incentive for goodness and spiritualism, must be only for its positive effects on a person's psyche and mind with no external implications, especially about afterlife. How can any person or supreme power goad people to consider this type of unorthodox mentality about religions and spirituality?

Our need for salvation and a more meaningful existence is in our spirits and deep consciousness, and spiritualism is merely the means of satisfying those basic needs. We seek spiritualism also because our spirit feels energized by some sense of connection to a larger entity outside our physical being. The big problem is that we usually do not know how to explore and fulfil our need for spirituality on our own in line with our inner strengths. Instead, we are easily drawn to religions or some enlightenment rituals to feed our inherent spirituality need superficially. Accordingly, few of us get a chance to either seek goodness and spirituality or grow our inner strengths and high spirits.

Throughout the history of humanity, we have neither grasped nor nurtured our need for spirituality properly, because religious leaders and scholars have misrepresented this concept. We do not realize that we can grow a sense of spiritualism naturally when we build our inner strengths to soothe our souls, raise our spirits, and learn to take life in our strides. Besides the direct benefits of self-grown faith, i.e., high spirits, goodness merits, and a peaceful contentment, we also acquire some degree of enlightenment.

Religions and new spirituality jargons have now in fact stirred lots of cynicism and confusion for people who are disappointed

---

[*] See footnote on page 129. The Role and Shortfalls of Spirituality are also explained in Chapter Three of *Doubts and Decisions for Living, Volume II*.

with traditional means of fulfilling their needs for divinity. Now, smart people have lost their trust in divinity and goodness fully, since they do not know how to explore their spiritualism through their own inner self and strengths. At best, people see spirituality and enlightenment as abstract and mystical concepts, like some fantasy about a supernatural power. Thus, they either submit to teachings of religions blindly to resolve their urges for divinity or fully dismiss the notions of spiritualism and enlightenment. Some even prefer to become atheists in order to subdue their inherent urges and curiosities about spirituality. They find this approach most convenient and fast for handling their inner conflicts caused by their subliminal urge for spirituality versus their basic logic refuting religious claims. In all, people's desperate efforts to adopt a religion blindly or stay rigid atheists show our ruined mentality about spirituality, although we crave it instinctually. Thus, we can conclude that the lack of a true meaning and means of spirituality has hurt almost everybody throughout human history.

In a practical, simple context used here, spirituality is merely a natural extension of the goodness regimen, as defined all along. And enlightenment is mainly our ability to resist shallow means of living in order to find our true self and authenticity. The only purposes for spirituality and enlightenment are to overcome our rooted naivety and become more realistic about life, and then play our social roles consciously and responsibly. We do not need to go overboard about the meanings of spirituality and enlightenment. The goal is to grow a personal wisdom for living in peace with oneself after admitting the impossibility of humans ever building a harmonious society and enough social wisdom due to people's innate flaws and social pressures to keep them in their shells. Spirituality is also a solution against the options of becoming either an atheist or a religious fanatic based on blind faith. Ironically, following our personal spirituality regimen might bring us close to God, too!

At a high level of spirituality, we also address our curiosity about the supernatural power that dominates the whole spectrum of existence. Thus, on the one hand, spirituality is a regimen to reach and redeem our inner strengths. On the other hand, it is for connecting to a mysterious outer power that seems to augment our wisdom and enlightenment. We can believe in God or not and still develop a personal type and level of divinity. Spirituality is also about love. Not love of one person or oneself, but rather the love of all people and nature despite their malice. This kind of selfless love cannot nurture spite and hatred even when our egos and pride are threatened. Clearly, reaching this level of wisdom and self-control is a huge task for us vengeful, haughty humans! It is also so contrary to religions' historical knack for hostility.

Goodness regimen might lead to an ultimate sense of divinity only as a natural process of mental growth. During the primary stage on the goodness path, the emphasis is placed on finding and nurturing the sources of our inner strengths. Then, as we proceed successfully on this path, we sense, and begin to explore, an outer power that appears to support our drive for goodness towards divinity and completeness.

Outer Power

Nobody can deny that each person, animal, plant, and all other organic matters are filled with amazing levels of inner strengths, beauty, and celestial complexities. Then, learning even basic things about the universe shows the magnitude and majesty of the supernatural that rules such a phenomenal process of life and creation. As part of our self-realization, many of us also feel the presence of this supernatural—outer power—within and around us. At least occasionally, we get experiences beyond our ordinary senses and logic, as if this outer power were interfering with our lives, often with sacred intentions. We get blessings, feel lucky, and gain incredible insights that we cannot explain in any normal way. They just feel like clues about an outer power supporting us, especially when we set our minds and energy to proceed on the goodness path. Then again, many of us seem to receive some form of warning or misfortune abruptly in line with our meanness and malice. We seem to receive our shares of bad or good luck, which often feel related to the kind of person we choose to be.

Amazingly, most of us believe in the outer power and the possibility of its connection to our daily lives. On the other hand, no sense or evidence exists for afterlife or a set reward system for our deeds in this world. Nevertheless, we can embrace any kinds of feelings and beliefs about supernatural—an outer power—for nurturing our self-developed spiritualism. We can be an atheist, believe in God, or define the outer power based on our specific grasp of some form of reality. Some may even wish to believe in afterlife in order to satiate their illusory hopes. We can define our spiritualism in any manner, as long as we realize that our *absurd* interpretations or attempts to sell our perceptions and preferences to others would be contrary to the purpose of spiritualism, like the bizarre practices promoted by religions and spirituality gurus.

Many of us might have wondered about the meaning and purpose of strict, showy rituals that religions have mandated. Are those stringent worshiping and praying regimens God's direct orders or merely people's self-impositions? It is hard to imagine God has made such detail demands about the way He should be worshipped or the way people perform their spirituality rituals. In particular, some religions' use of harshest form of radicalism and violence to force their infantile beliefs, rituals, and ideologies on others sounds weird and against any peaceful purpose for divinity or the type of wisdom any benevolent God might recommend.

On the other hand, past our freedom to define our spiritualism based on our personal beliefs and feelings, we must still develop and adhere to some rather strict personal principles and routines, in line with ideas in this book, to advance on the goodness path smoothly, develop our inner strengths, and approach a primary or remarkable level of spiritualism and contentment. We should create some form of rituals and routines for self-discipline and staying in sync with our spirituality intentions. We can have our ways of connecting with this outer power to boost our beliefs and nurture our spirits, e.g., by meditating over the contents and meanings of Table 9.3 regularly. Such personal rituals are useful for keeping our beliefs intact. These soothing moods also create brain chemicals that promote our health.

Ultimately, we can never ascertain God's likely intentions to create good or pure humans. Instead, our daily experiences keep confirming that God—this outer power—could not, or chose not to, create all humans good. Maybe genetic changes and evolution could not be controlled totally. Yet, it is rational to believe that He knew that a bunch of humans might end up with genes and talents to become better beings if they got the right guidance or insight to delve into their beings. This likely raw justification is the only way of stopping ourselves from doubting God's ability or intention to create pure humans, or give them enough inner strength to become one on their own.

On the other hand, God definitely knows too, like the rest of us, *if not more,* that only some people can be good according to their finer genes, rearing conditioning, and social opportunities. Therefore, imposing a fixed guideline for rewarding people or punishing them for their sins sounds unjust and ludicrous—and, most of all, contrary to any type of divine intention that any sane person can ponder, let alone a fair God. This idea reveals another primary flaw of religious beliefs. It also shows humans' gullibility in terms of making or accepting many bizarre, prevalent claims about God's expectations from humans, such as purity, amazing virtues, or willpower to become better beings.

Obviously, human logic is too primitive to find answers to our dilemmas about God's possible intentions for creating humans, if anything at all. We can never explain His goal for some (or all) humans growing the right characteristics, gaining divine wisdom, and fulfilling certain purposes! *Or if all our efforts are merely a naive humanistic initiative for making Him happy and proud!* In fact, we may have an easier time to accept that God has never had any specific design or goal for humans' capacity or chance for divinity. *He did not even care!* We may enjoy a more realistic life if we agree on the impossibility of even a few of us reaching the proper level of piety. For one thing, both humans' emotions and logic are too fragile to allow consistent goodness. Our deep idiosyncrasies and emotions often make us quite dogmatic and incapable to analyze even simple issues. Thus, we would never understand God's possible wisdom and intentions for creating humans for any purpose outside humans' primitive, predisposed mentality. Yet, our crooked logic makes us perceive ourselves so important at the centre of the universe as God's preferred species. This conceited, naive self-image, spread by religions and goaded by our misperceptions about the world and society, prevents the chance of exploring the meaning and value of both our inner strengths and outer power. We ignore the signs and possibility of a divine force running both within and outside us and helping each person privately—sometimes even with sacred sensations. In all, either our religious fanaticism or our dogmatic atheism stops us from developing our personal spirituality regimen and exploring God—the outer power.[*]

Inner Strengths

Learning about goodness and practising its somewhat complex regimen might have felt gruelling already. Thus, this chapter's elaboration of spirituality and inner strengths may overwhelm us. However, there is no need to memorize or digest all these ideas. Rather, the readers are encouraged to merely try to familiarize themselves with these general ideas and then delve into them step by step slowly. It is best to work only on goodness regimen for at least one year to understand and cleanse our basic quirks before stressing on our inner strengths and finally mastering spirituality.

---

[*] I must humbly confess that I often believe this outer power—our sole God—has been goading my nosy muse to push me write this book mainly for offering some hypotheses about the ***Outer Power*** and for conveying His categorical denial of being involved with any religions or spiritual cults, especially their violent principles or guidelines. Sorry…! Unless my muse has been fooling with me, God wanted me to insist He has nothing to do with any of these outrageous claims and mumbo-jumbo under His name, but He loves us all, anyway, *especially me!*

After all, the three concepts of goodness, inner strengths, and spirituality are interrelated and driven by our spirits for personal growth. They mix and often share the same elements stirred by our spirits for a common goal, although it is useful to distinguish their roles. Nevertheless, our efforts and progress in any of these areas would in fact help us in the two other areas simultaneously. Especially, our ability to succeed on the goodness path ultimately depends on our inner strengths, so a short description of inner self and inner strengths is necessary without complicating matters.

'Self' was explained in Chapter Four to consists of a person's 1) Instincts, 2) Ingenuity (intelligence and Ego), and 3) Identity. (See Diag. 4.1, page 99.) **'Inner Self'** is merely humans' *spirited* essence (Self) outside their superficial needs, dogmatism, and pretensions. It holds virtues that we can strengthen and draw on to achieve the goodness goals and elements listed in Table 9.3.

Merely boosting our inner self (Self + spirit) in our daily lives helps us build our inner strengths, including beliefs, vigour, and mind for pursuing a simple peaceful life on the goodness path, while our spirit soars, too. In return, our inner strengths induce the intuition for gaining our true freedom, self-reliance, a sense of the Outer Power, and all other attributes needed for a meaningful existence and pursuing the goodness regimen.

As we get absorbed in an addictive, corrupt culture, we ruin our inner self that reflects our natural needs and potentials, as well as our spirit that generates our physical and mental strengths. The virtues of 'inner self' erupt in terms of the level of goodness and wisdom a person radiates when s/he proceeds on the path of goodness, which might lead to some level of spirituality. Still, the concept of 'inner self' sounds abstract, so the best way to grasp it is to review its **four** rather general elements and effects.

Instincts and intuition hold our divine potentials and natural urges to sense our urgent needs and finer purposes of our being, along with a chance to connect to a sacred sphere—without any illusion or expectation about afterlife. Just a mix of curiosity and need for refuge goads us to seek higher principles and guidelines for self-expression and living. Humans' lasting disappointment about their systematic inability to design a harmonious social structure for coexistence also fuels their innate need for salvation. These natural urges in humans also offer hints regarding some form of innate capacity in humans for being pure and good if evil forces in their minds and communities did not affect them so deeply. We have divine potentials that we may exploit to become better beings if we learn to draw on our sacred inner strengths and perhaps even put our heads together to build a more effective social structure in line with some level of spiritualism.

Ingenuity is the second element of inner self and a source of inner strengths. It entails 'intelligence and ego' noted in Chapter Four as a 'Self' attribute. We have a high sense of curiosity and an intrinsic urge to express our *deep* feelings and thoughts in novel manners. Yet, we miss the chance of fulfilling these sacred urges, because an immense load of infantile feelings and thoughts overwhelm our psyches and damage our drive for ingenuity. We are usually too distracted by our daily obligations and needs to explore our inner self and activate our creative minds. Moreover, self-expression and true individualism are risky nowadays within the superficial social framework, as we face the high chance of being ridiculed, pushed into depression, or rejected. If we resist social norms, we may have a hard time finding employment and a companion. Instead, we feel pressed to think inside the box and act like everybody else in order to fit in and be accepted by the public as a normal person, mostly in hopes of getting rich and famous. Thus, we try to sound modern and imitate the phony routines that our friends and family members expect from one another. Our intelligence and ego dwindle and we do not even find out about this source of energy (ingenuity) within us.

Identity reflects one's natural traits and needs clear from one's naive perceptions and phony personality. Most of us live under the influence of our egos without seeing the depth of our narcissism and ignorance. We do not know who we really are, while our personalities evolve around a wide range of insecurities and superficial needs. Thus, the stronger our personalities grow around pervasive social norms, the more we lose our identities and inner strengths. Nowadays, the Ego and Model aspects of personality drive our thoughts, feelings, and actions, with no or very little influence of our inner Self. Therefore, our egotistical personality and crude identity clash regularly, while both remain unexplored and our inner conflicts grow all along.

Spirit is the root of inner self, although its main function is to serve our outer self—body and mind. It connects our Self with outer dimensions, including people and the universe. When our spirit is low, our body begins to falter and we cannot think straight. We get sick either physically or mentally. Conversely, our efforts to maintain a healthy body, positive attitude, and clear thoughts boost our spirits. Nowadays, we stress on body-mind connectivity and the way our mind and body affect each other. Healthy mind is in the healthy body and vice versa, we remind one another and ourselves. However, 'spirit' should be included as an essential dimension of humans that completes a person's being, in particular for pursuing the goodness regimen, as noted on page 129. In all, it is crucial to perceive body, mind, and spirit as three interconnected dimensions of our existence. In fact, spirit must be viewed and empowered as humans' dominant dimension to keep our minds vibrant and our bodies healthy. Without a fine balance and teamwork among these dimensions, we lose our identity, ingenuity, and a capacity to stir our divine potentials. As noted all along, spirituality and goodness are the best venues to keep our spirits high, not the superficial means propagated these days in society, including materialism and sexuality. In return, high spirit is the best venue to create *the self synergy*.

The Self Synergy

The above four elements of inner self fuel one another and create a high synergy to maximize our inner strengths and positive life experiences. However, we miss this innate blessing, since society has no mechanism or interest to teach us anything about our inner self and strengths that can help us manage our lives within our rowdy social structure. Instead, we are trained to fill our bodies and minds with junk. In fact, the more civilized we have allegedly become, the more tainted our physical and mental nourishments have become. We consume so much unhealthy foods, alcohol, and drugs due to the effects of social living, high depression, and commercialization. All along, we also absorb and spread all kinds of juvenile ideologies and socioeconomic propaganda in hopes of proving our freedom and parading our individualism. We grow bigger egos every day, believe to be so special, and talk as though we knew everything better than everybody else does. Our shoddy social values have turned us into robots following self-gratifying, meaningless plans at the cost of hurting other people, including our family members. We adopt social norms and religious rituals without even doubting or questioning the validity of their sources. We think our socioeconomic superstructure can serve humans' basic needs at least. We assume it has been built with proper scrutiny and intentions. Many of us cannot see and accept the sad reality about the nature of current systems and culture as addictive mechanisms designed mainly to control our minds and bodies for serving the interests of elite groups and corporations. We fill our minds and bodies with harmful thoughts and food at the expense of suffocating our spirits. Our sour feelings and crooked actions reflect the repercussions of this huge spirit-mind-body imbalance, besides the overall failures of social relationships and lifestyles in the new era.

If we study our inner self, we realize the vast physical, mental, and spiritual strengths that reside even in one person. Then, as two or more people collaborate on a project or their relationship sincerely, their collective strengths raise many folds quickly. The level of synergy and energy that people's teamwork induces is huge. Instead, we fight too often amongst ourselves to the point of ruining our spirits and draining the last grains of our inner strengths. We do not care or know how to use our strengths for everybody's benefit, and instead try to break other people's pride and hearts by our extreme demands and needs. In fact, we waste even our limited, undernourished inner strengths, including our ego, individualism, and pride in the process by humiliating and weakening one another, instead of enriching each other's life.

In all, our inner self is malnourished since we do not get the chance to grow our identities, spirits, potentialities, and ingenuity properly in society. We have no time, knowledge, or energy to attend to our authentic needs, while we struggle to fulfil many superficial ones, such as love, happiness, and wealth. In such a convoluted setting, most of us have never learned about the real person we could have potentially been if our spirits were not so dampened and our minds and bodies were not so badly infected from birth by advertising, propaganda, political disorder, and crippling socioeconomic systems.

In fact, we do not even realize the need to build our identities, spirits, ingenuity, and divine potentialities. Nowadays, these vital human dimensions get buried in our unconscious minds, while we abuse our bodies and minds, and we drown our Selfs with our oversensitive, pretentious personalities in line with mainstream's values and rules. All our lives, our distorted self-images and lost identities damage our spirits, mostly because we lack the time, incentive, and expertise to explore our potentialities and feel the power of spiritualism. The dire effects of this vicious cycle are evident all around us in the high level of personal depression, stress, disappointments, and loneliness.

Our spirits are very low usually also because we neither have productive relationships in society nor a powerful inner self to keep our being intact as a self-reliant person. Instead, our stamina and spirits deplete more every day due to inevitable, constant confrontations with malicious people and systems. The pressures of our daily obligations and struggles to fit within certain social norms also reduce the chance of attending to our deeper urges for ingenuity and divinity.

Losing one's identity and authenticity is the most damaging aspect of this mayhem, since we suffer in a world of delusions grown around our misperceptions about the world and what the purpose of our existence is supposed to be. We are disheartened about our being, since we either do not know who we are—our identity—or fear to reveal our vulnerable, insecure, or vicious character. We suffocate our identity, as everybody is forced to focus on building phony personalities to prosper or fit within our showy, shallow social norms and encounters. A person's identity depends on the power of his/her inner self to explore and redeem his/her inherent potentialities. Therefore, most of us do not even get a chance to learn about, or feel, our identities.

Ironically, we not only have the potential to perceive and live a productive and creative life, but also can feel and exploit the finer dimensions of the universe by learning about ourselves. We just need to build our incentive for goodness and raise our inner strengths, instead of cherishing social and religious teachings so eagerly and blindly. Besides realizing our inner self to live easier with peace, goodness would help us traverse outside our physical existence at times to explore our divine potentialities and maybe even find our link to the universe—the outer power—as well. In fact, we can grasp and benefit from this outer power only through a refined self and high inner strength.

Nevertheless, it is up to us to explore and nurture our inner self and strengths personally. Following the goodness regimen is a simple, gradual mechanism to find our spirits and spirituality. The process is not meant to be an overwhelming or strenuous adventure, but rather a natural way to connect with our inner self and strengthen it gradually over several years or a decade. If someone feels incapable of doing it alone—as a preferred option—s/he might consider getting into it and progressing together with a confidant.

PART III

Social Conscience
And Consciousness

In a cultureless, corrupt world, social conscience evaporates fast and people become least conscious of their beings and their purposes for living!

A wandering citizen

Chapter Eleven
American Dream

We dream about a better future, though we know the truths! We strive faithfully with hope to save our souls at least, if human salvation seems unlikely. Still, our pervasive incentives for badness subdue our random goodness efforts, while we feel trapped in an abyss. This seems to be the bottomline! So, where do we stand as individuals and societies, really?

Well, we stand on a shaky ground with some raw perceptions of reality and some idiotic notions of democracy and freedom in hopes of satiating our superficial personal needs. The truth is that humans' capacity for goodness has diminished, because even our basic flaws now clash rapidly in society and turn into colossal, reactive forces of evil that spread and overwhelm everybody. Building an integral character has also become tough, since the provocative results of every individual's evil grow exponentially and stir deep personal burdens and social corruptions. Therefore, we suffer, while too many wicked individuals lay the foundation of societies and deform humanity altogether. We are making our societies sicker personally every day and our dying societies are dragging down and killing us in return with more vengeance.

For many bizarre reasons, including the effects of American movies exported to the farthest corners of the world, we are lured to adopt juvenile mentalities and superficial lifestyles. With our immature imaginations of democracy and prosperity in the US and its super power, we have also come to perceive America as a symbol of civilization, at least in terms of its people's seemingly flourishing lifestyle. Thus, American values, especially sexuality and consumerism, have emerged as enviable, legitimate venues for achieving our dreams and freedom as modern humans. Yet, this American dream has in fact turned into a nightmare even for Americans themselves when poverty, racism, corruption, mass shootings, crimes, inequality, and natural disasters are uprooting any chance for civilization and peace in that nation. Now imagine how pitiful and desperate those who envy Americans are!

Anyway, some discussions about the global desperation and efforts for goodness had been planned for this part of the book years ago. Then, the rising global challenges in 2016, including the presidential election in the US, necessitated the expansion of topics covered in this chapter and Part IV. At this point, we have suddenly reached a big milestone in terms of human vanity, as new evidences reveal a much gloomier picture about the world affairs and the wisdom of entertaining even a moderate hope for global goodness and peace. Suddenly even our fragile hopes for some form of leadership and global trust have been shattered. It is now quite evident that both the public and leaders lack enough capacity and motivation to envision even a basic plan for social harmony, let alone a universal one to grasp humans' long-term needs to survive on a healthy planet based on some fair, practical principles. Instead, people are sinking deeper into their pompous personalities with narrower views of national interests versus the world affairs. Our leaders, in particular, are using all sorts of vile tactics to promote themselves, misguide the public, and tackle so many socioeconomic issues with their lousy plans and mindsets. Any narcissist or lunatic can become a leader these days in any country, thanks to our lame democratic processes. Meanwhile, these leaders' raw, radical mentalities are corrupting our societies further and faster by causing irresolvable conflicts around the globe towards human annihilation.

Many insightful, objective people feel these catastrophic new developments around the world, as well as people's desperations mixed with their naive reluctance to grasp and address the roots of the problems. At the same time, choosing, or even considering, a person like Donald Trump for the presidency of the US says a lot about American culture and the vanity of political system in the US. It reveals so much about humans' mentality in general, too, especially American citizens' in this particular case.

For one thing, it is just amazing how people are so drastically different in their values, even in democratic countries like the United States, where we expect the public have had a chance to find a common ground for dialogue, reasoning, and choosing a peaceful social direction and process for themselves. It is odd that the support for the Republicans and Democrats is usually 50-50 split and how Americans have such huge differences of mentality in terms of a fair, viable social process for their country. Even more amazing is that some people (mostly Republicans) cannot perceive the flaws of their outlooks and their selfish values in a modern society that boasts about liberty and humanity. Now, just imagine the extent of human weaknesses and differences around the world when supposedly civilized countries like Canada and the US are suffering such rooted, dreadful mayhems.

Surely, the saddest outcome of this growing global mayhem is that following a goodness path is getting harder and lonelier for us every day. Even if we believed in goodness for our own sakes, living within such a flawed social structure ruled by lame, wicked leaders elected by naïve, misled citizens remains a big challenge even for enlightened individuals.

Nonetheless, devising a personal philosophy to overcome, or withstand, these inescapable obstacles is still the only solution for gaining some relative freedom and peace of mind. Exploring this narrow scope for salvation, in line with the goals and challenges of *personal awakening* and goodness within an inharmonious, ineffective, and infectious society, has been the main theme and purpose of this book.

On the other hand, the wide, supreme view of 'being better beings' as a *global mission* cannot be totally ignored, although such target feels too fanciful to ponder seriously. Global morality is obviously a precious ideal in itself for building social harmony, besides providing a conduit for personal goodness. However, all the clues about human nature and logic, as well as our historical experiences, show that a global plan for becoming better beings is futile. In fact, it feels more rational to accept the high likelihood of not even God ever believing in such an ideal, i.e., a relative human piety—again judging by the failures of prophets and all humanistic efforts throughout the history. Irrationality and cruelty are too deeply ingrained in humans to allow enough compassion and reasoning to prevail during our encounters.

The rather critical review of American politics, policies, and the 2016 election, as noted in the following pages, might sound too pessimistic or unfair, yet the whole point is to merely depict the roots of human folly minimizing our chances of being better beings. Also, it must be stressed that these negative observations about the 2016 election and people's choice for a new president are merely based on the behaviour of many leaders causing such a shenanigan, including the election results. Still, people's idiotic choice of a useless, narcissist as their president has also proved a valid point about the huge mess Americans have been living in for decades—as Mr. Trump has asserted rather rhetorically, too. Americans might also prove to have been quite smart, ironically, in their naïve choice of a new president if the unconventional politics and appointments by Trump lead to radical revelations and maybe even useful changes in the world affairs inadvertently —after people accept how low they (and the whole world) have sunk! Such catastrophic political mayhems might finally lead to some form of global awakening, mass rebellion, social reform, and an opportunity for becoming better beings. Maybe a bizarre development actually leads to a revolution in the US, especially in people's minds about capitalism and democracy. At the same time, the chance of this terrible mistake making America messier and President Trump causing huge damages globally is much higher and disheartening. We humans love to prove our inherent idiocy again and again!

The Rise of a Global Perspective

During the last century, the limited trade and communication channels among nations began maturing into a universal venue for cooperation and coexistence. In particular, the two World Wars led to alliances with some common objectives for peace and prosperity for all. While scepticism and espionage never stopped, some degree of trust among unified nations, along with better mechanisms for exchanging their views and settling their disputes, were established over decades. Diplomacy and decency made sense and proved useful sporadically for settling world's animosities and avoiding radical decisions. We even created the United Nations with so much hope and enthusiasm. Still, in many cases, political sense and objectivity have been ignored and many wars have killed large numbers of people and displaced many others for no benefits whatsoever. We have still not learned to solve our conflicts peacefully and instead resorted to violence and criminal acts around the world out of dire ignorance and alleged patriotism. Still, the scheme to maintain some basic alliances and collaboration to curb unilateral actions has had positive effects. In particular, the US emerged as a global leader and role model for democratic efforts—for no tangible reasons perhaps other than its large military power and obsession for dictating some crooked laws of humanity in hopes of controlling the world.

All along, a fanciful view of American lifestyle and mentality was developed and portrayed to the outside world through crafty propagandas and deceiving movies. We built the perception of a democratic and wise society where people enjoyed their freedom, wealth, democracy, and intelligence. We imagined those cowboy movies were only a historical recount of events in which Indians were always the criminals and responsible for all that bloodshed and not the other way around. Thus, soon American way of life, as a symbol of success and happiness, appeared as a universal dream for people all over the world. We all imagined and envied the luxury and pleasure of living like Americans, perhaps in the US or at least within a replica of that glamorous society in our own countries. We looked up to the US as a model of civilization and the protector of other nations! Then, we got addicted to its inventions, including automobile, fancy dwellings and furniture, fashion, fast food, internet, and too many raw slogans about sexuality, pleasure, and positive thinking. Surely, these fanciful symbols of modern existence had already hypnotized American people themselves—most likely more than they had fooled the outsiders who were imagining the huge party going on in the US.

Sometimes, our views of Americans' fortune and mentality as well as America's values, economic viability, and politics had felt shaky. However, we still kept our faith and craved the American fortune and lifestyle. Most of us gave America the benefit of a doubt and ignored the ongoing human infringements that went on both inside and outside the US, too, including the slavery, racism, tortures, massacres in various wars, and even dropping enormous atomic bombs on helpless civilians intentionally.

With the fast dissemination of news in many forms these days, the grievances of people both inside and outside of the US have reached a boiling point gradually in the last few decades and all the clues indicate that we are now finally facing the hidden truth we had ignored for too long about the state of global unrest. All nations have similar socioeconomic and political disorders that they seem incapable of resolving. However, focusing on the US is due to, 1) the special role it has tried to play all along as a model for democratic values and social mentality for the rest of world, and 2) our amazing discoveries about the depth of social disorder in the US, especially after witnessing the 2016 election. We have learned a lot about Americans' mentality, mood, general dissatisfaction, and electoral deficiencies, and we wonder about the validity of the world's trust in the US to be a leader. The big shock to the world stems partly from the fact that allied nations had not anticipated the time when they would need plan B if their suspicions about the social and political instability in the US turned into a messy reality. Now, it is no longer wise for those nations to second guess themselves and doubt their cynicism about the US's long-term commitment to be a leader. Now, it has also become much harder to trust the US political systems, not to mention its deeply corruptive, instable financial mechanism that would continue to cause universal distress like the one in 2008. It is simply unconceivable for the rest of the world to not learn any lesson from the history of the US, even if going merely by the events in the 21st century alone.

The rooted social disorder in the US would cause not only vaster national and international conflicts and more wars, but also more misery for people all over the world. The level of personal evil and social mayhem would rise accordingly. The amount of distress and distrust, within governments and among common people, would exacerbate, while the US continues to insist on playing the role of the leader for the rest of the world. All along, the US also appears determined to dictate its interpretation of democracy and the politics of international coexistence even if the whole world decides that a new vision and process can help humanity better than letting any country, especially the US, do it for them mostly by force and bullying. Many nations would probably not find it too diplomatic and necessary to express their separation from the outdated image of the US as the world leader directly. However, the whole world thinks that way, not out of spite, but for practicality—merely because the US model cannot save even its own people, let alone the destiny of humanity. Maybe soon, some open resistance to the US mentality becomes inevitable, but the final objective is to save the world if possible, including the oppressed Americans. Clearly, they seem even more worried about their doomed situation than outsiders, so much so they even imagined an incompetent, inexperienced person like Donald Trump could grasp the state of the world affairs! Their anger mixed with misplaced faiths and naïve perceptions are enough clues about the vanity of the American dream that many people around the world had entertained for decades. Americans' own dream facing such catastrophic threats after all these years is most amusing. Now they are so desperate and confused they are nurturing an even odder dream: that lunatics like Trump can fix everything and make America great again for them!

The crucial fact this general picture reveals is that we all miss a vision for a sane humanity, society, and personal prosperity to look forward to with high hopes. We seek intuitively an image of good humans and societies. We need role model individuals and nations to affirm at least the possibility of being better beings.

The Clues and Lessons

Let us hope more people around the world agree that it is time to learn some good lessons from the faltering world affairs and sad human mentality that manifests itself best during special times, particularly at this historical point, at the early decades of the 21st century. We have been lost in our dreams and delusions during the last century, while severe damages have been inflicted upon our identities, societies, and environment. However, the situation is getting out of hand now at an alarming rate. As an example, the Britain's decision and division about leaving the European Union and the consequent uncertainty that would prevail for a long time, with some possible dire effects, would be educational for the rest of the Europe and world. However, more revealing has been the 2016 presidential campaign and election in the US. Actually, we can draw a general picture about Americans, America, and the world from the events during the 2015 to early 2018.[*] This topic is covered in Chapter Eighteen.

---

[*] This book was completed in the spring of 2018 except for editing. Thus, ensuing comical dramas and idiocies, including Trump's impeachment and dire global chaos after COVID-19, lost their chances of being analyzed and included.

The World's Big Dilemma

At the most critical moment in history, when humans were facing annihilation, when the majestic planet Earth felt most threatened by human waste and pollution, when all scientists agreed about the source of looming human demise, when all the nations came together to fathom a possible solution, when all humans' mental and emotional energies had to be focused, when we all worried about our last chance, …, the only nation that denied all scientific evidences, broke its official promise to be sensible like the rest, left the Paris Accord with no shame, stressed on more money at the cost of basic human decency, remained the most polluter ever on this planet, ignored all the humans' and nations' pleas, forgot its conscious and social duties so fervently, and let the whole world sweat in dismay, was the United States of America.

So, dear Americans, how would you expect the world ignore your apathy and hypocrisy, or forget your absolute disregard for human decency? Is American Dream in its deathbed?

How can we not have debates with our confused conscience these days about humanity and wonder if we could ever become better beings?

Debate with Our Confused Conscience

Humans and humanity are always in our minds, but only seldom we study them seriously when our spirits and conscience strive to rise and reflect on some existential questions at critical moments. On such precious, private occasions of encountering the truth, we strive to make sense about our Self and come to terms with our troubled conscience partially.

It is interesting to know the thoughts that must have circled in Trump's and Clinton's heads during and after the election about two big mysteries: 1) Human nature in general, and 2) Personal karma. Yet, we can imagine certain sardonic points in their heads.

Just for fun, I tried to imagine their thoughts and experiences and laughed even harder pondering a possible precious lesson that Trump might learn at the end of his hilarious presidency: that he cannot always win no matter how much he cheats. Even then, he would most likely still not learn much about humility and his nothingness as a foolish human like the rest of us.

Hillary Clinton's Debate with her Spirit

Why are we humans so mean and moron? Why people see me in such gloomy light, instead of recognizing my lifetime efforts to serve people? How can they enjoy some lowlifes calling me cunt[*] and dying to lock me up for what, I do not know?! I just cannot think of any crime worth being prosecuted for, save for my simple mistake of using a private server for sending emails, which people keep using as an excuse to hate me, instead of grasping my repeated explanations and requests for forgiveness. Well, maybe I have abused my power a bit, too. But, do I deserve this much hatred and insults merely because I wish to serve our nation sincerely some more? What is the value of all this money that Bill and I have accumulated after we die in a few years? What was the point of our struggles when my spirit is crushed from humans' low morality and integrity? It seems I have no luck at all, despite my sincerity and hard work a lifetime, while God seems so keen to support all these silly, pretentious crooks and evils in a mysterious way. Oh, God, I feel so terrible for wasting so much of my life and energy to serve these idiots! But are some people right saying I do not know what the heck I am doing?

> "Is Hillary really doing the most good that she can do, fighting for the best deal that's there to get for ordinary people?
>
> Or is she doing something that satisfies her definition of that, while taking tens of millions of dollars from some of the world's biggest jerks [mainly Goldman Sachs]?

---

[*] See Matt Taibbi's quote on page 382.

I doubt even Hillary Clinton could answer that question. She has been playing the inside game for so long, she seems to have become lost in it. She behaves like a person who often doesn't know what the truth is, but instead merely reaches for what is the best answer in that moment, not realizing the difference." *Insane Clown President*, Matt Taibbi, 2017, Spiegel and Grau. Pages 167-8.

Donald Trump's Debate with his Spirit

Are people really so dumb or I'm really such a good actor?! I can say and do anything I like and they still love me. *Let me tell you, lying works perfectly....!* I deserve an Oscar for the great role I have played as a leader for these naive people. But I know deep down how I have always exploited every single person when possible. People know it, too, yet rather accept my excuses than use their commonsense and conscience for a second. Well, I must not criticize them since I am such a phenomenal actor, after all! My character has apparently seemed sincere and solid to them, including these allegedly smart people in the White House and Senate obeying my commands so timidly. What a lot of pitiful Republicans! Do they really think I am the wisest President ever or coaxing me merely out of zero self-esteem? My narcissism does not seem to bother my fanatic followers, either. Still, it is so weird I keep getting more rewards for my lifelong atrocities, as though I had a special pact with the devil, or God enjoyed fooling with people in a mysterious way, no matter what they deserved. Therefore, I must keep doing and saying lots more crap after I am re-elected, although this job is getting a bit boring, too.

Still, I must certainly take care of some jerks, especially this Matt Taibbi who thinks I am an insane clown, cipher, cheap fraud, and con man!

"It turns out we let our electoral process devolve into something so fake and dysfunctional that any half-bright con man with the stones to try it could walk right through the front door and tear it to shreds on the first go.

And Trump is no half-bright con man, either. He's way better than average." Ibid. Page 134.

"The problem, of course, is that Trump is crazy. He's like every other corporate tyrant in that his solution to most things follows the logic of Stalin: no person, no problem. You're fired! Except as president he'd have other people-removing options, all of which he likes: torture, mass deportations, the banning of 23 percent of the Earth's population from entering the United States, etc." Ibid. Page 154.

"It's not an accident that his attention span lasts exactly one news cycle. He's exactly like the rest of America, except that he's making news, not following it—staring on TV instead of watching it. Just like we channel-surf, he focuses as long as he can on whatever mess he's in, and then he moves on to the next bad news or incorrect memory that pops into his head." Ibid. Page 107.

"Trump is a TV believer. He's so subsumed in all the crap he's watched—and you can tell by the cropped syntax in his books and his speech, Trump is a watcher, not a reader—it's all mixed up in his head." Ibid. Page 108.

"Trump sold hate, violence, xenophobia, racism, and ignorance, which oddly enough had long been permissible zones of exploration for American television entertainment." Ibid. Page xxviii.

"He can do plenty of damage just by encouraging people to be as uninhibited in their stupidity as he is." Ibid. Page 38.

Chapter Twelve
Culture Collapse

Humans' waning capacity for goodness, weak inner self, and vague sense of the Outer Power, as discussed in Parts I and II, plus socio-political analyses in the following chapters, show the sad prospect for humanity, as living will get harder and darker personally and universally. People's confusion and vanity will rise fast also due to: (1) The lack of a solid culture to guide citizens and stir some form of social harmony, and (2) Artificial Intelligence and technology replacing humans' limited mental and physical abilities. Soon, robots will take over our jobs when scientists and the exploiters of human spirits figure out cheaper and easier means of running our societies without the hassles of dealing with our occasional demands, complaints, and tendency for rebellion. At that point, we are turned into helpless and mindless robots ourselves with no intuition, intelligence, or a sensible culture to keep people together around some rules of morality. Instead, we just follow, even more obediently, the dire fate that our leaders, and the elites controlling them, set for us. All clues indicate we are rushing towards a dismal future mindlessly, while this grim picture makes us despair and feel helpless these days. Thus, the goal in Part III of this book is to delve deeper into societal and cultural incapacity as alarming perils to existence in line with humans' rising naiveté, evil, and idealism.

We used to have some evolving cultures at some parts of the world, especially in Asia and Europe. They helped people keep some levels of peace and morality (goodness) among themselves. At least they had hope and high spirits, despite their gullibility due to the high influence of superstitions and religions. Now, too many immoral and purposeless values have eradicated those few merits of old cultures, while our spirits and identities falter in rootless societies. We just nurture a variety of demented ideals and idols, feel so smart, and behave arrogantly. Our actions are based on spontaneous whims, social fads, and juvenile ideologies rather than well-thought cultural values. Now, kids do not even care about their parents' views, let alone those old cultures. In this delusional world, we merely strive to imitate the lifestyles and goals that alleged leaders, celebrities, and rich have created for amusing our susceptible sorry minds.

Every generation is growing up with more fantasies about life and exciting lives more than they learn and think about life's harsh realities, as well as the goals and manner of raising a family and keeping it together and happy. So most people end up living without a faithful family or suffer in a dysfunctional one, while enduring a great deal of depression and stress. Family values and relationships were driven by traditional cultures, which had come out of centuries of trials and errors, e.g., in Middle East, China, or Japan. In the last century, however, we have rushed to discard those traditions fast in hopes of creating better ways of defining freedom and being happier, while gender conflicts and quarrels have grown fast with no principles to guide couples. Instead, a shoddy neo-culture has emerged under the name of modernism to satiate mainstream's naive views of individualism, feminism, capitalism, consumerism, and similar symbols of social vanity.

Without a culture and social guidelines, all we can do now is to rely on our own crude logic and idiotic perceptions of life to follow some trifling goals within a dire social structure in hopes of success and happiness. Now, we are at the mercy of not only the ruling monsters making us behave mechanically like robots already, but also the monstrous robots that will soon take over our jobs and run our socioeconomic milieu vastly. Even worse, nobody seems to realize or care how fast our sense and drive for culture have been fading away. No desire and responsibility for building a meaningful culture exists now, while the whole world is merely embracing the hypnotic symbols of materialism at the expense of abolishing our chance to form a sensible civilization and sustain humanity in the long run. No authority seems to be in charge of societies and the world, while we have no personal will or wisdom, either, to push for a moralistic way of coexistence.

A Cultureless Social Structure!

The overall picture regarding the fifteen social elements explained in Chapter Eight shows how badly we have been failing, despite our claims for civilization and intelligence. Their collapse are due to humans' gullibility and low capacity for teamwork, while we have no true leaders, cultures, or plans towards global harmony. Actually, we are still living in primitive societies with a mentality not much stronger than our Stone Age ancestors' judging by the vanity of our religions, relationships, politics, etc.

1. Education	2. Learning	3. Occupation
4. Marriage	5. Parenthood	6. Health
7. Security	8. Justice & Fairness	9. Courtesy & Trust
10. Morality	11. Environment	12. Culture
13. Democracy	14. Economy	15. Authority

After millenniums of trials and errors, arguments and fights, technological progress, and crude democratic ambitions, we are still incapable of keeping basic peace and order even in a small corner of the world, in a confined community perhaps, or even within families. Instead, the whole world is in turmoil with all the clues pointing only to one direction—more chaos and human misery. People are dying in throngs in the streets all over the world, especially in so-called modern societies, from addictions, suicides, crimes, and drug overdoses to fight their physical and mental pains. Who is responsible for these miseries and how can we ever overcome this chaos? What kind of a civilization and society can we ever imagine would come to our rescue and help us mitigate our own deep badness, too? Can anybody become a better being in the middle of this social mayhem?

Finding even a global definition of good and bad, for a person or the world, has become a blur, due to modern lifestyles' mottos for happiness and love ruining people's sense of reality. How could a deprived, greedy person with raw ambitions distinguish goodness from badness objectively? Who makes that judgment for the sick, evil human race? What values are right?

Thus, the cultural collapse, rising social disorder, and people's sufferings accelerate. Meanwhile, as noted before, we should expect further annihilation of social structure when robots and technology replace many jobs, especially those needing human intelligence. The anticipated calamities of climate change will expedite the process of disintegration of economies and cultures around the world, too. The vast pressures for cleaner energy will diminish the need for labour-intensive sources, especially fossil fuel. The low demand for coal and oil will ruin many countries' economies and people will be forced to migrate to elude misery. Eventually, a robotic, ruthless setting will place a huge level of psychological pressures on most people to survive and still feel obliged to maintain their positive attitude as a symbol of social aptitude and adaptability.

Soon, the world economies will start to tumble and social structures collapse, since we have relied too much on capitalism for everything with no plan or culture to survive personally or globally. In the end, the repercussions of the growing pressures on socioeconomic structure will raise people's appetite and drive for both goodness and badness—depending on their mentalities and inner strengths—but mostly the latter.

People have been feeling increasingly useless and restless and losing their self-image, hope, and minds fast. Thus, their badness urges will keep accelerating across the societies and around the world in line with people's growing despair. Those with inner strengths and deep convictions strive to survive thru their faiths and spirituality in hopes of salvaging their souls. However, most of us find badness a more potent way of adaptation and releasing our frustrations, which in turn makes life difficult for everybody and ruins any kind of attempt to develop even a simple form of culture for coexistence. All along, the role of religions in modern societies will be largely diminished as well.

Surely, we feel responsible, and strive, to ponder and do many things on our own, cause our happiness or misery, make friends or alienate people, etc. Still, our psyches cannot overcome our habitual, high reliance on society to fulfil many of our needs and run a functional, orderly environment for us to live in harmony, discharge our duties, and pursue our ambitions peacefully. We are raised to believe that a good social structure has been planned and built to fulfil people's basic needs as well as their natural urges for mental and spiritual growth. Thus, when society fails to fulfil our needs even for basic security and subsistence, we lose not only track of our daily lives and sanity, but also our spirits and motivations to help the society or show compassion. Instead, only our urges for evil grow and we become erratically defiant, rebellious, or stoic in order to cope or retaliate.

Many people and governments are also concerned nowadays about large immigration damaging their cultures and economic welfare, yet our leaders are letting foreign investors do much worse to their societies in various manners. For example, the practice of letting foreigners, mostly non-residents, invest in the prime real estate of our cities has led to artificial housing shortage and affordability concerns for local residents. Now, real estate has become a new venue for capitalists around the globe to launder their dirty monies or park their vast wealth in lucrative properties in safer nations and to keep speculating on their values.

Our leaders are promoting these types of capitalistic schemes in their dire attempts to boost or save their local economies. Poor immigrants at least intend to work and contribute to economy if they were given a chance. Foreign investors are only exploiting other nations' resources and stirring long-term havoc for people and local economies, since our leaders cannot find nationalistic means of running their economies with less reliance on greedy foreign investors. They refuse to see how the evils of capitalism have already ruined the chance of nurturing any type of culture. Even worse, our leaders grasp and support—like robots already —only capitalistic principles for thinking and running a country, instead of finding a better means of using people's brains and labour more productively. In the end, the public must now endure many new sources of hardships due to the global symptoms of capitalism crippling their basic needs and lives, while they are also losing their chances to ponder or protect a viable culture.

Sadly, humans appear incapable of resolving the fundamental flaws, dysfunctions, and complexities of the fifteen noted social elements due to the lack of social culture, people's raw logic and intelligence, as well as their high emotional, egotistical urges. Without a viable culture, humans cannot create even a basic level of coordination among people and their social systems.

These strict conclusions about humans' inability to *ever* find suitable social systems or leaders to manage the world annul the rationale for wasting any time to study the prospects of humanity and social structure. Yet, gauging the ineptitude of these elements and leaders may convince more people to ponder the depressing outlook for humanity and the need to rely only on their personal initiative to salvage their own souls at least, if not get together for a revolution to redefine the whole social spectrum, if possible.

The Neo-culture Curse

Some evil forces have always played a powerful role in directing people's minds and emotions. Now, however, a special class of invaders have succeeded in imposing a greed-ridden *neo-culture* that pushes the public deeper and faster into ignorance with an intense aptitude for living merely based on hopes and promises. Over the last century, in particular, these masters of manipulation have successfully erased the last grains of morality and integrity that older cultures had strived to inject in people's minds. In this sad, hypnotic environment, idiotic economic systems and social values have evolved out of people's whims, modern visions, and naïve obsessions for success, love, and happiness, while becoming more oblivious of the need for a moral culture.

Culture has been a potent means of spreading worthy values and norms to raise people's sense of self, morality, and stamina to cooperate towards some form of social harmony and cohesion and to withstand life's hardships gracefully. Therefore, now, the word 'culture' has no sensible meaning and application, since no moral values support societies for any logical purpose. In effect, the present semblance of values and norms do not fulfil even humans' basic needs, let alone build a culture.

Instead, the hollow neo-culture emerging now around some ideologies, such as freedom, individualism, and happiness merely appeal to our deprived minds and trap our souls in a delusional world, while we try to prosper by pampering our fantasies and raw ambitions. This neo-culture is making people phonier every day at the cost of losing their souls and dignities, as we hope to satiate our needs for self-gratification and a bombastic image of individualism. We strive to cope with, or prosper in, this chaotic, humiliating setting at the expense of demolishing our helpless inner self. Even if we were wise and courageous to resist, or rebel against, this degrading way of existence, we feel helpless. Instead, we are rather forced to become a shallow person (sometimes against our inner tendencies and desires) in order to survive in the superficial society built around a corrupting neo-culture. The mainstream and leaders hate those who feel and behave outside the imposed norms. They abhor people who like to act somewhat more naturally or maturely.

The enormity of our misperceptions, challenges, and pains to cope with so many social demands within a faltering structure were noted in Chapter Eight, and the growing hardships of our wicked international neo-culture will be discussed further in Part IV. This cursed neo-culture and mentality has spread fast around the world and inflicted people and remaining cultures as well. Now, everybody is susceptible to its lure and in fact boasts about being part of the mainstream mesmerized by the demented global vision of life built around illusions and sexuality.

Nonetheless, humans' rising frustration and helplessness in the neo-culture with its dizzying acceleration towards the ultimate waste and vanity is evident all around us. We have lost even our primitive intuition and independence, while we obediently follow new patterns for thinking and behaving in so-called democratic societies. Under the name of human rights and democracy, we are too eager and persistent to import our doomed mentalities and means of living to all corners of the world. We attack other ways of thinking and planning for a fairer social structure. We fight with any group that defies the pervasive phony existence that we so-called civilized people like to cherish.

However we gauge the emerging culture, it is too shallow and dispiriting, despite our hypnotic eagerness to adopt its teachings and rules in hopes of some promised privileges. It has also been shaping too fast erratically for most of us to ponder its effects and realize its hollowness dragging us all towards a complete social fiasco. We are too helpless, anyway, to play even a small role in correcting the saddest and fastest cultural decline in history. All along, all kinds of social gimmicks for manipulating humans' deprived psyches and mental insecurities have ruined our chances for self-realization and goodness. So we might as well get ready to face the inevitable reality about our cursed neo-culture pushing us fast towards doomsday. The only question is, "How to cope with these sad facts, then?" Many of us have adopted progressive philosophies, such as 'positive thinking' or 'living in the now' with as much pleasure as possible to forget reality. People are pushed into this juvenile mentality by both their despair and the hypnotic slogans of the idiotic neo-culture. Without even noticing the neo-culture's curse or the viability of *living in the now*, people are already looking for an easy way to hide deeper in a delusional world that this freaky neo-culture keeps pushing on us.

Luckily, some groups around the world still resist the big load of demeaning international values, often for defending their own radical views or religious ideologies. In the end, though, humans have now been trapped within a variety of vain views, values, and wars. A few leaders' pride and persistence on traditional values is also slowing the spread of the neo-culture a bit. Still, the chance of any authentic culture surviving or erupting in the new world is almost zero. Sadly, soon we will all be slaves to this new baseless culture of deceit and domination.

For now, all we seem capable of doing is to just follow the crowd and engage in our robotic duties until the real robots are ready to take over completely and demolish the last grains of human dignity and identity. The idea of a world controlled by intelligent robots—lacking even the primary elements of human conscience, emotions, and sympathy—sounds so scary. Humans are bad and scary enough already, despite the consciousness and emotions they use fruitfully sometimes. So, just try to imagine how cruel people and a world dominated by robots and artificial intelligence would look like a few generations down the road!

The Neo-culture Forces

The death of our basic traditional cultures accelerated about two generations ago due to the youths' numbness and nonsensical preoccupations, but also their families' dire loyalty to capitalism and materialism, and then spoiling their kids with overindulgence and attention, too. Peer pressure and advertising have also been damaging children's brains, while no social models exist to warn kids about their hypnosis and lunacy. Thus, the cultural downfall would be too fast for the future generations.

The new culture that youths are growing up in stresses highly on self-importance and self-gratification. Their zest to imitate and propagate this mentality blindly within delusional lifestyles erases their chances for learning compassion, teamwork, and family values as the locus for personal and social health. Consequently, people's senses of insecurity and loneliness are growing too fast, too, which cause all sorts of psychological dysfunction, naivety, frustration, revulsion, negativism, wishful thinking, depression, etc. In return, these personal setbacks have increased personal and social mayhems, including addiction to alcohol and drugs, hatred, reckless killings, bigotry, sexism, racism, narcissism, cynicism and mistrust, endless wars and hostility, and a confused world with millions of refugees (71 millions in 2019) around the globe. Nonsensical violence is in particular expanding at so many levels. Random shooting and cruelty, bombing, and suicide have become daily news, while the police and people are killing one another senselessly, too. The rates of suicide among the youths and family murder-suicides have also gone up drastically. In the United States, the number of suicides went up from 29,199 in 1999 to 48,344 in 2018 (based on the latest statistics) and it seems to be rising even faster now. It was the second highest cause of death among the youths.

As another forceful feature of neo-culture, we are now letting internet and social media dominate people's lives and constitute the foundation for a global cultural demise. This pervasive tool is exploited very effectively by the US's unconditional devotion to commercialism and free enterprise values for controlling people's minds, too, especially the naïve new generation. A few quotes from Lee Siegel's book, *Against the Machine, published by Spiegel & Grace 2008,* offer some insight regarding the role of internet and related technologies on our culture.

> "Change happens fast in America. Claims of newness are intimidating, and the fear of being left behind is threatening. The result is that you suddenly find yourself meekly asking how a recent phenomenon (internet and Wikipedia) can be fixed or improved, rather than asking the more fun-

damental question: Why is it here at all? In the face of all this absurdity, which fifteen years ago would have been the plot of a science-fiction novel, you have to step back and take stock." Page 147.

"We are living in a popularity culture, where being liked is the supreme value." Page 154.

"Combined with the habit of living vicariously instilled in us by watching television and movies, our impatience with anyone higher than us is one of the fuels of internet interactivity." Page 142.

"In this strange, upside down world, words like 'democracy' and 'freedom' have lost their meaning. They serve only to repel criticism of what they have come to mean, even when that criticism is made in the name of democracy and freedom." Page 132.

The repercussions of social media craze (addiction) are not limited to the amount of time the youths wastes on sharing trivial information and petty emotions to promote their insincere, shoddy social habits. The level of misinformation spread in society and hindering the chance of mental and cultural growth is staggering. People's growing urge to parade their hedonistic mentalities on social media through fake news is demolishing the last residues of decency around the world. Accordingly, our mistrust of news and information is abolishing our senses and enthusiasm to listen to different viewpoints at least occasionally.

Our culture has faded also due to useless books and weird arts offered to the public. The interest level in reading, especially self-exploring or literary books has declined drastically, while the commercialization of books and arts is screwing people's minds and views about life. The fad to express and share our bizarre creativities has led to the introduction of outrageous art, music, literature, and sports with dubious meaning or value for building a sensible culture. We are merely hoping to amuse or distract ourselves for the moment, mostly through filthy pleasures, noisy music, mushy movies and novels, violent sports, or messy art. We throw lots of paint on canvas and get mesmerized, because the mix of colours looks both intriguing and perplexing like our aimless lives! Millions of supposedly artistic creations are offered as art and music merely for profit purposes, while people waste their brains and hard-earned income on raucous concerts, rough sports, and bizarre artistic venues recklessly and then nag about their distress and debts.

Surely, these neo-cultural creations and habits are causing vast confusion and diminishing the chance for creating a definable, productive culture. People are drawn to violent, odd amusements, since their mentalities are not cultivated properly beyond their hollow views of life and means of indulging themselves. They never learn compassion and integrity, but become more arrogant and dogmatic. Even when we sense real culture, e.g., in the 17th and 18th centuries regarding art, music, passion, and divinity, we just cannot maintain it. We cannot wait to create bizarre ideas and abolish our cultural achievements. Our obsession for chaos, even under the names of freedom, art, and originality has slowly led to more hatred and aversion towards any sense of culture, personal and social welfare, and learning from our mistakes.

Naturally, all innovative creations have some value and place for reflection and admiration, but considering them literature or art is detrimental for nurturing a soft, solid culture in the long-run. Especially, commercializing these venues in cultureless societies is an offence to human dignity. Promoting or being carried away deeper into a delusional world even through literature and art, as has occurred in recent decades, is preventing us to even ponder a culture that can help humanity. *But how can we elude this trap?*

So many symptoms of personal badness and social mayhem discussed in this book, especially Chapter Eight, reflect the lack of not only a basic culture and meaningful social values, but also an environment conducive to the growth of a moral culture. Now, our neo-culture boosts badness urges and goads us to adopt vain, pretentious habits and values rather than learn about the merits of goodness. Our educational system is corrupting our culture, too, since apparently the more degrees people collect, the snobbier, stupider, and greedier they usually become. Even when they gain some knowledge, their wisdom does not help them or others, since the neo-culture does not let them function outside crooked norms. Furthermore, they do not know how to be better beings or how to relate to others and enrich their spirits. Our friendships are getting shallower and more insincere. We brag about hundreds of so-called friends listed on the Facebook, but have no true, sincere relationship with even two or three of them. We crave for love and attention, but cannot relate to our spouses, parents, and kids. We are obsessed with happiness, success, and compassion, but destroy our lives and spirits by depending on sex, pleasures, and power to replicate happiness and success.

In all, the fundamental social problems noted in this chapter and Chapter Eight, as well as socioeconomic and socio-political issues noted in Part IV, reflect the annihilation of culture. Even worse, we do not even realize or worry about the lack of culture or the vanity of our lifestyles, nor do we have a plan to at least study the results of our current mentality and lifestyles. Simply, we do not seem to see, or care about, the effects of running our personal and social affairs so irresponsibly for a few more decades before our final demise.

At the same time, materialism and marketing are destroying people's, especially children's, mentalities and lives. With regard to this subject, the following quotes from Juliet B. Schor (*Born to buy*, Scribner 2004) provide further clues about the extent of damage to American society as well as the repercussions of the neo-culture on people's mental and physical health.

> "Marketing is fundamentally altering the experience of childhood. Corporations have infiltrated the core activities and institutions of childhood, with virtually no resistance from government or parents. Advertising is widespread in schools. Electronic media are replacing conventional play.

We have become a nation that places a lower priority on teaching its children how to thrive socially, intellectually, even spiritually, than it does on training them to consume. The long-term consequences of this development are ominous." Page 13.

"One of the most troubling aspects of viral marketing is that it asks kids to use their friends for the purpose of gaining information or selling products... Marketers are teaching kids to view their friends as a lucrative resource they can exploit to gain products and money. They even counsel kids to be "slick" with their friends... A serious consequence is the corruption of friendships itself... A major reason [for viral marketing] is that word of mouth from friends is one of the remaining sources of credibility in a world that is oversaturated by commercial messages." Page 77.

"More children in US than anywhere else believe that their clothes and brands describe who they are and define their social status. American kids display more brand affinity than their counterparts anywhere else in the world; indeed, experts describe them as increasingly 'bounded to brands.'" Page 13.

"Materialism is related to psychological distress and difficulty adapting to life. People who value money and conventional success are less likely to experience positive emotions, such as happiness and joy, and they are more likely to experience negative ones, such as anger and unhappiness." Page 174.

"Adolescents who have more materialist values are more likely to engage in risky behaviours, such as smoking, drinking, and illegal drug use. They are more likely to suffer from personality disorders such as narcissism, separation anxiety disorder, paranoia, and attention deficit disorder. Materialism is also correlated with carrying weapons, skipping school, and vandalism." Page 174.

"The marketing of violent products and their connection to violent behaviour has been widely described, analyzed, and debated. The frequency and severity of media violence continue to increase, and the cultural cultivation of a "taste for violence" among American youth has become a serious problem." Page 137.

Living for Today

Surely, a dire symptom of the neo-culture is our juvenile slogan and mentality about 'living for today.' This infectious philosophy has become popular for curbing our burdens by trying to take life easy, focusing on our immediate needs and urges, and pampering our pleasure-seeking habits. We try to live for today or even *in the now*—as the urgency for forgetting our obligations and ourselves seem to keep rising as fast as social mayhems and idiocies are! Hippies, sophists, philosophers, and varied cults have suggested similar ideas mostly as stoic means of resisting social norms and evading our entrapment in a rigid and stressful social structure. Yet, these shallow cures, including our misconceived, immature 'positive thinking,' have led to more disappointments, idealism, lower self-image, and loss of initiative to face abrasive realities and live proactively with insightful convictions.

Slogans like, 'you live only once, life is too short, live a little, make the best of your life,' have turned into scapegoats for our waning sense of morality and responsibility. They have become major obstacles now for building a sustainable culture, too, of course. Then, our positive thinking slogans, idealistic visions of the world, and emotional vulnerabilities about love, trust, and happiness, goad us to adopt these seemingly sensible ideologies and life philosophies. Thus, we resort to all kinds of perversions and amusements to curb our insecurities and social burdens.

Even without the neo-culture *forces* and ideas about living for today, we humans have a deep tendency already to focus on our immediate urges and needs, especially pleasures. The urge for laziness also motivates most of us to focus on the present time, instead of working harder and staying prudent to safeguard our long-term needs and security. Thus, this philosophy of 'living for today' is indeed nothing new, but rather a means of justifying our inherent urges for pleasure, passivity, and indolence, while trying to justify our existence in a delusional world. In fact, we humans have always, but more so in the last few decades, have lived too much in the now already. We have grown the habit of borrowing too much money without having a proper financial expertise or a secured means of repaying our debts in a timely and economical manner. We have grown an exaggerated mentality about 'living for now,' especially in terms of embracing all kinds of sexual freedom and perversions to maximize our chances for happiness today with little concern about the consequences of our shoddy pleasures, plans, and lifestyles on our spirits.

Ironically, living in the now often causes depression because we learn the most shocking reality about existence without proper preparation and mindset: We sense the vanity of life more readily when our endless struggles to define and live it render no results. Especially, the more we insist on finding a meaning and purpose for our actions and thoughts in every moment or a day, the more exhausted and frustrated we get for imposing such a strenuous demand on our psyches and spirits. We fuss over not only getting the most pleasure in this moment, but also our mission to keep this and all future minutes gratifying within the highly strenuous demands of 'living in the now.' In fact, the more we become an advocate of living in the now, the more we torture ourselves to prepare and fulfil our minute-by-minute plans for the highest possible self-gratification, especially by insisting to achieve this goal through our juvenile thoughts and routines. At the end, our failure to embrace a smidgen of happiness within a whole week, let alone in every second of the now, would feel just devastating.

The main goal of living for today is to allegedly relax and take life in our strides. However, even the basic demands, let alone the (ir)responsibility, of 'living in the now' exasperate any normal person, even if s/he could stop his/her thoughts about the past or future minutes of his/her life.

The sense of passivity and resignation that emanate from the 'living for today' slogan dampens our foresight and the urge for being proactive, which are the requirements for becoming better (active) beings. The struggle to make 'now' a useful moment also makes our lives stressful and purposeless. In fact, our lives feel even more boring when we fail so often—maybe around 80% of the time—to find anything useful to do during our idle minutes. Even the lucky minority who finds its niche and passion in life cannot maintain a continuous life of self-fulfilment. The mere fact of existence, the reality of belonging to a falling society, and our needs for belongingness and love, cause routine depressions that break our conviction to live with contentment in the now.

NOW is a static state, as its main goal is to stay clear from the next minutes—the next Now. This condition halts the insight and dynamism of human spirit. We cannot, and do not want to, live in so many static states since it drives us mad. We need and love dynamism, continuity, adventure, and even labour, in order to overcome our senses of idleness and boredom. We like to feel the flow of life, which comes from a right mix of past (memories and lessons), present (action and contemplation), and future (hope and plans). It requires an active mind to predict and plan our next steps and challenges almost constantly. We humans need a sign of activity and progress (tangible results) or else we go crazy and find our lives stagnant. Living in the present moment sporadically is not a bad tactic to defeat the stress of fast, chaotic social life. We need breaks from our erratic thoughts and plans. We need to be without thoughts (free in the now) maybe 20% of the time. However, that seems like the maximum limit that humans can tolerate without getting lazy or going crazy. Actually, the art of balancing our past, present, and future very consciously all the time is a main secret for happiness and it is crucial for building a proactive, productive life. Mainly, the lack of culture is making us so restless and reckless, thus we invent many foolish ideas, including the motto of living in the now, all in hopes of bringing more sense and fun into our lives. In return, all these juvenile mottos are demolishing any chance for building a viable culture.

In fact, 'living for today' causes both badness and sadness slowly, as it reduces our foresight and increases our stress during our strenuous, futile efforts to make every minute of our lives meaningful and joyous. As noted in Chapter Six, we need long-term vision and consistent vitality as main pillars of goodness.

Overall, the constant pressure on people to live for today, as a philosophy, out of laziness, for pleasure, or anything else, has confused them too much already. We try to grasp both the means and meaning of our amusements based on some practical, sound philosophies. However, most intelligent people often realize later in their lives that no ultimate value or uniform meaning exists for human life or their struggles, the same way we judge the lack of meaning or purpose for animals' existence for their own benefits. They may help the planet and serve us, but have no true purpose for themselves per se. Maybe human existence must also have only the purpose of helping other creatures! Are all creatures and plants merely for the purpose of helping others? Then, if so, what is the purpose of existence if not at least partly for our personal benefits? These odd, intuitive ideas are just too damn confusing and philosophical for us! However, we feel life's futility when we think and add up all the facts. Some enlightened individuals even realize their helplessness to stop their sinful, torturous urges that hinder their chances of becoming a relatively good person and exploring life's spiritual dimension at least.

Another repercussion of 'living in the now' is its devastating effect on our sloppy approach in teaching life's realities to our kids. As bad role models, we spoil them with our materialistic and addictive values infecting humans' new lifestyles. We give our kids the wrong advice and impressions about life, instead of teaching them the hurdles of social living nowadays and the need for a proactive mentality to go thru life with minimal shocks.

Sadly, we have let 'living for today' evolve into a prominent mentality nowadays merely for tolerating the mess and stress of the neo-culture. We are using it as a modern excuse to satiate our self-gratification urges within a rather loose lifestyle financially and emotionally, thus our mental decline and ensuing badness. We have forgotten that only solid faiths and outlooks might help us build our characters and a peaceful life.

Luckily, we have the choice of becoming a strong, self-reliant person instead of a confused robot living in the NOW in a fantasy world waiting for love, happiness, and all kinds of miracles to change the course of our lives.

Goodness Culture

Hoping to propagate a culture that promotes goodness within the corrupt environments we have created in recent decades would be merely a dream. Clearly, even our primitive traditional cultures had provided the atmosphere, incentive, and support to become better beings in order to sustain our tribal senses of cooperation, compassion, and harmony, and thus less urges for badness.

Cultural residues in some nations might give their citizens a better chance to adopt a goodness path, compared with people already lost in the neo-cultures' mishmash or whose culture had never rooted due to historical circumstances. As an example, the United States has had major difficulty developing a culture due to many factors, but mainly the enormity and variety of immigrants who have built this country within a short period without any common cultural principles and directions, except for Christianity amongst a larger group. At the same time, the big emphasis on capitalism, materialism, and guns has not merely impeded the opportunity for building a sense of culture in the US, but also led to wicked values and practices emerging in a bizarre neo-culture. Of course, nations like Canada have faced similar obstacles, yet a smoother integration of many cultures has availed a softer setting for open dialogue, understanding, and fairer relationships among groups and authorities with some patience and compassion.

Thus, as a rudimentary conclusion, we might say Americans have a lesser incentive to pursue the path of goodness compared with Canadians, for instance. Probably even such a tiny sense of culture helps Canadians think more selflessly and internationally rather than focusing mostly on personal and national interests. As long as a nation and its citizens are keen on making their own country great at any cost to other nations—such an old-fashioned, infantile mindset—they cannot create the atmosphere, incentive, and support to build a simple culture even for themselves and work on personal goodness. A bigger catastrophe, of course, is that American lifestyle and values have been imitated widely around the world and besieged their senses about life's realities, thus making the prospect of human survival very remote as well!

Now, our neo-culture—or no culture at all[*], depending upon upcoming global affairs—would only stir more evil and gloom. If this theory sounds reasonable, merely more corruption and badness would spread in the future decades and we will fight among ourselves until humanity or most of us are removed from the face of this planet. Then, maybe other creatures and nature get a break and a chance to reverse the course of corrosion caused by humans, too. The best we can hope for is that at least some of us find a relative sense of peace eventually, despite our entrapment within a soulless, malicious society. Maybe some leftover smart groups also learn to master some level of goodness to survive a few more millennia.

Still, let us dream the neo-culture can and will be revamped before humans' brains and social order become irreparable!

---

[*] The Neo-culture evolving around present social values and mentalities is most likely more harmful to humans than a simple No-culture option.

Chapter Thirteen
Lonely Social Humans

How sensible our primitive tribal notion about synergy and security in large cities sounds nowadays? This is a fine, existential question to pose now that we know much better about humans' nature and the world's affairs. We need an answer fast considering how societies are threatened and how deeply they are causing humans' stress and agony. Meanwhile, we now have less options, aptitude, and appetite for living in smaller communities or even less advanced countries, mostly because we have become addicted to new symbols of modernity and phony lifestyles. We are simply trapped in our fantasy worlds amidst a cultural mess with our vast expectations from society and life.

Humans are social by nature, but proven unable to envision and develop a social structure suitable for their collective needs in a civilized manner. Actually, their historical tenacity to prove this embarrassing fact can be noted as their biggest achievement and irony at least! Of course, this deficiency makes some weird sense considering the difficulty of fulfilling even basic human needs consistently, e.g., food and lust, let alone all the artificial needs we have grown and demand from society. The huge hardships we endure during our struggles to satisfy all these real and imaginary needs have skyrocketed in the new era. Our basic needs for food, shelter, and security demand lots of labour already. Yet, we pain ourselves too much more nowadays in hopes of fulfilling our misguided impressions about our middle and higher needs, such as wealth, love, status, fame, etc. We just do not appreciate the vanity of our expectations in such a chaotic civilization, while our societies' consciousness and conscience have also kept eroding.

In fact, it must be reiterated that, despite our highly inflated egos and self-images, our social and personal mentalities are not any stronger than our Stone Age ancestors' considering the rising level of mayhem overwhelming people and societies. This claim sounds outrageous, but it is justifiable, judging by the objectives, contents, and effectiveness of our religions, political systems, relationships, and all the other social elements and processes. In fact, the overall human maturity has declined in recent decades, as we have gotten ourselves immersed in more idealism, tyranny, materialism, and vanity in line with the slogans that capitalism and consumerism inject in our heads since birth. We see all the misery and poverty around the globe and still think that everybody can be wealthy and healthy because we imagine these ideals are our rights, feasible, and valuable. We have built a huge sense of entitlement despite our declining commonsense and compassion. Even worse, we believe our present mentalities and mechanisms can fulfil our personal and social needs, where in fact civilization has so far caused humans only more pains and turmoil. We have not even taken the time to define the meaning and parameters of 'civilization' before using this word so liberally.

Therefore, we live in limbo forever. Surely, we cannot ignore history and current clues about humans' inability to build a viable social structure and a harmonious life. On the other hand, we cannot stop dreaming about salvation and global peace, despite all the negative signs. We just cannot give up our hopes for social harmony and peaceful coexistence as two reasonable and feasible human ideals. Most of us sense these conflicting truths and suffer for them deep down, while remain baffled about our life choices. We feel stuck with this big dilemma, yet try to stay positive about reshaping our societies and mentalities eventually. But how?

A major dilemma for many of us is the type of relationships we wish to keep with people and society, especially if we prefer a moralistic life philosophy and like to explore the goodness path for survival or enlightenment. As much as we can try to remain patient with people and family, conforming to prevalent values and demands would be hard for anybody seeking peace, while some level of stoicism feels more practical and peaceful.

Social coping is tough, because humans' mere gullibility and pomposity make the prospect for a bearable environment too slim. Still, we are mainly in fault for our hardships by choosing wrong objectives and structure to fulfil our social and personal needs. Only humans' nature, logic, and teachings have prevented the creation of proper social elements and processes. Thus, it is hard to anticipate a harmonious life, unless most people's mindsets are reformed by a miracle to grasp relevant social values and personal needs, and then plan to fulfil them through teamwork gradually. After all, only people have the power, interest, and duty to build a functional society to improve their living conditions along with a better chance for salvation. Despite their nasty minds and habits, humans must ultimately develop viable societies or accept their looming demise. This requires an immense level of wisdom and sacrifice to effect such a huge social and personal reformation—to give up our present way of thinking and dreaming.

To study even the possibility of this radical transformation and revamping humans' mentalities, plenty of research and personal learning about the obstacles, including the negative forces noted in Chapter Four, are needed. Meanwhile, making practical choices about society and humans remains a major personal challenge.

Sadly, we are lonely social humans bogged down by our growing modern obsessions and oversensitivity, while our raw perceptions and personalities stir endless frustration, oppressions, sour sentiments, erratic mood, and depression in society.

Humans' anguish due to their daily struggles with numerous personal and social issues has been reviewed all along from many angles. Nevertheless, a deeper discussion about the nature and implications of our frustrations and social obsessions leading to general oppressions seem useful in this chapter.

Endless Frustration

Clearly, everybody has his/her hang-ups and frustrations due to the difficulties of relating to people even within their own small circles, let alone with opposing groups in terms of mentality and attitude. We all feel helpless relating to so many odd personalities stuck in a soulless, oppressive social structure. Thus, everybody ends up being tortured nowadays by, i) the constant pressures of social demand for compliance as a normal manner of existence, ii) idiotic and specific cruelties we impose on one another during our regular interactions, and iii) general social oppressions. At the same time, it is useful to know the degrees of the overall mayhem that different groups' mentalities cause.

The effects and symptoms of social disorder among people vary radically. However, three main groups can be identified in society based on people's consciousness and conscience levels, besides their personal prejudices and socio-political ideologies. **First,** those *fixated* with social norms and promoting them in spite of their bad experiences in terms of depression, insecurities, or loneliness. They simply cannot see any other way of thinking and living. **Second,** those who remain *perplexed*, perturbed, and paralyzed all at the same time. They ponder the pervasive social behaviour, grasp the shortfalls of people's mentality and values, and fret over their own unsettled relationships with people and their attachments to society. Yet, they blame mostly themselves for their failures or inadequate social recognition that they believe they deserve. Thus, they strive harder to fit within social norms as the only means of success. **Third,** those *resolutely cynical* about social values and unwilling to accept the humiliation of following a phony and showy lifestyle that the majority imposes on society. Yet, they end up paying a big price for their lack of enthusiasm and participation in the prevalent social mayhem and promoting it. A small fourth group also exists, which consists of individuals with shaky personalities, merely trying to imitate one or more of the top three groups randomly with no conviction. The first group constitutes the majority, while the second and third groups hold about 20% and 10% of the world's population respectively.

Nevertheless, the majority's actions and attitude—the first group—promotes the foundation of human depravity recklessly, while the tyrannical social structure debilitates and disheartens us. And, proudly, we call this democracy, too! In particular, the effect of our capitalistic mentality pushing a big chunk of population to sell so many useless products to the public is devastating. Our fixation for lying to convince people to purchase worthless stuff, including risky financial securities and products, has turned us into robotic devils. Accordingly, people have become too tense and sceptical about everybody else's intentions, business tactics, and social and financial institutions, while sporadically also suffer their own regular lies and hypocrisy that show their own lack of professional integrity and personal identity.

Usually, logic does not work in this oppressive setting, either, because every time we strive to reason calmly with people and attempt to be fair and nice, they just take our approach the wrong way and abuse us further. Thus, it seems prudent to do not rely on reason and commonsense too much. Then again, logic is the only civil tool we seem to have for making our arguments and defending ourselves, while its growing impotency is another big source of frustration and social concern.

Now, bearing our senseless, illogical world has become quite cumbersome and frustrating, while we wonder if commonsense would ever work, or else, how to live without even a basic sense of logic. Especially, our communications and teamwork dwindle when the repercussions of egologic (humans' low logic and high ego, as noted in Appendix B) vastly hinder our personal, social, and global chances for peace and sanity. Instead, our fixations increase, since we just cannot overcome our egological tendency to make a better world for all or at least a group who prefers to build a small community based on moral values.

In such a cold, calculating environment, handling people has become too frustrating, so we act rudely or insult them in return. It has become difficult to keep our composure and spirits when we are struggling with so many personal and social issues already and then must face people's apathy or gimmicks for money as well. In fact, it seems the only way of eluding so many crooks hoping to exploit us is to become rude ourselves. Then again, our frustration pushing us into anger and losing our basic virtues so often—just for fending off others (e.g., endless telemarketers)—is sad. All along, our rather justifiable rudeness towards these social pests has ruined our characters and mindsets, as the whole situation has now developed into a demeaning, endemic social behaviour and causing endless frustration.

Surely, people's levels of consciousness and conscience affect their varied ways of reacting to social disorders the most. The first —*fixated*—group do not spend time and energy to second-guess the validity of our social norms. This often implies they are hardy conscious of the wider range of issues facing people in a nation or around the world, or simply do not have time or compassion to care. Their trifling conscience matches their low consciousness as well. They are merely absorbed in their own immediate interests, including the best means of exploiting the present socioeconomic systems and maximizing their wealth and success at any cost to others and society. The second—*perplexed*—group has a rather higher consciousness regarding life's realities and essentialities, instead of focusing only on personal urges and interests. They have a better conscience, too. The third—*cynical*—group has a rather high degree of both consciousness and conscience, though they feel abused the most. Thus, it seems that the more a person is conscious of his surroundings and himself, the more cynical and conscientious he becomes, which together goad his/her urge for isolation, while raising his/her frustration and chance of facing the ominous social chaos more realistically.

In all, the second and third groups' higher consciousness and conscience—along with their cynicism, isolation, and inability to adapt to this chaotic social charade—usually cause them a sense of desperation and deeper frustration compared to the first group. On the other hand, it is also reasonable to imagine that the third and second groups have a higher chance of seeking and finding a more suitable path of life, eventually, and becoming better beings compared with the *devoted or absorbed* first group.

Meanwhile, we all struggle with yet another dire dilemma: On the one hand, we cannot rely on bullying and abuse to resolve personal, social, or global issues, or even for deterrent purposes. On the other hand, people seem to hear, or even respect us more, only when we are illogical and rough—and maybe even more so when we intimidate them. *This is sad, but a growing reality!* So, soon people grasp one another and each other's language only through rudeness and distrust all in vain. Then, of course, it just feels too embarrassing to be an active participant of this abusive, manipulative society amidst humans' showy claims of civility!

Our endless frustrations to fulfil our daily obligations at work, at home, and in society are excruciating. Ironically, however, we try to soothe our pains through more socializing, which leads to vaster personal conflicts and social oppressions.

Socializing Obsession

Without a proactive, guiding culture, our basic 'socializing need' has been deformed in the new era like most other human needs. Like other symbols of modernism, our social interactions have been expanded unnaturally. They have become showy, insincere, and useless for satisfying our authentic needs for compassion and companionship. The old socializing principles have been eroded due to people's obsession for popularity, more sexuality and love, and partying at the cost of our obligations for comradeship and family loyalty. Instead, now a competition is out there for more friends and popularity as a fad without recognizing friendship and courtship purposes and handling them with integrity and care. Now, we focus mainly on quantity rather than quality, although we nag about our relationships' low quality with family, friends, colleagues, etc., anyway.

In fact, people's over-socializing fad has turned into a funny addiction all over the world. We devote ourselves to this cause as an obligation to build a peculiar social identity and self-image— and for portraying ourselves as wise, concerned individuals. The number of friends people have on Facebook is quite large. In fact, it appears the youths these days consider any number below one hundred rather inadequate!

A few days ago, a 'friendship request' arrived on Facebook from a stranger who apparently lived in London and had over 3,400 friends already. This info alarmed me about the possibility of relating to her, anyway, whether I knew her somehow or not. Still, my curiosity goaded me to check her profile, wondering if I knew her from my youth in Iran. But her background and friends did not suggest this possibility. Maybe she had a professional or artistic interest she wanted to share with me, but her profile did not support that possibility, either. Why did she need still more friends, anyway? How could anybody imagine this person was serious about her friends or even finding time to at least chat with these many people occasionally directly, let alone in person. The chance she had some commercial goals was even more insulting.

By the way, my curiosity and cynicism about this friendship request and her intentions felt somewhat silly later when I learned that one of my existing Facebook friends had over 4,000 friends.

The amount of time people, especially the youths, spends on internet for socializing is staggering, as another by-product of our neo-culture. Like everything else, now socializing, is no longer smooth and natural. We must spend 80% of our time and efforts to attract and keep friends for 20% of real socializing, while the whole exercise adds no value to our sense of being or stir any true friendship. In fact, our obsession with this fad is unproductive, as we not only gain nothing from spending time with these quantity-oriented people, but also lose more trust in human judgments and values subconsciously. Our psyches wonder about the purpose of wasting our brains and precious lives around insecure, insincere, and insensitive people, even about their own lives and needs. This shenanigan depresses our spirits about the rising vanity of social and personal mentalities as human history proceeds along a bizarre risky path. It also poses another mystery about humanity when no benefits or friendship values can be expected from our obsessions to gather so many lousy friends or a list of strangers. Meanwhile, of course, we are losing our chances for being close to our families and a handful stabler people to build meaningful relationships and appreciate one another sincerely.

Supposedly, more friendships indicate one's importance and social skill, while making one feel more secure as well. In reality, however, this trend shows just the opposite: The shallower and phonier people become, the more friends they accumulate, and vice versa. Accordingly, their lingering or subconscious sense of loneliness and mistrust in the integrity of their friendships raises their insecurity and makes them anxious and needier for yet *more* friends as their only refuge! This phenomenon mostly affirms the faltering human senses and the growing vanity of social affairs. Surely, it is unlikely for these busy buddies to build the mental and emotional capacity needed for helping each other with real friendship and a sense of security.

At the same time, people who do not have time or patience for these kinds of pretentious behaviour are left out and viewed as outcasts, while they strive to know how or why to belong to such a pathetic social setting, anyway. In the end, we have become idiotically obsessed with socializing for two main reasons: First, we feel pressured to make more friends because we are too needy for attention and showing off our popularity. Second, the more time and energy we waste on socializing, the more anxious we get about i) losing our friends, and ii) the humiliation and hassles of humouring their inane values and expectations.

Our strenuous efforts to fit better within the phony social norms and handle our friends' and families' superficialities ruin our identities and self-images, while we also lose our chances and capacities to build proper families and friendships. Nevertheless, we often yield eventually and become insensitive and shallow like the majority, just in hopes of getting hurt less often at least. Accordingly, everybody feels helpless or suffers somehow with regard to his/ her socializing and courtship needs unless s/he finds a means of salvation personally. It is just difficult for any person, especially those with particular insecurities and needs, to choose a suitable option for living and coping with this social issue that is getting out of hand. All along, our struggles to absorb or cure so much humiliation, pressure, and pains related to our socializing and companionship needs alone exhaust our psyches and spirits.

Social scientists have attributed the low quality of education in the United States to loose social values and students' obsession with socializing, despite the fact that the US incurs the highest expenditures on education in the world.

Now, we humans have become just too insecure, insincere, and insensitive to perform our main responsibility for developing both social structure and personal integrity based on our healthy perceptions, convictions, and relationships. Ironically, we have also become oversensitive and demanding from our families and friends, society, life, etc.!

In all, the over-socializing fad nowadays is a time-consuming, soul-depleting addiction ruining our senses about comradeship and communication. This horrendous amount of struggles to fit in society consumes too much of our inner strength, mind, and time that could be used on gauging our being, society, humanity, and nature. Besides hurting our psyches and spirits, over-socializing has made our social structure and culture less stable and reliable, as the number of authentic individuals and friends have declined fast during the last four or five decades. Our socializing obsession has now raised general oppression in society drastically as well, as will be discussed in the next section.

General Oppression

Ironically, people's socializing obsession has also raised the level of social and family oppressions a lot in many bizarre ways for a large variety of reasons. Indeed, it is weird that not even our new obsession for socializing has taught us teamwork to avoid so much chaos and oppression! Instead, we have reached an impasse in terms of social harmony and justice, economic stability and fairness, political integrity, environment, family relationships, gender identity, etc. In return, social systems are less able every day to satisfy our basic needs or stir goodness.

We are all victims of social and parental oppression in some form. In return, we hurt others, even our family members, out of sheer naivety or even misplaced sense of love, e.g., towards our children, parents, or spouses. Yet, too often nowadays, oppression is deliberate by some people or groups who instigate various types of crude social mentality and disorder for personal interests. They exploit people's naiveté and vulnerability casually with no conscience about the damage they cause the public and society. They contaminate people's mindsets and society with their vile ideologies, spread misinformation on social media, and increase social mistrust. Thus, we all, including those devils themselves, lose our chances to find inner peace or a sense of decency. All that conceit and distrust have made people oppressive and cruel.

Ironically, people have also become both oversensitive and insensitive, which has caused a psychological paradox at personal and social levels in itself. We are oversensitive when we get hurt or feel insecure, but insensitive when judging others. We become offended fast, but do not realize, or care, how our attitudes insult, humiliate, or hurt others. This new paradox is just another source of growing oppressions in society.

Therefore, it appears civilization and social living have caused more oppression, disappointments, and loneliness for all, since we and social systems cannot goad cooperation and peace among us as a venue to spread order. Instead, authorities running social systems merely focus on keeping our minds and personalities susceptible to their exploitation. Accordingly, a dire epidemic of global oppression and apathy is killing humanity speedily, as we suffer from the setbacks of civilization and modern existence—yet another embarrassing achievement of 'social humans.'

Besides spreading wicked values around the globe so casually, modern societies punish those who defy mainstream's deformed lifestyles and mentalities. Thus, the acceleration of social badness due to a large variety of ways that people and society oppress one another like a plague. In return, people's inabilities to resist social allure, mature, or gauge their mounting defects, are breaking their spirits and resolve to define their individualism and lives.

We do all this disservice to ourselves out of sheer foolishness and arrogance, often innocently. Then again, the rising oppression pressing our psyches and spirits might awaken some responsible people to gauge the silliness of their characters and the impact of their crude perceptions, raw ambitions, phoniness, cruelty, and naiveté on others, social health, humanity, and themselves.

Socioeconomic Sources of Stress, Confusion, and Frustration

A major source of our endless frustrations is materialism and our refusal to admit that capitalism cannot work much longer. We do not even wish to see the need for research to gauge our social and existential options, as well as the chances and risks of capitalism and materialism failing soon. We, especially our scholars, have surely contemplated these ideas, but it is now clear that a group of elites prevent any second thoughts about the future and value of capitalism. We are dissolved within our socioeconomic systems and overwhelmed by our naïve minds and egological attitude.

How cannot we recognize that any economic system that keeps discriminating between groups (poor and rich, for instance) so vastly is bound to collapse? How much longer can we allow special groups thrive on keeping the public in dark and exploiting their naivety? Until when and for what end our economies must depend on the production of such enormous amount of weapons for global wars and public killings in streets? How much human energy and lives should we waste on our wars and ideological conflicts? When are humans going to grow up? What should be done about capitalism, before it is too late and societies are out of control fully? Nobody seems to know or care! Instead, we appear quite mesmerized and impotent to do anything about these dire social realities of the 21st century. Nobody seems to know or even ponder the required changes. Nobody seems capable or interested in defining even the basic theories for designing a peaceful social structure and a sustainable economic system. Actually, many of our subservient academicians are forced to research only those narrow areas their sponsors want them to focus on for maintaining our flawed socioeconomic systems, rather than using their brains to find long-term solutions.*

Our influential social entities, including the United Nations, simply refuse to acknowledge and propagate the need for a more viable economic model for international and societal coexistence. For example, Nobel Prize for economics is given regularly to narrow, side topics related to capitalism, whereas this committee should have at least known by now that the whole concept of capitalism is doomed. Cannot our economists think deeper, more creatively, to save humanity by predicting and preventing all the social issues caused by such extreme economic inequality and corruption? Cannot they focus to affirm or refute the viability of any socioeconomic system that must rely on endless growth in population and consumption worldwide to satiate its need for an endless expansion? It simply does not sound viable.

Even if we cannot find a better economic system to replace capitalism and keep people motivated to work, we could at least make it more practical and civilized, e.g., by preventing wealth

---

* A book about *the mystery of humans' debility* to build a manageable global socioeconomic system, despite their intelligence, needs, and desires, seems urgent in hopes of stirring some interest and ideas about humanity.

concentration at such extreme. People could still get rich, but not filthy rich as the phrase goes, or by destroying the planet through pollution and climate change crises. Even a highly generous tax system can remedy the situation somewhat by imposing a ceiling on personal income exceeding 100 times of average personal income in developed nations. Even this lousy example sounds generous and more than fair, considering that no human being is smarter and deserving not even ten times more than an average active human being. However, this type of moderate capitalism is called communism and resisted. Our rich elites hate even hearing these socialistic options. Surely, better social mechanism can be devised to prevent such degrees of greed, waste, and inequality.

Barack Obama's farewell speech was passionate and logical, as he appealed to Americans to stay hopeful and keep working on freedom and democracy based on traditional principles. Yet, that kind of logic would not do any good for enlightening the huge population misled by propagandas about freedom, equality, security, and prosperity. People are both brainwashed and spoiled in line with their dire, naïve imaginations about so many ideals, while systematic racism, violence, human idiocies, economic pressures, social injustice, and inequalities are making them more helpless and frustrated.

People's desperation for a more harmonic and healthy social environment and smarter leaders is rising all over the world. Some of these symptoms and social discontents became evident during the 2016 US election in the way desperate citizens were drawn to both Bernie Sanders' and Donald Trump's promises at opposite sides of the scale. It showed the public's frustration with present socioeconomic and political structures and the pervasive abuse in our presumed democratic settings. It revealed people's discontent with the symptoms of capitalism and related social values. In return, people's growing demands for social services to help them bear the repercussions of rising general oppression is crippling socioeconomic systems. In all, capitalism and lifestyle pressures nowadays in western culture manifest as the ultimate symbols and symptoms of human exploitation within a crippled structure. People are more depressed and whining in the US and Europe despite their seemingly more favourable socioeconomic means and democratic values. Ironically, these nations criticize Russia, China, Cuba, and others about human rights and abuse so arrogantly, too, as though they had ideal societies and practical systems in place with solid proofs of moral success and social welfare. Their arrogance and mentality is utterly weird!

Americans and Trump dismiss that only the long history of crude capitalism in the US is responsible for jobs going overseas, too, among all other social havoc it has caused, especially the huge gap in social class. Capitalism causes high costs of wages, production, and living, while competition gets too stiff, especially now that other countries produce the same goods cheaper and often better. Mexico and China are not the cause of job losses and economic problems in the US. Rather, the Americans' obsession for consumption and waste has induced the growing economic imbalance and doomed prospect for the US's competitiveness and productivity. Merely people's demand for higher paying jobs —to afford the constant rise in cost of living—has declined their industries' edge and raised trade imbalance and national debt. Naturally, more jobs would be lost, people's purchasing power would decline, and pressures for cost savings through automation would reduce the need for labour drastically, too. So, in the end, Americans must only condemn their beloved capitalism for their social chaos and endless frustrations, and blame only themselves for electing a catastrophic symbol of capitalism and corruption as their president to fix their economy, society, and lives.

The devastating effects of capitalism are emerging all over the world already, mostly in the way older cultures are subdued by both economic pressures and people's growing thirst for luxury, sexuality, and happiness. Now even China has fallen in similar capitalistic traps in spite of its struggle to maintain its socialistic ideology. For one thing, they require lots of new work force to replace old people just to maintain the growth that their ambitious economic machinery demands for its survival. They are already partially trapped within the constraints of capitalism.

A major damage of commercialism is its dire impression on children about life and the kind of lifestyle they are building around materialistic values and sexuality with no vision in terms of their long-term needs as thoughtful, peace-loving humans. In particular, advertising and TV have been influencing children directly and parents cannot play an effective role to prevent this abusive intervention in our neo-culture. Society is putting deep burdens on parents and kids to cope with so much vanity, while social media and marketers are allowed to manipulate kids' minds and personalities. Thus, basic social principles and culture are damaged along with people's values and relationships at all levels. Especially, spousal and parenthood obligations are mixed up, while parents fight in their families over their children's needs in line with prevalent social trend to spoil kids.

Mothers might have derailed our culture a bit more, not only with their higher flexibility and crude materialistic view of life, but also their faster support and imitation of their kids' misguided fads. Thus, maybe we can say that women are a higher advocate of capitalism through their vaster appetite for, and addiction to, consumerism. But let us not blame only women for destroying the world!

Governments are unable and unwilling to control the process of commercialization and the effects of advertising on people, especially kids, thus all the consequences of social demise. We are at the mercy of commercial and advertising entities for the way we think, eat, dress, build our families, etc. In a way, we may say parents have been disrespected and duped by advertisers, authorities, society, and children. On the other hand, we can say that, ultimately, it is parents' (the public's) weakness (badness in a way) that allows such high level of child commercialization and youth-directed advertisements ruin the parents, children, society, culture, and human life in total. Thanks to this new culture, it is estimated that more than 60% of the youths have some kind of mental and addictive disorder. But who cares, eh?!

Even more disturbing, nowadays advertising is deeply mixed with news in nations' top newspapers, online, on internet, TV, and everywhere else. Exploiting scholars and academic studies to introduce and promote sales, lie outright, and conceal product defects for vaster profits is making us lose confidence even in our research entities and the role of science. Now children are hired as subjects for marketing research or as inconspicuous marketers to manipulate their classmates.

The following few quotes demonstrate the symptoms of our fixations to shallow ideologies and visions.

> "American children are deeply enmeshed in the culture of getting and spending, and they are getting more so. We find that the more enmeshed they are, the more they suffer for it. The more they buy into the commercial and materialistic messages, the worse they feel about themselves, the more depressed they are, and the more they are beset by anxiety, headache, stomachaches, and boredom. The bottom line on the culture they're being raised in is that it's a lot more pernicious than most adults have been willing to admit." *Juliet B. Schor, Born to buy, Scribner 2004,* page 173.

> "Schools are selling ad spaces on buses and stadium walls, and even inside school building and classrooms." Ibid, p. 89.

> "High consumer involvement is a significant cause of depression, anxiety, low self-esteem, and psychosomatic complaints. Psychologically healthy children will be made worse off if they become more enmeshed in the culture of getting and spending. Children with emotional problems will be helped if they disengage from the worlds that corporations are constructing for them. The effects operate in both directions and are symmetric. That is, less involvement in consumer culture leads to healthier kids, and more

involvement leads kids' psychological well-being to deteriorate." Ibid, page 167.

"The prevalence of harmful and addictive products, the imperative to keep up, and the growth of materialistic attitudes are harming kids. If we are honest with ourselves, adults will admit that we are suffering from many of the same influences. That means our tasks should be to make the world a safer and more life-affirming place for everyone. Reversing corporate-constructed childhood is a good first step." Ibid, page 211.

"Television induces discontent with what one has, it creates an orientation to possessions and money, and it causes children to care more about brands, products, and consumer values." Ibid, page 169.

"Parents who are interested in reducing the influence of commercial culture on their children need to walk their talk, especially as children age. Preaching against expensive athletic shoes isn't credible with a closet full of Manolo Blahnik shoes. Restricting television is much harder in households where parents watch a lot. Surveys show that highly materialist kids are more likely to have highly materialistic parents. And highly materialistic parents are likely to have kids with similar priorities. To transmit values effectively, you need to live them. Parents who desire less commercial lifestyles for their children need to change with them." Ibid, page 210.

The symptoms of socioeconomic failures in the US appear in so many places. For example, the popularity of Ultimate Fighting Championship (UFC) around the world, especially in the US, shows people's fixations and mentalities when they spend their time and money on such wild, inhumane sports. UFC was the largest pay-per-view audience worldwide—1.1 billion household in 156 countries. Its revenue in 2019 was $900 million (6 times of 2014). The two brothers who bought UFC for only $2 million, sold it in July 2016 for $4 billion. This type of social fad reveals human mentality at its lowest value and wildest nature. It shows the menace of capitalism and people's crude mentality (ferocity) to turn such a sickening human urge into a global disease.

Housing market is another simple example about the effect of capitalism, when many rich people, including non-residents, are using this basic human need as another means of increasing their wealth or hiding their monies, mostly in other countries. They are causing widespread housing shortage, unaffordability, and all kinds of related social problems in major cities around the globe for hardworking local people.

Our societies have tainted all aspect of humanity by attaching extreme monetary incentives to any object they can exploit. For example, some rich people's rivalry to pay outrageous amounts, e.g., $200 million for a rotting painting shows the vast degree of greed, gullibility, arrogance, and wealth distribution in society— to the point of people losing their senses regarding the aesthetic or cultural value of art per se. Most of these people do not even appreciate the artistic values of their acquisitions, anyway. They usually hide them in vaults instead of letting the public enjoy them! Like real estate, art is another means of rich hoarding and hiding masterpieces only for reselling it at a more outrageous price to another filthy rich later. These extravagances and social diseases are total insult to humanity and art itself. Yet, our elite capitalists are only bragging and enjoying themselves with these lucrative symbols of human folly. They are just laughing behind the scene regarding their knack for evil and exploiting common people's immense gullibility.

A rapper makes $25 million by the age of 25 and then brags to a reporter, so haughtily, that he wants to make 250 million by 29. For one thing, his mentality reflected the narrow nature of the youths' character and social absurdity. We witness similar clues daily about the depraved nature of our culture, since for every successful, buoyant person, a few million frustrated and confused kids feel worthless and failures when their similarly crude visions of self would never materialize or when they sense the vanity of their being even if they happened to succeed and become rich. Watching people's juvenile ambitions, although honourable in some respects, makes some of us deeply sad and embarrassed about our neo-culture and being.

Any conscientious, conscious person can see these clear signs of humans' looming demise in the absence of a culture or action plan for coexistence, while no hope exists for people ever getting less gullible and finding wise, competent leaders with goodwill to build a more efficient social structure.

The above few examples and the upcoming discussions in Part IV show how out of balance society has become due to the dire effects of capitalism. Meanwhile, people's chronic obsessions, oppressions, and frustrations are rising fast, since we all cling to superficial means of finding success and happiness, while lacking real passion and fulfilment in our lives. The lives and mentalities of people like Donald Trump and our seemingly accomplished friends demonstrate that wealth, relationships, and success within present social context are never fulfilling. The richer they get, and the more successful they appear, the odder, shallower, greedier, and more unfulfilled they become. Donald Trump is still in need of daily and hourly praise to satiate his incurable vast insecurities and amazing inability to become a decent being. His whining and worrying about not winning the popular vote and about some people's low view of him show that success and wealth cannot make a person any wiser, better, or happier. In fact, history may judge Trump as the saddest and maddest accomplished person that ever lived. A perfect symbol of humans' utter idiocy!

Still, we must thank Donald Trump for becoming the greatest example of the modern world's vanity and helping us make our *educational* points quickly!

Chapter Fourteen
Mental Restoration and Revolution

Are humans doomed? Well, how can anybody feel safe and sane when so many of us have lost our spirits or gone crazy about our choices of lifestyles and leaders? What can we do when businesses are so unethical, most officials and scholars are lame or corrupt, the world's political milieu is dysfunctional, and the model nation is in such comical disarray?

Trapped in such a chaotic world, we feel dejected and stressed by so many quandaries, including job insecurity, meaningless relationships, and a muddled identity, all due to the convoluted life structure in the 21st century. Mostly, however, our juvenile image of society's capacity to fulfil our fantasies obstructs our chances for embracing a simpler, realistic existence. Furthermore, our crooked lifestyles, misled mindsets, and crude dreams about the meaning of life are draining our spirits. In fact, we would only pain ourselves in vain until we accept life's innate vanity along with a spiritual mindset. We need resilience and brain to bear a lifetime of failures and hardships, instead of fantasizing love, happiness, success, afterlife, etc.

Salvaging the society would be an even bigger challenge, as it requires a highly unlikely universal mental restoration and social revolution. Only if we grasp the misery we are imposing on our grandchildren and future generations, perhaps enough people get the incentive to challenge the senseless status quo and reform the society even if a major bloody revolution is needed.

Surely, this author's naiveté about people's will and ability to refurbish their nature and fight social norms is clear in his wishful thinking in the above two paragraphs alone. Most people cannot entertain such a sacred transition, think less materialistically, and become a better being. Still, many of us ultimately feel the vanity of social temptations and resist the values and teachings imposed upon us under the auspices of democracy and capitalism.

Part IV elaborates on socio-political shortfalls, though a brief discussion of these issues is useful in this part of the book to complete the picture about the depressing state of humanity and our duty to rebel for human survival. Chris Hedges and Naomi Klein state these facts delicately:

> "We must do the hard work of stepping outside the system and building our own radical structures to fight back. It will not be easy. We have to build powerful, anti-capitalist movements…" *Unspeakable,* Chris Hedges, Hot Books, 2016, Page 65.

> "Put another way, only mass social movements can save us now. Because we know where the current system, left unchecked, is headed. We also know, I would add, how that system will deal with the reality of serial climate-related disasters: with profiteering, and escalating barbarism to segregate the losers from the winners. To arrive at this dystopia, all we need to do is keep barrelling down the road we are on. The only remaining variable is whether some countervailing power will emerge to block the road, and simultaneously clear some alternate pathways to destinations that are safer. If that happens, well, it changes everything." *This Changes Everything, Capitalism vs. Climate,* Naomi Klein, 2014, Alfred A. Knopf, Canada, Page 450.

> "… we need to take a much closer look at precisely how the legacy of market fundamentalism, and the much deeper cultural narratives on which it rests, still block critical, life-saving climate action on every front." Ibid. Page 63.

Climate change is only one of numerous disasters caused by capitalism already and the scope of related crises is only going to expand as Naomi explains in her big book devoted to this subject. Varied catastrophes of capitalism are obvious in the manner it exploits people and the vast inequality it has created, but mostly the way it has made everybody very bad individuals out of either greed or necessity to struggle for survival. The average CEO in the US earns around 300 times more than an average worker. Is this a new kind of slavery or what? Slavery in the US supposedly ended only in 1865 after 250 years. But it has been going on all along in an unobtrusive manner, anyway. Thus, a big war will soon begin to end this deepening stalemate. It will be between us desperate, frustrated commoners and them, arrogant, tyrannical capitalists. Who will win is hard to predict, though this gloomy destiny itself is inevitable and necessary. As Naomi Klein says,

"… there will be things that we lose, luxuries some of us will have to give up, whole industries that will disappear. And it's too late to stop climate change from coming; it is already here, and increasingly brutal disasters are headed our way no matter what we do. But it's not too late to avert the worst, and there is still time to change ourselves so that we are far less brutal to one another when these disasters strike. And that, it seems to me, is worth a great deal. Ibid. Page 28.

"… the culture that triumphed in our corporate age puts us against the natural world. This could easily be a cause only for despair. But if there is a reason for social movements to exist, it is not to accept dominant values as fixed and unchangeable but to offer other ways to live—to wage, and win, a battle of cultural worldviews." Ibid. Pages 60-61.

We can have either a moralistic or a materialistic worldview. Presently we are only focusing on the latter with no compassion about the damages we are inflicting on one another and the planet. Even physicians have lost their traditional, expected sense of compassion, since they also see the world through a business lens like everybody else. Marriages have become calculating like a business; so are politics, family relationships, friendships, etc. Pharmaceutical companies pay doctors to prescribe addictive painkillers to their patients. Now many thousands of people die from these drugs around the world. In 2018, 67,367 died from opioids overdose in the US with 168 million prescriptions, almost one bottle of opioids for every American adult. More than 48,000 commit suicide in the US every year—one every 10 minutes. All these crimes are symptoms of capitalism. Yet, the corporations, people, and officials cherishing their capitalistic mentalities and goals do not give a damn about the public and their sufferings as long as they keep exploiting them in every manner possible.

The thwarted youths are toying with the idea of a revolution tentatively—to fight socioeconomic systems and capitalism that are goading greed, arrogance, and fashion, while causing climate and human crises. They might rise and make their movement serious until conscience leaders are elected to change the world. The sad youths have the power and duty to end this oppressive parade of human folly and social vanity. Their power to give up fashion and extravagance per se can break the back of capitalism. They should define finer social values for themselves, rather than following the norms or merely amusing themselves with their whimsical obsessions. Maybe they could even boycott their high schools and colleges for a few years, while working actively to raise their voices for a big revolution even if they must fight their parents or die of hunger. This is their last chance to get serious!

Humans' tenacity to pursue idiotic ideologies and religions under the guidance of fanatic leaders has been evident throughout the history. We have always put our faiths in the wrong places so naively in hopes of salvation and as a refuge from worldly pains. However, our trust in crooked political systems and leaders to improve the socioeconomic state of a country and save the world, too, is an ultimate proof of humans' vulnerability and gullibility. In particular, our faith in democracy and the big bunch of vastly corrupt leaders in charge nowadays says a lot about humans' desperation and idiocy. It only reflects the effects of materialistic propagandas on our naïve, distressed mentalities.

> "... [The] numbing reality of how completely corrupted the modern American political process is bends the brains of those whose job is to cover it. What happens over time is that you lose hope, and you begin to view everything through the prism of the corruption to which you're so accustomed.
>
> When you stop believing in the electoral process, then the only questions left to interest a professional observer are who wins, and how many laughs there will be along the way. We've gotten good at thinking about these things.
>
> Conversely, we've been trained not to care about which old ladies are freezing to death this week because some utility somewhere is turning the heat off, or who's having their furniture put on the street by a sheriff executing a foreclosure order, or who's losing a leg to diabetes because they didn't have the money for a simple checkup two years ago, etc." *Insane Clown President*, Matt Taibbi, 2017, Spiegel and Grau. Page 77.

It is just too hard even to imagine a day when we can define a practical political system and restore our images of our leaders. Now, even defining the meanings of human rights and freedom is a delicate, complex task for setting logical social objectives. For one thing, we wonder what rights such a conceited, naïve species might have! On the other hand, we are still obliged, as part of our mission of becoming better beings to: 1) Envision practical social mechanisms that respect people's rights as long as they do not impede the long-term welfare of the society. 2) Resist personal predispositions about democracy and the vain values that lame, pathetic leaders and the Western culture propagate recklessly to brainwash humans' minds for capitalistic ends. The best way anyone can now help to expand a sense of democracy is to elude propagandas and materialism largely. We could at least stop our obsessions with fashion and luxuries.

> "Social and economic life will again have to be rationed and shared. The lust of capitalism will have to be curtailed or destroyed. And there will have to be a recovery of reverence for the sacred, the bedrock of premodern society, so we can see each other and the earth not as objects to exploit but as living beings to be revered and protected. This recovery will require a very different vision for human society." *Wages of Rebellion*, Chris Hedges 2015, Alfred A. Knopf, Canada. Page 220.

Linking democracy to capitalism in our heads is another flaw. They have no common thread or purpose, except that capitalism hinders our chances of grasping and fulfilling so many humanistic needs and maybe even inventing an effective democratic process.

The large variety of issues reviewed in this book regarding the US political shenanigans in 2016 are mainly for reflecting the public's naiveté and infected mentality on top of humans' flawed nature in general. People's behaviour during this period clearly confirmed the doomed destiny awaiting us and our helplessness to do anything about the major social and economic divide that has crippled the US and the world. This election and its aftermath have provided plenty of proof about the frailty of our mentalities, which is responsible for the present social chaos, but mostly for our own sufferings. This election revealed the enormity of human folly and hypocrisy. After all, regular people are choosing leaders like Trump and supposedly brilliant congressional representatives who behaved so feebly and foolishly, as noted in the Washington Post's article (see pages 343-5). Their support of Trump with absolute pride merely for their own selfish agendas and needs have not been merely educational and entertaining, but mostly frightening. Those leaders' choices and adaptability to praise a bully and justify his deceits and lies have been quite depressing and comical. These pitiful proofs of humans' fawning capacity further revealed the impotency of so-called democratic processes that most Americans boast about arrogantly. Meanwhile, many moral, intelligent Americans suffer the effects of living in such a corrupt and convoluted setting, like the rest of the world.

Surely, the depth of mass's infected mentality is disheartening and worrisome the most. The possibility, let alone the enormity, of so much social hypocrisy is unbelievable! How could anybody miss the fact that no person so illiterate about basic principles of society, economy, and world affairs can make sound judgments, let alone decisions, for leading a nation? Still, a huge mass of mesmerized people did it so keenly! For a nation claiming to be the world's role model for democracy and civilization, especially, the way a pathological liar and hypocrite became a major political party leader and president revealed the mentality and nature of its citizens the most. The way a narcissist and his empty promises could cripple a big nation—both commoners and political leaders —reveals the vulnerability of the world's present social structure and democracy. It is hard not to wonder about people's sanity to accept a lifetime exploiter and loser as their leader and refuge! It has been a major revelation for another large group of people, including the author, to witness people's persistence to disregard their leaders' continuing hypocrisy. This phenomenon has looked fundamentally bizarre, educational, depressing, embarrassing, appalling, and perplexing all at once, especially to outsiders with a crude view of the US. Mostly, these experiences confirm the fundamental frailty of human nature overall, besides the effects of crooked political systems on stirring people's naive brains and their systematic failure to realize the true causes of social chaos. Are not our leaders so pathetic like all humans?

Obviously, it is also unfair to expect commoners to realize the complexity of national and world affairs in order to make sound judgments and better political choices. For one thing, they just cannot recognize that our alleged leaders are helpless, as they do not have the knowledge and conviction to do something positive for others and society, while socioeconomics' complex problems are not solvable by any leader or nation in the new era. We have created a world so entangled within idle principles and ambitions that no solution seems plausible before human mindset is vastly revamped, practical social systems are developed, and universal relationships are rather moralistic—through a magical revelation maybe! As long as we love capitalism and materialism so blindly, our problems would increase, social chaos would get more out of hand, and human nature would deteriorate further. Therefore, our leaders cannot solve even one of the varieties of problems they pledge to resolve quickly.

Arlie Hochschild offers a big paradox about the Americans' mentalities, especially their baffling obsession with capitalism:

> "If I were a small business owner, I would welcome lower company taxes, sure, but strengthening the monopolies that could force me out of business, I didn't get it.
>
> Wrapped around these puzzles was a bigger one [paradox]: how can a system both create pain and deflect blame for that pain? In 2008, reckless and woefully underregulated Wall Street investors led many to lose saving, homes, jobs, and hope. Yet, years later, under the banner of a 'free market,' many within the growing small-town right defend Wall Street against government 'overregulation.' What could be going on?" *Strangers in their own Land*, Arlie Russell Hochschild, 2016, The New Press, New York. Page 10

"As a powerful influence over the views of people I came to know, Fox News stands next to industry, state government, church, and the regular media as an extra pillar of political culture all its own." Ibid. Page 126.

…Fox News stokes fear. And the fear seems to reflect that of the audience it most serves—white middle- and working-class people. During the series of police killings of young black men, Fox reporters tended to defend white police officers and criticize black rioters. It defended the right to own guns and restrict voter registration, and it continually derided the federal government.

George Russell, a Fox commentator, spoke of the 'green energy tyranny.' Business anchor Eric Bolling referred to the EPA [Environment Protection Agency] a 'job terrorists' who are 'strangling America.' Fox News Business Network commentator

Lou Dobbs commented in 2011 that 'as it's being run now, [the EPA] could be part of the Soviet Union.'" Ibid. Page 127.

According to Arlie Hochschild, too many Americans, mostly Republicans, feel as if 'Strangers in their own land,' so get carried away when a loose-mouth like Trump shows up and plays with their naive, agitated minds about the US and their old way of life —*when the US had supposedly been great!* This opportunity triggers their emotional and financial ambitions.

The fact is that those Americans feel 'Strangers in their own land,' since they see the world and their land only in terms of Christianity, free enterprise, wide inequality, guns, government's lowest possible role in business regulation, and other issues that mainly Republicans insist on as America's fundamental values. The roots for feeling 'Strangers in their own land' lie in this group's same old deep senses of racism, bigotry, greed, disregard for the looming climate disaster, and apathy towards a long-term vision for humanity, as long as they profit from capitalism and their crude freedom. A big irony is that not merely rich thinks so selfishly and materialistically, but more so most ordinary people. Thus, both rich and poor miss their chances to grasp the meaning of goodness or ponder the relevance of being better beings.

Besides humans' immense naiveté and vulnerability, people's frustration with social mayhem and desperation to sustain a basic life goad many of them put their last grains of faiths in the hands of idiotic leaders or dictators repeatedly. They cannot see these leaders as the horrific symbols of capitalism, which creates social pains and problems, including radicalism and terrorism within their countries and worldwide. Even the youths' mass murders, addictions, and suicides are direct symptoms of their frustration with our failed social structure, capitalism, and so much immoral values propagated in this environment.

Any chance for social salvation requires the public's grasp of facts about the risks of their materialistic worldviews, tenacity to ignore the big picture, and shoddy lifestyles causing the social mayhem, such as climate crisis. Only their apathy and numbness are causing humans' sufferings and looming demise, although they cannot help themselves much, since the society has made them this way. Instead, they are rushing to teach the same values to their children. Still, they might rise up one day and challenge the leaders who are paving the short path to doomsday or join in a long, nasty, but necessary, revolution eventually as humans' last option. And, of course, this desperate, radical option would most likely burden our spirits further in the process and cause deeper global pains unless and until it succeeds by a miracle.

Naomi Klein believes, rather so optimistically, that some level of uprising has already begun:

> "Yes, the ice sheets are melting faster than the models projected, but resistance is beginning to boil. In these existing and nascent movements we now have a clear glimpses of the kind of dedication and imagination demanded of everyone who is alive and breathing during climate change's 'decade zero.'
>
> Because the carbon record doesn't lie. And what that record tells us is that emissions are still rising: every year we release more greenhouse gases than the year before, the growth rate increasing from one decade to the next—gases that will trap heat for generations to come, creating a world that is hotter, colder, wetter, thirstier, hungrier, angrier. So if there is any hope of reversing these trends, glimpses won't cut it; it will need climate revolution playing on repeat, all day every day, everywhere." Ibid. Page 452.

> "Fundamentally, the task is to articulate not just an alternative set of policy proposals but an alternative worldview to rival the one at the heart of the ecological crisis—embedded in the interdependence rather than hyper-individualism, reciprocity rather than dominance, and cooperation rather than hierarchy. This is required not only to create a political context to dramatically lower emissions, but also to help us cope with the disaster we can no longer avoid. Because in the hot and stormy future we have already made inevitable through our past emis-

sions, an unshakeable belief in the equal rights of all people and a capacity for deep compassion will be the only things standing between civilization and barbarism." Ibid. Page 462.

Another big irony about capitalism, in fact, is that both poor and rich are victims somehow eventually: While poor must suffer for a simple subsistence *most hours* of their lives, rich must worry *every minute* about expanding or protecting their wealth. As Saadi, the Persian poet, utters, "The bigger one's roof, the more one's snow to plough." Yet, people are hypnotized by their dreams and phony lifestyles to see the evils of capitalism ruining so *many hours* or *every minute* of their lives *(in close proportion to their wealth)*. Another irony about capitalism is that many people strive a lifetime to get rich and then suffer for not knowing what to do with their wealth, since they cannot find a worthwhile cause or honest person deserving their generosity.

Strangely, the rich elites do not care (or realize) how their dire greed would hurt their children's and grandchildren's fates soon, despite all the wealth they inherit. New generations, in particular, should fight not only the effects of climate change—no matter where they live, in a hut or a mansion—but also the anger of revolutionaries who would find the rich and give them a deserved retribution—no matter how hard they try to hide or only blame their parents and ancestors. Those revolutionaries have no other option, *then*, but to be equally bad and vengeful if the rich, greedy capitalists refuse to be a bit better beings *now. Is this unlikely?*

While feeling helpless, we are amazed of humans' tenacity to stir so much stress and bear so much suffering all by their own faults. We do not know how and why we are pushing ourselves into such a tight cocoon with no chance for solace, yet unwilling to abandon our absurd dreams! Why are we so keen to ignore the option of living more naturally in a simpler lifestyle for easier goals? Why are so many leaders crooked, useless, and powerless and why are they fighting amongst themselves like idiots within the divisive and ineffective political systems and vile democratic facades and processes? Why are even our famous and rich idols grappling with their own discontents and miseries? Are not the dire perils of democracy and capitalism clear enough yet? How can we waste so much mental energy and time on futile hopes in a fantasy world to cherish and justify our materialistic values, corny beliefs, and petty ideologies? How can so many of us come and go and live so uselessly and sadly?

Hopes for a Miracle!

Aiming for 'human salvation,' as our highest ideal at such a large scale, requires, i) an unprecedented global wisdom and unity, and, ii) a magical overhaul of people's raw ambitions and minds. Most embarrassingly, though, we should admit that humans have failed badly so far to prove their intelligence, despite all their incredible scientific discoveries. We have failed to envision humans' vital needs and means of fulfilling them. We have failed to develop a functional socioeconomic structure to nurture and choose capable leaders for managing our nations and the world. We have failed to build a moralistic culture in sync with educational systems that teach life's essentialities to the youths. Instead, we have merely invented crooked means and mechanisms to serve some elites' or nations' interests, regardless of the sufferings that people and the world keep grappling with. What a pathetic species!

We have built political parties and parliaments to impose checks and balances, but these entities and the officials running them have no guts and integrity to resist the power of elites and evils of capitalism. They do not know how or refuse arrogantly to cooperate for the common interests of people, nations, and the world. Instead, they waste most of their times and energies to fight and humiliate one another.

Therefore, we humans must eventually acknowledge that we have failed to invent practical constitutions and social mindsets to run our personal and political affairs rather realistically towards a global outlook for humanity.

Can we redesign everything, starting with our constitutions, a bit more practically now?

Well, we still hope for miracles to bring timely inspirations, social maturation, peace, and harmony. We imagine and cherish role models to affirm our sacred aspirations and show us how to attain the wisdom, wealth, health, and serenity humans might deserve, after all! We strive to overcome our setbacks during our search for ideals and idols, which has only caused us depression and stress. Societies have become so unstable and immoral with no foresight to develop a more compassionate environment, but we still pray for humans' chance for coexistence. Is this likely?

For these global aspirations, to facilitate human salvation, we must mainly find better means of electing our leaders, especially in the US, where the urges for world dominance and immorality seem to be accelerating. Good US leaders are also essential for the role they still play in the world for a while longer. The US has the chance to prove itself gradually over the next few decades as a true leader of morality that the world needs so badly, or destroy itself and all humanity by further dissemination of materialistic views globally. Surely, for being a great nation and the world's moral leader, the US's biggest task is to recognize and accept the huge responsibility and enormous work and sacrifice required.

At personal levels, we must clean our conscience about our personal prejudices, instead of just sitting back and basking in our idiotic ideals and wasteful lives. Maybe we could even stop our leaders' tenacity to spread their vile ideologies and policies around the world and cause so much pain and frictions. Many compassionate people, including selfless Americans, are already serving humanity around the globe with sincere convictions. Yet, most Americans and their leaders should stop stressing on their 'greatness' while the world is suffocating. Instead of raw patriotic jargons and ideals, only a nation's mentality regarding humanity and global goals is the sign of its greatness. Greatness erupts from people's efforts to discover long-term solutions for our survival and salvation rather than focusing only on power and wealth, while ruining the environment and people's minds. A patriotic mentality is now impractical and embarrassing.

Oh, gosh, how some of us, especially this disillusioned author, keep insisting to prove our naivety by even suggesting all these fantastic dreams about humanity and personal salvation! A big hazard of pursuing a goodness path is that we also become quite romantic and revolutionary at the same time!

Sadly, a big majority cannot find salvation without some form of miracle changing their mindsets and lifestyles. Human demise instead of salvation is a sad, most likely reality, while we seem to have no other option besides whining and dreaming. We can only resort to people's senses of decency to partake in the upcoming revolution needed for changing social mentality and instilling some level of morality, at least for their grandchildren's sake.

Luckily, many of us still have decent options to escape the abyss we are trapped in somewhat easier. We can help ourselves and maybe society by changing our views of life's essentialities. The best place to start is to learn how to curb our superficial needs and infantile perceptions of fanciful lifestyles. We could fight our obsession for materialism to minimize the power of industries in shaping our cultures and personalities. We can free our spirits from the society's imposition of vanity. Actually, our efforts for becoming better beings, with high conscious, compassion, and conscience, can ironically reduce the need for industrial growth, wars, and all the other games that leaders must play nowadays in hopes of fulfilling capitalists' agendas. We could curb our urges for idealism and showiness. This self-containing mindset sounds radical, but appears like our last chance to redeem our spirits and build a sustainable, healthier social structure.

We humans must also realize eventually that the only way to unite, think harmoniously, build a more compassionate and moral society, resist our obsessions for consumerism and capitalism, and make better personal choices, is to become better beings.

Chapter Fifteen
A Solemn Conclusion

So, in the early 21st century, we stand baffled at the last, historical stage of finalizing human demise or salvation depending upon our critical choices during the next few decades. Every individual and leader around the world should ponder this reality and make very tough decisions if we wish to use humans' brains and last chance for survival. Yet, picturing the barriers is painful, in particular the needs for exceptional leaders and global cooperation. It appears we would never get smart and brave enough to face facts even at the cost of our own definite demise.

Main Facts: Dire Goodness Shortage

The meaning of 'being better beings' and its objectives have been explored from many angles all along. Yet, as this book's gist, the following three facts support humans' looming demise readily:

1. Not good enough beings (due to poor human **nature**)
2. Not being good enough (due to poor human **mind**)
3. Not enough good beings (due to poor human **nurture**)

Together, humans' poor nature, mind, and nurture (including parental and social teachings) hinder their welfare as well as the health of society and nature. As a solemn conclusion, therefore, we can say humans taint and hurt one another habitually—like another one of humans' embarrassing achievement! Or maybe as a natural mission bestowed upon us, like another mystery about God's intention for creating humans!

Not good enough beings

As a whole, we humans are not good enough beings, mainly due to our poor nature and historical forces growing our obsession for corruption and immorality over millenniums. This severe human deficiency is reducing individuals' ability to be better beings for finding peace and building a viable social structure, culture, and moral values. Still, understanding human nature is at least useful for gaining higher self-awareness, especially when our interests and egos goad us to ignore ethical principles and our conscience. In particular, human nature's inclination to adopt social badness so fast needs our special attention, as a primary human shortfall and a big obstacle to find our Self and boost our spirits.

Not Being Good Enough

Despite our crooked nature and a corrupt society pushing badness into our psyches, many of us have the capacity to be better beings if we build the incentive and make some efforts and sacrifices. Thus, while we internalize (thru awareness) the first hurdle, i.e., 'not being good enough beings by nature,' we can strive to use our brains to overcome that debilitating condition (our innate badness) and succeed. We might even classify a large group of people as 'good' relative to the majority who behave within or beyond humans' natural wickedness. As a rule, however, almost nobody is good enough to steer a peaceful existence in his or her daily encounters and maybe even reach a divine salvation. We are not taught how, nor do we develop a personal incentive, to become better beings. We are good, maybe, sometimes, but not good enough regularly, mostly because we are not trained to use our brains diligently and wisely. We personally ignore the power within us as well.

Thus, we can say that our personal lack of interest and efforts to be better beings is the second big hurdle for goodness next to our vile nature. We prevent our chance for salvation personally, while our societies have fallen apart from human malice.

Donald Trump and his supporters during and after the 2016 election provide a fine example of the sheer size of people who are 'not good enough' for themselves and society. Even if Trump had good intentions, too, his naiveté to believe in the possibility of fulfilling his infantile promises is a sin and a reason for not being good enough. His ignorance about the impracticality and futility of his crude ambitions are already too harmful to him and others, as would soon be proven to the entire world. When people like Donald Trump believe and insist that climate crisis is a hoax, they mislead the public and we miss our last chances to save the environment and humanity. It is a great clue about their minds' malfunction. In all, Trump may not be an evil and he might even have some goodness in him, but he is not good enough by any moralistic measure. *Still, the opportunity of using Trump as a fine anecdote to explain the meaning of 'not being good enough' has been both quite timely and amusing!*

We might even consider Trump a good person for his minute interest to fight the bureaucracy and corruptive social elements. While 70-80 percent of his followers were misled by his empty words, the rest chose him for his alleged qualities. He may even succeed to do some good things for the US, despite his bizarre behaviour and ignorance about the socioeconomic and political complexities of the new era. Some people may claim that he has been kind and maybe even smart *a few times* in his life, which could be considered a big deal for an unlearned person. Still, only his *weird* charisma drew such a big naïve crowd to believe in his gibberish messages and ignore his immense character flaws that the whole world has witnessed. Unlike charisma, huge conscious efforts and mindfulness are needed to attain goodness, after all.

Trump has proven useful as not only a big example of human idiocy, but also its extent by the number of people following him!

Nevertheless, even if we assume that Trump is a good person for the sake of argument, his kindness and charisma cannot help anybody if he is also stupid and his brain is fully dysfunctional. He is not a good enough being by a long shot for all the lies and low ethics he has spread throughout the nation. In fact, his deep hypocrisy and empty promises alone must be considered crimes, because they create false (painful) hopes for people, plus more frustration and distress when their infantile expectations remain unfulfilled again. The more he keeps promising how *everything would be beautiful,* as he has been saying like a teenager, the more he is responsible for all the new uglier realities and agonies that he and American people shall face soon.

Two major dilemmas also cross our minds in these instances: 1) How fate and God's wisdom operate to let some (immensely) narcissist idiots gain so much power and prosperity when a huge number of better people keep suffering their whole lives just to survive?, and 2) How terribly dysfunctional our socioeconomic mechanisms and people's mentalities must be to let this happen? *Something very peculiar is manifesting about both God's wisdom and humans' nature!*

Again, as noted before, the phrase 'being better beings,' also implies that, while we are not good enough beings for reasons noted before, we have the potential to be much better for our own sake and for building a better society, if we begin using our brains about life's essentialities at last. The idea is to recall our inherent ability to overcome our egos and acknowledge the high chance of our naivety about the world, people, and social issues, despite our usual conviction about being experts, especially when pondering and expressing our perfunctory solutions so hastily. We can learn to monitor and manage our egological tendencies and shoddy attitudes that prevent us from being good enough. We must learn and remember how our gullibility, judgments, crude ambitions, and hypocritical promises can hurt others and us very deeply.

Not enough good beings

Obviously, the third hurdle for creating a higher level of morality and conscience in society is that not enough good beings are around to form a formidable force for ruling a part of the world at least, but also become role models for the rest of us. We might hazard a guess and proclaim that if even 30% of humans were wise, good, and eager to build a viable society, the picture about humanity would change largely within a few centuries. On the contrary, the majority, especially our leaders and scholars, have low incentive and capacity to be better beings themselves or work on principles that might encourage a more compassionate mentality among the population. We do not have enough good leaders to inspire us, while our neo-culture and social values are incapable of nurturing enough good people to serve humanity. The reason so many people are drawn to lame, phony leaders like Trump is that most of us think and feel like them. We are raised to be phony, naïve, idealistic, vengeful, and hypocrites, and stress on our short-term personal needs and interests. In all, not enough good beings are around nowadays. Social pressures to survive and adapt have ruined us all. Yet, if enough of us try to become better beings, we might become a major force to reckon with. We may even get a remote chance to build better communities.

Our Tricky Role as a Human

Alone, the best we can do is to seek inner strengths and the outer power's support to navigate life's rugged journey safely with positivism, and maybe even an idiotic grin, while defying endless disappointments, rejections, and the prospect of a gloomy fate. We feel *obliged*—like revered robots—to grasp and follow life's challenging routines, day after day, in a cloud of confusion. We try to cope with malicious people and social tyrannies somehow, in spite of an inevitable sense of vanity and entrapment within a soulless society. *That is how I feel more often now at old age!* If even partly enlightened and conscious of our baffling existence, we thank God and our high spirits for aiding us in this fateful, binding journey, and hope to get at least a clue about the purpose of it all at some point before dying. Yes, death...! It sounds like a decent option on some days, too, but we fear it enough to give up life yet. We still long for a solemn salvation. Sometimes, we pray for human salvation overall, too, against all odds.

Luckily, we all have a chance to contemplate the facts and our options about our 'being,' as reiterated in this book. We could at least admit that everyone is capable and responsible ultimately to cleanse his/her mentality and find salvation personally, despite his/her heavy professional and social obligations. For one thing, we could stop buying so much stuff to satiate our self-gratifying urges. We could learn humility and curb our naiveté. We could resist the lure of superficial lifestyles that merely goad greed and extravagance. We could boycott American products if the US's policy to impose its failed ideologies worldwide persists. Any nation striving to maximize its hold over the world or punish other countries for not following its lead and crude ideologies (including capitalism) must (and would) be restrained somehow. At the same time, we can always hope that the highly intelligent half of Americans would eventually prevail in enforcing a more viable, healthier means of relating harmoniously nationally and globally within a spirit of sharing and the power of morality rather than military.

The tough, tricky role we should play, as active members of society and humanity, but also for personal salvation, are:

1. We, especially any aspiring leader, should suddenly find the urge, wisdom, and power to envision a new political system driven by some standards of morality and peace. Cherishing humans' prevalent drive for domination and conflict through threats or military manoeuvres is futile and juvenile.
2. We must find a practical type of socialism to replace the outmoded, greedy, and oppressive values of capitalism. We need an innovative economic system that can offer jobs and

dignity to people, while sustaining itself without the need for constant, cancerous growth. We have enough resources and intelligence to keep the mass active within compassionate societies, rather than working so hard with great humiliation in populated societies for no sensible end. We must discard the mentality and means that allow a tiny fraction of people get filthy rich at the expense and misery of the world.

3. We should spread social morality through self-development and spiritualism, instead of depending on religions per se. In particular, humans' mentality must be turned 180 degrees to focus on humility instead of pomposity, greed, and malice.

4. Our views of religions, afterlife, and God require an overhaul. In particular, any religion goading violence is invalid in its roots. Tolerance of even basic greed or exploitation of people is against any type of faith. Sadly, these deficiencies apply to most religious leaders who tolerate or promote social vanities somehow. Opportunistic leaders in politics and religions are only crooked hypocrites ignoring the incapacities of religious and current social teachings to help humanity a bit.

5. We must personally surrender and accept the truths about the flaws of our mentalities and lifestyles. This is hard since we love the perceived reality we have learned to cherish all our lives and are attached to so helplessly. It is hard to admit that our dreams are quite infantile, e.g., about afterlife, happiness, a reliable companion, or a meaningful materialistic success.

6. We should develop and propagate a completely new set of family values, curb our obsession for sexuality and pleasure, and facilitate gender communication and connection.

7. We should stop immediately all our economical excuses for polluting the environment.

8. We, especially the US, must nurture a truly civilized culture free from capitalism. We should plan for raising national and global teamwork and coherence, instead of goading people's senses of rivalry, racism, and isolation that current ideologies about nationalism and individualism have forced upon us.

9. We must revamp our personal and social mentalities in order to replace consumerism with conservationism. We must find means of reducing people's gullibility, instead of allowing special groups and businesses exploit them.
10. When we go to vote, we should think a bit more globally for humans' long-term welfare, instead of focusing only on our immediate needs or ideals. We must learn to think about our country, world, and vulnerable citizens all at the same time.
11. The barrier for social and personal salvation is humans' low incentive and capacity to study themselves, tame their egos, raise goodness, and build a peaceful world for coexistence. We have let societies and their lousy leaders mislead us with crude ideologies raw ambitions about success and happiness. Clearly, this hypnotic setting has also distorted our sense of reality and reduced our chance of finding ourselves.
12. We are barely conscious of our divine needs and spirits or conscientious about other people's needs and rights. Instead, our rising arrogance, greed, and showiness have turned into an epidemic worldwide and leading to personal confusions, social chaos and gullibility, and global conflicts. People have also become oversensitive and raised their expectations from people and society, instead of preparing their brains to endure life's natural hardships and a growing social chaos, like all creatures, in addition to the pains related to our social efforts in hopes of tentative joys of being a human.
13. In brief, we should become better beings!

******

Part IV offers extra material about the depth of socio-political malfunctions nowadays. The general, fresh guideline in Appendix E, under the heading of *A Social Reality Check* (page 425), is a useful recap about the 'Goodness Path' to read even if you would like to skip the technical materials in Appendices A-D. It may be a good tool to stir another good layer of consciousness and insight needed during the long, tough journey of becoming better beings.

PART IV

World's Political Impasse

This civilization is causing all the social mayhem and people's distress, but this modern world is itself the creation of too many pathetic leaders and substandard socio-political systems we humans have been able to put together after millennia of thinking and developing!

A badly cynical philosopher

Chapter Sixteen
Leadership Mishmash

The political analyses in Part IV might help, since humans' survival and chances for goodness depend on our ability to elect or become brilliant leaders. Globalization, especially, has raised an urgent need for open-minded, wise, and selfless leaders to gather around a unified long-term plan. They should build a stable and moral social structure and enforce harmony within a civilized, efficient lifestyle that stirs order, contentment, peace, and self-realization.

Sadly, the prospect does not look good, as though humans are obsessed with their crude mentalities and routine cruelties. Most leaders still prefer to fight amongst themselves forever and look incapable of leading us within the vastly dysfunctional, complex political machinery of the new era. Actually, governments and leaders are harmful nowadays, as capitalism concentrates the power in the hands of select groups running the world behind the scene. Ironically, we have also strived so naively to justify this directionless, doomed social structure by calling it democracy.

Our leaders' narrow worldviews and inability to establish a proper long-term direction for humanity have been affecting us in two major ways. First, the ensuing socioeconomic impasse and our leaders' failures to manage the world affect us personally, as we must endure and suffer so much immorality, social chaos, and deprivations. Second, so much social corruptions turn us into wicked, calculating creatures to survive in this wild environment. We have now lost both our senses of identity and morality as well as our conviction about our future due to a lack of reliable social setting. When leaders focus only on means of maximizing their power and tightening their grip on the rest of the world, we all feel entitled, or forced, to be selfish and power thirsty. When superpowers stir so much tension around the globe for personal and corporate interests, we behave the same way—ruthlessly—towards other human beings, including our family members and friends. We lose interest in ideas such as coexistence, harmony, morality, and peace, despite our erratic shows of goodness.

Even those few leaders with enough intelligence, conviction, and conscience to recognize the needs of people and society are helpless and victims of social chaos themselves. They just waste their lives and achieve nothing, since our political systems are so convoluted nobody can envision, or follow, long-term plans to bring some moralistic and progressive notions into the governing principles. The whole world is stuck in a stalemate due to the ineffectiveness of our political systems and our shoddy views of national and world priorities, or the practicality of democracy. Even good leaders soon recognize, but still hide, their helplessness to fulfil the public's real needs. The never-ending conflicts in the US's political machinery about an affordable health care or gun laws are good examples of political impasses around the world. How many more decades would you bet these struggles among leaders of this supposedly democratic, civilized, and rich country would continue in vain, while over half of its population suffer poverty and other consequences of capitalism?

A true leader needs extremely rare, high qualities, especially in terms of decency, a strong drive to serve humanity, vision and conviction, devotion and purity, etc. These are strong enough reasons why hardly any qualified leader lives amongst us or chooses to take on the challenges of being a leader nowadays and then be humiliated and harassed for his/her efforts, too. In fact, any potentially capable leader has now acquired enough sense to know s/he does not want to be a leader, since changing people's demented mentality and nature to develop a peaceful society is impossible. S/he knows his/her efforts to lead people would be in vain within such a broken socio-political setting, so why bother when s/he could focus on simpler personal plans and activities to fill his/her life. Instead, too many small-minded, vengeful people are always on hand to join the political system for prestige and personal ambitions and do a lousy job without grasping or caring about the gravity of their responsibilities.

Most alarmingly nowadays, however, if the US and Trump are supposed to lead the world, by force and bullying perhaps, no doubt we are all in big trouble. Trump has now shown the world how easy Hitler had paved his way into dictatorship and crippled the world for a long time. Actually, Americans have proven to be even lamer than Germans falling for Hitler, who was at least way smarter and steadier than Trump.

In response to Obama's decision to abstain the US's vote about the UN's resolution about Israel's settlement activities (see page 401), some US leaders stated the following comments:

> *"This is absolutely shameful,"* House Speaker Paul Ryan (R-Wis.) said in a statement, promising that next year, *"our unified Republican government will work to reverse the damage done by this administration, and rebuild our alliance with Israel."* The Washington Post, December 23, 2016.

> Senate Armed Services Committee Chairman John McCain (R-Ariz.) said abstaining made the US, *"complicit in this outrageous attack"* on Israel, and predicted the resolution *"will serve as yet another roadblock to peace between Israelis and Palestinians, and embolden the enemies of Israel."*

> Meanwhile Sen. Lindsey Graham (R-S.C.), who chairs the Appropriations subcommittee that deals with foreign aid, threatened earlier on Friday to reduce the U.S.'s contributions to the United Nations and any country that voted for resolu-

tion. After the vote, Graham tweeted that *"Obama-Kerry foreign policy has gone from naive and foolish to flat-out reckless. With friends like these Israel doesn't need any enemies."*

America's blind support of Israel appears too pathetic and perturbing all in itself, in spite of some presidents, like Obama and Carter, redeeming themselves at times by making objective judgments and reflecting the farce of the US's pitiful puppet-like support of Israel and the Jewish elites of the US.

Sadly, Obama's efforts after all the work he and his devoted, intelligent wife did for the US and the world is disappearing. That is the reality of politics in the US and almost all other nations nowadays. It is a pity that his contributions are obliterated and so much more he wished to do was never appreciated. Instead, some capitalists and lame leaders are now reversing his decisions and policies out of spite and greed. Even when a genuine, insightful leader emerges miraculously to give humanity some hope, all kinds of evil forces stop him/her in his/her tracks. Or some devils quickly undo everything s/he had achieved with sweat in such hostile political environments.

Of course, good leaders' deeds and memories still enlighten some humans. Their genuine efforts and sincerity inspire those of us who strive to become better beings ourselves, though no lasting benefits emerge for humanity without enough good people. Now, the world is trapped in a huge impasse, while personal survival and salvation have become tougher daily. People and leaders feel stuck in an abyss due to so many irresolvable shortfalls and the situation is deteriorating very fast.

We need leaders with the capacity to enlighten the dogmatic, ignorant public, instead of exploiting their naive minds and raw sentiments. They must have a knack for calming people, instead of raising their rage just for getting their votes and becoming a useless radical leader—something like what Trump has become. Something like what Rubio and Cruz did and failed, especially during their pathetic 2016 presidency campaigns.

Certainly, it is hard to imagine so many idiots could gather anywhere in the world and talk so much nonsense to support one another so insincerely, especially in a supposedly civilized nation like the US, never mind in the White House itself!

Pathetic, Lame Leaders

Our leaders become ineffective since they should make tentative compromises constantly and find shortsighted, quick fixes for feeding our capitalistic economies, while struggling to respond to both people's demands and industries' interests. They appear pathetic and lame when they try to justify their shoddy decisions so childishly or when they ignore their promises to work for the public and not the elite groups and companies. Of course, we commoners look pathetic with our naive attitude and desires, too. Yet, our leaders' idiocy and hypocrisy demonstrate the depth of humans' failure to develop themselves and a constructive social structure around compassionate, ethical values.

Leaders appear pathetic for two completely different reasons, though: 1) For failing to execute their honest, humanistic plans, like President Obama, because of partisan resistance in congress, pressures by elite groups running the country, or when all their achievements are reversed by the next administration, and 2) For the lack of integrity and character, like President Trump and those supporting him for boosting their positions with their constituents and elite sponsors. Actually, this second group should be referred to as pathetic puppets (instead of leaders) who merely exploit the public with their campaign promises. They look pathetic due to the lack of integrity and solid beliefs, talking foolishly to deceive voters and protect their pitiful careers.

Accordingly, democracy has proven useless and dangerous when leaders and people are behaving erratically in line with their naive, short-term visions of the world affairs. This democracy is in fact counterproductive for all the additional problems that the election of so many lame, pathetic leaders by stupid or naive people causes in the first place.

Rachel Notley, past Premier of Alberta, and Trudeau had to compromise about imposing carbon tax in Alberta in exchange for federal leniency on pipeline projects that benefited Alberta—a project opposed by environmentalists. To fulfil business interests of a province or country, Notely and Trudeau most likely felt obliged to forego their personal convictions merely for keeping the oil industry happy and creating more jobs. They just ignored environmental protection principles and approved the Kinder-Morgan pipeline that would carry such vastly contaminating oil sand productions from Alberta to BC harbour in Burnaby. In the meantime, two seemingly devoted leaders appeared pathetic and lame, because they not only had to compromise their principles somewhat to satisfy various political groups and agendas, but also lost their chances to remain faithful to their constituents. At the same time, people in Alberta demonstrated and shouted in the streets 'Lock her up, Lock her up,'—the phrase Trump had taught Americans to chant in their streets about Hillary Clinton.

Aside from the above noted compromises, Trudeau had to make concessions in British Columbia with other groups as well in order to allow the Trans-mountain pipeline go through BC. He had to satisfy the proponents of the Liquid Natural Gas in BC, including Christie Clark, then premier of BC, while attaching 192 conditions for project implementation to keep environmentalists on board. Still after all these compromises, it is quite doubtful that any one of these projects would go ahead with all the oppositions surrounding them, especially by the public in BC and Alberta.

Both Trudeau and Notley are decent, competent leaders. Yet, they were often unable to either decide like a learned leader or balance the public's and various interest groups' demands fully. Therefore, in the end, they just looked lame and pathetic.

Even in small scales, such as Trudeau's zeal to entice a group of foreign billionaires during Nov. 2016 to invest in Canada's infrastructure looked rather pathetic to some of us for a country that has many eager investors and a capable industry to do these infrastructure projects nationally. Countries like Canada must be able to rely on private, instead of foreign, capital and initiatives, while keeping billions of dollars of profits in local economies. Of course, foreign investment is a common and practical necessity, at least for developing nations. Yet, at times, it reflects leaders' lameness and low initiative in affluent countries.

Clearly, another cause of leaders' lameness is their insecurity about re-election and their self-preserving submissiveness to their constituents' short-term whims. Even when they learn something about the world, society, economy, and themselves, and gather enough conviction and integrity to help the public, they are voted out due to the lack of progress or under the influence of deceitful propagandas and corruptions in society and political systems.

Our seemingly necessary political machinery, e.g., parliament and senate, to avoid the abuse of power, impedes the leaders' power, too, for alleged good reasons often. Surely, checks and balances are preventing abuse. Yet, they often reduce a leader's effectiveness. Then, these monitoring means are often ignored, like what Trump did during his impeachment with no retribution. Thus, often even our honourable attempts to safeguard political systems cause our leaders' lameness. Instead, our representatives in the parliament spend a great deal of their times finding dirt to taint the opposite party or hinder their efforts, rather than putting their minds and energies together to cooperate and find long-term solutions for a nation and the world. These are some inevitable negative side effects of democracy, apparently! *Hooray....!*

In a very short period, Trump has made a mockery of himself, his officials, Americans, America, executive orders, and the US Constitution. His erratic opinions keep showing his lack of grasp of the job people have elected him for so naively. White House has now turned into a kindergarten, where Trump keeps bullying a bunch of toddlers even more pathetic than himself, like Pence, Barr, Pompeo, McConnell, etc., to fool and amuse the public.

Still, the effects of Trump's jargons, lies, and hate-mongering will keep raising even deeper bitterness and hostility within the US and around the world, while many Americans remain fearful about the spread of radicalism within the US as well as more alienations, retaliations and aggressions by others countries. Quite comically, the events during the 2016 US election, and Trump's subsequent showy executive orders, mostly reveal the impotence of the country's political system.

Surely, a new president's power and eagerness to repeal his/her predecessor's decisions demonstrate the vanity of our leaders' initiatives and actions. It reflects the discontinuity of policies and visions preventing a nation's progress. Instead, political parties and leaders keep fighting over their policies and views, overruling the old ones as soon as they are in power, and re-inventing the wheel over and over regularly when a new president or prime minister is elected. Their idiocy and spite to discredit previous officials and justify their own agendas, to please corporations and elites, show the lameness of leaders and political systems in the US in particular. A new leader feels obliged (and expected) to know so many crooked leadership tricks to replace the previous regime's policies, rather than drawing on some moral principles, vision, and personal integrity to develop a long-term plan for a nation. The whole history of humanity has suffered from these types of idiocies, but not being able to solve these clear obstacles to progress and peace, while claiming democracy, freedom, and civilization, is comical and embarrassing.

Striving not to laugh at the President of the United States showing off his signatures on every executive order or bill, like a kindergartener parading his new drawing, is really tough, even if those orders or documents' contents were not often too idiotic already! The chaos in the White House is irrelevant for this book, but a few hints here shows how Trump is only another pathetic, lame leader just by his demented character, struggling to survive politically instead of helping the US honestly. A few of his words provoking Americans before and after the election follows:

1. Leave Paris climate accord. He said climate change is a hoax.
2. Ban Muslims from coming to the US. His showy, conceited words were simply pathetic, "Donald J. Trump is calling for a total and complete shut down of Muslims entering the United States until our country's representatives can figure out what the hell is going on."
3. Not settle the lawsuit that Trump University students had launched against him—*because then everybody would like to sue me*, he proclaimed so decisively and proudly.
4. Continue water boarding of political prisoners.
5. Revoke Obama's affordable healthcare.
6. Renegotiate or abolish the North American Free Trade and some other trade agreements.
7. Cancel the nuclear deal with Iran.
8. Get out of NATO. He said NATO is obsolete.
9. Deport illegal immigrants.
10. Build a wall along the US/Mexico border at Mexico's cost.
11. Get Hillary Clinton prosecuted and locked up.
12. Sue, after election, all the women who had accused him of sexual assault.

Making these contentious promises proved the shallowness and shortsightedness of political settings, the public, and leaders, especially Trump, already. Then, the matter got even worse when he began reneging on many of them quickly to prove both his hypocrisy and the public's naiveté. Some of the promises he has already broken so quickly or keeps going back and forth on them often, right after the election, are as follows:

- After his repeated promises before the election to release his tax return after the IRS audit, on Jan 22, 2017, he said that he would not release it, after all.
- Just one week after election, he instructed his lawyers to settle the lawsuit regarding his fraud at Trump University.
- On Nov 22, 2016, only two weeks after election, he said he might not get out of the Paris accord, although he kept making

inconsistent comments about this matter, and finally did it with a comical fanfare. Parading and proving his lack of empathy, so foolishly and energetically, about this looming catastrophe along with his immense illiteracy was horrific.
- He changed his mind about water boarding terrorist suspects, since he now says it does not work. Nov. 22, 2016.
- He changed his mind a few times about cancelling the nuclear deal with Iran, while saying inconsistent and incoherent things about his real goal, mostly to please Israel. Then, he finally did it in another showy, irresponsible manner. His pathetic tactics to get Iran to return for renegotiation have failed, though the US's withdrawal will cause more pains for the US and its allies.
- He changed his mind about repealing Obama's health care totally after talking with Obama and saying that he would keep some aspects of it. Meanwhile, the congress failed, despite so much fights and struggle, to get enough support and vote even from a majority Republican Party to consider a new health care bill. The confusion about this matter continues and would lead to major conflicts and disasters in the years to come.
- We are still waiting to see when he would act on his promise to sue all the women who have accused him during his campaign of sexual assault.
- He changed his position about NATO and now says it is not obsolete. So, he sent Vice-President Pence to clean up his mess.
- He changed his position on the first day of his presidency about labelling China as currency manipulator. However, his trade war with China and the entire world continues erratically.
- He backed off his promise to prosecute Hillary Clinton. He knows he has no grounds for prosecuting her and now offers new excuses for not doing it.[*]
- He changed his words on Nov. 13, 2017 about the Mexican wall and said it will be mostly fencing, which is the way it is

---

[*] Many people think Trump is obliged to lock up Hillary by proving his claims about her crimes, or else Hillary Clinton should sue him to prove her innocence.

already. Yet, he keeps changing his words erratically about this matter, anyway. The confusion about the possibility of doing it and his persistence to make Mexico pay for its cost continues.
- He backed away from *total and complete* banning of Muslims from coming to the US. He issued an executive order only to retaliate against certain Muslim countries. On Jan. 27, 2017, he signed an executive order banning only people from Iran, Iraq, Libya, Somalia, Sudan, Syria and Yemen from entering the United States for 90 days. Many Muslim allies, such as Egypt and Saudi Arabia, with which Trump has business dealings, are excluded from his ban. It all shows what a big sham and shame this unsuccessful (legally defeated) ban has been, as well as the US's integrity and infantile foreign policy. Some related news releases regarding this matter are:

Judge halts deportations as refugee ban causes worldwide furor The Washington Post Jan 29 2017
A federal judge in New York blocked deportations nationwide late Saturday of those detained on entry to the United States after an executive order from President Trump targeted citizens from seven predominantly Muslim countries.

Countries where Trump does business are not hit by new travel restrictions The Washington Post Jan 29 2017
Earlier in the week, Norm Eisen, the group's chairman and a former ethics adviser to Barack Obama, tweeted: "WARNING: Mr. Pres. your Muslim ban excludes countries where you have business interests. That is a CONSTITUTIONAL VIOLATION. See u in court."

The above brief examples of Trump's words and actions also show the public's vulnerability, illiteracy, and apathy regarding important global issues. Within an emotionally charged political environment, people jump to elect a new leader who shows his/her talents in lying, discrediting the existing leader, and giving the public many radical, empty promises. The big irony is that people believe all these phony promises again and AGAIN, instead of learning a lesson from their past experiences.

Socio-political Illiteracy

Does not the US's current political environment suggest that its constitution needs an overhaul right away to address the nation's and people's new civilized needs, instead of arguing about some old worldviews forever? All these chaos and controversy are the outcomes of people's crude mentality and confusion about the capacity of any society to keep everybody happy in many respects regularly. People do not even wish to consider the need for a new vision based on the realities of the 21st century.

It is weird humans cannot fathom their rudimentary needs for civilization after many millenniums of failures! It is amazing how our allegedly smart societies and leaders cannot see the causes of chaos, invent social principles that can be managed, and rebuild the world together according to a master plan for humanity.

Our current worldviews that stress on our self-interests and shortsighted needs cannot work, and our reliance on our leaders' quick-fix promises during elections is naive. For humanity to survive, a long-term radical vision is required and tough, novel principles must be implemented within a few generations with patience and sacrifice—towards relative social order, morality, and harmony.

Surely, the absence of moralistic values and social structure has impeded the training or use of wise, honest leaders. Yet, the main hurdle for social progress and civility is people's naivety about the viability of present socioeconomic systems and electing useless leaders in our lame democracies. We are also guilty for not realizing our leaders' general limitations to make real changes in fully broken societies or a world so incapable of pondering a practical process for human relations and cooperation. We still brag about our outmoded constitutions, instead of thinking more holistically and realizing the need for an overhaul of humans' mentalities about life, society, and global coexistence.

Even if we dare to assume a chance for humans' survival, a functional social structure would not evolve if people and leaders are not objective, unselfish, and active. Yet, humans' naiveté and socioeconomic barriers appear insurmountable for sensing our entrapment in an abyss of social vanity and developing proper mentalities. Our methods of choosing our leaders cannot be valid if we have not done enough self-analysis and soul-searching first to set our life outlook with compassion in a universal framework and revamp our raw, bigoted mentalities consciously. We should grasp the complexities of the fast-changing world's affairs and accept that no country can isolate itself from the rising miseries on this planet, especially our nations' poor. We, especially elites, must stop thinking we can keep all the good things for ourselves, while holding others inside some arbitrary borders away from us.

To mention just a few fine examples of social recklessness, we waste and destroy over 50% of our food yearly when half of the world suffers from famine and malnutrition. We have lots of land and resources to exploit, but keep fighting over small pieces of land for selfish purposes, territorial disputes, and traditional prejudices. We fight over foolish religious ideologies and ponder afterlife so fanatically like idiots, while ruining our lives now. We have millions of vacant houses and villas that rich people keep only for investment or pleasure, while half of the world populace live in the streets, refugee camps, or awful dwellings.

We have some smart leaders and scholars around the world, too, who like to sort out so many social conundrums of various natures, but they are stuck in a stalemate much worse than we commoners are. This global deadlock cannot be resolved until the public's overall mentality around the world is revamped and they are ready to face the new realities growing out of centuries of bad leadership, exploitation, and capitalistic views around the world. The global havoc besieging us now is the result of decades of our leaders' atrocities and abuse of people, nations, and nature.

We must deal with our socio-political illiteracy somehow first. But how can anybody play a role in fighting such horrendous obstacles by just revamping his/her mentality? As a start, we can ask ourselves, 'Why do we still elect leaders whose narcissism and hypocrisy has been evident? Or those who ignore, or cannot grasp, the reality regarding the rising global interconnectivity and growing social complexities? How can we trust leaders like Trump and Romney, who suddenly get cosy after insulting and accusing each other of all kinds of treachery? How can they look at each other, let alone work side by side, after considering and calling each other phony, fraud, and other stuff? They do not have enough integrity to stick to their earlier assessments of each other at least. How can people feel confident about these leaders' ability to help their countries and the world, then? How can we be expected to ignore so much duplicity, lie, and spite in political systems? At best, these leaders' diplomatic show of tolerance, after insulting each other enough already, is only another proof of their hypocrisy and the political charade killing our spirits. More crucially, though, all these atrocities are our faults, as we ignore these facts and elect them based on our old-fashioned mentalities and juvenile needs!

Surely, a civilized society cannot emerge without many wise, caring, and conscientious leaders. Then again, ironically, not even smart, ethical leaders can run the world nowadays, due to the public's socio-political illiteracy crippling those leaders' chance to do the right things for the long-term benefits of all.

Sadly, it is just becoming impossible even for caring, capable leaders to do the right things without worrying about losing their powers. They may even feel guilty and worried (but pressed) for doing wrong things (e.g., disregarding climate and environmental catastrophes), and often even feel justified, too, in fact—just to stop some evils from taking over and making even a bigger mess of the world. The fact that our leaders feel obliged to compromise for keeping various groups and people happy regularly is a big challenge and often a necessity, yet they look pathetic and lame even if they happen to have some conscience and competence. In the end, humans seem doomed by their own fault—merely for forcing this situation upon society and themselves. Only people's naiveté about the reality of the world and their insensible demands ultimately cause their own pains and frustrations, while disabling a few good leaders that come around from time to time, too. As stressed in Chapter Eight, our educational systems' failure to teach these basic social facts to the youths is most disheartening and a sign of our failure.

Some hypocrite leaders in the US, like Senators Marco Rubio and Ted Cruz, criticized Justine Trudeau, the Prime Minster of Canada, for praising some of Fidel Castro's qualities when he passed away. Their self-serving diplomatic reactions looked truly pathetic. It felt ludicrous that such hypocrites kept misrepresenting a revolutionary hero like Castro and calling him a dictator merely for their own self-serving purposes. Just for pleasing their voters, these lame, pathetic leaders gave themselves the right to criticize Canada's prime minister for his liberalism and expressing his points. These big shot US leaders do not even understand the basic principles of democracy or dictatorship. They do not grasp, or care, that it is up to Cubans to judge Castro and the value of his revolution for their nation, not the pathetic leaders of the US or some capitalist Cubans living in Florida. However, they make their foolish judgments about Castro and Trudeau. While Obama realized Cuba better and initiated a wise reconciliation process, now all his efforts have been wasted since Trump has retracted all those precious developments, too.

It is hard not to wonder about the depth of Rubio's and Cruz's integrity and hypocrisy when condemning Trudeau's civilized praise of Castro and for expressing a personal opinion (which sounded legitimate in many people's minds). These lame US leaders look pathetic when they insist on seeing the world only from their selfish, narrow capitalistic minds. Then, the situation got worse when Trudeau felt obliged to moderate his position after so much pressures from the US and Canadian capitalists. Thus, at last, he said Castro was a dictator, instead of defending the reasons for his dictatorship. He even changed his mind about going to Cuba for Castro's funeral, though Canada's Governor General attended instead. Nevertheless, Trudeau looked lame and pathetic as well for not adhering to his personal, objective views of Castro and defending him as a hero that he had been within his limits for the ultimate, sincere purpose of serving poor Cubans. Trudeau just felt obliged to remain politically correct merely for protecting his national and international image.

Ultimately, a leader should be a good being with a natural leadership quality, able to demonstrate the virtues of a peaceful coexistence for all humanity by example. However, we humans choose our leaders or become one with confused sentiments and values. Ironically, everybody, including American leaders and political scholars, considers Robin Hood a hero. We do not call him a dictator or a communist, although at the end his main goal was to redistribute wealth fairly, which had been Fidel Castro's ultimate goal as well. In fact, considering the wicked nature of humans, often dictatorship and force appear necessary for larger social causes in the long run, as the US itself has been doing it— wrongly mind you, just for its own benefits per se—all over the world in order to deter world agitators or to spread its demented capitalistic values.

Are not we humans, especially our leaders, so pathetic?

The public's choice of a pathological liar as president is weird enough, but Trump's ability to gather such a big group of liars to serve him seems even more bizarre, although we have always suspected the enormity of substandard humans willing to sell their integrity and pride merely for gaining an image of power. While Trump looks more pathetic every minute by his tweets and comments, those pathetic leaders serving him timidly, including VP Pence and Paul Ryan, trying so hard to sweep his daily mess under the rug, look quite pathetic.

> "Ryan's cowardly play was reflective of the party as a whole, which has yet to own its role in the Trump story. Republican ineptitude and corruption represented the first crack of in the façade of a crumbling political system that made Trump's rise possible." *Insane Clown President*, Matt Taibbi, 2017, Spiegel and Grau. Page 264.

The following article shows how so many of our leaders are lame and pathetic. It is a rather long article, but quoting it here felt necessary for reflecting the depth of human idiocy and problems.

Former Trump critics make up a parade of shame at Trump Tower The Washington Post, December 10, 2016

House Speaker Paul D. Ryan made the pilgrimage Friday morning that many former critics of Donald Trump have made since the election: up to Trump Tower in Manhattan for a meeting with the president-elect and then a walk through the lobby to address reporters wanting to know how it feels.

"Very exciting meeting," Ryan (R-Wis.) said in remarks that lasted mere seconds. *"I really enjoyed coming up here and meeting with the president-elect. We had a great meeting to talk about our transition. We are really excited about getting to work and hitting the ground running in 2017. And getting this country back on track."*

Over the past month, the president-elect and his team have been mending relationships within their party, meeting with former rivals who resisted the idea of Trump becoming president but are now willing to work with him. But forgiveness often comes only after accepting a heap of humility.

The parade of shame has included GOP primaries opponent Sen. Ted Cruz (R-Tex.) and the previous Republican presidential nominee, Mitt Romney. On Monday, Trump's team expects the arrival of Carly Fiorina, the former business chief executive and presidential candidate who Trump suggested was unattractive. And the ritual isn't reserved just for Republicans: Trump invited a group of television personalities and executives to the tower soon after the election, and then yelled at them for underestimating him and accused them of dishonest reporting about his campaign, surprising and unsettling many attendants.

John Weaver, a strategist for Gov. John Kasich (R-Ohio) who has been critical of Trump, said he understands why former critics are having these meetings — but he worries that embracing Trump has led some to embrace his approach and policies, abandoning long-held Republican principles. Weaver said he has already seen it happen with free trade and federal spending, and he worries that it could also happen with the country's approach to Russia.

"Some leaders are rolling over for Mr. Trump," Weaver said.

Sometimes Trump's guests secretly slip upstairs without being seen, but they frequently have to run the gantlet that has become the Trump Tower lobby — a maze that twists through packs of tourists with cameras, a horde of reporters screaming questions and a C-SPAN live feed. Part of pleasing the president-elect often involves public praise.

When Cruz visited a week after the election, he managed to slip upstairs undetected. During the campaign, Trump compared the attractiveness of their wives, suggested that Cruz's father was involved in the assassination of John F. Kennedy and raised questions about Cruz's eligibility for the presidency, since he was born in Canada. Cruz refused to endorse Trump at the Republican National Convention but did so just before the election.

After the Trump Towers meeting, Cruz took a more direct route through the lobby. It was nearly 7 p.m., and most reporters had left for the evening. But the few that remained shouted questions and, when ignored, followed Cruz outside, where his escape was slowed by a heavily armed guard who wanted a photo.

Cruz continued down the block, followed by reporters who wanted to know how the meeting went. He finally stopped.

"This election was a mandate for change," Cruz said. *"The American people rose up and spoke overwhelmingly to say that the path we're on, it didn't work. And they want change, and they have given Republicans a historic opportunity."*

Cruz didn't directly answer a question about whether he would want a position in the administration, and then took off down the street.

Romney, on the other hand, is interested in becoming secretary of state and willingly went through this exercise several times. Trump railed against Romney throughout the campaign, mocking his wealth, accusing him of having "choked" during the 2012 election and being "stupid," and joking that he walked "like a penguin." Romney called Trump "a phony, a fraud," said Trump's "promises are as worthless as a degree from Trump University," and predicted there was a bombshell in the tax returns Trump refused to release.

Romney first met Trump at his golf club in New Jersey on Nov. 19, where the two were photographed together and where Romney took a turn in front of the cameras. Ten days later, they publicly dined at a French restaurant. Photos of the evening were quickly memed on Twitter. One photo was manipulated to show a huge crow on Romney's plate. Another compared the dinner with a subplot from HBO's "Game of Thrones" involving a psychopath's grotesque physical and emotional debasement of a nobleman's son.

But Romney was nothing but smiles and praise as he spoke to reporters after his "wonderful evening with President-elect Trump."

"President-elect Trump is the very man who can lead us to that better future," Romney said that night.

Despite these acts of contrition, the president-elect widened his search for secretary of state this week, saying he still wasn't ready to decide.

On Friday evening, another contender for the position — former New York City Mayor Rudolph W. Giuliani — publicly withdrew his name for Cabinet consideration, perhaps rendering pointless many of the cringe-worthy comments he made on Trump's behalf over the past six months. Giuliani memorably said that "everybody" cheats on their spouse, that the Black Lives Matter movement is "inherently racist" and that Trump would be "better for the United States than a woman."

New Jersey Gov. Chris Christie (R) went through a similar experience after losing to Trump. Christie became a trusted Trump adviser, only to be cast aside when the "Bridgegate" scandal blew up. A Vine video of Christie staring uneasily into the middle distance as Trump spoke a few feet away in March has been played nearly 20 million times.

"No, I wasn't being held hostage," Christie later had to tell reporters. Some Republican critics have stayed away, although the list is shrinking. Former Florida governor Jeb Bush, Sen. John McCain (Ariz.) and Sen. Lindsey O. Graham (S.C.) have not been spotted at the tower.

Those who show respect or deference in private may still be publicly exposed: Kasich was booed by his own state's residents during a post-election Trump rally in Cincinnati.

"In the great state of Ohio, we didn't have the upper echelon of politicians either, did we?" Trump said, which prompted the boos. But he added, *"Your governor, John Kasich, called me after the election and was very nice. He said, 'Congratulations, that was amazing.'"*"

Surely, these pathetic leaders have left their amazing legacies in history! In all, most leaders are too arrogant and incompetent

to make any social impact, but then get trapped in stagnant and inefficient socio-political systems as well. Big bottlenecks, such as national conflicts and unrests, international competitions, cheap labour markets and automation in manufacturing, wars, corporations' greed, and the public's obsession for waste and extravagance, hinder initiatives for social harmony. All these clashing forces around the globe have crippled leaders to achieve equilibrium in any nation and among people. Even when some leaders are good beings somewhat, national and global conflicts quickly make them lame and helpless to serve people. In return, this universal corrosion has made the prospect for humanity dire and dramatic, and raised everybody's frustration and desperation. All along, many people are becoming too wicked themselves, while striving to exploit this mayhem. The rise of extremism and terrorism is mostly due to humans' incapacity to lead the world properly as well.

Now, our socioeconomic and political systems have paralyzed all of us, indeed, while the reality we are facing is too complex and chaotic already to warrant any hope for social solutions and human salvation. We suffer witnessing our leaders' helplessness to do anything for people, especially when some exceptional leaders' talents and intentions go to waste due to global downfall driven by people's socio-political illiteracy. Overall, we can say that the mix of naiveté and conceit among the public and leaders is bringing humanity to its end hastily.

Scholars' Complicity

The role of scientists, academicians, and scholars is extremely vital for saving humanity by guiding people and society revamp their mentalities, as well as our educational and political systems. However, many of them appear equally as pathetic and lame as our leaders. They are only humans, after all! The deliberate role some of them play to influence, instead of enlighten, the public, is depressing. Their systematic collaboration with ruling capitalists, including lobbyists, pharmaceutical firms, financial organs, food industry, political parties, etc., is beyond reproach and simply too embarrassing. Some economic academicians in the United States covered up the fraudulent schemes that US bankers and financial entities were running prior to, and during the 2008 financial flop, and the misery it caused for ordinary people.

As a political scholar, George Friedman predicts the future of world affairs in the 21st century quite favourably in terms of the rising US power and position in the world. In particular, his view of the US grand strategy to rule the world is interesting. He says:

> "US defeat or stalemate in Iraq and Afghanistan is the likely outcome, and both wars will appear to have ended badly for the United States. There is no question that American execution of the war in Iraq has been clumsy, graceless, and in many ways unsophisticated. The United States was, indeed, adolescent in its simplification of issues and its use of power. But, on a broader, more strategic level, that does not matter. So long as the Muslims are fighting each other, the United States has won its war." George Friedman, *The Next Hundred Years*, 2009, Doubleday, Page 49.

Many points in this short phrase reflect Americans' mentality, including its scholars'. While he admits the dire result of the US's wars and adolescent use of its power, at the end he still justifies all these oppressions as a necessity for the US domination. His support of the notion of causing tensions around the world (in his last two sentences above), as long as the outcome benefits the US, is simply deplorable. He believes the misery America causes globally is irrelevant, since it is a grand strategy for making the United States win the ultimate war for controlling the world. *This is how most Americans apparently envision their greatness!*

This is exactly the type of conclusion that many nations and people around the world have arrived at about the US and its grand strategy. Meanwhile, other nations' reactions to the US have manifested in many novel forms of resistance that would continue to annul the US's so-called grand strategy and most of Friedman's predictions about it. Ironically, we can agree with and argue against many of his alarming analyses and conclusions from different perspectives, yet that is not within the scope of this book. In particular, his prophecy about the Russia losing most of its power by 2020 appears shoddy. On the contrary, it appears that Russia's power and influence in the world would increase drastically. Meanwhile, it is plausible that the US will lose both its appetite and influence for controlling the world at such high cost when its national debt and domestic concerns keep rising, too. Friedman is being proven wrong already even about the US's rise in the 21st century. The US would in fact lose its grace and power now that the nature of American mentality and its broken political system is becoming clearer even to its allies.

The world, mainly the US, is spending too much energy and money on military, instead of finding ways of helping the poor citizens and maybe even playing a useful role for coexistence around the globe. Indeed, it is a pity we cannot use all that money and energy—all that alleged greatness—more productively on social welfare, infrastructure, humanity, and environment.

Friedman also reiterates the fact that the US should and would exploit its power despite various challenges it faces in a few parts of the world. Nowhere he considers the likelihood (or option) of the US and the world relating in a more civilized, moral manner. His conclusion is that the world should continue with power struggles forever, while the US keeps imposing its will over the globe and the world would tolerate this condition forever, at least during the 21st century! However, some of us doubt the validity of his assumptions about the world's fear of the US, even if it remains the strongest military and economic power. Nevertheless, it is troublesome that most of his analyses stress on the immense power of the US and the importance of its military might at any cost to other nations and humanity.

We are all hoping—despite inadequate reasons for optimism—that future disputes will be intellectual, instead of hostile, and driven by compassionate ideologies for social stability and at least a minimal global morality. Then again, this vision maybe too sophisticated for human mentality and their thirst for guns, aggression, and power. It is apparently too much even for some scholars, although Friedman's blunt statement of facts about the state and role of American politics is admirable! It offers a clear proof about the mentality of many American scholars and a large portion of Americans who share similar sentiments about ruling the world at any cost.

Friedman's ideologies and conclusions are quite educational for reflecting our scholars' role in the fast decline of cultures and humanity. Especially, they demonstrate the sad reality about both American leaders and scholars being obsessed with power more than compassion. Many of them are already basking and boasting in the Trump administration, striving to show the US's true face and agenda to the world. Nevertheless, the following statements by Friedman are reflective and true, thus warrant a deeper review of his very educational book by readers. Italics are my comments.

> "The United States is socially imitated and politically condemned. It sits on the ideological fault line of the international system. As populations decline due to shifts in reproductive patterns, the United States becomes the center for radically redefined modes of social like. On the other hand, those who don't adopt America's ways can't have a modern economy. This is what gives America its strength and continually frustrates its critics." Ibid. Page 64. *I disagree totally.*

> "Certainly, as is usually the case, the United States currently appears to be making a mess of things around the world. But it's important not to be confused by the passing chaos. The United States is economically, militarily, and politically the most powerful country in the world, and there is no real challenger to that power." Ibid. Page 4. *I disagree totally.*

> "… the argument I'm making is that the world does, in fact, pivot around the United States." Ibid. Page 4. *I disagree totally.*

"The United States doesn't need to win wars. It needs to simply disrupt things so that the other side can't build up sufficient strength to challenge it." Ibid. Page 5. *Foolish thinking.*

"Psychologically, the United States is a bizarre mixture of overconfidence and insecurity. *Totally agree.*
... How else should an adolescent feel about itself and its place in the world?" Ibid. Page 28. *Totally agree.*

"Rhetoric aside, the United States has no overriding interest in peace in Eurasia. The United States also has no interest in winning a war outright. As with Vietnam and Korea, the purpose of these conflicts is simply to block a power or destabilize the region, not to impose order." "The United States is so powerful that it is almost impossible for the rest of the world to control American behaviour." Ibid. Page 46. *Totally disagree.*

"So long as the Muslims are fighting each other, the United States has won its war." Ibid. Page 49. *Totally disagree.*

"The computer was the most effective introduction to American culture, far more profound than movies or TV. The robot will represent computer's logical and dramatic conclusion." Ibid. Page 220. *What culture?*

"The radical shifts that have wracked Europe and the United States, transforming the role of women and the structure of family, will become a worldwide phenomenon. Deep tensions—between supporters of traditional values and new social realities—will become intense throughout the second-tier countries, all major religions will be wracked by then. The traditional values are going to collapse in Europe and the United States, and they will then collapse throughout most of the world." Ibid. Page 221. *Totally agree about this sad prospect.*

Despite Friedman's nationalistic optimism, a gloomy future is awaiting humanity, no matter how powerful the US is militarily. That is, without a basic peaceful culture and sense of morality, all nations, especially the US, are doomed by immense human evil expanding fast. Actually, the rising global mayhem and mistrust mostly relate to the US's failure to fulfil its self-proclaimed, and widely misperceived, role as a democratic, moral world leader—another great symptom of human naivety. All such claims are now widely challenged and slowly addressed by global aversion towards the US's dire policies, lifestyle, and immorality. Some of the reasons and examples of the US's socio-political failures are noted below:

1. People's lack of security and routine killings in the streets and schools all over the US.
2. Loss of credibility both nationally and internationally due to its instable internal affairs and the discontinuity of its political direction, financial markets, and banking system.
3. The only nation that has used atomic bomb, as a war tactic, on helpless civilians of another country, in full knowledge of its dreadful consequence.
4. Making massacres and human rights violations everywhere, including in Vietnam, Philippines, Iraq, Afghanistan, etc.
5. Widespread slavery for 250 years openly along with racism, and now in an indirect manner.
6. Torturing prisoners from all over the world with all kinds of self-serving excuses. The idea of CIA paying psychologists $81 million to design and monitor tortures at Guantanamo Bay detention camp and in Afghanistan shows the US's deep disregard for human rights and decency. The foreign prisoners in Guantanamo Bay have been kept there without criminal charges, but only with the excuse that they are dangerous.
7. Incessant exploitation of the third world countries for their natural resources and ruining their political destinies. (See the example on page 362.)
8. No affordable medical services and coverage for at least one third of its population.
9. The role of wall street and banking system, including the Federal Reserve Bank in the financial crisis and recession all over the world in 2008, and most likely in future years.

10. Spread of social greed and hypocrisy, for example in 2008 letting the CEOs of financial industry pocket millions and billions in compensation for their deliberate schemes to cheat the public and abuse the lack of banking regulations. Not only those CEOs were not prosecuted, they were allowed to stay in power and even work for the White House. The US did not even adopt some rules to put limits on those greedy executives' compensations the same way Europeans did after learning their lessons.
11. Causing the largest amount of pollution in the US and around the world and now refusing to partake in any form of climate change initiative.
12. The highest inequality of wealth than any other country.
13. The highest number of prisoners in the world at 724 per 100,000. In Russia, the rate is 581.
14. Probably the most ineffective and corrupt political system among modern countries.
15. The most publicly armed country with commercialized and comical gun laws. With 4% of the world population, the civil gun ownership in the US is at 40%.
16. The most pompous, self-promoting nation and people for no apparent merits other than military and economic powers.
17. Almost all people and leaders are driven solely by capitalistic ideologies and lifestyles instead of contemplating a long-term vision for humanity and moral values among all nations.
18. Americans do not seem to believe in, or respect, their alleged democracy, either, as they easily conspire to sabotage or even dispose of elected leaders or their achievements whenever they can.
19. Both the public's and government's obsession with guns is ruining the basic social fibres of American society, let alone allowing any chance for cultivating a civilized culture.
20. In fact, the whole concept of democracy in its present format is questionable, as political processes and outcome in the US best demonstrate its impotence.

Chapter Seventeen
Democracy Mess

The hazards of democracy and our present means of aiming it can be analyzed extensively from many angles, though that is beyond this book's mandate. Still, we should at least grasp and agree on our main intention when talking about democracy. Are we just interested in a society, a) governed by the rule of the majority, or b) driven by ethical principles for a rather peaceful, enduring coexistence? These two goals are incongruent and need unique political mechanisms and leadership approaches. Do we wish to fulfil humans' innate greed, self-serving mentality, and focus on their immediate needs, goal (a), or think globally and plan for the long-term welfare of societies and humanity, goal (b).

Democracy might achieve objective (a) somewhat at best, i.e., governing by the rule of the majority. Yet, it has no mechanism or capacity to stir moral values, peace, and justice—objective (b) —which is the most urgent and desired human ideal. Ironically, people assume democracy has an inherent capacity to achieve objective (b) automatically. This is the most misperceived and harmful aspect of democracy, even if people were rather smart and elections were honest without too many influential groups brainwashing people's minds. Thus, our present application of democracy is aimless **at best**. Nowadays, nations cannot even fulfil the lame goal (a) by their presumed democracies.

Accordingly, a big confusion has spread in societies as people use the word democracy as an ideal target *idiotically* against even their own ultimate intention. They do not grasp its meaning and implications even under the best circumstance—if the majority ruled. We are not eager, or equipped, to initially define a system capable of achieving our real intention, which is supposedly for instilling justice, morality, and a harmonious global coexistence. Yet, almost everybody agrees with this vision—to run a political system capable of spreading equality and peace. Focusing on the rule of the majority that is not learned and objective enough is harmful. The idea is in fact idiotic when people are too naive and biased. This flaw alone gives us a reserved, polite right to view this political system as 'idiots democracy,' even if many other *outlandish* misperceptions about democracy could be ignored.

Instead, we need a scientific, strict mechanism if we wish to develop a civilized society that can best fulfil people's long-term desires and needs regardless of how we must go about it—most likely in non-democratic ways without the majority's direct role in electing their leaders. Surely, this sounds like a communist or socialist ideology, which people are told to avoid like a plague! But why? Why are our elites, scholars, and universities afraid of discussing the merits of an orderly society where charlatans and devils do not control the entire socioeconomic principles with the aid of naïve, shortsighted, and easily manipulated population?

Anyhow, we can say that, after all this time, humans have not been able to at least define their intentions properly first before starting to invent a mechanism for achieving them. They have failed to invent a social system with potential to fulfill their basic intentions. They have merely adopted the silliest conclusions and easiest solutions—a kind of idiots' democracy that elites have duped us with. Thus, we witness and suffer our failure to know the first thing for social living: What do we wish democracy or any political system achieve for us, after all?

The so-called democratic process in America has elected a president who would cause so much mayhem and immorality worldwide by his erratic policies, thus inflicting more suffering for all, including the majority who allegedly ruled this outcome. Trump's supporters have ruined everybody's lives. Democracy in America has resulted in 50% of people voting for Republicans that always betray the poor to serve the rich like themselves, e.g., Obama's affordable healthcare bills that Republicans are trying repeal and are estimated to result in about 400-600 billion dollars in tax cuts for the 2% richest in the US at the expense of the rest. These examples show the vanity of democracy and citizen's dire incomprehension of its purposes. How can anybody presume this so-called democracy sensible?

Besides its incapacity to spread moral values, the prevailing practice of democracy stirs many potential obstacles for creating at least a minimum level of justice and peace for the public. These added flaws require a book of analyses all by itself. Even an honest democracy, where people's freewill and votes become possible, would not have much value if, for example, too many ill-natured, pompous humans have voted or controlled this crude process. The point is that democracy could have *some* value only if we could count on at least some minimal degree of people's integrity, morality, and intelligence all at the same time. Only a tiny minority has one or two of these personal virtues, let alone a combination of all three across the entire population. Therefore, nurturing a productive socioeconomic environment based on democracy alone is impossible, especially when the majority of people are resolute to remain so naïve, crooked, and careless. Humans' mentality hinders any attempt to maintain an overall sense of dignity and equality for people merely based on the rule of the majority. The entire voting exercise is clearly futile and meaningless, then, if we get the gist of it. Actually, it is hard to imagine humans ever becoming learned and objective enough to make the rule of majority a viable option for any social purposes.

In his book, *The Dumbest Generation,* Penguin Books Ltd. 2009, Mark Bauerlein states the basic requirement of democracy:

"Democracy requires an informed electorate, and knowledge deficits equal civic decay." Ibid. Page 212.

"Most young Americans possess little of the knowledge that makes for an informed citizen, and too few of them master the skills needed to negotiate an information heavy, communication–based society and economy. Furthermore, they avoid the resources and media that might enlighten them and boost their talents." Ibid. Page 16.

In his book, *Griftopia*, Spiegel & Grau 2011, Matt Taibbi also explains the American democracy in the following words:

"We get a beautifully choreographed eighteen-month entertainment put on once every four years, a beast called the presidential election that engrosses the population to the point of obsession. The ongoing drama allows everyone to subsume their hopes and dreams for the future into one all-out, all-or-nothing battle for the White House, a big alabaster symbol of power we see on television a lot. Who wins and who loses this contest is a matter of utmost importance to a hell of a lot of people in this country.

The presidential election is a drama that we Americans have learned to wholly consume as entertainment, divorced completely from any expectations about concrete changes in our own lives. For the vast majority of people who follow national elections in this country, the payoff they're looking for when they campaign for this is that political figure is that warm and fuzzy feeling you get when the home team wins the big game. Or, more important, when a hated rival loses. Their stake in the electoral game isn't a citizen's interest, but a rooting interest.

Voters who throw their emotional weight into elections they know deep down inside won't produce real change in their lives are also indulging in a kind of fantasy. That's why voters still dream of politicians whose primary goal is to effectively govern and maintain a thriving first world society with great international ambitions. What voters don't realize, or don't want to realize, is that that dream was abandoned long ago by this country's leaders, who know the more prosaic reality and are looking beyond the fantasy, into the future, at an America plummeted into third world status." Ibid. Page 10.

"People aren't really needed for anything in the Griftopia, but since Americans require the illusion of self-government, we have elections." Ibid. Page 34.

"When you have a system with an electorate divided up into two fiercely warring tribes, each determined to blame the country's problems on the other, it will often be next to impossible to get anyone to even pay attention to a problem that is not the fault of one or the other group. Moreover, it is incredibly easy to shift blame for the problem to one of those groups, or to both of them, if you know how to play things right." Ibid. Page 150.

Besides the excruciating facts reiterated above about the risks of democracy, we have successfully made life many folds harder for ourselves by introducing even some weirder notions into the equation. For one thing, mixing the meanings of democracy and free enterprise to make deceiving propagandas has caused added social complications and agony. This second most misperceived aspect of democracy has brainwashed people's simple minds by assuming that capitalism is the best way of achieving democracy and democracy gives us the right to be a greedy capitalist at any cost to the society and the world. Thus, capitalism is now raising humans' hedonism and self-serving attitude, while abolishing any chance or hope for democracy, especially when people's minds and votes are easily bought by elite capitalists. A democracy that cannot offer a fair healthcare for poor people in line with rules of morality is worthless. It fact, it is merely embarrassing.

Our obsession for democracy is shameful, instead of laudable, as it shows we have not still realized the fact that giving people, especially the rich, too much liberty would jeopardize the rights and welfare of the public. The political systems many nations call democracy are designed just for the benefit of a small group at the expense of the majority. All these talks about democracy only reflect humans' obsession to justify their addictions to unfeasible ideals, while some jargons are more appealing to the naïve public and easier for propaganda. In all, it is just impossible to give any serious value to the present means of democracy in societies driven by selfish, simpleminded, and greedy people. Even sadder, of course, is the capitalists' abuse of democracy to brainwash and dupe the public for their objective of spreading consumerism and social vanity. Both democracy and human rights are overrated concepts and in fact stir more division among people and damage people and society, at least while people are so haughty, naïve, or mentally sick. It is very easy to prove all these claims in a book, including the meaning and implications of 'freedom,' as another juvenile jargon amongst such gullible, selfish humans.

However, mainstream cannot fully grasp or care about these facts as long as elite groups have the power to exploit the public. Nor do (can) supposedly democratic governments do anything to stop business gimmicks and atrocities in our capitalistic settings with unregulated, abusive pricing systems, e.g., by oil, insurance, and pharmaceutical companies.

While we are naïve and wicked by nature and through social teachings, we are asked to go vote, choose a leader, and build a democracy. No wonder our democracies are so crooked like us. We merely waste so much time, money, and energy to elect and keep ignorant, useless leaders. We love to boast about democracy when we know deep down how unreliable our leaders are for solving social issues. Even if our elected leaders were as good as we think we are ourselves, we are in big trouble, since all of us are somewhat flawed if not vastly crooked and naive.

A big irony is that nobody has yet defined a set of parameters for a practical political system (democratic or otherwise) where morality and humanity's welfare supersede people's self-interests. Religions have also failed to address people' spiritual, mental, and survival needs together. In fact, nobody questions the value of our current democracy and religions for a moralistic humanity, instead of only serving personal or national interests sloppily.

The points raised above demonstrate that even an imaginary true democratic society (free from influence peddling) has many limitations, as various groups' interests and ambitions always clash with governments' intentions to provide social services at affordable rates to everybody. Governments' effectiveness would be in jeopardy, even if our leaders were not so lame, corrupt, and incompetent, and if bureaucracies were not so much manipulated and wasteful. Grasping at least these obvious limitations or evils of democracy is crucial for becoming better beings.

The Marvel of Democracy!

You need not go beyond the White House these days to find the biggest marvel of democracy. He is usually sitting in the Oval Office or his bed at 2 or 3 A.M. twitting lots of nonsense and lies. This example alone is enough to close the case for democracy for good, but the manner other Republican leaders and people cajole him can put the last nail into its coffin.

The kind of democracy that elects people like Donald Trump and George Bush, Jr. is in fact a menace for human existence and building a civilized society. Even the process of nominating and choosing a Supreme Court judge is supported by dark money that people behind the scene contribute to it. It was noted that $10 million of such money was behind Neil Gorsuch's nomination. Then, Brett Kavanaugh's appointment was another disgrace to democratic process. The absence of real conflict of interest laws for a US president is another odd feature of American democracy. Thus, a crook like Trump now has all the excuses and liberty to do as he wishes with his business conflicts all over the world, defy the congress, and make silly decisions and appointments as President, *never mind his silly twits!*

Stephen Harper was the Prime Minister of Canada based only on 40% of popular vote, while the other 60% abhorred his guts and policies. They call this democracy, but when a small fraction of people in Syria, Iran, or China demonstrates, outsiders talk about human rights and lack of democracy. The failing Western democratic societies are quick to disregard the majority in those countries who support the government. They suddenly ignore the majority's wish and that kind of democracy, so that they can just rush in to change the government for their capitalistic interests. If political divisions and quarrels in the US get as much attention, its officials must be changed daily. Especially, in the case of *this* Trump, the majority of people are unhappy with the outcome and continue to demonstrate (maybe even more violently soon) to express their displeasure, but the covert dictatorship in the US would not care about their voice. Instead, the US goes to war in Syria, Iraq, Afghanistan, or other places just because it wishes to interpret a group's dissent as a sure sign of human rights violation and lack of democracy. Most US leaders condemn Cuba and Fiddle Castro as a dictator, while the US has been dictating its demented perception of democracy on the rest of the world on top of its own naïve citizens.

In particular, the US has no legitimacy or credibility to advise other countries about human rights when its dire racism, wealth inequality, health care, crime, social depression, gun laws, false news on social media, propagandas, political instability, poverty, suicides, drug addictions, and general unrest are the highest in the world. It is in fact quite hypocritical and funny when the Western world rushes to impose the guidelines for democracy or accuse other countries, like Cuba and China, of human rights violations. They cry foul when a nation is enforcing order and rules to stop a radical or greedy group from stirring unrest to impose demented Western values. Then, the matter becomes comical when these allegedly democratic nations strive to define and impose human rights within the mishmash of a capitalistic democracy. Now, this mixing of 'human rights' with democracy is still another sham.

Ironically, the US democracy and its citizen's rights remain unchallenged when over 50% of Americans resent their president, his staff, and political setting in general. Nobody raises human rights or objects to the US's acts at Guantanamo Bay Prison or when the police keep killing innocent people in the US casually. Nobody seems to care about the US's political system being in such total disarray and incapable of serving the public. Instead, people trust leaders like Trump to make America great again and resuscitate the American Dream. While mixing human rights, democracy, and capitalism so arbitrarily, their call for these ideals is bizarre, as if those concepts were well-defined, sustainable, or proven in their own supposedly democratic nations. These goofy jargons are merely too embarrassing, instead of praiseworthy, while a uniform definition for democracy becomes impossible and the majority of Americans are stuck with a broken political mechanism that dictates their lives on the assumption that the democratic system and voting process have been fair.

A few volumes should be written about the vanity of the kind of democracy that US has boasted about and demonstrated to the world for many decades. In fact, the way humans have become mesmerized by the idea of democracy requires major analysis and practical remedies. More relevant and infuriating, however, is to enumerate and remember the level of the US's systematic disregard for other countries' autonomy and political preferences. The only purpose of the US's democracy so far has been for propagandas and means of exploiting other nations, e.g., Saudi Arabia and Gulf nations these days, at the cost of ignoring the absence of basic human rights and democracy in those nations.

As a direct example of the US intervention in other countries democratic processes, a large volume of documents have become available in which CIA has confirmed its role in the 1953's Iran coup for US oil companies' benefit. Various documents provide new details on Mosaddeq overthrow and its aftermath, as posted on August 19, 2013, edited by Malcolm Byrne mbyrne@gwu.edu

The CIA has publicly admitted for the first time that it was behind the notorious 1953 coup against Iran's democratically elected prime minister Mohammad Mosaddeq, in documents that also show how the British government tried to block the release of information about its own involvement in his overthrow.

"The military coup that overthrew Mosaddeq and his National Front cabinet was carried out under CIA direction as an act of Us foreign policy, conceived and approved at the highest levels of government," reads a previously excised section of an internal CIA history titled The Battle for Iran.

Britain, and in particular Sir Anthony Eden, the foreign secretary, regarded Mosaddeq as a serious threat to its strategic and economic interests after the Iranian leader nationalised the British Anglo-Iranian Oil Company, latterly known as BP. But the UK needed US support. The Eisenhower administration in Washington was easily persuaded.

British documents show how senior officials in the 1970s tried to stop Washington from releasing documents that would be "very embarrassing" to the UK.

One document describes Mosaddeq as one of the "most mercurial, maddening, adroit and provocative leaders with whom they [the US and Britain] had ever dealt". The document says Mosaddeq "found the British evil, not incomprehensible" and "he and millions of Iranians believed that for centuries Britain had manipulated their country for British ends". Another document refers to conducting a "war of nerves" against Mosaddeq.

The Iranian-Armenian historian Ervand Abrahamian, author of The Coup: 1953, the CIA and the Roots of Modern US-Iranian Relations, said in a recent interview that the coup was designed "to get rid of a nationalist figure who insisted that oil should be nationalised".

US officials have previously expressed regret about the coup but have fallen short of issuing an official apology. The British government has never acknowledged its role.

The depth and variety of issues related to the 2016 US election and its foreseeable repercussions are simply amazing, especially about the meaning of democracy and human rights when more than 40% of eligible people did not even vote, since they have lost their trust in their democracy, leaders, and political systems. Even then, the majority voted against Trump, anyway. Therefore, we cannot wonder if this travesty is supposed to be the marvel of centuries of democracy? Are Americans now happy and proud of their nation being run by a lame, pathetic dictator like Trump, while he would not be able to accomplish anything due to his idiocy augmenting the impotence of political process within the US democracy (dictatorship). As Matt Taibbi says:

> "Trump's populism was as fake as everything else about him, and he emerged as just another in a long line of Republican hacks, only dumber and less plausible to the political center.
>
> ... after all that we went through last year, after that crazy cycle of insults and bluster and wife wars and penis-measuring contests and occasionally bloody street battles, after the insane media tornado that destroyed the modern Republican establishment, Trump concluded right where the party started 50 years ago, meekly riding Nixon's Southern strategy.
>
> ... after all the fantastical performances in the ring, the ultimate showstopper: emptiness, an endless black sky, 'nothing, nothing, nothing—nothing at all.'
>
> Trump's finale was like that. When we finally pulled the lid off this guy, there was nothing there. Just a cheap fraud and TV huckster who got in way over his head, and will now lead his hoodwinked followers off the cliff of history." *Insane Clown President*, Matt Taibbi, 2017, Spiegel and Grau. Page 224.

The validity and goals of democracy, human rights, the US's political system and electoral process are in serious doubt more than ever after the 2016 US election, all thanks to Mr. Trump. Accordingly, humans' inability and resistance to think of plan B or even research about an alternative socioeconomic and political system is another major conundrum facing humanity now.

Now, we know better that hoping for democracy and human rights to help people sort out their socio-political and economic needs is useless—even if judging only by the dire disarray in the US as the role model nation and symbol of democracy in the world. Now, we can believe that these concepts are only human fantasies until we can at least determine their practical purposes and applications.

Ignoring these plain facts shows our lack of a social sense and conscience for building our mentalities and lifestyles realistically. After all, we are such naïve, lazy citizens, letting capitalists and political opportunists brainwash us with their vain, self-serving propagandas regarding a materialistic democracy that we might as well refer to as 'idiots democracy' merely as a reminder of humans' highest accomplishment in their naïve minds!! Or, in fact, we may call it devil's democracy, because it is more like a furtive dictatorship, where more of people's dignity and freedom are robbed every day stealthily in cunning manners.

Accordingly, despite all the fuss about democracy, three types of dictatorships besiege all societies now. First, the kind prevalent in Saudi Arabia and other kingdoms in the Persian Gulf, where some sheikhs dictate their nations' affairs based on their personal whims, often for the interests (and by the support) of international corporations and superpowers—mostly the US. Second, the kind where leaders and states try to dictate some principles to prevent capitalists domination of the country and exploitation of people, while striving to make wealth distribution and access to public services fair and affordable. These societies are usually labelled communists and dictatorship by the Western nations, because capitalists do not get as much freedom to exploit the public as they can in the Western societies. Third, the so-called free market countries where elite groups, and hypocrite leaders serving them, exploit people's lives and minds under the name of democracy.

Obviously, none of these three types of dictatorships can instil a fruitful political process and society for the benefit of the public, especially the one in the US. Yet, for mere discussion at least, we must realize that even communism is keener about human rights and equality than our capitalistic view of democracy, despite so much propaganda. China has already proved that communism does not necessarily mean poverty, as its economy is on its way to surpass the US's very soon. Ultimately, we must accept that leaving our future and planet at the mercy of capitalists under the name of democracy is our own (humans') big failure.

With the present irresolvable social and political impasse for a universal harmony and peace, we can wait for the whole world to perish or save at least half of the population who could be better beings under the right circumstances—if they were exposed to moralistic values instead of fighting a lifetime with the corruptive social norms prevalent nowadays.

The world's daunting, tough challenge is to acknowledge that we have now reached a global impasse and we have no plan, while the US seems incapable of leading the world anymore. In fact, the United States is now emerging as the main obstacle for our last chance to explore humanity and possibly save the planet, too. Despite its zeal to insist on its self-imposed perception of greatness, many signs of failure in the US worry most nations about the rising chaos in a leaderless world. We cannot depend on various coalitions among a group of nations and the United Nations to lead the globe effectively, either. Our trust in leadership abilities around the world has been mostly abolished. The only silver lining is that we can now look up to the US as a perfect socioeconomic and political model to avoid at all cost. Now, a horrendous challenge amongst all nations is to find a moralistic and fair socioeconomic system mostly based on what to avoid with absolute conviction, after many decades of wishful thinking and viewing the US as a leader for civilization.

The most depressing facts nowadays (the 21st century's sad reality) are:

1. Our world has no direction, plan of action, or leaders to offer a decent life path for people, let alone a fulfilling existence.
2. Our ideals and ideologies for social progress and prosperity, including the notions of democracy, freedom, human rights, capitalism, individualism, and equality, are extremely naïve and impractical considering humans' wicked nature fostering in cultureless societies.

3. Reaching a consensus amongst nations for creating even a basic level of cooperation and harmony seems impossible. Meanwhile, the likelihood of inventing and forcing a solution to prevent human demise appears slim, too.
4. Our obsession for capitalism and our lack of vision for a more viable socioeconomic system would prove fatal.
5. The value of democracy depends on people's high cognition and aptitude for goodness. In most societies nowadays, three groups can be distinguished in terms of knack for goodness: First, a small group is either good naturally by some fluke or finds the incentive for goodness for personal sake. Second, a rather large confused group that is driven by its conflicting, erratic urges for both goodness and evil. This group is most susceptible to peer pressures and follow social norms in line with an easygoing life philosophy. Third, the mass with no interest or urge for goodness, thus live selfishly with only one main goal of exploiting others and society. As a result, most societies are driven by devilish forces and mentalities that the majority of citizens adopt to adapt.
6. Capitalism, freedom, and human nature stir a lethal mix and prevent peace and harmony, even if humans could envision social systems capable of goading morality and equality.
7. Accordingly, democracy within such environment is simply a useless, impotent concept even if the majority ruled. It is just a fad in modern societies used to engage and fool people.
8. Meanwhile, the notion and wide application of democracy is another major clue about humans' failure to invent practical and purposeful goals as well as mechanisms for coexistence. No wonder we are at the brink of extinction!
9. Considering the irreversible social chaos and humans' dire destiny, we are on our own to find a viable life path.
10. Many of us may conclude that the only, and easiest, way to find at least some peace of mind and possible salvation is to make a solid personal plan for becoming a better person.

Chapter Eighteen
Need for a New Role Model

The growing political instability and social distress in the United States have shocked and disturbed the world. For a role model nation eager to boast about its high standards of living and freedom, facing such widespread, social disarray is surely quite unsettling.

Accordingly, a review of the world affairs and the need for a new role model for humanity appears urgent. The questions are how we can make the world agree about the process and urgency of doing this enormous research and reconciliation, and who can lead this huge mission of saving a chaotic world.

The reality the world sees nowadays is that the US is still very influential in the world affairs, but also destroying the chance for global harmony and peace by electing presidents like Donald Trump and George Bush, Jr., and by its obsession for capitalism. While the world is struggling to move forward out of the misery that capitalism and fossil fuel have caused for humans, America is going backward and wishes to be great like the old times by continuing its exploitation of the world and the planet. They are persisting to build more walls and ignore the looming effects of the climate change. Yet, other nations' capacity to save the world without the US's help is also minimal. Thus, humans are facing a major historical impasse at this critical point in 2020.

Accordingly, a fast review of the problems hurting Americans and America may be useful as a general background for studying the rising global issues. Sadly, Americans seem stuck in an awful abyss, while still struggling to define America after all this time. At the same time, most conclusions about the US's political and social shortfalls somewhat affect, or apply to, other nations, too. They show the social mayhem worldwide due to humans' crude nature and idiosyncrasies flourishing fast in modern societies tainted by a mishmash neo-culture and impeding our chances of becoming better beings.

The observations in the following pages about Americans and America are mostly based on the US experts' remarks, as noted references indicate. Besides making general points in line with established facts and evidences, this author has strived to avoid expressing personal judgments about a foreign country.

About Americans

A comprehensive observation of the 2016 US election, in line with daily events in the US and American experts' conclusions, suggests the following facts about Americans:

1. A majority of people are quite dissatisfied with the standards of living, social services, inequalities, and socioeconomic conditions. Accordingly, they are quite frustrated and furious.
2. They believe their country is in shambles and needs a major overhaul, without knowing how, in what form, for what end, and by whom.
3. They believe their corporations and financial industry, as well as the state and federal governments, have been corrupt, incompetent, and unable to provide the basic socioeconomic needs of citizens.
4. Yet, they like to believe America can be great (again), as if someone could magically uproot corruption and greed, and then everything becomes not merely acceptable, but indeed quite great again in a few years.

Need for a New Role Model 369

5. They are reluctant to admit that nobody knows how to make America, or the world, even a bit better within a century, 'forget being great!'
6. They also seem unable to see or acknowledge that the roots of personal and societal issues relate to their socioeconomic structure built merely around capitalism and consumerism. This is due to people's naivety, the tight grip of capitalism, the power of elite groups' propagandas, and the domination of idealistic ideologies, values, politics, and social structure tainting the whole spectrum of American life.
7. Accordingly, people get carried away fast when a presidential candidate makes shallow promises. They rush to trust his/her magical ability to fix everything, restore the socioeconomic environment, and make their farfetched wishes come true.
8. People's overall social naiveté and desperation appears in the way they still want to keep their trusts in free market slogans and practices, as well as unconditional personal freedom, yet keep whining regarding the tyranny of authorities and social orgasms that must serve capitalism.
9. The irony is that they chose a president who has exploited people and society so greedily and arrogantly all his life. It shows how people's obsession with capitalism overrides their senses about the risks of letting a self-serving person, like Trump, control their minds and fates, as though craving for self-destruction.
10. Before making any more comment about Mr. Trump as the oddest president of the US, it is relevant to quote only a small sample of comments that prominent sources made during 2016 election about his ineptitude for leading even a decent organization, let alone a whole nation known as super power. The main point is that the entire world knew all the following facts about candidate Trump months before the election and still Americans rushed to give another corrupt capitalist even more power to direct their nation and the world:

"…most ostentatiously unqualified major-party candidate in history." The Atlantic said about Trump.

"Trump is unfit for the presidency." "Erratic, Ill-equipped to be commander in chief, serial liar." USA Today's Editorial Board: Sept. 30, 2016-10-02

"A sexual predator who lost the popular vote and fuelled his campaign with bigotry and hate." Senator Harry Reid (from Nevada).

"Trump used $258,000 from his charity to settle legal problems." The Washington Post.

"There are some jarring similarities (between Lyndon Johnson and Donald Trump) — two big, fleshy men given to vulgarities and gauche behaviour, boastful, thin-skinned, politically amoral, vengeful, unforgiving and, most important, considered illegitimate presidents. For Johnson, that took some time to sink in; Trump is already there." The Washington Post, January 17, 2017

"His bellicose pussy-grabbing vulgarity and defiant lack of self-awareness make him, unfortunately, the perfect foil for reflecting the rot and neglect of the corrupted political system he conquers. A system unable to stop *this* must be very sick indeed." *Insane Clown President*, Matt Taibbi, 2017, Spiegel and Grau. Page xxxv.

"He takes us for idiots." Colin Powel, the former Secretary of State, said about Trump.

11. So, just based on Colin Powel's comment above, at least 50% of Americans supporting Trump are presumably idiots!
12. Or else, at best, we could say that Trump supporters have an enormous sense of humour. They like to laugh a few years, even if it would be at the cost of deep damages to the US's already frail social structure and international relationships.

13. On the other hand, people's persistence to overlook their president's vast mental incapacity and personality flaws, in particular his knack for bullying, lying, and even the lack of basic intelligence or integrity, shows the mentality of the American public per se. This is an important clue about the oddity of human nature in general, too, as if we all prefer to support and spread irrationality and ignorance rather than use our minds to find fundamental solutions for society.
14. Trump's disqualification was so clear and extreme that most political analysts only laughed about his chance of winning.

    "Trump can't win. Our national experiment can't end because one aging narcissist got bored of sex and food. Not even America deserves that." *Insane Clown President*, Matt Taibbi, 2017, Spiegel and Grau. Page 277. Matt had made this prediction on Oct. 16, 2016, three weeks before the election.

15. People's depth of desperation and frustration regarding social conditions is so extreme they resort to any bizarre option to improve the situation even if it means believing in the kind of nonsense that a candidate tells them without offering tangible solutions or means of achieving any of his goals with lasting useful outcomes.
16. People's naiveté is also evident in their lack of appreciation of the fact that social and personal problems cannot be solved without an overhaul of socioeconomic and political systems in the US and around the world.
17. Enough eccentric and unqualified people have taken on the post of presidency in the US. In particular, with Bush Jr.'s presidency everybody assumed that a low enough standard for such high office was set. Then, the results of the 2016 election proved that Americans would never stop amazing the world with their choices. Now, maybe we have reached the lowest level of eccentricity in politics possible. Or not! Most likely, not!

18. Neither the public nor their new president has a grasp of the intricacy of national and international mechanisms, rules, and relationships. Therefore, while a candidate delivers so many empty words, the public gets excited and fooled repeatedly.
19. In particular, Americans' perfunctory patriotism and ongoing propagandas about the strength and position of the US in the world have made them unaware or insensitive about the real socioeconomic issues in the US and the rest of the world, while also ignoring the repercussions of trade and financial market deregulations, capitalism, the power of elite groups, and corporate corruptions in the US.
20. Something must be vastly wrong with the mentality of voters who miss or just ignore even a candidate's direct confessions about his/her lifelong hypocrisy, lies, and corruption. When a billionaire like Trump brags in his first political debate about his knack for outsmarting the taxation system and abusing loopholes to cheat, something is terribly wrong with him and his supporters, besides the tax system. It is another evidence about the vanity of democracy and leaders like Trump.
21. Intelligence and sincerity of a leader are easily detectable from the way s/he talks and curbs his/her ego to concentrate on national interests and responsibilities.
22. Trump's low character became evident also when his tactics for not paying his contractors and employees, abusing his charitable foundation only as a scheme to serve his personal interests, and operating Trump University only for scamming students were made public. Still, not all these clear evidences influenced people's conscience and judgments. The manner Americans have so often trusted people with such wicked characters, and in fact elected them as their leaders, reveals a lot about people's overall mentality.
23. Trusting any person who talks so childishly and conceitedly like a fool also shows the extreme frailty of human logic. "Nobody knows the system better than me," "Which is why I alone can fix it," "I will build the wall; I will make Mexico

pay for it," "I will make all your problems go away," "It will be so beautiful," "I will make America great again," etc. The world had never heard so much nonsense before Trump! Are not people and social mentalities in total disarray?

24. People's ignorance about the limited power of a president or even the congress to fulfil even a small portion of citizens' desires is the cause of making so many juvenile assumptions. Especially, their imagination is amazing about the possibility of any president achieving any tangible outcomes before the US's political and economic systems are revamped largely, people are much wiser and saner, and conscientious leaders emerge by a miracle perhaps.

25. Americans' high susceptibility and low objectivity was proven in 2016 also by the weird way they assessed their candidates for presidency. While fussing over Clinton's emails that FBI had already rejected as a proof for any wrongdoing, they just ignored Trump's overwhelming hypocrisy and lies, which showed the vast frailty of their objectivity and judgment.

26. Moreover, in 2016, the true character of a significant portion of Americans became evident when they considered bullying and vulgarity so readily acceptable or admirable, especially for such a high job. Their senses of judgment and ethics have become highly questionable now in the manner they allowed a demagogue get the highest job in the country just by lying, bullying, and making idiotic promises. The following quote shows the American society's declining civility.

> "Yes, Trump's win was a triumph of the hideous racism, sexism and xenophobia that has always run through American society." Insane Clown President, Matt Taibbi, 2017, Spiegel and Grau. Page 285. (See also his quote on page 382)

27. Americans' division now appears too deep and vicious to let any cooperation or reconciliation towards national unity. This would be another force crippling any president or congress to

work out and achieve a national plan, especially for a country like the US with capitalistic roots already crippling its social structure on both financial and emotional grounds.

28. The 2016 outcome revealed the idiocy of election process in the US. In fact, demonstrations across the US and some parts of the world showed that 50% of Americans feel their nation has been hijacked by a demagogue and misguided citizens (half of the American population) who were doped or duped by a clown, characterless actor.

29. Americans do not take at least their basic democratic rights seriously, especially during elections, as only 55% of eligible people voted in 2016 election. This is most likely just another sign of people's cynicism and frustration about their political systems and candidates. Yet, their negligence resulted in the election of the most ridiculous president in the US history, if not the whole world. This outcome also shows that even the basic goals of democracy are unattainable—even in a nation that brags so much about democratic processes and values.

30. Especially, the youths' apathy or laziness to vote at least for exercising their alleged democratic rights is odd when social disorder and climate change crisis must concern them deeply nowadays. They only whine about the election results and social chaos. They promise to vote the next time, forgetting that the daily damages that existing systems are causing, e.g., regarding climate crisis, will become immensely harder to overcome later, if possible at all.

31. Meanwhile, the above revelations, especially the immensity of population mesmerized by Trump's vanity and illiteracy, confirms Americans' mixed desperation and naiveté.

32. Americans' choice of an angry clown with such antagonistic approach towards the world also reveals an amazing reality about this nation's, and its people's, lack of appreciation of the world affairs. How Americans and Trump imagine other countries can and would work with an unstable liar leading a conflicted nation with so many duped citizens?

33. The depth of political systems' frailty nowadays is clear when even the allegedly experienced American leaders sold their honours and souls during and after this outlandish election and showed their hypocritical essence by supporting a crook, all in hopes of abusing his popularity with their voters. This mass of officials revealed the enormity of hypocrisy and self-serving mentality of many alleged US leaders—striving and hoping to fool the public by following the crowd, instead of showing signs of personal integrity and principles.
34. Humans' tenacity, besides naiveté, to avoid learning anything even from so much open hypocrisy is surely most amazing. Trump's fraudulent promises and silly rhetoric, e.g., about the Obama's Medicare and the Mexican wall, did not seem to affect Americans a bit. Meanwhile, his inconsistencies and more chaos would continue to amuse and amaze us for years. How much longer are people going to trust their presidential candidates' empty words and elect so many lousy presidents or representatives to lead and save them?
35. Even worse, citizens' avid, blind support of Trump has now created misperceptions for other leaders and nations to copy the US's juvenile, populist slogans. In fact, the repercussions of the US political mood on the world affairs could be huge when many arrogant, shallow politicians around the globe try to imitate Trump. They will incite and dupe the distressed public with their foolish, radical initiatives by insisting they can help their nations and the world. After all, humans seem easily swayed by empty, idiotic words nowadays, much more than logic works. Then, the meaning of democracy in the US boggles our minds again as well.
36. A big irony is that Americans cannot solve their basic issues with violence, poverty, healthcare, clean energy, guns, climate change, and abortion in their own country, but insist on being recognized as a great democratic country and a trustworthy leader of civilization for the rest of the world.

37. It is doubtful if Americans would ever grasp the roots of their nation's vast internal chaos realistically. Will they notice and act upon their speedy social decline in many fronts, including their gun laws, outdated constitution and justice system, deep racism, social and economic inequality, and on and on? And then maybe enlighten the world, too, or at least stop insisting on teaching their kind of democracy and civilization to the rest of the world?
38. Will Americans appreciate what is happening in the world, what is crucial for humanity and not the US alone, and how the world's perception of the US is shaping? Will the current self-appointed leaders around the globe awaken and grasp the futility of their current policies and worldviews?
39. In particular, Americans' reluctance to find a more peaceful manner of managing their society without so much reliance on their outdated Second Amendment and guns is so bizarre. Still, they keep thinking and talking about peace, civilization, and being the greatest country, too.

> "The US town preparing to go 'gun crazy' if Clinton wins." Headline in the Independent by David Usborne on Oct 29, '16.
>
> "An unlicensed vendor [in Louisiana] can sell handguns, shotguns, rifles, or assault weapon, and large-capacity magazines. A person can buy any number of guns and, except for handguns, need not register them, or report a theft of one, or hesitate to take them into parking lots and state parks. Louisiana also has a 'Stand Your Ground' law, permitting a frightened homeowner to shoot first. A man can walk into a bar on Bourbon Street in New Orleans with a loaded gun.
>
> Indeed, a gun vendor in Louisiana can keep no records, perform no background checks, and sell guns to an array of customers forbidden in other states: those with violent and firearm-related misdemeanours, people on terror watch list or 'no fly' list, abusers of drugs

or alcohol, juvenile offenders, and criminal with a history of serious mental illness or domestic violence. In 2010, the governor passed a law that permitted concealed handguns in churches, synagogues, and mosques. Louisiana has the highest rate of death by gunfire in the country, nearly double the national average." *Strangers in their own Land,* Arlie Russell Hochschild, 2016, The New Press, Pages 67-8.

40. Hillary Clinton's reference to the 'deplorable' Americans supporting Trump was considered offensive or untrue. She was forced, or felt obliged, to apologize for it, too. Yet, her honest and accurate assessment should not annoy people. This group's fantastical perceptions of life's realities and the chance for an honest, effective government is deplorable—definitely nothing to be proud of or celebrate! (See next point.)

41. As a big clue, gun control opponents' excuses in the US are juvenile for any nation that even thinks about civilization. Blaming school shootings only on mental diseases cannot help anything, yet their leaders want to arm their teachers in hopes of stopping school shootings. They refuse to look into the sources of these mental diseases! More guns to fight shooting epidemic merely demonstrates how NRA and other conglomerates run the US and its presidents. Many find this silly idea only a clue about a nation's cultural vanity. There are more gun stores in the US than Starbucks all over the world! Meanwhile, more people are getting mentally sick in the US, mainly due to the lack of a civilized culture. Maybe the next step would be to arm the students themselves!

42. Of course, Trump's supporters have a valid point about the catastrophic decline in American socioeconomic systems and politics. Yet, they not only have no grasp of socioeconomic variables in play for running a country and relating to other nations, but also insist on ignoring the fact that people like Trump are the root of the problems due to their hypocrisy, greed, self-serving business tactics, and narcissism.

> "We're more divided than ever, sicker than ever, dumber than ever. And there's no reason to think it won't be worse the next time." *Insane Clown President*, Matt Taibbi, 2017, Spiegel and Grau. Page 277.

> "How could the electorate not care that a billionaire admitted to not paying taxes? Why was no one troubled by a child rape lawsuit? How was the 'pussy' thing not fatal? What about the mountain of lawsuits —75 open cases, according to some reports—for offences ranging from simple nonpayment for services to sex discrimination? Why did no one care?" Ibid. Page xxii.

43. If we wished to be extremely optimistic and give Americans the benefit of a doubt about their choice of a president, we could say that many of them elected Trump mostly out of spite for the other candidate, or just to show their frustrations with the crooked establishment in the US. They did it even though they realized Trump could not do anything for them. Yet, this option means that too many deplorable Americans are more spiteful and masochists than even slightly practical.

44. Trump summed up a main source of social problem around the world: "I speak from my head and heart." Most people, including Trump as an expected responsible leader, want to judge and rule based on their dogmatism, crude instincts, and emotions. With their supreme arrogance and ignorance, they do not even consider the need for understanding the world's complexities, consultation, compromise, a valid worldview, etc. Instead, they believe to know it all, while misleading the confused public by spreading fake news or giving them too many idiotic promises. Should not we expect the public to know at least these basic human tendencies and stop being manipulated so easily, especially when voting for leaders?

45. It is necessary to reiterate that when Trump talks, it is hard to detect the slightest sign of intellect or honesty in his words. This is a painful fact in itself, but again, such huge population

believing in so much nonsense that a lunatic utters shows the depth of human naiveté and misery. It shows the sad state of affairs in the US and the world that America had been trying to lead. It is just unfathomable how Americans could elect a leader so reckless and foolish like Trump.

46. Trump does not like America, as he let his idiocy hurt their nation probably knowingly, like his peers in the White House. They all probably feel this irony, too—that crooks like Trump would sell even their mothers or country for personal gains.
47. Ironically, most of us are quite naïve when we still think that some solutions might actually exist for ending human misery or that anybody (including any leader) might gain the power or capacity to solve humans' complex dilemmas. We are all so naïve, especially hopeful Americans, when we try to trust our lame leaders, especially arrogant, silly ones like Trump, to save us. The problem is that we, mostly Americans, do not get serious about grasping the causes of rising social chaos, the evil of our chronic naiveté, the need for restructuring the social structure, and perhaps even becoming a better person.
48. The saddest fact to reiterate here is that so many Americans who are, or could be, very good beings—including present or potential effective leaders—do not get a chance to help the public due to the system's horrendous shortfalls and people's growing dire naiveté. What a deplorable waste!*

About America

The following weaknesses in America that damage its strengths apply to many other nations, too, which show the extent of global and humans' inherent inability to build functional societies.

1. The growing crimes, public's frustrations, and social division show that America has failed to build a basic vision of social

---

* Just in case Americans re-elect Trump in a few months, after this book is finally published, the gravity of the above 48 points about people's naiveté should be multiplied by two, if not ten!

unity and morality. It has also failed to envision real remedies against humans' apathy towards ethics and teamwork, while people are getting crueler every year, despite their superficial show of compassion and religious habits.

2. The increasing number of public shootings, mental disorders, addictions, suicides, mass demonstrations, and homelessness in the US reflects its socioeconomic and political systems' incapacity to address its citizens' security and primary needs.

3. Accordingly, the disorder and confusion in the US nowadays —a nation posed for civilization after centuries of efforts and propagandas—feels like an awakening clue about a looming global anarchy towards humans' demise. It shows chaos rises in any nation when greed drives the public, corporations, and elites at the cost to society and humanity. These revelations announce a historical point to contemplate realistically.

4. America is still unable to provide basic social necessities of a large portion of its population, including affordable housing and medical services. The number of homeless is staggering.

5. No reliable authority or mechanism addresses citizens' needs consistently, thus people are duped every few years when someone gives them empty promises about saving the nation and then serves the elite entities supporting his/her election.

6. America has no interest or plan to study and adjust its trite ideologies, including democracy and capitalism, in terms of their potencies for building a sustainable civilization.

7. All along, never-ending fights between political parties over social deficiencies, instead of achieving long-term, tangible results for the public, continue. They cannot agree even on their healthcare needs after many poorer nations, such as Cuba, are vastly advanced in this regard already compared to the limited, profit-oriented medical services in the US, not to mention the outrageous cost of drugs.

8. The ineffectiveness of its political mechanisms, including the election process, has now been proven in many fronts during the 2016 election and Trump's administration.

9. For one thing, the fact that people had to choose between two drastically unpopular, polarizing candidates is another proof of severe political disorder in the US.
10. Both presidential candidates in 2016 appeared unacceptable for different reasons to one half of the US population. Thus, the question is, "Why the US political system is still so frail and incapable of finding even a few suitable persons out of a population of 300 million to serve their country properly?"
11. In fact, it appears that no fully qualified and moral individual has a chance or desire to run for the presidency of the US!
12. Accordingly, people compare the evils, instead of the merits and characters, of candidates as their justifications to vote for the least undesirable one. They argue about candidates' flaws instead of nobility. Yet, even then, they are too subjective in terms of weighing their candidates' types and degrees of crookedness. Thus, the whole society and citizens' welfare is in limbo in this aimless setting, while the public and leaders always think and act according to some tentative, interim compromises, rather than finding real long-term solutions.
13. The sheer size of population voting for a candidate just out of spite for the other candidate's idiocy or corruption in itself shows how useless these elections and presidents are.
14. The fact that both presidential candidates in 2016 had real or perceived deficiencies caused a big mayhem, but allowing some fake news, propagandas, and misperceptions change the course of an election is depressing and bizarre in itself for a supposedly modern country.
15. Political parties in the US do not even have a mechanism to screen and choose their leaders according to some practical merits, maybe by people's input, too, perhaps a few years in advance of elections, like in Canada. Then they can let him/her prove his/her capacity and sanity instead of nominating a narcissist, liar at the last second as the leader of a major party and then their president, as it occurred in the 2016 and many other elections. Especially, the candidacy and election of

such a vastly unqualified person in a short time to represent a major party and run the affairs of a prominent country shows the basic, deep deficiencies of the US political mechanisms. Even Trump showed his disbelief in a news clip!

16. The way propagandas and false news alone can incite people so drastically also reveals the vulnerability of the US political system, for example in the way the FBI and media made a fuss about Hillary Clinton's duplicate emails on someone's computer just a few days before the election. This immense influence showed another big flaw, if not a deliberate means, for manipulating people and votes. Furthermore, while this news was abused to raise cynicism about her trustworthiness, no authority or media argued effectively in her defence to show no criminal activity was ever related to those emails. The main issue again is that people were provoked, and they let themselves be duped, without any understanding of the significance or effect of Clinton's alleged email mishandling.

17. The liberty that people, especially a supposedly qualified presidential candidate like Trump, give themselves to insult and lie about others, especially the other supposedly qualified candidate for presidency is quite shocking. It is amazing how irresponsibly politicians can disrepute one another without any consequence or basic civility, especially in a country where people sue each other for the smallest libel all the time. Besides, is it okay or ethical for an alleged civilized nation, and its president, to be so rude and vulgar?

> "Trumpian license has pushed hatred of Hillary Clinton beyond all reason. For grown men and women to throw around words like 'bitch' and 'cunt' in front of their kids, it means things have moved way beyond the analytical." Insane Clown President, Matt Taibbi, 2017, Spiegel and Grau. Page 269.

> "America was so divided, so alienated from itself, so vulnerable, that even a zero like Trump could penetrate

our political system without breaking a sweat." Ibid. Page xxxv.

"America is like a giant manor estate where the aristocrats don't know they're aristocrats and the peasants imagine themselves undiscovered millionaires. And America's cultural elite, trained for so long to think in terms of artificial distinctions like Republican and Democrats instead of more natural divisions like haves and have-nots, refused until it was too late to grasp the meaning of the rage-storm headed over the wall." Ibid. Page 284.

18. Quite bizarre, of course, is the absurdity of mechanisms for political contributions and propagandas—to lure people elect leaders that serve only the interests of corporations and elite groups. Presidents and representatives being sponsored by big industries and special groups inside and outside the US defies even the basic rules of democracy and decency.
19. The lack of a mechanism to control a president's financial or business interests and conflicts nationally and globally is surely another big, bizarre weakness in the US.
20. The fact that these kinds of possibilities are not prevented in the American constitution and political process reveals the roots of socio-political problems, not to mention the tenacity and apathy to do anything about the matter.
21. The irony is that even if a conscientious, qualified president is elected, his/her ability to accomplish his/her goals is too limited because of the way the partisan politics and congress can block his/her personal or populist initiatives. Instead, the debilitating principles of capitalism always supersede and become stronger and corrupter in this muddied setting.
22. Then, even when some worthy initiatives are implemented occasionally, such as Obama's climate control initiatives, the next administration or congress soon revoke them, maybe even by a simple executive order.

23. Creating a unified plan and picture for the future of America appears highly unlikely while the public and major political parties have such big differences about socio-political issues and fight with such rude, hostile attitudes.
24. Accordingly, no continuity prevails either within the US's convoluted administration or with regard to its relationships with other countries. This is particularly getting riskier every year as political parties and ideologies for running the US are becoming more unstable, hostile, obscure, and absurd. The main reason for such large division among its citizens is that no long-term visions for the public's and nation's welfare exist to give people and authorities a unique focus. With the emphasis always given to short-term goals mostly for elite corporations' benefits, the officials' chances for re-election depend on their knack to lure people with only juvenile promises.
25. Similarly, international accords with the US are too shaky and risky as each administration has its own agenda and power to revoke their previous commitments.
26. The process of presidential campaign for two years is quite exhausting, demoralizing, and debilitating, especially for the candidates. In fact, it seems the whole nation—people and new presidents—need at least one year to recuperate after hearing so much nonsense and sustaining so much anxiety. Even then, it is hard to assume all the negativity during the campaign and after the election can be removed from the presidents' and people's psyches, and hoping all that added animosities among people and political parties can be curbed and people's ripped spirits mended.
27. It appears that even the US Constitution needs fundamental adjustments to reflect the kind of modern, model state the US is aspiring to be. In particular, the obsession for the Second Amendment—the right to wear arms—is terribly outdated, while stirring so much conflicts and crimes in the nation. The purpose of wearing arms is no longer justified for a country with a strong police and army already to defend its citizens in

mostly urban environments. The old doctrine to goad people defend themselves against one another does not make sense for any civilized society; unless all these guns are only for the purpose of a looming inevitable national revolt against the government when things get totally out of hand! It seems that Americans need a much less violence-oriented Constitution! More strangely, they sound as if modifying it would be a sin!

28. Gun ownerships as a right, *merely because it is noted in the Second Amendment,* is even a sillier idea or excuse for any nation aspiring to aim for civilization eventually. The endless fight over gun control in the US appears like an embarrassing topic in itself for people and leaders of any progressive nation to waste their energies over forever.

29. Overall, the political and socioeconomic systems in the US have reached a frustrating stalemate, while the president and the congress fight and hinder progress. Amidst these power struggles, only the public and nation suffer, while elites abuse this mayhem and people further every year.

30. In fact, mood disorder (depression, bipolar) is the third most common cause of hospitalization in the US for people under 45. Antidepressant is the most prescribed drug in the US, as the public face all kinds of financial and social distress.

31. While wealth inequality in the US is the highest in the world, its government relies on borrowing and raising its national debt—about 1/3 of it from outside the US—to run its affairs. They borrow idiotically just to give the rich more money!

32. Discussing the depth of social corruption in the US is beyond this book's scope. It is also futile to state the awful statistics about crimes, poverty, and drugs. Many excellent books have already addressed these matters adequately. For example, read *Griftopia* by Matt Taibbi 2011 (Spiegel & Grau) to learn about the horrifying depth of corruption in the US.

> "These [American] leaders are like the drug lords who ruled America's ghettos in the crack age, men (and some women) interested in just two things: staying in

power, and hoovering up enough of what's left of the cash on their blocks to drive around in Escalade or a 633i for however longer they have left. Our leaders know we're turning into a giant ghetto and they are taking every last hubcap they can get their hands on before the rest of us wake up and realize what's happened." Ibid. Page 10.

"There are really two Americas, one for the grifter class, and one for everybody else. In everybody-else land, the world of small business and wage-earning employees, the government is something to be avoided, an overwhelming, all-powerful entity whose attentions usually presage some kind of financial setback, if not complete ruin. In the grifter world, however, government is a slavish lapdog that the financial companies use as a tool for making money." Ibid. Page 30.

"The mistake our politicians so often make with the [US's] industry leaders is in thinking they are interested in, or respectful of, the power of government. All they want is to keep stealing. If you can offer them the government's seal of approval on that, they'll take it. But if you can't, well, they still take that too." Ibid. Page 205.

"Big money already has a stranglehold on the process of government. It outright owns most of the members of Congress, and its lobbyists write much of our important legislation." *Insane Clown President*, Matt Taibbi, 2017, Spiegel and Grau. Page 76.

33. In all, no sense of accountability exists in the US, despite all the *alleged* mechanisms for checks and balances in place. Letting the crooked US CEOs who caused the horrific market crash worldwide in 2008 off the hook shows the chaos, while those CEO's pocketed billions of dollars of compensations and some got lucrative jobs in the Presidents' administrations,

including in Trump's after he criticized the same policies during his campaign.
34. Trump and the public make legitimate claims about the high level of corruption in the US, but people like Trump are the roots of it. Moreover, narrow-minded people like him are the least likely leaders capable of even grasping the problems, let alone admitting and solving them.
35. A big reason America cannot unite or lead the world in the new era is its lack of a culture with humanitarian mottos and morality intentions to nurture human nature to a higher level.
36. A country that lacks a basic affordable healthcare system, cannot control crimes, must use guns freely, has so much mental disorders and suicides, sustains the biggest levels of poverty and inequality, and faces such a big divide, cannot foresee and pave the way to greatness or lead the world.
37. People and reporters in the US refer to the US Presidency as the biggest job in the world! While America likes to believe and boast about this privilege, the rest of the world wonders about the criteria behind this prophesy considering the high corruption, immorality, and the vast social chaos in the US, especially nowadays with Mr. Trump at the helm. Why is the US so important for itself or the world? Even its economic principles are in big jeopardy, while its military power has also failed all over the globe in the end, anyway, despite the decades of atrocities in many parts of the world so uselessly.
38. America will fail economically and politically fully within the next 4-5 decades if it does not adopt a socialistic attitude and approach, instead of getting greedier with capitalism. But the chance that this could happen is infinitesimal.
39. America is hesitant to inform people about the fast-changing socioeconomic environments. Thus, people have difficulty adjusting their mentalities to the inevitable drastic economic changes in the 21st century.
40. The US has the largest wealth disparity among its population, thanks to capitalism crippling its socio-political stability.

41. In the short term, Trump's major tax relief for the rich as well as the reduction of the public sector and regulatory mandates would most likely lead to a major budget deficit, recession, further social chaos, and unrest.

Pondering the above points, we also wonder quite urgently if the situation in the US, as the model for human civilization, is an indication about the best we humans can ever achieve! If yes, are not we doomed?

As a fine recap about America and Americans, it seems useful to quote a few of Chris Hedges' straight comments in his 'must read' book, *Wages of Rebellion*, 2015, Alfred A. Knopf, Canada.

"We [Americans] suffer from a dangerous historical amnesia and self-delusional fantasies about the virtues and goodness of ourselves and of empire. We have masked our cultural propensity for widespread and indiscriminate murder. ... a universal truth about the American soul and the naturalness with which we turn to violence at home and abroad."..."Violence in America is not restricted to state violence. There is a tradition of vigilante violence that is used, usually with the state's tacit if unofficial blessing, to crush dissent, to keep repressed minorities in a state of fear, or to exact revenge on those the state has branded as traitors. It is a product of hatred, not hope. It is directed against the weak, not strong. And it is deeply ingrained in the American psyche." Ibid. Page 145.

"Vigilante groups in America do not trade violence for violence. They are mostly white men who often prey on people of color and radicals. They are capitalism's ideological vanguards, its shock troops used to break populist movements and tyrannize the oppressed." Ibid. Page 146.

"Our mechanical drones still circle the skies delivering death. Our attack jets still blast civilians. Our soldiers and marines still pump bullets into mud-walled villages. Our artillery and missiles still raze homes. Our torturers still torture. Our politicians and generals still lie. And the soldier who tried to stop it all is serving a thirty-five-year prison sentence." Ibid. Page 186.

"We are not conscious of the long night of collective humiliation, repression, and powerlessness that characterizes existence in Israel's occupied territories, Iraq, and Afghanistan. We do not see the boiling anger that war and injustice turn into a cauldron of hate over time. We are not aware of the very natural lust for revenge against those who carry out or symbolize this oppression." Ibid. Page 187.

"Why should we respect a court system, or a governmental system, that does not respect us? Why should we abide by laws that protect only criminals like Wall Street thieves while leaving the rest of us exposed to abuse? Why should we continue to have faith in structures of power that deny us our most basic rights and civil liberties? Why should we be impoverished so that the profits of big banks, corporations, and hedge funds can swell?" Ibid. Page 192.

"Keystone XL is part of the final phase of extreme exploitation by the corporate state. The corporations intend to squeeze the last vestiges of profit from an ecosystem careening towards collapse. Most of the oil that can be reached through drilling from traditional rigs is depleted. In response, the fossil fuel industry has developed new technologies to go after dirtier, less efficient forms of energy. These technologies bring with them a dramatically heightened cost to ecosystems. They accelerate the warming of the planet and contaminate vial water sources. Deepwater Arctic drilling, tar sands extraction, hydraulic fracturing (or hydro fracking), and drilling horizontally, given the cost of extraction and the effect on the environment, amount to ecological suicide." Ibid. Page 208

By the way, the Keystone XL that Chris Hedges is referring to above is the project that President Trump reinstated through another executive order on his first week of presidency. President Obama and environmental studies had rejected this project.

About the World

The world affairs as well as people's welfare and perceptions are damaged radically when no viable, long-term plan for humanity is envisioned. Some of these lasting effects and emerging trends are outlined below:

1. The need for global trade and cooperation has grown rapidly, while the chance of any nation prospering alone or exploiting others is declining fast, although some nations are still a bit more civilized and inhabitable for a few more decades.
2. Accordingly, the world has become too unstable and hurtful no matter where we live, while the rising cultural connections and migrations are also causing new headaches.
3. The global socioeconomic superstructures are incompatible, ineffective, and vulnerable, while population growth, climate change, and pollution would stir more sufferings for humans due to growing pressures on all social mechanisms.
4. The world's political systems are quite chaotic, while people are getting less capable of identifying and promoting sincere leaders who can grasp the world's problems, invent practical solution to address citizens' concerns, and explain the flaws and potentials of a fair global coexistence to people honestly. In fact, no true leaders seem to be around or eager to waste their lives on pointless politics and naïve people.
5. Selfless, honest individuals find less incentive or opportunity to work for the public when the majority does not seem to grasp reality and the need for a humanistic and sustainable worldview, while cherishing only some raw nationalistic and capitalistic objectives.

6. We had imagined that some parts of the globe, mainly the US and Europe, offered some senses of security, justice, and freedom, but it has become obvious now that we have been wrong on this matter, too.
7. These dire realities are getting clearer and sadder every year. They also make us somehow more alarmed and sceptical about global peace and humanity.
8. In particular, the 2016 US election and ensuing events have taught the world a lot about Americans, the US, democracy, and human nature in general. Accordingly, the world's view of the enticing American dream has vanished.
9. Now, nations have realized that their hopes for the US to prove the merits of capitalism towards economic equalities, high standards of living, social order, fairness and efficiency of political processes, and human rights have been in vain.
10. To grasp America, just consider that its closest and possibly sole allies now are Israel and Saudi Arabia! That is the USA!
11. With the viability of American lifestyle and future in doubt, nations are scrambling to find a new leader or a novel, decent means of international cooperation with mutual respect.
12. In fact, the political events during 2015-2020 have been quite informative for the world to understand the true mentality of alleged civilized nations, especially the US and the majority of its people. Now more people grasp the cause for so many oppressed countries' misgivings and resistance towards some exploiting regimes, especially the US, for many years.
13. The world is worrying about the vast, rising polarization in the US politics, and the huge division among Americans about their country's basic principles and values. This social instability has also rattled Americans themselves somewhat, although they still seem to be in denial about the depth and roots of their problems. They appear lost in their delusional aspiration about 'Greatness'.
14. The world may get a timely awakening from the frustration of vastly divided people in the US about the vanity of values,

economic models, and processes that modern countries have been propagating so keenly during the last century.

15. Yet, sadly, the political instability in the US and discontinuity of its policies would keep infecting the whole world for now, since no role model exists for nations to follow.

16. Especially, the world cannot trust the US leaders' words after direct evidences in the last few decades about their lousy sense of commitment in foreign affairs and internal politics, especially during and after the 2016 election.

17. The world had assumed George W. Bush Jr. had harmed the world enough with his petite political sense. Now they are more amazed by Trump's election—a person with even lower sense and intelligence needed for running a nation and contributing to the world's order and peace, including the big efforts and goodwill required for saving the environment.

18. Even the US's historical allies have now become wiser, in particular after 2016 election and 2008 financial meltdown around the world due to the US's market collapse. The rush to reassure the world cannot help, either. The long-term harm is made and the deep scepticism about the viability of the US as a reliable ally or model would most likely be a lasting one.

19. In fact, we have reached a dangerous point in history where a country with such political instability and colossal leadership deficiency also has such disproportionately huge amount of arsenal and war machines and often showing a tendency for violence just for proving its *alleged* superiority *(Greatness!)*

20. Even more worrisome would be the US's probable resort to retaliatory measures to crush the world's resistance towards its claim of leadership and superiority.

21. The world's tolerance of the US's claim of leadership all along has been mostly due to its monetary contributions to the world affairs. Without such incentive, as Trump promises to stop American generosity, the world would not accept the US, or any nation, as a leader before the morality and quality of such leadership are proven.

22. A rather reverent old image of the White House is also now tainted for good after characters like George W. Bush, Jr. and Donald Trump have occupied it and damaged the world as a result of the Americans' bizarre choices of presidents.
23. Naturally, many world leaders would still not show negative sentiments openly for diplomatic and self-interest purposes, but the truth is that the US's influence around the world has now received its final blow.
24. Meanwhile, weird international relationships, such as the one between Trump and Netanyahu would further reveal the depth of the chaos and hypocrisy in the world. It is funny and depressing to watch the way Netanyahu's sly flattery satiates Trump's narcissism and proves his childish idiocy, not to mention the horrific outcome of co-conspiracies and actions by these two leaders all along due to their petty politics.
25. At the same time, many good-natured and mature people, especially Americans, are distressed about the way societies and political systems have gotten out of control and wonder why such a large population is so odd, arrogant, ignorant, and stir so much hostility within and outside their nations.
26. The world also gets anxious when an alleged leader like the US cannot keep its commitments and promises due to a lack of continuity within its political system. For instance, Trump's decisions about NATO, nuclear agreement with Iran, Paris environment accord, and trade agreements with other nations have created a lasting effect around the world. This global damage—inflicted mostly upon the US itself—would not be repaired before an overhaul of its political systems, if at all.
27. Surely, the outside world is forced to judge and trust the US according to its overall political stability and not the attitude of mature portion of its population victimized and suffering from their nation's lack of direction and leadership.
28. In fact, the world would no longer bear or ignore the way the US government bullies other nations and even its own people for various goals as its only consistent policy.

29. The events during the 2016 US election revealed humans' absurd tendency towards lunacy, besides showing the frailty of American political system. The ultimate lesson is about the fallibility of human nature in general, while social and global distress augments people's dire naiveté as well. This is also another clue about the depth of people's *egological* [*] tendency growing faster in modern societies.

30. One evidence for the growing global disorder lies in people's bizarre reactions, e.g., during the 2016 US election, in line with their rising distress due to the faltering world affairs.

31. This loop would accelerate fast and lead to colossal social hostility and personal anguish universally. As an example, Trump's threat during his political rallies to prosecute Hillary Clinton and vulgar chanting by Trump and his supporters, "Lock her up… Lock her up…," revealed people's growing agitated mindsets and characters—both the supposedly civil citizens and their president.

32. Meanwhile, the whole world has been waiting for Trump to fulfil his promise—to prosecute Clinton and *lock her up*, as he had yelled energetically along with people in the streets and Republican conventions so shamelessly and arrogantly.

33. The world was amazed by two facts about 2016 presidential candidates the most: First, both had seemed severely flawed, incompetent, and arrogant to Americans. Second, people's tenacity to chose the one with the lower character, after all, even when he showed his meanness openly and provoked the crowd into wild behaviour with his lies and creepy spite.

34. Also puzzling to the world was that most Americans chose to ignore the fact that Clinton's alleged wrongdoing remained unproven without any legitimate cause for investigation by the FBI. Yet, Americans refused to see the truth, and instead turned the issue into such a vulgar show and another proof of the US's political infancy.

---

[*] Explained in Appendix B, page 413.

35. Accordingly, a deep scientific curiosity arises when a modern population, e.g., in the US, have such opposing ideas and mentalities about their common needs: We wonder if these differences are due to genetics or intellectual deficiencies. How can two big groups in a developed nation be so divided intellectually about such rather simple issues, and why?
36. The speed American society and politics could get so oddly instable and confusing, even for the US public, warns other nations to doubt their citizens' stability as well as their affairs with America. Swiftly, the need for a practical socio-political system feels too urgent but harder to fathom, while the signs of humans' deep desperation and naïveté have alarmed the world. We wonder what magical measures and models for social and personal morality might ever provide a reliable path for social unity and humanity. Now, the entire world is also struggling to learn how to prevent their societies from becoming equally divided and chaotic like America.
37. Trump's presidency would probably prove to be a historical turning point in international relations and search for a viable plan for civilization, sustainable socioeconomic and political systems, and final efforts for saving the planet, *if these ideals are possible for such ill-natured humans.* Now, we confused humans have much more dilemmas to ponder and suffer.
38. A major question is whether Americans will learn anything now and do something about their society, electoral process, and Constitution. In particular, the 2nd Amendment regarding citizens' freedom to bear arms needs an urgent review before the world's faith about Americans' mentality is abolished.
39. Ironically, Americans demand gun ownership as a sign of democracy and constitutional right. Just imagine a world with free arm markets and the kind of civilization and democracy we could expect. The US would be the first nation opposing such a gun-driven democratic freedom. This double standard, e.g., about gun ownerships or global nuclear power, is yet another symbol of some nations' hypocrisy and imperialism

set to dictate the destiny of other countries according to their anarchic, bigoted views only for self-interest.

40. The world wonders and worries about Americans' obsession for guns and their zeal for economic and military dominance destroying humanity if they prove incapable or reluctant to connect nationally and globally in a more compassionate way.

41. Let us hope Trump's presidency has warned everybody about the depth of social distress and humans' fallibility. Has this historical revelation awakened the world to get together and envision a practical path towards the world order without the US or any other nation playing the sole leading role model in any terms, ethically, economically, militarily, etc.? Is it time to upgrade the UN and maybe even move its headquarters to a different location outside of the US as well? It would be a wise and productive step, but also a great symbolic gesture for the US.

42. The irony is that while most Americans, including its leaders and scholars, love to insist on the US's greatness, Trump and half of the US population supporting him believe that the US has lost it, but now wants it back—to be great *again*. So, there is a big confusion even in America about its greatness, never mind around the globe! *Of course, the only point of dwelling on the "Greatness" rhetoric in these pages is to stir some fun amidst so much cynicism in this chapter!*

43. Meanwhile, many people around the world wonder about the criteria for any country's greatness, after all. What had made America great, if ever, according to what merits, etc.? After all, it sounds too arrogant for any nation to assume and insist on being great in such a chaotic world led by some allegedly advanced nations. This crude point offers another clue about modern humans' dire egological tendency, *especially during such a confusing state of affairs in the US, to say the least!* Anyway, *if really necessary*, only outsiders can judge about a nation's greatness; not the people of any nation or its rulers, if not meant to be merely rhetoric or patriotic.

44. Contrary to the current attitude, a nation's greatness depends on its moral values, culture, and level of compassion; not the size of its military, zest for bullying, or even huge economy.
45. Now just imagine the idiocy of several nations also fighting, savagely or furtively, for some idiotic images of 'greatness' based on the prevalent criteria!
46. Sadly, the spread of crude political sentiments, e.g., a nation's greatness, and populist jargons would cause further divisions and conflicts nationally and globally.
47. Especially, we Canadians must be careful and disallow the spread of sentiments similar to those percolating in the US due to Trump's views of the world and politics. We must also strive to build a more viable socioeconomic and political system of our own. We must avoid the Trump Effect, though it might be too late already!
48. For example, Canada must rely merely on proper policies for immigration based on national and international needs and views, instead of letting people or officials abuse this subject as a gimmick for promoting political and personal agendas—like the mayhem Trump has caused in the US. Hopefully, we will not need a wall to stop the flood of American refugees!
49. An important lesson for the world from the 2016 US election and Britain's exit from the European Union is that every one of these revelations can infect other countries fast, too, due to people's pent-up frustrations with their lives and leaders. On the other hand, hopefully the world would soon realize the need for a global rebellion and cooperation to build a unified, functional planet. The problem, however, is that we have not even envisioned the need for a plan and proper mechanisms to replace the existing systems and start a fruitful dialogue among nations. Mere rebellions for changing governments and leaders cannot help much until our socio-political means are redesigned to minimize the chances and incentives for human corruption, incompetence, and greed.

50. Now, political systems in all nations seem in shambles and in need of major overhauls. In Canada, for instance, the role of senate and too many representations might require a review in terms of its effectiveness. Still, the US wins the prize for this worldwide marathon of political instability by ten miles!
51. Youths all over the world seem ready for a revolution, too, but they also seem lost. Their frustration is evident, e.g., their resort to Bernie Sanders and Donald Trump in hopes of a presumed social overhaul, yet they have not still built enough vision and conviction to unite and proceed.
52. Youths' lethargy and distraction by shallow ideals, instead of focusing on building a society and planning proactively for their threatened future and humanity, is depressing. The 2016 election in the US and the Brexit's referendum were affected by the youths' negligence to vote and ponder their welfare.
53. The growing social mayhem also relates to the dire influence of social media and the effects of the neo-culture on people, while people are provoked and mobilized by misinformation and lies. Especially, during the 2016 US election, fake news and propagandas were more influential on voters than regular official news. Fake news went viral closer to the election date and it can most likely be blamed for the shoddy outcome and a shaky political environment around the world. Around 62% of US adults were estimated to have gotten their news from social media during the 2016 election.
54. Certainly, all countries have similar problems due to the wide use of internet and social media. Yet, these sources of social confusion and chaos usually percolates in the US and spread around the world fast. Meanwhile, the American youths nag about their lives the most, while the chronic depression in the US has proven the legitimacy of people's senses of misery and frustration already.
55. The amount of nonsense and lies that leaders like Trump and his supporters deliver to people and the amount of time and energy their opponents waste to disclose and fight all these

vanities and stupidities are just staggering. No wonder no time and ingenuity are left for real progress and civilization.
56. Accordingly, people's naïve beliefs built around dreams, lies, and deceit are threatening the world's sanity and humanity.
57. Then again, maybe the world and humans deserve the doom fate awaiting them due to their incurable naivety, obsession for vanity, and narcissism.
58. Trump's election offers another plausible clue about people's weird proclivity towards bullies and abnormal role models, including rich and celebrities. Meanwhile, they usually find thoughtful individuals with simple notions about life boring or a threat to their adored mindsets. This pervasive tendency affirms again the frailty of human nature and our planet's vulnerability the most.
59. Surely, humans' search for peace and prosperity would fail as long as they refuse to develop a practical setting around some rules of ethics. But, we do not have time and mind to do this, all thanks to vast social conflicts, growing global alienations, and environmental disasters that will overwhelm our lives— just because we abhor the idea of being better beings.
60. Meanwhile, the rising division in global vision of humanity would stir further alienation towards the US and more radical attempts by religions to inject some morality into this messed up world, most likely in vain. However, some individuals and groups might seek some level of morality for personal salvation and peace after feeling sceptical enough about the superpowers' emphasis on military, materialism, and human exploitation. They might grow and emerge as role models for spreading some degree of peace, decency, and social stability before it is too late.
61. Therefore, soon the whole world might unite against the US and other modern nations, openly or covertly, exactly at a critical point when no more principles exist in the world to avail peace treaties or simple compromises to handle even basic conflicts.

62. Surely, the world's biggest dilemma is that both capitalism and communism seem deficient for helping us develop a healthy, practical socioeconomic structure. Yet, capitalism destroys humans' limited sense of morality, too. It turns us into vile, arrogant, and depressed humans as evident in the US and other parts of the world where capitalism has rooted. As a last resort to elude this gloomy trap, perhaps some form of progressive socialism can be built if the ruling capitalists in the world allow such humanistic schemes get a chance.
63. Meanwhile, the tyranny of capitalism around the world will sabotage people's efforts to fulfil their basic socioeconomic needs, aggravate their perceptions of social affairs, and ruin their sense of judgment. For example, people's subliminal tendency to trust rich, arrogant crooks like Trump, despite their proven hypocrisy and greed, seems puzzling when they envy and detest rich overall, e.g., Clintons, for making over $100 million after leaving the White House. While people's general cynicism is logical, their ignorance or dismissal (at the exact moment) of the other candidate's dire crimes and lifetime financial gimmicks to enrich himself reflect people's mixed-up criteria and views even about wealth and greed.
64. The United Nations is becoming ineffective as well, due to members', mainly superpowers', disregard for its principles and rulings, and even invading other nations against the UN's ruling. It has failed to satisfy its basic purpose of instilling some level of stability and harmony around the globe. Its failure to enforce peace in the Middle East has caused a global volatility and raised the threat for another major war among nations.
65. In particular, the UN seems so powerless when a country like Israel keeps defying any kind of global solutions for bringing peace to the Middle East. With the support of the US, Israel continues to expand its settlements in occupied territories with total disregard to the UN's Security Council resolutions. Some US Presidents like Obama and Carter have been more

vocal about this atrocity, but they have failed to change the US's unconditional support—like a petty puppet—of Israel's bullying attitude in the Middle East. The Washington Post reported the following on December 23, 2016

U.S. declines to veto U.N. Security Council resolution for Israel to stop Jewish settlement activity

The U.N. Security Council on Friday passed a resolution demanding Israel cease Jewish settlement activity on Palestinian territory in a unanimous vote that passed when the United States abstained rather than using its veto as it has reliably done in the past.

The resolution declares settlements constructed on land Israel has occupied since the 1967 war, including East Jerusalem, have "no legal validity." It said settlements threaten the viability of the two-state solution, and it urged Israelis and Palestinians to return to negotiations that lead to two independent nations.

The United States' abstention Friday was a rare rebuke to Israel, and reflected mounting frustration in the Obama administration over settlement growth that the United States considers an obstacle to peace.

"In the absence of any meaningful peace process, as well as in the face of the acceleration of settlement activity that put at risk the viability of a two-state solution, we took the steps we did today," said Ben Rhodes, the White House deputy national security adviser.

66. The UN's International Criminal Court (ICC) has now lost its legitimacy as many countries, including the US, Russia, and Israel have not committed and many African countries are giving up membership, too.
67. The United Nation is losing its credibility even in terms of propagating its main role and principles. For example, its choice of the Wonder Woman as its ambassador—maybe as

a gesture to empower women—angered many people inside and outside the UN, while many suggested that the whole scheme had been for promoting the new Wonder Woman movie and introduce the character to the youths. Even these simple gestures merely increase people's cynicism about the UN's role and the depth of social and global issues in the 21st century. A few weeks later, the UN reversed its decision about choosing the Wonder Woman as its ambassador.

68. We know human nature is crooked, social mechanisms are ineffective and hurtful, our political systems and leaders are useless, and we have no mind, facility, or a plan of action to build a true civilization.
69. The role and legitimacy of religions (actual or potential) to develop practical social agendas and move people towards a harmonious society is seriously doubtful as well.
70. Thus, only a magical social enlightenment and movement (in whatever miraculous form or mandate) might be able to save humanity.

It is rather unseemly to mention America and Trump so much in Part IV—in a book written mostly for discussing the merits and means of becoming better beings. However, it seems that recent world events, especially in the US, will have an immense impact on the future of humanity, while the possibility of people being better beings will keep declining very fast due to all these new developments. Trump has started something that will not end well —for him, for America, and for the world!

Epilogue
A Divine Being

As noted in the Author's Note, I had a lengthy, perturbing debate with my conscience for writing a book about the merits of goodness—a topic sounding like an old rejected cliché. Promoting an ideal with so little chance of materializing at a large scale felt futile. Then, I consoled myself that I was only trying to say three things about 'being better beings': **First,** it is a soothing and satisfying method of bearing life's inevitable hardships—way more productive and practical than usual options available to us nowadays, especially drugs, alcohol, and sexual indulgence. **Second,** many of us can learn and master the tricky, long process of goodness, though as a tough, sacred mission beyond humans' normal capacity and against our bizarre belief about being perfect individuals already. It is plausible that some special people get an insight, and build the incentive, to become better beings against all odds if they only get serious and brave the big challenge of getting there! **Third,** our experience might prove to be enriching, entertaining, and maybe even highly enlightening.

Now, after years of reflection and labour on this book, I still have two big hands! On the one hand, I am glad I undertook this challenge and offered my views, anyway. My three reasons noted above are still valid. On the other hand, I feel sadder now about human nature and future. It feels harder every day to ignore the accelerating mayhem declining the chance for personal, social, and global goodness and peace. I am now even more sceptical about people's knack to gain inner peace or the chance of any book making even a small effect on our mentalities or lifestyles we cherish so much. The chance of any guru or religion instilling enough goodness in people and society to stir harmony amongst a sizeable group at least feels remote as well. Sadly, my doubts and dilemmas still linger even more poignantly… Simply, we like to make one another sick!

"How can we expect people become better beings in a society like ours?"; "Does my conviction about many people's chance of finding inner peace, perhaps thru a high degree of goodness, hold water?"; "Can enough people build the incentive and courage these days to learn goodness at all, given the highly tainted nature of humans and their naïve, hypocritical character evolved within a vile neo-culture during the last few decades?" I still wrestle with these fatalistic questions, although I also push myself to remain rather optimistic and fight my urge to throw away the book.

Nevertheless, the damage is done and the book is complete, so I might as well publish it and hope for the best!

At the same time, it feels surreal to witness such absurd social decay and human suffering *merely* due to our persistence to stay the course and promote juvenile hopes and ideals about wealth, power, happiness, extravagance, and love. It feels stupid to lack enough sense or incentive to get along somewhat civilly. It is foolish to let our exaggerated obsessions for individualism and pleasures obstruct our grasp of basic family values and personal integrity. It is sad to witness our opportunity for inner peace and spiritual prosperity evaporating due to social values and norms goading evil and corruption so widely. Surely, morality, justice, freedom, security, and peace cannot grow in our dying societies, in this chaotic, vile world. Still, we often feel obliged to elude all these obstacles, idiocies, inconveniences, and cruelties and just keep on ploughing. Therefore, we might as well try the option of goodness personally to endure life easier and hope for a miracle!

Most stressfully, I have become very sceptical about the world leaders' ability, sincerity, or intention to spread peace, morality, and harmony for building a civilized way of existence. They have no vision or power to stop industries from ruining social morality and the environment. They are merely driven by their traditional agendas and mindsets for ruling the world by abusing people's naivety. They seem blind or duped, as if hoping that eventually some super-intelligent leaders or aliens would arrive to stop the course of human demise magically in the last minute! Maybe too many mushy movies have ruined their perceptions of reality, too. Our greedy scholars' loss of incentive, power, or brains to find solutions for socioeconomic and political obstacles of the 21st century and help humanity is also painful. We have supposedly tried to be civilized and happy, yet achieved neither. Nor are we willing or competent to learn anything from our endless failures. Rather, we simply seem numb, stuck in a thick web of ignorance and arrogance, as though we love the present stalemate too much to think in a *completely* different realm for a likely salvation.

Surely, the sombre discussions in this book mostly reflect my pitiful, chronic pessimism about human race's vision and ability to build a harmonic means of coexistence. After all, humans' dire obsession for fighting amongst themselves over everything seems eternal! I wish I could be more optimistic about things, the way Al Gore sounds about 'climate change' initiatives and humans' prospect. I envy him, although I have strived to stay positive and stopped whining as much as I did a few years ago, at least for keeping my spirit intact and staying on the goodness path.

Amidst my crude cynical views, in fact, I hope my reserved optimism is also apparent about some individuals' capacity to be better beings for their own sakes and perhaps even spreading a moralistic and peaceful culture in small corners of the world. I believe some of us might grow the courage and enthusiasm to pursue this sacred mission. After all, this book's goal has been to stir hope and incentive for being better beings in a practical way. We could try to be good *for* ourselves at least, regardless of the outcome, rather than focusing merely on being good *to* ourselves at any cost to others, society, and the planet. Especially, I truly hope, the way most parents always dream, that my kids find the conviction to become better beings with solid minds for their own sakes, despite the bad genes we have bestowed upon them. That would prove their immense intelligence and stamina beyond all achievements that any parent could possibly aspire for his/her children. I hope they make me proud for their own and their kids' sakes—with more personal peace towards a solemn salvation.

Often, we question our being, anyway! At some critical points, life feels like a vain endeavour that we are stuck with unfairly. One day, we realize that this world, this life, and these people are not what we can face in good faith, as sincerely as we have now obliged ourselves to behave. Can (must) we go hide somewhere remote, in a cocoon, to at least witness as little of this world's atrocities as possible? Merely because we still love living just a bit, or a lot, longer perhaps?! Because death feels just so hideous, unfair, and painful *already*, even the thought of it?! We might consider living only for today, follow many amusing adventures, adopt and enjoy solitude, be a better being, or just get it over with and die, after all. Any of these options has its own challenges and appeal, thus choosing requires the highest level of contemplation, wisdom, commitment, and conviction all by itself! Often, we do not even know what we like or is good for us![*]

Similar existential thoughts and philosophical choices have amused me personally, too, to explore the possibility of finding a less intimidating option for living than a routine survival. Some of us cannot satisfy or dismiss our obsession for finding a logical resolution, although only some idiotic ideas jump in my head, like going to live in Paris for a while at least—just for a change of scenery or something, or maybe even finding my beloved Farida

---

[*] By the way, some tentative answers regarding humans' general cynicism about living (being or not being) are discussed in the three-volume book by this author, *Doubts and Decisions for Living*.

there to resume our old love affair! Then again, all that growing unrest, terrorism, and pollution in Paris deter me. All these silly analyses merely make any logical person only more confused, paranoid and exhausted.

How many times has God made us mourn the loss of people we have loved so much—even the ones still alive? Why has He made even the thought of death so disgusting when living and suffering are so humiliating already? Yet, our mission to learn the wisdom of existence can move us forward, maybe with a divine insight after years of self-cleansing and contemplation. Sadly, this long journey is lonely, long, and intimidating too often, due to all the controversies and defeats we must still face regularly.

Still, I have at least realized that 'being a better being' and 'living at all' are related, precious notions. Luckily, I have never stopped believing in the chance of some of us eventually finding the right option for living and justifying our existence on most days at least, perhaps by becoming just a bit better beings, which often helps a lot for boosting our spirits and maybe others', too. Building this mindset feels like a useful strategy for sustaining at least a less painful existence even if we never get a chance to feel love again. Some of us may learn to ignore social burdens just by relying on our inner strengths and *that* outer power nourishing the essence of our being. Faith still drives some people to look for salvation even amidst the social turmoil nobody can avoid.

Many people may feel my sentiments now, yet not be swayed by this book or any rationalization. They may *still* ask, "What's the point of being a better person, anyway?" In fact, many of us can never elude the main depressing thought, "What is the point of living altogether or fussing over it so much?" This pensive group cannot fool itself with fleeting pleasures or even bask in the joy or soothing wisdom of goodness permanently.

Sometimes, we look at our boring lives and feel their vanities regardless of the level of our goodness or badness. Then, we think of other options to elude our boredom, yet realize wisely that any of those other remedies would be a creepier option even when we have all the money and energy for new adventures. Thus, we try to stay content with our painful, odd fate, since a simple mistake, such as choosing a companion to change our dull routines—*maybe even as a writer or philosopher*—might push our destiny into a messier abyss quickly. We might sink so deep we miss our past shoddy routines we had not appreciated enough before. Then, we curse our creators and ourselves for the idiotic trap we have jumped into only out of desperation. We abhor the new baffling existence bestowed upon us suddenly—usually just by one horrible, hasty mistake! How about that?

Of course, goodness is not a remedy for our misfortunes or depressing existential thoughts, which no wise human can avoid, as he hopes to capture peace and enlightenment at last and enjoy life cautiously. However, goodness—once its essential attributes are mustered—raises our contentment and tolerance enough to take both our fates and faiths in our strides.

We might even goad our wild imaginations, only for humour and distraction, to invent any likely means for human salvation. One such amusing idea is to divide our planet into several remote regions based on people's mentalities and values—and then let them live as they wish in their unique, calm societies. Especially, if the US is divided into two harmonious states based on people's ideological preferences, instead of fifty controversial regions, the world's problems will reduce immensely. People could move to the side of their preference and live happily rather than fighting forever with a group that has opposite sentiments and ideologies. They *might* explore and handle their own affairs better, too, *for a while perhaps! Yeah…,* knowing human nature, soon each group would find new conflicts to fight over among themselves and their societies become chaotic again in a decade, if not a month.

The Beauty of Betterness

Our efforts for 'Being Better Beings' stir a divine sense of beauty as well. Besides a higher grasp of life and nature's splendour more consciously and delightfully, we discover the two opposite realms of our blessed self. On the one hand, we start to experience the wholeness of our self, as our lively spirits explore our inner potentialities and attain inner peace. On the opposite spectrum, all these self-explorations and achievements may make us realize our nothingness and attain selflessness with humility. Thus, in effect, our efforts for being better beings—betterness—give us a chance to infuse our self-wholeness and selflessness and reach a state of divinity—a sacred sense of beauty just by being better beings.

We could do it for God's sake, too, I guess! Again, it seems He really wants us to be better beings than how He has created us! Recreating ourselves better than He had been able to manage originally is a big incentive in itself—just to show it to Him! Still, grasping His interest in our goodness remains a mystery! *What's in it for Him?* Is He feeling lonely in Heaven? Is He so desperate for some amusement, creating all these routines, dispatching so many prophets with tricky messages, all in hopes of enlightening a few humans, including a lot of wicked bastards who repent in the last minutes to join Him in Heaven before showing their true nature soon again? He goes through all these hassles and waits billions of years for the judgment day when humans are allowed at last to arrive in Heaven for what?

These and similar questions occur to many of us sometimes, as we wonder about God's divine intentions. Yet, a big dilemma, for a cynical jerk like me, is still whether he *couldn't* or *wouldn't* make us as good as He wanted us to be when he set out to create humans. If He *couldn't*, then, of course, it is rather unfair of Him to expect us achieve something that He couldn't do Himself. And if He *wouldn't*, then why is He trying now to make us defy our nature, be stronger than our genes, fight our urges, perform a lot of worshiping rituals, and other stuff just for the sake of some peculiar game He is playing with us, including all these hell and heaven threats? Is He just having some fun with us, or is this idea of piety just a figment of some humans' imagination without any pertinence to God? Ironically, these seemingly logical thoughts still haunt me, although I acknowledged adamantly, in Chapter Three, the absurdity and frailty of human logic to tackle even much less complex issues. Yet a major regret for me all along has been my inability to understand God or communicate with Him!

Just one last point, I promise, about God's logic and approach for making better human beings: Why has He been so persistent to stay mysterious and keep us in suspense about His intentions? Why not be transparent about such a crucial matter in His opinion at least? Why not talk to everybody, maybe thru internet now, to tell us how He wants us to behave and find enlightenment for a chance to go to Heaven, too. If He could talk to a few prophets sporadically, He could surely speak louder for everybody to hear Him, too, couldn't He? Directly or through Jibreel or whomever! Now, just imagine, if He did just that: The Earth will turn into Heaven overnight! *So why wouldn't He?! He likes mystery a lot or prefers keeping us confused, maybe?! He created mystery!!*

My dilemmas and lasting curiosity about God are probably related to the deep bitterness that life has etched in my psyche, although I have learned over the years, through my goodness regimen, to deal with my bitterness largely. So, maybe betterness is only for overcoming our bitterness about being and the agony of living. Then, perhaps leave God alone as well before He gets really upset! Ironically, as stated on page 242's footnote, He might have made my muse goad me write this book for a scared purpose, so I hope He forgives my daft logic, trying to be both pensive and witty about His intentions regarding humans! To be honest, all these gibberish and wondering about God's game have hurt me a lot. *But I'm sure He knows I love Him.*

Anyhow, aside from all these cynical thoughts and words just for our last minute fun, I often contemplate John Lennon's poetry in *Imagine* where he is merely asking people to be just a bit better beings. That is what I am hoping to convey and accomplish, too. What if so many of us could imagine a saner world rather clearly the way John did? Wow! Just Imagine!

Appendices

Appendices A through D offer technical topics to support the theories and opinions offered in the main text, but they include some supplementary analysis and points, especially in Appendix D, as well. Some or many readers may find them of less direct use, and thus prefer to skim only. Appendix E, however, is a good summary for a deep, final reflection; or maybe as a venue for routine meditations during goodness regimen.

Appendix	Page
A: Human Cognition	412
B: Humans' Egological Conditions	413
C: Humans' Logic Aversion Drive	416
D: Human Instincts' Vulnerability	421
E: The Summary; Reality Check about Humanity	425

Appendix A
Human Cognition

A person's genetics (nature) and upbringing (nurture) influence his/her character and cognition mainly by developing his/her brain (mind), which, in turn, directs his or her urges, feelings, thoughts, and actions. Accordingly, a person's health and brain capacity are vastly crucial for his or her cognition level. This simple concept is shown in the following diagram, where:

A: Shows Nature (biological construct/genetics).
B: Shows Nurture (family and social environments).
C: Shows Mind (logic and analytical capacity).
ABC: Shows Cognition (one's ability to grasp and process data.)

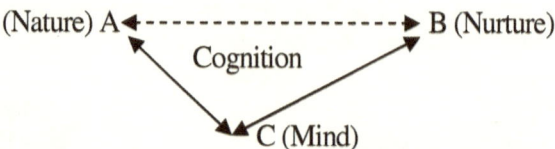

The area ABC, one's cognition, is constantly influenced by one's biological and environmental variables, as well as one's mental ability to receive and utilize various stimuli. The mind, as a tool developed by A and B, in turn assists one's 'cognition,' to serve A and B. That is, our active efforts to boost our cognition raise mind's analytical capacity to serve A and B, maintain a person's biological needs, and face environmental issues, including his/her relationships and career effectively. The notion of 'healthy mind in healthy body, and vice versa' reflects this principle.

In the above diagram, the broken line AB indicates that A and B are semi-independent sources of mental development. Still, A and B affect each other to some degree as well, even though A (nature) is an inherent aspect of man and B (nurture) reflects the effects of external forces. For example, anger caused by someone or an event induces chemical reactions in our body. In turn, our reaction may affect B—people or events surrounding the person.

Appendix B
Humans' Egological Conditions

Besides its harmful effects noted in Chapter Three, our crude logic makes us think too highly of ourselves, cherish our juvenile personalities and views, and boost our egos constantly. Then, our ego returns the favour by making us think that our logic is perfect about everything and it is superior to everybody else's. Therefore, together, our ego and logic are constantly boosting each other and making a complete fool of us—our poor Self!

Our communications and sense of cooperation decline when humans' demented logic and inflated ego mix and mess up each other constantly. This destructive force, called 'egologic' in this book, causes personality quirks or even psychosis for most people.

The effects of egologic can be studied in five groups of people shown in Diagram B (next page.) The first four groups reflect the outcome of extreme interactions of ego and logic and contain about 30% of the world population. The fifth group, the majority about 70%, have varied degrees of ego and logic, which lead to infinite types of mindsets and personalities. However, this group shares some of the fatal idiosyncrasies that the first four groups have, besides the specific egologic effects that usually besiege the fifth group with varied mixes of narcissism and eccentricity.

Low logic and high ego are mostly common and inherent among Humans, especially nowadays. However, people can be divided into these five general groups according to the following readily detectable symptoms:

I. Extreme Ego in opinionated people makes them dogmatic.
II. Extreme Ego and average Logic make a person arrogant.
III. Average Ego in opinionated people makes them cynical.
IV. Average Ego and average Logic make a person dumb.
V. Varied levels of Ego and Logic create people's unique minds and personalities with various qualities and idiosyncrasies. Everybody holds some levels of all the typical idiosyncrasies

noted for all five groups in Diagram B. These combinations show varied mixes of narcissism and eccentricity in people along with the traces of dogmatisms, arrogance, cynicism, and dumbness that the first four groups demonstrate deeply and directly more often.

Diagram B: Humans' Egological Conditions

Effects of Human Ego + Logic ↘		Logic	
		Opinionated	Average
Ego	Extreme	I **Dogmatic** 10% ↘	II **Arrogant** 10% ↙
		V **Narcissist Eccentric** 70%	
	Average	↗ 5% III **Cynical**	↖ 5% IV **Dumb**

The suggested percentages of people in each group, as shown in Diagram B, are very rough estimates and merely hypothetical for the purpose of discussions in this section. However, it seems plausible that at least 30% of people have extreme egological defects, whereas the majority (around 70%) suffers from some types of egological flaws, plus some lesser degrees of other kinds of idiosyncrasies, including dogmatism, arrogance, cynicism, dumbness, narcissism, and eccentricity.

Naturally, our logic and ego have some useful properties that we use for managing our lives and dealing with people. Yet, the negative impacts of egologic on our personalities are much more severe and noticeable, especially in terms of encountering and humouring people in society. Humans are controversial mostly due to the effects of their innate egological tendencies.

Human ego and logic enforce each other's potency and cause further deterioration of personality within one of the five noted categories above. Egologic raises humans' vanity exponentially as well, beyond what our ego and logic would usually do on their own already. In effect, egologic makes us a bad person since our demented logic makes us feel so important and our inflated ego makes us trust our logic and self-image wholeheartedly. It makes us lose our objectivity and it kills our incentive for exploring the path of goodness and becoming a better being. The only way to reduce the egologic effects is to learn some humility through the goodness path explained in Chapter Six.

Furthermore, egologic effects are many folds more critical in younger people in terms of causing wrong viewpoints and flawed personalities. The younger a person, the more s/he is susceptible to his/her egological tendency for three reasons: 1) the youths' logic and objectivity are substantially undeveloped due to limited life experiences, while s/he is also threatened by high emotional tendencies, 2) his/her ego is much more inflated and he/she feels smart, wise, and invincible, and 3) decisions during the youth are potentially too destructive and most potent for derailing one's destiny. When these three reasons mix, the effects of egologic during a person's early ages are much riskier with high potentials for catastrophe. Therefore, it is even more important for younger people to realize and beware of the repercussions of egologic as explained in this Appendix.

Accordingly, the youths' apathy for the elderly's wisdom—as a tool to mitigate the effects of egologic—is a big disservice to themselves and a major cause of cultural and social demise. They think they are smart, but are really setting the grounds for ruining their own and their kids' lives with their low senses of reality.

Overall, if human logic worked, they would have realized by now that arrogance cannot help anybody. It only reveals humans' depth of stupidity and inability to help themselves. Most of all, however, humans really have no ground for being so haughty, especially since most of us are extremely naïve and characterless.

Appendix C
More about Human Logic
Logic Aversion Drive

The following discussions and suggested statistics are theoretical. They augment the discussions in Chapter Three and Appendix B. They are mostly hypotheses for further studies and speculations.

****

Factors of Human Logical Defects

Besides humans' emotions, logical limitations (noted in Chapter Three), and egological symptoms hindering our decision-making capacity already, we suffer from a condition, which we may call Logic Aversion Drive (LAD). This happens when we defy our logic adamantly with weird tenacity. That is, even when our logic provides a solid ground for judgment and decision-making, and we manage both our emotional and egological tendencies, we consciously ignore the truth and our sensible options due to our preconditioned mindsets, habits, idiosyncrasies, sickness, pride, biases, obsessions, dogmatism, raw ambitions, prejudices, spite, and many other psychological deficiencies. A good example for this pervasive condition—humans' logic aversion drive—is our wealth-gathering obsession. After we accumulate enough wealth to guarantee a rich life even for our grand-grand children, most of us still cannot apply our sound logic that screams at us to stop worrying about, or hustling for, more, even at the expense of damaging our body, mind, and spirit even further. Any kind of addiction is another example of our aversion to use logic, or even fighting it often doggedly. Even artistic and scientific endeavours, when a person devotes his/her entire life to them, often feel against our logic, as we seem to be wasting our precious lives away. Yet, we, the artists or scientist, writers and philosophers, cannot stop ourselves at the cost of missing many privileges of existence.

Many reasons exist for our inability to abide by even our own sound logic, but the outcome and our pains for this shortfall is simply bizarre and educational, especially for self-awareness. For one thing, spite and arrogance often stop our brains from working altogether, let alone using logic. We often even feel our stupidity later and hate ourselves for sabotaging even our own long-term interests on top of killing our spirits, yet cannot stop our spite and pride. Then, some of us wonder why and suffer even more!

Thus, the following four types of logic-related defects cause a great deal of problems in our lives all by themselves:

- Logic limitations (as discussed on page 82)
- Emotional tendencies (e.g. love) overwhelming our logic.
- Egological symptoms (as discussed in Appendix B)
- Logic aversion drive (discussed here)

It might be interesting to guess the effects of each of the above factors on the overall degree of humans' decision inaccuracies or insensibilities merely due to our inability to i) appreciate the role of logic and related decision factors, and ii) seek possible means of handling each factor *logically*. The author has taken the risk of proposing some rough estimates of people's decision inaccuracy in general due to the effects of the four human tendencies related to logic as depicted in Table C. He estimates that 60-90% of our decisions are tainted by at least one of these four factors.

Table C: Decision Inaccuracy Ratings

Factors of Logical Defects (Causes of Bad Decisions)	Within the rules and values of:	
	Perceived Reality World	Real Reality World
1. Logic limitations	10%	15%
2. Emotional tendencies	15%	25%
3. Egological conditions	15%	15%
4. Logic aversion drive	20%	35%
Total tainted decisions	**60%**	**90%**
Fully sensible decisions	**40%**	**10%**

Thus, only 10-40% of humans' decisions are fully sensible for their ultimate, lasting welfare in the overall scheme of things. The insensibility of humans' decisions can also be measured in terms of the two worlds that we live in, i.e., the perceived versus real realities as explained in this author's book, *Doubt and Decision for Living, Volume I,* Chapter Two.

As one or a mix of the four logic-related deficiencies obstruct our decision-making ability, our daily lives and psychological welfare are compromised, just because we cannot think straight. Any of these four areas of logic-related flaws stirs dire imbalance and damages our routines and decisions, yet the fourth one, i.e. Logic Aversion Drive (LAD), interferes with our thought process more often and affects our way of thinking and behaving most directly even against our own welfare and logical perceptions. We keep doing things that we do (or must) suspect to be useless and unethical, thus ruin our spirits and a chance for redemption.

If we could invent a process to help people overcome their LAD at least, their miseries would be reduced substantially, the entire social structure would improve drastically, and our chances for becoming better beings would increase substantially as well. For example, just imagine humans realizing that their greed is merely ruining their lives as well as the foundation of human thoughts and social structure.

In fact, if somebody could invent a process to help people overcome their LAD, s/he would become a billionaire!

Human Logic in Perceived and Real Worlds

Both our logic and science remain limited by human intelligence, which is functional mostly within our perceived world, and only for speculating about some of the simpler natural laws. Of course, humans' collective logic and science have followed a systematic, proven track. A continuous development of ideas has turned into workable theories, tools, and machinery to fulfil specific goals. The advance of science has been cumulative, disciplined, and methodical (limited to laws and principles we have created in our perceived world, of course). Moreover, scientific rules have been tested within the natural settings of the universe and they have complied rather nicely with some of the specific laws of nature.

However, human brain and logic seem viable merely to the extent they fit nicely with the natural laws of the universe, e.g., building an airplane to defy gravity, finding a cure for a disease, etc. Human logic is not driven by some mysterious, inherent power within us, but it is only a tool for making an inference based on past results and specific methods to verify what is out there in Nature. Even at this scientific level—for making reliable inferences—our logic has not helped answer the majority of questions and phenomena that the universe throws at us.

The validity of our logic and science outside of humans' raw perceptions is debateable from many different angles, though that is not the purpose of this book. The goal here is only to stress on our random inclinations to believe in, or doubt, the validity of our logic and science. This rather whimsical mindset is equally at play when we wish to establish our personal beliefs and life choices. Thus, we cannot be easily persuaded to engage (and believe) in a philosophical notion or abstract sensation that feels illogical to us, opposes the existing scientific knowledge, or defies our personal beliefs. Personal intuition and cognition also mix with a person's unique experiences and genes to build his or her peculiar logic, perceptions, and preferences. Therefore, while logic is for finding common grounds amongst humans, it usually causes conflicts when people perceive the same points and principles differently based on their subjective personal criteria.

Overall, outside its application to natural laws for scientific purposes, we have no other criteria for measuring the meaning and power of human logic for deciphering complex features of our daily existence and thoughts. Even for applying human logic to scientific research, we must usually go through a long process of trials and errors, and experimentation of random ideas (e.g., for finding a cure for cancer), until finally someone stumbles upon a solution. Therefore, at best, we are only fitting our logic to some scientific methodologies to prove natural laws. Again, this means that our logic is not an inherent and reliable tool, but merely a dynamic means of focusing our thoughts and processes.

On the other hand, human logic and knowledge have evolved purposefully and systematically over millenniums, despite its vast limitation due to human brains' frailty (mainly our perceptions). We cannot refute the validity of events and things that happen to us in the perceived world on the grounds that things we do and see in this world are only dreams or illusions. It sounds *illogical* to believe we may be awakened from this dream to enter the real world—e.g., to go to heaven. Even our basic logic stresses that using an analogy, e.g., night dreaming, to create an illusion of an unknown phenomenon is most likely a fallacy and leads to other forms of illusions. Relying on the possibility of being awakened magically from our present state of delusions and ignorance would not help our urgent need to grasp who we are and what our relationship to the real world is. We need a plan to discover it on our own mostly through our spiritual goodness regimen.

In the end, we must haggle with our dilemmas about human logic and science and find reasonable criteria for developing our personal faith and purposes in order to direct our lives. For sure, we cannot, and should not, discard our urge to explore exotic ideas that have been called supernatural, spiritual, or myths in spite of our logical scepticism. We should assume that, with an open mind, we always have a chance of finding other life paths that could never become obvious to a rigid mind, even if all kinds of evidences were in front of the person. Thus, it seems we can (should) never trust our logic fully. Our misleading logic cannot be useful or make enough sense, e.g., for grasping supernatural, and God when in fact our intuition or imagination goads us to believe in myths or some other reality beyond the overwhelming perceived world we are familiar with due to specific teachings in society, in our families, and by religions.

Appendix D
Human Instincts' Vulnerability

A major obstacle for self-awareness and reducing our gullibility is that the new patterns of social living have numbed our instincts. For one thing, our instincts are suppressed during childhood due to either rearing overindulgence or deprivations. In our complex societies, children are exposed to a vast amount of superficial ideals and fantastical visions of life through media and public interactions. Meanwhile, parents are themselves driven by similar phony values and too busy to have a useful and natural contact with their children. Instead, they spoil their kids with too many privileges and low discipline. They merely follow the shoddy trends of childrearing propagated in modern societies in line with commercialism. In our new culture, parents do not know any better means of educating their kids other than explaining the social patterns designed for goading materialism. At the same time, they are too pressed by their own life priorities to give the right level of attention to their kids' natural needs, even if they knew what they were. Thus, they only engage their children's brains with trivia, toys, and dreams. With all the stress and agony parents must deal with already, children would be lucky to evade severe physical or mental burdens and tortures. Nowadays, family and relationship conflicts are growing faster than ever and have become the causes of crimes in modern nations. On the other hand, many children are left unprotected and helpless in the streets and refugee camps all over the world. They rely mostly on their basic animalistic instincts to survive in this hostile world. Therefore, although their basic instincts are better instigated in those environments, their more sophisticated talents and instincts would never get a chance to flourish.

Even families who strive to discharge their parenthood duties more responsibly usually emphasize too much on teaching social values and norms, which revolve around the themes of sexuality, materialism, happiness, pomposity, rivalry, and winning at any cost. Parents' teachings are vastly driven by their own shallow minds, especially about success factors and individualism that are defined wrongly in our cultures. Their outlooks and principles, which they find useful for their kids, are tainted with materialistic ambitions and social routines that have brainwashed the public in full scale already. Thus, kids' power of intuition is vastly subdued by parental and social brain washing forces as well.

Our surviving (primary) instincts are getting least applicable to artificial settings, feelings, and dealings that define human life in the 21st century, too. 'Instincts' reflect the essence of humans, which manifests naturally for coping with our comprehensible needs, problems, and surroundings. They respond to, and become useful only in, natural settings in line with the needs of a simple human being. Yet, the intricacy of prevalent social systems and relationships nowadays, as well as people's mental and emotional instability, makes personal encounters too unnatural to grasp and handle instinctually. Our instincts become idle when we have no natural impulses for handling our superficial needs and situations. Then, out of desperation and frustration for the lack of effective solutions, we merely retaliate or create more frictions to cope with our wacky surroundings and relationships. Most likely, our agitated minds make our instincts less accessible as well.

Conversely, it is getting harder, if at all possible, to rely on our instincts to handle our erratic needs and feelings in the new era, which are inconsistent with our inner conception of humanness and our urge for a pure, peaceful existence. Thus, we rarely grasp and use our intuition and instincts. The only role and significance that our *primary* instincts can play in our unnatural life settings nowadays is to somehow (rather magically) trigger and enhance our awareness about the artificiality of our present lifestyles, which might then aid us in redirecting our minds and values. The immense problem with the prevalent speedy social growth is that our instincts are dampened more every day, and we do not know how to evoke our deeply sunken spirits to protect ourselves. In the meantime, society and parents keep spreading more egoism, superficiality, and gullibility, because parents are themselves so helpless to elude social norms or teach their kids anything useful.

Sadly, we do not appreciate our real 'being,' because we have been raised in a crooked neo-culture and alienated our instincts and spirits in pursuit of phony lifestyles unrelated to our natural feelings and needs. We lack awareness and inner strengths that erupt from humans' spiritual dimension through self-fulfilment by following our instinctual and creative urges. Therefore, we can safely say that undermining or losing our instinctual abilities to handle life situations is both a direct symptom and cause of deterioration in overall human capabilities.

Most people and anthropologists consider 'human nature' and 'human *primary* instincts' the same thing as the roots of human behaviour. However, as noted before, it seems plausible to view human nature as an evolving phenomenon rather than an inherent property related to humans' primary instincts. We can theorize that 'primary instincts' consist of basic, inherent, fixed urges, while 'human nature' covers a larger array of humans' mental attributes that keep evolving forever. Humans' progressive needs, feelings, and reactionary behaviours reflect their evolving nature, but not their primary instincts. The difference lies in the fact that culture and environment can tame or improve human attributes through history. This human capacity to display flexibility and change distinguishes 'human nature' from 'primary instincts' that seem similar to humans' innate, rigid characteristics. To the extent that only external forces and environment stir some aspects of human behaviour, those behaviours are only transitory reactions, which we may choose to call the nature of man, but only at this limited scope and subordinate to negative stimuli that activate them. They are not innate, primary instincts, nor are they stable and permanent human attributes.

To explain it still in another context, we may say that although some of our basic reactionary habits reflect our instincts, the roots and causes of our reactions depend on the type of external stimuli and the way we perceive and react to it. Moreover, people do not react uniformly to similar external stimulus, which is contrary to the definition of 'primary instincts' that are allegedly uniform and consistent. In fact, we have learned enough about psychology to know that we perceive and react to a stimulus not only based on our basic instincts, but rather through our personality and level of intelligence in line with our crude perceptions and emotions. Thus, as general population matures over a long span of history, human nature changes gradually in terms of means and methods of perceiving and reacting to situations or stimuli. Many people may call this nurture instead of nature, since they believe social teachings and conditioning create personality and intelligence, which in return build humans' reactionary habits. The difference is that while 'nurture' covers individuals' unique personality traits within each generation, 'nature' reflects people's dominant habits and attributes developed during a long span of history.

Overall, it is more realistic to assume that humans' nature is susceptible to our surroundings and conditions over centuries and millenniums. Like chemical reactions in a laboratory experiment, our mind is constantly reacting to varying mixtures of positive and negative forces stimulating it. These syntheses and processes change human nature very slowly. We can assume that human nature changes along with humans' overall evolution, and that neither nature nor nurture of humans per se is responsible for humans' sad state of existence and the process of deterioration that is threatening humanity nowadays. Instead, only the mixed, erratic effects of all these brainstorming forces account for social and personal distress. Therefore, for studying human mind, we must focus on the circular effects of these forces accelerating the overall imbalance of our minds and loss of control over human affairs. We can review each group of forces first and then try to propose some examples of their interactive consequences. We did some of these analyses in Chapter Four.

Appendix E
The Summary
Reality Check about Humanity

The following summary reiterates the, i) realities, ii) dilemmas, iii) bottomline, and iv) choices facing humanity nowadays. It can be used as, a) a long synopsis for readers eager to get the gist of the book first, and/or b) a platform for regular reflections.

****

Dark Realities

Societies are immensely volatile and vulnerable nowadays due to, 1) humans' petty nature and minds fixated by crooked social teachings, 2) the lack of culture and social conscience to guide people, 3) people's apathy for self-awareness and goodness, and 4) the absence of enough good people, especially wise leaders, to impose civilized principles towards a healthier coexistence for all.

At the same time, ultimately, the only hope for personal and human salvation is that more of us find good reasons and the guts to become better beings even slightly. The means of raising our awareness and incentive to pursue a path of goodness have been discussed throughout the book, including the goodness purpose, elements, and regimen. Still, the following brief guidelines might stir another fresh layer of consciousness to help meditate during the long journey of becoming better beings (BBB).

1. We should admit that Humans' pervasive suffering is due to their impiety and inability, or reluctance, to be better beings than they have been so far. Ironically, we have always known this basic fact about the high relation between human wickedness and their pains. Prophets have also tried to make us conscious of this main cause of human misery. However, we seem to be deaf and adamant to hurt ourselves. *Such an intelligent species we have proved to be, after all!*

2. We should figure out humans' essential needs, instead of fussing and fighting over so many artificial ones.
3. We must learn about teamwork at personal and global levels, which our civilized societies lack seriously. Furthermore, we should explore the basics of humanity for our salvation as well as connecting to nature and other beings with humility.
4. Our zeal for glamour, fashion, and extravagance is unnatural and a big hindrance for becoming simple, good beings.
5. At best only 50% of people have the capacity for being better beings (BBB) if they try. There is no hope for the rest. Thus, we need a creative means of dealing with these untameable souls and devils effectively in order to raise the chance of building a rather liveable, moral society and coexisting with patience and compassion.
6. Humans are not God's privileged creature with the right to exploit all aspects of nature merely because they can or are allegedly more intelligent than other beings.
7. Minimizing the effects of advertising and consumerism on our children and ourselves raises humans' chances for BBB.
8. Too many people are both mean and moron nowadays, since they not only give themselves the right to abuse and confuse others, but also believe everybody else is stupid like them to fall for their gimmicks and games, including their phony shows of friendship or sympathy.
9. We need better values, economies, leaders, societies, and, most important of all, a somewhat wiser populace. We must stop being so naïve with our dreams and unrealistic outlook. For a better society, *some ethical authorities,* but not clergies or prophets, are needed to reassess our priorities for social health, people's basic needs, socio-political systems, personal rights, faiths, and global affairs in a realistic way. Religions cannot achieve that.
10. Society and people spoil our being little by little directly or inadvertently, including our sanity, feelings, compassion, and

health. But we should at least stop their attempts to take away our dignity and integrity or spoil our spirits.
11. At the same time, we are such peculiar people, punishing desolate individuals for doing minor crimes, but reward and respect big crooks and make them heads of major nations. We are the ones, as individuals, allowing these kinds of deep-rooted, long-lasting travesties grow and continue.
12. Life feels just unbearable too often, yet we must also learn to muse over many painful, philosophical questions that boggle our minds every day, such as, "Is this meant to be a world for naïve people with dreams and hopes, a world for crooked populace hoping to fool and abuse others forever, or a world for wisdom and compassion? Can we ever focus on a more viable option for humanity?" In the end, we should come to terms with such dilemmas thru personal growth and wisdom.
13. Many people, especially the youths, are insecure and anxious about their relationships being in such big disarray, but also obsessed with love and happiness at the cost of losing their identity and interest in life's main endeavours, including self-awareness, cultural development, and spiritual growth.
14. Accordingly, a big dilemma for people, especially the youths, is that they are good neither together as couples for building functional families, nor alone as independent persons. Thus, their big mission is to defeat this deficiency personally and learn to build the right characters for living independently, while hoping to find a right companion if they are lucky.
15. We can also help and stir goodness in our kids by teaching them life's hardships and essentialities, especially in light of the looming catastrophes related to climate change and social systems' failures to cope with new demands. We must learn to be better parents, instead of spoiling our kids with fantasy, phony values, vanity, and crude ideologies.
16. People must realize that world economies would become even more dynamic and vulnerable, thus they should stop expecting local industries to support them forever. Instead,

they must prepare themselves to go around, perhaps even outside their countries to find suitable jobs.
17. Our leaders' promises are often empty and unachievable, in particular when they sound idealistic and immature already. Many obstacles, including the conflicting interests of various elite groups, as well as the bureaucratic protocols within various branches of political systems, cripple even devoted, honest leaders, let alone all those incompetent hypocrites who lie and cheat shamelessly to lure the public.
18. We must make some major personal life decisions that affect us and others deeply and permanently, e.g., related to child rearing, marital affairs, career, and lifestyle. They require wisdom and high conscience, as our lousy emotional choices often have lasting repercussions. Our hasty judgments during those stressful occasions are major causes for us becoming substandard humans, instead of focusing on the mission of becoming better beings.
19. Humans are destroying 2/3 of wild life population through their irresponsible environmental policies and actions. Playing a role to stop this dire proof of human selfishness is vital.
20. We are accelerating the annihilation of humanity merely with our naivety and arrogance without the help of atomic bombs.
21. Thus, we must at least stop being either selfish or impulsive about creating children, who must then face the dilemma of living or gathering the nerve to suicide as life keeps getting weirder, unhealthier, and sadder in the future. Creating and raising children require lots of wisdom and contemplation nowadays at this very critical point in human history.
22. In fact, we should stop bearing so many kids or any at all. The population increase presently required by capitalism to sustain growth and demand for goods would not be justified any longer, either, especially with the growing use of robots. The sad realities noted in this book about the dire prospect of humanity confirm that making more people is a disservice to children, parents, society, and the planet.

23. One main reason our marriages fail is that we are not good (strong) human beings as we used to be even two generations ago. We are becoming lousier human beings every year.
24. The only sign of success in one's life is how humble one has become as a person and how early during one's existence.
25. It is merely amazing and wonderful that life exists—and it is even more splendid that human intelligence has created such array of fantastic thoughts, arts, and innovations.
26. But a better thing about life is that we all eventually die, rot, and all that arrogance goes to hell.
27. Life is now for finding enough courage to laugh at ourselves after realizing humans' nothingness and growing stupidity all along, especially during the last 50-100 years.
28. Actually, life is so funny it makes you cry idiotically and it is often so glum you can only laugh hysterically.
29. It may feel strange and sad—but often a reality—that the more we stay away from people, the better beings we turn out and feel to be. This is a bizarre condition for humans who are such social beings and still destroy each other's life and spirit either intentionally or inadvertently through socializing.
30. We must learn, as individuals, how to deal with the sense of loneliness because many of us no longer can, or wish to, live with a lousy spouse.
31. Self-awareness is mostly for raising our consciousness and learning about our idiosyncrasies. However, it is also for learning how to treat people and bear their evil, mainly by raising our compassion and tolerance.
32. Our hardest job as an enlightened person is to learn how to be good in a stressful society among crooked people, despite endless provocations to become mean and phony like others.
33. It is a sad society when we witness even decent people being turned into uncompassionate individuals and disregard even basic social etiquettes as a new snubbing fad, for example, not answering their phones or returning our calls or emails.

34. Then again, a good thing about humans' varied, rigid natures is that most 'good ones do not change' their true nature easily in the long run, even when exposed to bad things and people.
35. Sadly, however, still many of these good-natured humans are eventually damaged when they are pressed to adapt and feel obliged to mingle among the regular people a lifetime.
36. The history of humanity has been terribly sad with so much cruelty, since we (humans) have failed in all fronts, including educational, societal, economical, and politics after centuries of civilization and philosophizing about life.
37. In contrast, all animals and plants have played a major role in sustaining nature's growth through a sacred process, on top of their beauty and grace. Then, we wonder desperately about humans' real role within, and for, nature. Are we here just to destroy it so mulishly? Are we *really* wiser than animals?!
38. It is sad to imagine that the world would have been much prettier and healthier if humans did not exist to pollute nature with fossil fuel and kill animals for their ivory, horns, etc., out of greed or for amusing themselves. Thus, our extinction might not be a bad thing, after all! Then, we wonder why, *or if,* God would choose humans as the privileged species, or even create them to destroy his creations and poor creatures! God's wisdom is so mysterious, in particular, if prophets' claims about His views of humans are legitimate! How can He still love such a thoughtless, vile species, especially after giving us a big brain to think and make good choices, too? *Never mind killing His son as well!*
39. We let life mould us gradually into confused, crude creatures with bizarre feelings, thoughts, and personalities.
40. We get ourselves stressed out in society more every day for many weird reasons, but our struggles to become (or pretend to be) happy and positive put lots of extra pressures on our psyches for no good reasons or outcome. In fact, it only makes us feel a deeper sense of failure and confusion about our luck and ability to find happiness.

41. Whenever we encounter a good human being, once in a blue moon, we get confused and all the logical equations seem to collapse for a moment because of our baffling discovery—although we return to reality soon enough when we turn and face hundreds of regular defective people.
42. It is pathetic to feel obliged or needy to humour a bunch of idiotic people (as colleagues, family members, or friends.)
43. Sometimes, we try to behave peacefully and be forgiving of people, like Martin Luther King or Mahatma Gandhi maybe; but usually we fail eventually, because people do not take us seriously or actually intimidate us in return.
44. We are such a weak species that must invent some sort of faith and hope for some reality beyond our present existence, e.g., about afterlife and heaven, to make our lives even barely tolerable and less terrifying in our delusional world.
45. Yet, we also feel a need for a more meaningful existence to fill the void of our daily lives in our soulless societies and cultures that are built upon lies, illusions, and corruption.
46. In fact, wondering about our existence feels like a spiritual urge, possibly in our DNA, maybe even instrumental for our occasional loathing of our satanic urges and arguments. This is a big irony, though, considering that humans, including our leaders and clergies, have a high propensity for hypocrisy.
47. The more we search for general happiness blindly nowadays, the more we lose our identities and capacities for finding at least a sense of divine contentment, due to all the phony roles and games that we accept to play regularly to fit in.
48. Childhood experiences make us alert, smart, silly, crazy, or funny. Yet, the ultimate goal is to become somebody special worth all the hassles of living a childish existence forever.
49. We often must choose between companionship and freedom, since these two privileges hardly mix, while each has its own value and procedure, *although some geniuses can mix them!*
50. Some of us have difficulty adapting to the vastly superficial social norms and people. We cannot tolerate phony people as

a fruitful means of socializing, but the fact that they cannot tolerate us, either, feels even odder and funnier to us.

51. Naturally, hundreds of personal idiosyncrasies, such as our urges for spite, rivalry, and deceit prevent us from becoming better beings. However, some of our simpler habits, such as chronic envy and cynicism, already make it difficult to gauge and explore our goodness capacity.

52. The goodness regimen helps people recognize the purpose of natural affinity some people can grow and offer, because we either lack enough compassion to care about people truly or do shoddy, showy jobs just to get by. A big hurdle for being better beings nowadays is people's dire incompetence and apathy for helping each other in society and their families.

53. Goodness regimen is also the best mechanism for a person to grasp the importance of complementary, productive gender roles for creating harmony and peace in family and society.

54. Surely, complementary gender roles are crucial for relating and communicating, nurturing authentic family values, and creating synergy in teamwork settings. In return, this peaceful environment provides a great chance for BBB.

55. Being better beings is just an attempt to be a bit more realistic about our needs instead of striving to be too opportunistic (and idealistic) in terms of taking advantage of life in full.

56. Ultimately, the main goal of Being Better Beings is to raise people's awareness, intelligence, realism, family cohesion, passion, and compassion. We can prepare (and drive) people and their mentalities to strive for becoming rich and famous like 0.1% of the population, or be a normal individual within a society that should accommodate the 99.9% of people. It feels weird that nowadays people and society merely focus on and value the former—the life of the minute minority. Are we a demented and tormented species or what?

57. Accordingly, leaders and governments must fight the roots of social gullibility driven by superficial values and systems.

They must help people grow their senses and independence somewhat, instead of exploiting and misleading them.
58. We should beware of the screen (e-technology, all digital world) that makes our minds work too fast without enough contemplation, and then often decide and act prematurely as well. In fact, the youths' brainkillling habits are growing due to their high dependence on social media for building their opinions, instead of reading books and seeking reliable sources of real knowledge and information.
59. This new social attitude for fast, crude thinking is destroying humans' brain, while we are also getting lazier to read books, which is a necessity for our brains' sporadic chance to relax, contemplate, focus, and learn some useful stuff about life. Then again, these ideas feel too farfetched nowadays.
60. Instead, children mock their parents' ineptitude for allegedly modern means of learning and communicating.
61. Meanwhile, internet has also become a means of intrusion into people's lives and minds. It seems we are paying the outrageous internet fees only for being exploited more, as our privacy is attacked through these devices regularly. So many organs seem to be spying on people and reading their words and thoughts through internet. At least we are often paranoid about this matter, i.e., somebody downloading or reading our files every time we turn on our computers!
62. Instead of imitating and envying the luckier or privileged people rather obsessively, we could learn something about life by reflecting more often on those less fortunate humans and possibly helping them, too.
63. With longer life expectancy, more sickness, and the rise of social mayhem and citizen's incurable psychosis, people like to have the option to call it quits on their terms. However, no concrete principles or means of helping them exist so far other than suicide, which often ends up being too messy or humiliating. We put animals like a horse, dog, and cat to sleep to terminate their suffering, but do not extend similar

courtesy to old, tired humans even when the person begs for mercy to end his/her suffering and confusion.
64. Ultimately, adopting the goodness regimen, as we strive to be better and more useful beings, might prove be the key to find the mystical, mythical happiness for many of us as well.

Our Dilemmas

Humans appear incapable of creating a society to serve people consistently and fairly. Rather, every generation has become more idealistic and sunk deeper in a delusional world, while the society has overindulged elites at the cost of misery for the rest. We have never had the insight to build a long-term vision and practical mechanisms for promoting social harmony and personal solace. However, we have now proven beyond any doubt our ineptitude for coordinating our needs or cooperating for useful, common goals. The more civilized we have supposedly become, the more controversial and selfish we have become. Thus, the chance for building a harmonious life on earth feels infinitesimal, while even the basic purposes of humanity are now corroded, judging by the growing levels of corruptions, crimes, and conflicts in all facets of socioeconomic systems and global affairs, not to mention the dire impact of humans' wasteful lifestyles on nature.

Our dilemmas will keep rising, as nations strive to grow their GDPs to sustain their dying socioeconomic structure, produce lots of junk food and useless stuff, waste more than 50% of their good food, and raise the world's helpless population to work as slaves for enduring such nonsensical ways of living, all at the cost of polluting the biosphere and killing nature! Humans' dilemmas will keep rising as we witness people's despair and dismay, while a huge number of people live in refugee camps or in the streets around the globe, especially in so-called civilized societies, or are dying from addictions, crimes, and drug overdoses!

Obviously, the most catastrophic aspect of humans' gloomy prospect is that we have neither a culture nor a plan of action for social coexistence. Nor do we have any hope for ever finding the wisdom, helpful leaders, and goodwill to develop a more efficient social structure. Indeed, we are still living in primitive societies with a mentality not much stronger than our Stone Age ancestors' judging by the vanity of our religions, relationships, politics, etc. After millenniums of trials and errors, technological progress, wars and debates, and alleged democratic ambitions, we are still unable to keep basic peace and order even in a small corner of the world, in a small community, or even within our families.

Altogether, the way we humans have become is simply too embarrassing! But who is ultimately responsible for all these miseries? How can we ever overcome this mayhem?

Ironically, most of us realize the absurdity of social conditions intuitively and seek solutions innocently during some precious moments of reflection. Accordingly, the biggest global dilemma is whether societies can *ever* uphold a reliable set of guidelines or basic ethics to congregate people within manageable boundaries and curb their gullibility at least. The big question is whether our primitive tribal sense about higher synergy and security in larger communities still holds water.

At the same time, we have become addicted to new symbols of modernity and phony lifestyles with less alternatives, aptitude, and appetite for living more independently. We are trapped in our fantasy worlds amidst a cultural mess with our vast expectations from life, society, and one another. Simply, humans' mentalities nowadays are shaped around shoddy principles and plans to serve their egos and maximize their self-gratification. Therefore, even our diligent efforts fulfil neither people's expectations enough, nor our own spirits. Rather, our lives feel too stressful and meaningless, while we struggle to play many idiotic roles for a decent existence, or at least an easier subsistence.

Still, we strive to make sense of it all and cope! But all we see is an intimidating world, where the majority of people wake up everyday merely focusing on the evil roles and games they must play all day to satiate their egos and greed. They strive to find new gimmicks to sell more stuff to people and exploit them with lies, propagandas, and relentless advertising. Everybody ponders how best to manipulate others for satiating his/her vast emotional or financial hunger, without fussing about the outcome of his/her actions on other people and humanity.

In all, we encounter too many dilemmas about existence and society, as we have simply become prisoners of ghastly societies built around our frivolous perceptions and fallacious ambitions. We feel lost in a world where too many officials and scholars are corrupt or inept, business practices are so deeply unethical, the world's political milieu is so dysfunctional, and the model nation is in such comical disarray nowadays. It is simply getting harder every day to live peacefully in a world where most people have gone crazy about their choices of lifestyles and leaders.

Our relationships and careers have become major sources of our inner conflicts and sufferings, too, because of our idealistic needs and demands on people and vice versa, although we often also become victims of our crude delusions and decisions. Thus, we face more dilemmas, despite our good intentions, positivism, and perseverance to plough on, while our efforts to understand our being also fail.

We often blame ourselves for our sense of entrapment and hardships. With a great deal of self-pity, we blame our inability to cope with people and society. Therefore, we just try harder to be more like others in order to be accepted in their circles, which in turn makes us more superficial, showy, arrogant, greedy, needy, competitive, and all other traits of weakness and wickedness. In effect, we cause our own deformation and sufferings with our gullibility and craving to be like others—so selfish and wicked. We ignore our random insights about the silliness of mainstream's mentality and the vanity of prevalent social values.

Still, many other fundamental questions boggle our minds sporadically. We wonder why humans' lives have become so shallow, arduous and stressful, for no rational reasons, and all for nothing. We wonder if living could be less painful if not joyful.

Reality Check about Humanity 437

We are baffled by people's obsession for malice and the manner we supposedly intelligent humans hurt one another so naturally. We seek the wisdom of living in peace personally at least and the chance of capturing the secrets of the elusive happiness that we crave both intuitively and traditionally. Yet, it is hard to imagine anybody ever achieving these ideals in modern societies. We try to find the roots of these mayhems and possible relief. Yet, our struggles to free ourselves from this universal madness merely sink us deeper into the abyss due to our raw perceptions of life, the world, and personal options with a conditioned mindset. Our mundane solutions are also ineffective, since they revolve around the same shallow values and desires that we hypnotically apply to think and behave with little insight or sincerity.

In all, an endless chain of niggling dilemmas sours our spirits a lifetime, as we wrestle with our deepening fears and agonies in our dense, cruel societies. Then, we eventually feel like prisoners of life per se now, for a long life that we *still* desire so idiotically, despite all the pains we endure daily. Thus, we live in limbo with major dilemmas a lifetime. On the one hand, humans' systemic inability to build a viable social structure and enjoy a moralistic coexistence is now more evident than ever. On the other hand, we can never stop seeking personal salvation and global peace, no matter how desperate and dismal the situation looks. We still imagine a wiser humanity enjoying their beings within a peaceful, functional social structure. We simply do not like to give up the idea of social harmony and effective coexistence as a reasonable and feasible ideal. This raw optimism feels like a genetic disease, or a spiritual drive, which we simply cannot dismiss, despite all the evidences demonstrating our pitiful naiveté.

Many evil forces, both social and inner conflicts, always push our nerves and cause us deep psychological disorders, while life's erratic impositions keep an upper hand and besiege our psyches, too. In the end, this growing sense of helplessness within a cruel, broken social structure cripple our psyches, while people seem adamant to break each other's pride and spirit.

Accordingly, the humility of living in vain generates a socio-personal paradox that singes our spirits, too, while resolving so many torturous dilemmas feels tough. Now, we feel stuck in a society that goads only terror and tyranny, as we feel obliged to abide by social rules and norms in order to fit in and prosper.

Our spirits question and abhor humans' apathy for goodness and building sounder societies. They sense the vanity of our crude optimism for personal salvation and social harmony, too. Deep down, we realize and suffer these sad truths. Still, we prefer to push our psyches to remain hopeful about reshaping our societies and mentalities eventually, while we wonder erratically about the possibility of ever finding a practical, personal choice for living! Amazingly, we remain largely optimistic about some miracle or our leaders saving us finally! We think humans can eventually mature and become better beings. Our naivety is just astounding!

The bottomline

In the end, many of us cannot simply ignore our curious spirits and accept status quo. Ultimately, only we can help ourselves, while we must also accept blame, as lousy humans and citizens, for the rampant social chaos. After all, social mayhems relate to humans' crude nature, genetic flaws, and rearing damages that lead to such a vast variety of odd personalities and quirks.

How many of us or our leaders are willing, or dare, to speak up against the conglomerates' interests around the globe in order to save the environment or help humanity? Thus, ultimately, it is our own varied weaknesses and gullibility, including our choices of leaders, that cause social chaos and damage the environment, too. We are guilty of wasting food, energy, clothing, etc., and for supporting corruptive social norms and mechanisms so blindly with our hypnotized mentalities. In particular, our addiction to consumerism and capitalism is quite deplorable, while most of us wonder if humans might finally mature. We let industries, and society in general, destroy our planet, while they keep fooling us about our superficial needs and potentials to become rich and happy by being too greedy, ambitious, and ruthless regardless of other people's pains and dignity. Almost all of us embrace this selfish mentality like our constitutional right nowadays with no conscience or interest to ponder the horrific social demise. In the end, our materialistic mindsets, spiritual weakness, and rooted gullibility are the main roots of social and environmental collapse. Many people learn to show sympathy sometimes, too, mostly for cleansing their burdened conscience, but only a small group has enough goodness as a basic human quality. The 64 dark realities listed above reveal the sad state of humanity and the varied roots of this chaos, but mostly the depth of humans' innate evil.

While personal incentives and efforts set the foundation for becoming a better being, social values and environment, as well as national and international politics, play vital roles in providing the right motives and atmosphere for individuals to take on the challenge of being better beings and succeed. On the other hand, social stress or desperation might goad a person to think a little deeper within him/herself and feel an urge or need to find a novel way of living, instead of only trying to cope with social demands and hope to adapt. *S/he might renounce his/her constitutional right to be as naïve or wicked as our societies now make us!*

In our neo-culture, any person or nation that resists Western propagandas and values, including commercialization, is attacked or labelled undemocratic and uncivilized. Meanwhile, the world is being demoralized and demolished by allegedly modern social values and ostentatious mentalities of citizens and leaders. Our neo-culture's vanity and people's numbness in this environment are ruining the meanings and purposes of election, democracy, society, economy, and other social systems. Now, the world must face many unsettling conflicts and suffer the consequences of actions by narcissistic leaders like Donald Trump forever, merely because Americans believed he could make America great again!

Anyway, grasping the social issues and politics at national and international levels, particularly in Part IV, is crucial, because the global state of affairs, especially in the United States, affects people's social outlooks and personal lives around the world very deeply—in bad ways, unfortunately, nowadays.

Sadly, the risks of global total demise and lack of direction would not end even when Trump is gone, the US democrats are back in power, etc. The socioeconomic and political systems in the US are instable and unsustainable, and other nations cannot survive without a moral leader forever. This is the bottomline! So what is the remedy for the world? How can a stable, reliable role model and geopolitical mechanism be devised and implemented? It is probably impossible! Yet, we can become better beings!

The bottomline, as a sardonic observation, is that maybe we humans deserve this turmoil and all the sufferings we inflict upon one another due to our malice and ignorance. This is another sad reality, especially, since we also know that humans have curious brains and spiritual urges to avoid so much pains, distress, and hassles of living. All they must do is to use their brains to become just a bit better beings.

Our Choices

So, what are our choices as intelligent individuals and humans? While most of us prefer to remain as we are—so dogmatic and naughty—it is crucial to at least know why we cannot, or refuse to, be better beings, even at such huge costs to ourselves. Does this mean that humans have no capacity for salvation, or merely social corruption is killing our spirits and our basic intuition for goodness? Do not we have any option to live a bit easier?

Surely, the absence of a reliable source of social guidance is a big obstacle and a sign of human failure to grasp our real needs and capture our spirits. In particular, nowadays, parents, schools, and religions are useless in that regard. Thus, personal, social, and environmental issues are deepening fast with no smart leaders or plans at hand to help people relax a bit and reflect on their options for living. Another barrier for being a better being, of course, is that dealing with such big variety of humans' personalities and natures across the greedy population living in cruel, materialistic societies has become a daily challenge and mental burden for us.

Still, our lack of incentive or self-discipline for grasping our being and becoming better beings (BBB), as a potential refuge for a simpler, more peaceful life, is a personal failure. While social and personal limitations suffocate our urge for goodness, some of us have a chance and capacity to redeem our inner Selfs. We have a spiritual curiosity and an eager spirit to explore our knack for BBB and ponder our options for redemption. Many of us feel a need for salvation, despite many obstacles, including humans' crude nature, people's genetic flaws, and our rearing damages leading to our vast variety of odd personalities and quirks. In the end, many of us just cannot ignore our curious spirits.

Perhaps one day we get a mysterious inkling to become a bit better, maybe after a divine experience or reading some reflective books like this. We may be awakened by a spiritual notion or feel the need to elude the crooked reality crippling our existence all along. So, we now find a strong incentive to explore our better side of being, but do not know how to do it and what to expect along the way. We like to grasp the basic elements of goodness, adopt the right process and principles to follow, and develop a constructive lifestyle and mentality, while maintain a practical relationship with our families and society as well.

Of course, it is impossible to build a general path of salvation considering the complexity and variety of human needs, natures, insecurities, and interactions. No universal solutions exist, either, since only we can, and should, discover our being (Self) privately and develop our unique life paths individually. We must make personal choices and take calculated risks. We must admit that something is fundamentally wrong with humans' mentalities and lifestyles, as well as our societies, when most of us are disgruntled with our lives, if not deeply disheartened already.

For salvation, we should gauge our options for living more peacefully in a simple, civil manner and muster enough personal incentive to adopt the path and goals of BBB despite the society's knack for sabotaging our efforts. We have a chance to boost our spirits with a positive attitude towards life, thru personal beliefs and faith, until our inner strengths and potentialities are enlivened to drive our minds and actions. In the end, personal solutions and wisdom emerge from our pious minds and potent spirits directly. Professional help at some extreme psychological dysfunctions is surely helpful, but ultimately, we must discover our 'spirit and being' only through self-awareness and faith in both our inner strengths and *that* mysterious outer power.

The main objectives of goodness are to: 1) fortify our psyches and spirits through self-awareness, while testing and boosting our being independently, and 2) try to understand what has gone so drastically wrong with our cultures, relationships, and mentalities, as a smart species. Then, we must make a sacred personal choice to cope with our sad social reality and personal lives.

Accordingly, the goodness path we adopt consists mainly of a vigorous regimen for self-development with the aim of gaining our soulful identity and individualism outside corruptive social values, while maintaining a civil connection to people, too. This requires a sacred wisdom to replace our vile habits with vivacious beliefs, while realizing the difficulty and necessity of making major concessions and sacrifices a lifetime. The big challenge, of course, would be to give up certain social privileges and absorb people's apathy towards those who choose to live outside the mainstream's rules and values. At the same time, an awakened individual seeking salvation and peace would be willing to make all these sacrifices to embrace an independent (and rather stoic) existence, while promoting social coexistence as well.

All these challenges have been addressed in this book with the aim of exploring humans' natural flaws, existential dilemmas, and social barriers to find the path for becoming better beings.

www.ingramcontent.com/pod-product-compliance
Lightning Source LLC
Chambersburg PA
CBHW021916180426
43199CB00031B/39